T.F. Torrance,
Moderator of the
Church of Scotland
General Assembly
1976-77

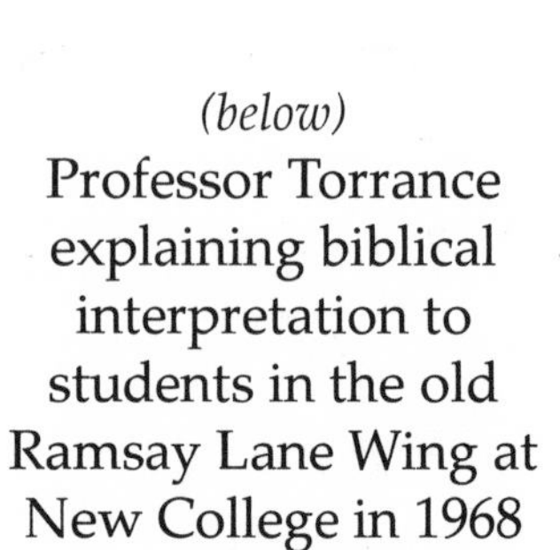

(below)
Professor Torrance
explaining biblical
interpretation to
students in the old
Ramsay Lane Wing at
New College in 1968

INCARNATION

The Person and Life of Christ

Thomas F. Torrance

Edited by
Robert T. Walker

First published 2008 by Paternoster in the UK
First published 2008 by InterVarsity Press in the USA

Paternoster is an imprint of Authentic Media
9 Holdom Avenue, Bletchley, Milton Keynes, Bucks, MK1 1QR, UK
1820 Jet Stream Drive, Colorado Springs, CO 80921, USA
Medchal Road, Jeedimetla Village, Secunderabad 500 055, A.P., India
www.authenticmedia.co.uk

Authentic Media is a division of IBS-STL U.K., limited by guarantee, with its Registered Office at Kingstown Broadway, Carlisle, Cumbria CA3 0HA. Registered in England & Wales No. 1216232. Registered charity 270162

InterVarsity Press, PO Box 1400, Downers Grove, IL 60515, USA
World Wide Web: www.ivpress.com
E-mail: mail@ivpress.com

British Library Cataloguing in Publication Data
A catalogue record for this book is available from the British Library
UK ISBN: 978-1-84227-607-5

Library of Congress Cataloging-in-Publication Data
A catalog record for this book is available from the US Library of Congress
US ISBN: 978-0-8308-2891-3

Scripture quotations are taken from the King James Version or the Revised Standard Version of the Bible, or are the author's own translation.

Cover Design by J.G. Tordai / Panos Pictures
Indexed and Typeset in 11pt Palatino by the

HANDSEL PRESS
EDINBURGH

Printed in the United States of America

InterVarsity Press is committed to protecting the environment and to the responsible use of natural resources. As a member of the Green Press Initiative we use recycled paper whenever possible. To learn more about the Green Press Initiative, visit http://www.greenpressinitiative.org

CONTENTS

The help of the Hope Trust, 32 Moray Place, Edinburgh, and
the Drummond Trust, 3 Pitt Terrace, Stirling
is gratefully acknowledged.

Thanks are expressed also to the Revd George Hastie,
and to Life and Work, for permission
to reproduce the photos at the front of the book.

AUTHOR'S FOREWORD

This volume comprises my lectures on Christology and Soteriology delivered in my classes on Christian Dogmatics at New College, Edinburgh University, during the years 1952–1978. These were new lectures, considerably expanded and substantially revised from the course which I had previously given on the Doctrine of the Person of Christ, at Auburn Theological Seminary, New York, in the years 1938-39 and which have now been published under the title *The Doctrine of Jesus Christ*.

On graduating from New College in 1937, I began research at the University of Basel on *The Doctrine of Grace in the Apostolic Fathers* under the supervision of Karl Barth. My research there was interrupted, however, by a request from John Baillie that I go to Auburn. I returned to Edinburgh in 1939 at the outbreak of war. As regulations did not permit an army chaplaincy at that stage, I went up to Oriel College, Oxford, to complete my doctoral dissertation for Basel. Following several years in parish service in Alyth, Perthshire and in Aberdeen, punctuated by war service in North Africa and Italy 1943-45, I was called back to the University of Edinburgh and the Chair of Church History in 1950. Here, lecturing in church history from 1950-52, I was particularly concerned with Patristic, Reformation and Scottish theology. In 1952, with the retirement from the Chair of Christian Dogmatics of G.T. Thomson, who had translated the first half volume of Karl Barth's *Christian Dogmatics*, I requested transfer to the vacant Chair.

John Baillie, then Principal of New College and Professor of Divinity in the University of Edinburgh, lectured on philosophical theology with particular attention to the doctrine of God. He had wanted me to remain in the Chair of Church History but to my delight I was transferred to the Chair of Christian Dogmatics, the same chair which had previously been held by Hugh Ross Mackintosh, my beloved old teacher, to whom I was greatly indebted spiritually and theologically. It was he who had first encouraged me to read and study the theology of Karl Barth. I began the preparation of lectures and week by week lectured on dogmatics. In time, I also began to prepare for the use of students copies of some of my lecture material, but had not thought of publishing all my lectures as such. Now, however, at the urgent request of some of my students I have prepared them for publication with only minor changes. I hope they may still be found helpful, not only to my former students but to others in different parts of the world.

I would like to thank Mrs Nancy Robinson, as she now is, very warmly for her secretarial help in New College, and not least my elder son Thomas who has given me enormous help and constant assistance in the handling of the computer and in preparing these lectures for the press. I am also most grateful to my former student Jock Stein of the Handsel Press, Edinburgh for agreeing to help oversee and arrange the final preparation and publication of this work. I want to express my gratitude to my dear wife Margaret above all for her patience with me as I prepared this and other books while shut away in my study upstairs.

Edinburgh, Easter 2002

PREFACE by Thomas S. Torrance

In 2001 and 2002 my father, Thomas Forsyth Torrance, gathered together material from his Edinburgh University lecture notes and other sources that he planned to publish on the Incarnation and Atonement. The resulting manuscript, however, subsequently proved to be in need of extensive editing before it could be considered for publication. Unhappily, during the afternoon of Tuesday 28th January 2003 my father (then aged 89) suffered a stroke that brought his long and immensely productive academic life to an abrupt end. I am most grateful to my cousin Robert Torrance Walker for agreeing to undertake the complex editing task which my father was unable to accomplish after his stroke. Robert was well suited for this role in that he had been a student at New College, University of Edinburgh, from 1966 to 1969 and had attended my father's lectures in the form in which they had evolved by that period. I believe that the outcome of Robert's sustained efforts from 2003 onwards, not only in editing the main text but also in meticulously verifying the accuracy of each reference, is a faithful and accurate presentation of what my father originally intended to publish. I should add that my father himself, shortly before his death on Advent Sunday 2007, expressed his great satisfaction with Robert's skilful editing.

Department of Economics
Heriot-Watt University
Edinburgh, January 2008

EDITOR'S FOREWORD

These unforgettable lectures on Christology and Soteriology made a vivid impression on generations of students at New College. Every day after the morning coffee break, apart from a Wednesday when there were no college lectures, second year students made their way along to the Ramsay Lane Wing in New College to the dogmatics class. A prepared typescript formed the basis of the lectures which were a tightly packed introduction to dogmatics and the classical doctrine of Christ. They covered a great deal of ground, from the nature of theology and the Old Testament to the person of Christ and the nature of the atonement.

While they made considerable demands on the listener's attention, the lectures were riveting. Students found themselves deeply challenged and made to think, not only about the central issues of faith but about science and philosophy as well. If at times they found themselves stretched to the limits, they also found the lecturer making time to answer questions or regularly laying aside his notes to speak simply and personally about matters of faith. On such occasions, one could hear a pin drop in the class. It was clear that while academic, hugely stimulating and informative, the lectures did not separate mind and heart, or intellect and faith. The short prayer at the beginning of the class, when "TFT" closed his eyes really tightly (as though he was shutting out all images foreign to the word of God), was invariably a beautiful and succinct summary of the whole lecture.

Although only now published for the first time, the lectures contain the heart and core of the author's thought. Brought up by missionary parents in China, where he was steeped in the bible and encouraged to think about theology from an early age, Torrance trained in theology at New College under H.R. Mackintosh. With his thinking then further deepened through study at Basel under Karl Barth, extensive personal reading of theology and several years in pastoral ministry, the author communicates in these lectures not only his understanding of the doctrine of Christ but of scripture and theology more generally.

Torrance's books cover a wide range of subjects expanding on some of the issues raised in the lectures and exploring in depth new fields far beyond them. These lectures, however, represent the starting point and centre of all his thinking. If the focus of his later work appeared to be on issues such as the relation of science and theology, or on more detailed expositions of the doctrine of God, that was only because the doctrine of Christ and the biblical understanding behind it remained the foundation from which he was thinking out other issues. It is the lectures which more than anything else unfold the biblical and theological roots of his thought.

While much of their content formed recurring themes in his writings, nowhere is this material brought together as a whole and explored in a more sustained, connected and detailed way than in these lectures. They contain by far his fullest biblical exposition of Christology and Soteriology. A key aspect of their significance is the way in which they reveal his knowledge of scripture, enabling the reader to appreciate the extent of the biblical study and interpretation which lay at the root of his thought. Here we have spelled out for us the way in which he saw different themes and passages of the bible connected together and serving in an integrated way to interpret the person and mission of Jesus.

Former students will have the opportunity to read and study in full, material they were only able to summarise in notes. More importantly, a broader readership, the wider church and the inquiring laity now have the opportunity to share in what excited and motivated a generation of students. They will discover a challenging introduction to theology which opens up a deeper and richer understanding of Christian faith as a whole and the person and work of Christ in particular.

The contribution that these lectures offer to the understanding of their author's theology can be summarised here as:

i) readability and accessibility – in contrast to the books prepared or written specifically for publication, the lectures are much less literary and easier to follow in content and style;

ii) centrality of Christ – the doctrine of Christ is the centre of Torrance's thought and informs all his writings, whether explicitly or implicitly, whatever their subject. Unfolding the doctrine of Christ in detail, these lectures present a defining account of the heart of the author's thought;

iii) biblical commentary – the lectures provide what is effectively an extended theological commentary on the bible. This means that they not only supply Torrance's understanding of scripture but in so doing the theological interpretation which informs it. They thus demonstrate the essential inter-relation between theology and scriptural understanding;

iv) a '*one volume dogmatics*' – in the absence of a dogmatics from his own pen, the lectures on Christology and Soteriology provide the most systematic and complete presentation of Torrance's thought and represent the nearest equivalent to the dogmatics he had hoped to write himself;

v) new material – although there is considerable overlap between the lectures and the author's writings, the lectures contain significant new material as well as material which complements and helps to amplify that in the published works;

vi) the best introduction to his thought – taken as a whole, the lectures provide the most readable, accessible and comprehensive introduction to Torrance's theology.

If the lectures do not always have the polish of a book prepared for publication they nevertheless possess a simplicity, a passion, and the freshness of material delivered direct to the class. Their overall effect is to create an indelible impression. Presented here all together and incorporating additional material given to students in written form, these lectures are not only an invaluable introduction to the thought of T.F. Torrance himself, but a major account of the classical and reformed doctrine of Christ, ecumenical in perspective and very much in the classical tradition of Christian theology.

Robert T. Walker
Edinburgh, Easter 2008

SYNOPSIS

Chapter One

INTRODUCTION TO CHRISTOLOGY

The task of christology

The starting point of christology

The nature of 'scientific dogmatics'

1 *The relation of Christ to history*

The inseparability of the historical from the theological in Christ

(a) It is the once and for all unity of God and man in Jesus Christ that preserves his humanity

(b) The unity of God and man in Christ is accomplished from the side of God

(c) It is impossible to move from the historical Jesus to God

2 *Jesus Christ and the New Testament* kērygma

The New Testament presentation of the Jesus of history as the Christ of faith

A fact-in-interpretation, Christ clothed with his own gospel

(a) Controlling factors in the New Testament witness

(i) The historical factuality of Jesus

(ii) The historical context of Israel

The compulsive Old Testament purpose behind the New Testament witness

Jesus himself is under obedience to the will of God and the Old Testament scriptures

(iii) The self-proclamation of Jesus

(b) The self-presentation of Jesus in the apostolic *kērygma*

(i) Inseparability of the word and deed and presence of Jesus

(ii) Inseparability of the *kērygma* from the rabbinic teaching of Jesus

(iii) Jesus' transmission and extension of his own *kērygma* to the apostles

The Jewish concept of the apostle-shaliach

(iv) The relation between faith and the *kērygma* – the relation of the church's faith and understanding to the faith and obedience of Jesus himself

The nature of faith: Kierkegaard on the apprehension of God in time

Faith is an act of appropriation and trust which is wholly based on Christ and his decision for us

The early church's piety and *kērygma* controlled by Christ and his obedience

3 *Procedure in christology*

(a) Knowledge of Christ by revelation through the Spirit

Philippians 2: the classic passage on the servant Son

The self-humbling of the Son to become servant , obedient unto death

(c) The descent and ascent of the Son

(i) A movement of revelation
(ii) A movement of reconciliation
(iii) Salvation through the whole course of Christ's obedience
(1) The active obedience of Jesus
(2) The passive obedience of Jesus
(3) The importance of both the passive and active righteousness of Christ
(4) The union of God and man in the life of the Son

OUTLINE OF THE DOCTRINE OF THE PERSON OF CHRIST

(1) The mystery of true God and man in one person

(2) The mystery of Christ only capable of negative definition

(3) The inseparability of *anhypostasia* and *enhypostasia*

(4) The hypostatic union to be understood dynamically and soteriologically

(5) Reconstruction of the classical doctrine of Christ: integration of Patristic and Reformation Christology, and of Christology with Pneumatology and the doctrine of the Trinity

Chapter Three

THE ONCE AND FOR ALL UNION OF GOD AND MAN IN CHRIST: HIS BIRTH INTO OUR HUMANITY

1 *The biblical witness to the virgin birth*

(a) The synoptic Gospels

(b) John – the Gospel and the Johannine writings

(c) St Paul

2 *The doctrine of the virgin birth*

(a) Preliminary observations

(i) The virgin birth not a theory of explanation
(ii) The virgin birth not to be separated from the whole mystery of Christ
(iii) The virgin birth not to be separated from the resurrection
(iv) The virgin birth and empty tomb as pointers to the mystery of Christ

(b) The positive teaching of the virgin birth

(i) The reality of the humanity of Jesus
(ii) Disqualification of human capabilities
(iii) A recreation out of the old creation
(iv) The setting aside of human autonomy
(v) The virgin birth the pattern of grace, the model for faith
(vi) Demonstration of the virgin birth only through the Spirit
(vii) Necessity and importance of the virgin birth

(ii) The uncovering of man and the unveiling of the human heart
Romans 1.16 – 3.20: revelation of righteousness and judgement to Jew and Gentile
Hebrews 4.12-16: the word of God that exposes all the thoughts of the heart
The high priest who uncovers and bears our sin, and answers for us to the Father
(iii) Christ's ministry as shepherd and king leads straight to the cross
The violence of the kingdom
The meekness of Jesus, his gospel of grace and vicarious suffering, is the most powerful deed the world has ever known
The agony of Jesus in bringing the truth to bear on humanity
(iv) Final judgement and salvation
The nearer the cross came, the more Jesus pressed the people to decision
Jesus' deliberate forcing of events to the climax on the cross and the hour of atonement
(v) The building up of the messianic community and the creation of the church
The three stages in the formation of the disciples
The reconstitution of the disciples in the power of the resurrection and of the Spirit

Chapter Five

THE MYSTERY OF CHRIST: the mystery of the union of God and man in the person of Christ

The mystery of Christ's person unfolded only at the end of his mission
John's apocalyptic vision of the glory of Christ
Paul's understanding of the mystery of Christ that goes back to eternity

1 *The mystery of Christ:* mystērion, prothesis, koinōnia

The mystery of the union in Christ, purposed, set forth and creating communion

(a) The mystery of Christ – *mystērion,* the union of God and man

The mystery of Christ and his kingdom revealed to the disciples
The unfolding of the mystery in the apostolic *kērygma* and the growth of the church

(b) The mystery of Christ – *prothesis,* the election of Christ

The eternal purpose is set forth in communion that reaches beyond the barriers

(c) The mystery of Christ – *koinōnia,* the communion of Christ

Koinōnia as participation in the mystery, and fellowship in the mystery
The mystery is inserted as *koinōnia* into the midst of our knowledge and our being
A summary of *mystērion, prothesis* and *koinōnia*

2 *The mystery of Christ and the holy Trinity*

(a) The 'pre-existence' of Christ

What Jesus is toward us he is antecedently and eternally in himself, in God
The person of Jesus is eternal, not his humanity

(b) The eternal election of Jesus Christ

Election is the eternal purpose of God that is identical with Jesus
Eternal election becomes temporal event confronting people in Jesus

Chapter Six

THE HYPOSTATIC UNION

The need to integrate the being and work of Christ, patristic and reformed theology
Hypostatic union and atoning reconciliation cannot be properly expounded apart from each other

1 *The humanity and the deity of Christ*

(a) The humanity of Christ

(i) Christ's humanity is the guarantee of the coming of God
(ii) The humanity of Christ essential for revelation
(iii) The humanity of Christ essential for reconciliation

(b) The deity of Christ

(i) Christ's deity is the guarantee that salvation is the work of God
(ii) The deity of Christ essential for revelation
(iii) The deity of Christ essential for salvation

2 *The hypostatic union in revelation and reconciliation*

The divine and human natures and acts are truly and completely united in one person
The deity and humanity of Christ have no revealing or saving significance for us apart from their hypostatic union in him

(a) The hypostatic union of God and man in one person is the heart of revelation, and its full substance

The incarnation of the Word in human form and language
The hypostatic union of God and human language is the basis of revelation
Analogy and the hypostatic union

(b) The hypostatic union of God and man in one person is the heart of reconciliation and its full substance

In the humanity of Jesus, God veils himself to save us and draw us to faith
The hypostatic union, worked out in atonement, is the objective heart of reconciliation
The one action of the God-man, of God as man, is fulfilled in atoning reconciliation
The hypostatic union is the mainstay of the doctrine of atoning reconciliation

(c) Outline of the main stages in the development of the doctrine of Christ and of the hypostatic union

3 *The Patristic doctrine of Christ*

(a) The differing strands in Patristic theology

(i) Defence of the deity and humanity of Christ
The full humanity of Christ the ultimate danger point
(ii) The council of Chalcedon
The difficulty behind the Chalcedonian concept of 'human nature' and 'divine nature'
(iii) The meaning of 'nature' and *physis*
'Physis' refers to the nature of things in their being – the parallel with 'alētheia', truth
The use of 'physis' in the Greek fathers – 'alētheia', 'ousia' and 'hypostasis'

(iv) The nature of Jesus' humanity – fallen humanity redeemed and perfected
The Chalcedonian hypostatic union must be stated dynamically in terms of the twin assumption and sanctification of fallen human nature by Jesus

(b) The significance of the Chalcedonian 'hypostatic union'
(i) The hypostatic union an act of grace
(ii) The twofold movement of condescension and elevation
(iii) The uniqueness of the hypostatic union
(iv) The integrity of both natures – correction of Alexandrian extremes
(v) The union of both natures – correction of Antiochene extremes
(vi) *Communicatio idiomatum* – the communication of properties
The properties special to the divine or human nature may be predicated of the other through their sharing in the one person of Christ
(vii) The weakness of the *logos* christology

(c) Factors helping to safeguard the humanity of Jesus
(i) The condemnation of Apollinarius
(ii) The condemnation of Eutyches
(iii) Leontius of Byzantium – the '*enhypostatic*' humanity of Jesus
(iv) The condemnation of the Monothelites

4 The Reformation doctrine of Christ
Return from medieval to Patristic theology and the living God of the bible

(a) The different emphases in Lutheran and Reformed theology
The Lutheran stress on the union of divine and human, and the Reformed stress on the Son as God and man
The hypostatic union interpreted more dynamically in terms of the whole life of Jesus

(b) The problem of the '*extra-Calvinisticum*'
Greek 'container' conceptions of space
The Patristic conception of space as 'relational'
The difficulties of the Lutheran concept of space
The truth behind both the Lutheran and Reformed positions

(c) The communion of natures - *communio naturarum*
Divergence between Lutheran and Reformed teaching on the nature of the communion

(d) The communication of properties - *communicatio idiomatum*
(i) The Lutheran doctrine of *communicatio idiomatum*
The danger of deifying the humanity of Christ
(ii) The Reformed doctrine of *communicatio naturarum*
The problem of the 'immutability' and 'impassibility' of God
The biblical view of God freely humbling himself to become a creature

(e) The doctrine of *anhypostasis* and *enhypostasis*
(i) The humanity of Jesus has no independent reality
(ii) The humanity of Jesus has full reality in the person of the Son
(iii) *Anhypostasis* and *enhypostasis* taken together
(1) Jesus was at once man, and a man
(2) The anhypostatic union and solidarity of Christ with all humanity, and the enhypostatic encounter with people in personal relation
(3) The anhypostatic assumption of fallen humanity, and the enhypostatic purity of Jesus and personal responsibility for sinners
A note on the use of theological terms such as '*anhypostasia*' and '*enhypostasia*'

EDITOR'S INTRODUCTION

The purpose of the introduction

The purpose of the introduction is, i) to explain the nature of Christian dogmatics as understood by Torrance and ii) to summarise the theology of these lectures on Christology and Soteriology and outline their leading characteristics. It is also, finally, to give an account of the text of the lectures and the process of editing them for publication.

1 The nature and purpose of the dogmatics lectures

An outline summary of the lectures

Torrance's lectures on the doctrine of Christ span the sweep of biblical history. They summarise the interaction with and gradual training by God of Israel in the Old Testament, shaping her concepts and institutions in order to create the tools and categories of thought through which Christ when he came could be understood. They focus on the life of Christ, from birth to crucifixion, resurrection and ascension into heaven, as the fulfilment of all the long Old Testament preparation.

They argue that the whole life of Christ from birth to death on the cross and right through into resurrection, ascension and the sending of the Spirit, is of saving significance. They argue that Christ's work of revelation and reconciliation can only be understood when the person and work of Christ are not separated but held together so that what Christ did is interpreted in the light of who he is.

Christ's work of salvation, of atonement, reconciliation and redemption needs to be interpreted in terms of the unity of his person, as the work of real God and yet of real man in the one person of Christ. For Torrance, the person of Christ, understood dynamically in terms of his work, is the centre of the Christian faith. As true God and true man in one indivisible person, Jesus is himself our salvation, the living and permanent union of God and man. The indivisibility of the person of Christ and his inseparability from the Father and the Spirit are the foundation of Christian theology. Salvation in the incarnate person of Christ is the work of Father, Son and Spirit.

The lectures outline the development of the doctrine of the person of Christ in the early church and argue that its concern with his person needs to be balanced by the modern concern with the work of Christ and eschatology. Torrance gives a full theological account of the life and work of Christ and presents an integrated understanding of his person and work in which insights from the early church, medieval, Reformation and modern theology are all given their place in a developed doctrine of Christ.

Torrance begins the lectures with an introduction to the nature of theological thinking and method and the relation between the Jesus of history and the Christ of faith. He concludes them with an emphasis on the eschatology of the New Testament and the way in which Christian faith must always look upwards and forwards to the coming again of Christ in glory and the full manifestation of the kingdom.

The logic of the lectures

The lectures are challenging in content and depth, span a wide field and integrate so many strands of theological thought, that while at one level they are easy to follow, it takes time to put them together and see them as a whole. Torrance used to encourage students to keep listening until they began to put the different elements together and follow the logic of the lectures. He was interpreting the bible in terms of its dynamic, which in the Old Testament reached forward and in the New Testament looked back to the coming of the Messiah. Interpreting the bible theologically in this way, as a whole, in its relation of depth, means seeing Christ as the ultimate focal point of all the scriptures and of all Christian faith and doctrine.

As Torrance goes through the bible, selecting the most important elements of its teaching and covering different strands of the doctrine of Christ, he is building up a picture of how the bible and Christian doctrine relate to Christ. As they listened to the lectures, students used to find that he would often return to the same point. Torrance used to say that the process of comprehension is spiral in nature. It involves seeing the connections between different parts of the bible and the relation of scripture as a whole to Christ. One comes back to the same point, but from a different angle and with a richer understanding.

The setting of the lectures – university and church

The immediate setting for Torrance's dogmatics lectures was New College, the divinity faculty of the University of Edinburgh and one of the Church of Scotland's historic four training colleges for the ministry.

In the tradition of Scottish theological education, university faculties and church training colleges were not separated. Academic rigour and Christian faith and belief existed side by side. During Torrance's time as Professor of Christian Dogmatics at New College, from 1952 until his retiral in 1979, the majority of students were candidates for the ministry of the Church of Scotland. For their Bachelor of Divinity degree, students were required to study Old Testament, New Testament, Church History, Practical Theology, and Dogmatics and Divinity for the first two years of their study, after which honours students could specialise in the field of their choice. The second year Dogmatics class was therefore attended by all candidates for the ministry as part of their training. It gave them a very comprehensive account of the whole doctrine of Christ and the nature and purpose of dogmatics.

The nature and purpose of Christian dogmatics

For Torrance, Christian dogmatics works alongside the other essential theological disciplines. Old Testament and New Testament study lay the foundation for biblical theology in its task of understanding the concepts and teaching of the bible. Church History, as part of its task, studies the development and history of church doctrine from the earliest years of the church and the time of the ecumenical creeds and councils. Christian dogmatics is the discipline which attempts to express the essential content of Christian faith and doctrine as an aid to the church in her teaching and preaching.

Christian Dogmatics overlaps with biblical theology and like biblical theology endeavours to be faithful to scripture but has three further features: i) it thinks with all the saints in the tradition of the church and in faithfulness to apostolic tradition, church creeds and ecumenical decisions on doctrine; ii) Christian dogmatics recognises that church tradition, creeds and dogma must always be subject to scripture and open to further development or amendment in the light of scripture; iii) it endeavours to express faithfully the doctrine of Christ and to bring all doctrine, preaching and ministry of the church into agreement with scripture and above all with Christ.

The aim of Christian Dogmatics can be summarised as:

(a) faithful interpretation, with all the saints, of scripture in the light of Christ;

(b) careful development or amendment of church teaching, doctrine and practice according to Christ;

(c) orderly articulation of the doctrine of Christ.

The 'inner logic' of the bible

In these dogmatics lectures Torrance is interpreting scripture in the light of Christ and with the help of past and present interpretation in the church. He is interpreting scripture in terms of the thought and intention of scripture itself, seeing it as Christ and the New Testament writers interpreted it, as referring to him. Such interpretation in terms of the '*inner logic*' of the bible as Torrance called it, is reached through following the language, context and thought of the bible and above all the apostolic interpretation of Christ. The lectures are an extended summary of the teaching of the bible in terms of its inner intention, of the Old Testament in terms of its slowly unfolding reference to the coming of Christ and of the New Testament in terms of its presentation of Christ as the revelation of the Father and redeemer of the world.

Articulating the inner logic in dogmatics

For Torrance, one of the primary tasks of dogmatics is articulating the inner logic of the bible. Without distorting it or forcing it into an alien framework, its task is to follow the inner logic as it comes to fulfilment in Christ and coheres around him. It is then to understand and express, as far as it is possible to do so, the logic of Christ and how Christian doctrine is structured around him.

Once brought to light and articulated, the inner logic of the bible and of Christ gives dogmatics its basic structure of thought and becomes an interpretative framework for the church to guide it in understanding the bible. It functions as a 'key', as Calvin put it, to understanding the whole of scripture. There are two points here:

i) dogmatics is a human activity, open to human fallibility. It attempts to be faithful to what the word of God is saying in scripture but is always open to revision and correction by it.

ii) in discovering and expressing the inner logic of scripture, dogmatics is discovering something which is not just a human structure of thought but a divinely given and inspired one. By grace and through the Spirit, dogmatics interprets scripture and summarises its divine content. Human activity though it is, it articulates for the church the doctrine of Christ.

The relation between preaching, dogmatics and Christ

Preaching and Christian dogmatics both present Christ. Preaching does it in a way which is simpler, more pastoral and with more emphasis on vivid presentation which brings home to listeners the reality of Christ and his relation to them. Dogmatics does it in a way which is more theological, more detailed and with more emphasis on understanding the full truth of the doctrine of Christ. Torrance's lectures are a theological presentation of Christ but in a real sense they are also preaching. Their aim is to lay bare the essential structure of the biblical doctrine of Christ and in so doing they are preaching him. Or to put it the other way round, in their preaching of Christ theologically, the lectures are using and supplying a structure of understanding which enables the truth of Christ to be grasped and Christ himself to be known.

For Torrance, there should be no gap between preaching and dogmatics. One of the aims of the lectures and one of Torrance's dearest wishes was to help bridge any such gap and give students a theological grasp of the gospel to enable them to preach Christ in a richer and deeper way. Torrance used to quote James Denney's dictum, 'If only all our evangelists were theologians, and all our theologians evangelists.' As a parish minister, Torrance preached the same theology that he later lectured on. Profound though his theology was, the heart of his dogmatics could be preached simply, as the books of his published sermons show.

The inner simplicity and structural complexity of the dogmatics

Torrance's dogmatics combines an inner simplicity with a structural complexity. In its evangelical presentation of Christ, his dogmatics has a profound unity and simplicity. It is also structurally complex in its combination of scriptural interpretation with theological insights from the history of the church. Interpreting the bible in its depth, he sees the different elements of the person and work of Christ and the many biblical images and doctrinal presentations of Christ in the New Testament as an integrated whole. His dogmatics is an integrated presentation of the whole biblical picture of Christ. Its shape and structure is deeply informed by the theological structure or framework of understanding first developed by the early church in the period of the ecumenical councils and creeds. But while the basic structure is that of the early church, Torrance incorporates many subsequent developments and insights, further extending and integrating them into a developed whole. His dogmatics is thus also an integration of theological understanding from different periods of the church.

The inseparable relation between Christ, the bible and dogmatics

In Torrance's lectures, there is an inseparable relation between Christ, the bible and dogmatics, in which they are bound up together and understood together, each through the other two:

i) Christ is understood through the bible and the bible through dogmatics.

ii) the bible for its part is understood when Christ is known and then it makes sense, but it is also only understood when dogmatics (or as may be, preaching and biblical interpretation) succeeds in interpreting it and making Christ clear as its inner content and meaning. The bible stands in the middle, as the mediator of Christ, but it needs to be illuminated from both ends, as it were, or from behind and in front, in order to be itself understood and make sense.

iii) dogmatics can only be understood when the Christ it presents is known in person as the meaning of the bible and therefore also of dogmatics. A knowledge of the bible is an essential prerequisite. Dogmatics is then understood when its structuring of the biblical message brings Christ to the fore, revealing him and making him known as the centre of the bible and of dogmatics. The light of Christ shines through, making the meaning of the bible and dogmatics transparent.

The circle of knowing in theology

In Torrance's view, there is in theology a circle of knowing into which we must enter. We know and understand Christ through the bible and dogmatics, and we understand dogmatics and the bible when through them we know the Christ to whom they refer. The same is true in other fields of knowledge. We understand any reality through language and a human structure of understanding. At the same time it is only through knowing the reality that the structure or framework of understanding makes sense. Understanding the structure or framework of knowledge and understanding the reality grow together, and little by little, our grasp of each increases, though there may often be a sudden and dramatic moment or moments of illumination.

The same process occurs when children learn language: they only understand the meaning of words when they understand the realities they refer to, but at the same time they only come to be able to think and understand the realities by means of the language which refers to them. Understanding of language and of reality occur side by side. So in theology, knowledge of Christ and understanding of the biblical and dogmatic structure through which he is known grow side by side. Little by little each unfolds the other.

Knowing Christ through the bible, dogmatics and the transformation of mind

Now to take the various elements involved in the knowledge of Christ separately and in more detail:

i) ***knowing Christ*** – the ultimate purpose of the bible and of dogmatics is knowledge of Christ. Unless we know Christ in his reality, neither the bible nor dogmatics make sense. He is known *in* but also ***through*** the word of the bible and theological structures of understanding. The *in* and the *through* are both important. We know Christ *in* the bible and theology but also *through* them, which means that we have to pass beyond them to the reality of Christ if we are to know him. We need to pass through them in such a way that our thought is not just resting in the statements of scripture and dogmatics but resting on Christ and knowing him in his own person and reality.

ii) ***the written word of the scriptures*** – Christ the living Word is known *through* the written word of the scriptures but also ***in*** it, which means that the written word has a unique and normative authority in our knowledge of him. It is holy scripture, with implications for the way we approach it and know it:

a) there is an imperative to *know the scriptures* and know them well. The more we do so, the easier it becomes to follow the thought of scripture, see the connections between different parts of it and come to know Christ through it. In revealing Torrance's own intimate knowledge of the bible, the lectures help to open it up for others.

b) Torrance stresses that in knowing the bible we must *learn to think in a biblical way*. We must learn to think in a godly way, in a way appropriate to what the bible is, the word of God speaking to us at our level and lifting us up to know him in accordance with his majesty. Such godliness, where human reason learns to know the truth of God in a way appropriate to him, Torrance found to be particularly characteristic of the great fathers of the church.

c) For Torrance, the bible is the result of the long wrestling by the Word of God with the human speech and thought forms of Israel. It is the training and adaptation of human word to be the bearer of his Word. The bible contains language, images, institutions, customs and metaphors chosen, adapted and welded together to be the vehicle of his revelation. It is through these specially moulded ways of expression and not others that God has chosen to speak to us.

That means that it is not only *in* the written word of scripture that God is known, but *in terms of it*. The bible, in other words, is not only the window *through* which we know him, but *the way we are to know him*. *This* is how God is to be known, in terms of these concepts and this set of metaphors: steadfast love, righteousness, covenant love, sacrifice, atonement, king, priest, shepherd, Father, etc. Culturally conditioned and localised as the biblical metaphors and way of thinking are, the bible contains the specially adapted means and categories by which God is to be known and understood.

iii) ***dogmatics*** – the role of dogmatics is to articulate how the various metaphors and expressions of the bible fit together and are understood. Dogmatics interprets the language and thought of the bible in terms of its immediate human context, in terms of the way the bible customarily uses the same language and images elsewhere in the bible, and in terms of the meaning of human language when applied to God. Torrance examines the principles of biblical interpretation in detail in some of his essays and books and in his earlier days spent considerable time studying the meaning of biblical words, as is apparent in the lectures. On the basis of careful linguistic and textual study, the task is to summarise the essential thought of scripture and articulate its structure. Five factors, overlapping to an extent, are central throughout:

(a) linguistic and contextual examination of the biblical text;
(b) learning the biblical mind and how it operates;
(c) following the intention and inner logic of the bible;
(d) interpreting biblical language through the Spirit in the light of the reality of God;
(e) interpreting the bible in the light of Christ.

Through all this, dogmatics aims to put into words the biblical structure of thought from its beginnings in Israel to its fulfilment in the doctrine of Christ so that he may be better known and the bible better understood.

iv) ***the transformation of mind*** – knowing Christ requires a transformation of mind, a reorientation of our natural ways of thinking so that we begin to think in a new way in accordance with his mind. The word *metanoia*, commonly translated repentance, means literally 'change of mind'. Coming to know Christ means a change in our whole way of thinking and Torrance did not hesitate to tell students on occasion that they needed to be converted. Without such a conversion and continual transformation of mind, Christ cannot be known nor the bible and dogmatics understood. While change of mind is something that needs to happen in us, for Torrance it is not something we can make happen ourselves but something we find in Christ and that is given to us. It is part of the relation between Christ and ourselves and part of the doctrine of Christ.

Theological language and faith

In the language of faith, Christ is known through the language of the bible, through the gospel stories of Jesus' teaching and healing and through the New Testament preaching of who he is and what he has done for us. Christian theology and dogmatics know the same Christ through language which is more technical such as incarnation, the deity and humanity of Christ, divine nature, human nature, person and work, two natures in one person, etc. The use of such a language enables us to see connections and pinpoint features of the doctrine of Christ, making it easier to discern its essential structure and know Christ with a richer understanding.

Torrance uses theological language, co-ordinated with biblical language and that of faith to present Christ and his gospel. The language of faith is based on biblical language which itself is everyday language enriched with specialised terms such as justification and atonement, the meaning of which has to be learnt. Theological language is a further enrichment, which by itself or when first used appears abstract, but which once learnt provides faith with deeper understanding. The theological language that Torrance uses extensively takes time to learn, but it is always dovetailed and continually translated into biblical and normal language. In his theology, the three languages function inextricably together and all three are the language of faith and prayer and worship.

2 Leading features of Torrance's theology

Its general nature

i) ***biblical and unitary*** – Torrance's theology is deeply biblical and like the bible his thought is unitary, combining head and heart. In the bible there is no separation between them and no such thing as knowledge simply with the mind or simply with the heart. The human person is a unity and the whole of the human person is involved in faith or knowledge, at once with the head and with the heart.

For Torrance, theology is personal knowledge of God in which mind and heart together are equally involved. God is personal, or 'personalising person' as Torrance used to say, the one who makes us personal and can only be known personally. One cannot therefore study theology without personal knowledge of God in faith. It can never be simply an academic exercise. Theology involves faith and worship and can only properly be done on one's knees.

ii) ***systematic but not a system*** – while Torrance's theology is highly systematic, it is not a system. There is no one key systematising principle and although key elements of it can be enumerated as basic principles, these cannot be neatly systematised. That is because the unity of his thought is to be found not in any logical consistency of important principles as such, but in the object to which his theology points, the incarnate Christ in the heart of the Trinity. Theological statements point beyond themselves to the reality of God in Christ and it is only in the reality of God himself that all we try to say about him is held together in one. For Torrance, dogmatics must be systematic and orderly in its articulation of the doctrine of Christ but in the nature of the case cannot be a system. Dogmatics points to, but falls short of, the reality of God in Christ and cannot reduce it to a human system. Human systems must go as far as they faithfully can without distortion but then they must break off and find their completion in the reality and truth of God.

While we try to understand Christ systematically, we have to be faithful to what he is without pushing our logic to the point where it begins to distort what we know of him through the scriptures. Torrance's theology points to but does not try to encapsulate the knowledge of Christ in a system or tie up all the ends. They are left open for it is only in God himself that all the elements of theological articulation can be held together.

Torrance therefore holds together positions which scripture holds together, such as the completed work of Christ and the need for faith, without logicalising them into a system such as universalism, limited atonement or Arminianism, all of which were for him distortions of scripture. For Torrance we must be faithful to the logic of scripture, learning to hold together what it holds together and endeavouring to understand how and why it holds different conceptions together which to natural human logic can seem inconsistent or contradictory.

(a) The Trinity and the deity of Christ

The heart of Torrance's theology is the Trinity and the deity of Christ. In the coming of Jesus Christ, the God of the Old Testament is fully revealed as Father, Son and Spirit, three eternal persons in one God. The truth of the Trinity, 'more to be adored than expressed', and the deity of Christ belong inseparably together. It is only because he is fully God that he can reveal God and as the eternal Word and Son reveal the Father.

The deity of Christ is the guarantee of revelation

Torrance stresses that it is the full deity of Jesus Christ as the Word and Son which reveals the Father. As the eternal Son in the heart of the Trinity it is the Son who knows the Father in the Spirit. There is an eternal communion of knowing and loving in God and only from within that communion can God be known. It is Jesus Christ who knows God from within that communion and it is only he who can impart that knowledge to anyone outside it. Torrance used to quote as one of the most important verses in the bible, 'No one knows the Father except the Son and any one to whom the Son makes him known'. Only God can know God and only through God can God be known. It is the full deity of Christ the Son which is thus the guarantee that through him we know the Father. Because he is God and comes out of the heart of God to make him known, we know that the knowledge of God which he gives us is ultimately and finally true.

The deity of Christ is the guarantee of reconciliation

Because Jesus Christ is God, he not only makes God known but what he does is the work of God. His word and deed is the word and deed of God. His love and compassion is the love and compassion of the Father. When he forgives that is the very forgiveness of God. This is likewise a point on which Torrance lays immense stress, the identity between the act of Jesus and the act of the Father. What he does is what God does. Torrance would often say, 'There is no God behind the back of Jesus'. In other words, there is no other God than the one we see in Jesus and no act of God other than the act of Jesus. The word and act of Jesus and of the Father are identical. The deity of Jesus is therefore the guarantee that the reconciliaton we see and receive in him is the reconcilation of God himself.

(b) The incarnation and full humanity of Christ

The incarnation of Jesus, in which he the eternal Word and Son of the Father became flesh and took on human form, is the beginning of his incarnate work of revelation and reconciliation. It is the miraculous event in which the Word through which the universe was made out of nothing became himself one of the creatures he had made. In love and compassion for the creation which he had made but which through sin and rebellion was in the process of disintegration, Jesus came to undo sin and death by himself becoming human.

(1) The nature of Jesus' humanity

Here the full humanity of Christ is of equal importance with his deity. If Jesus is not God then it is not God that has saved us, but equally, if Jesus is not man then man has not been saved. The deity and the humanity of Jesus are equally important and neither without the other can bring salvation. For Torrance, therefore, following the early Greek fathers, it is of critical importance to believe in the full humanity of Christ and failure to do so consistently has been a damaging weakness in the history of theology.

Torrance often quoted the famous saying of Gregory Nazianzen, 'the unassumed is the unredeemed'. In other words, whatever Jesus did not assume has not been redeemed. If Jesus did not become flesh, assuming a human body in the incarnation, then the human body has not been redeemed. If Jesus did not assume a human mind, then the human mind has not been saved. In order to save us, Jesus has to become what we are, assuming our humanity to the full. There are several points here:

i) ***Jesus assumed fallen flesh*** – since the humanity that we have is fallen, it was fallen flesh and humanity that Jesus assumed, taking on himself the nature of Adam as it had become after the fall. Sinless though he was, Jesus assumed sinful flesh and humanity, the whole fallen nature of man, body, mind and soul. For Torrance, theology has no option but to say this since otherwise Jesus would not have reached us in our actual condition. He took on himself the sin of the world and as Paul says, God 'made him to be sin who knew no sin'. While the climax of this, as referred to by Paul, was on the cross, Torrance sees it as beginning at Bethlehem and he quotes Calvin's statement that from the moment Jesus assumed flesh he began to pay the price for our liberation. Our redemption began right away in the incarnation with Jesus' assumption of our sinful human nature, but for Torrance we have to immediately say something else also:

ii) ***Jesus sanctified fallen flesh*** – in taking on himself our fallen flesh, sinful as it was, Jesus did not sin, but sanctified our fallen humanity. He the second Adam took on himself fallen adamic humanity but by his life of obedience in it undid its sin and restored it to fellowship with God. Torrance sees the human life of Jesus as one of wrestling with the nature he had made his own in order to bend it back into obedience and love to God. Living in sinful human nature, Jesus wrestles with it 'with strong crying and tears' and through his life of prayer and unbroken obedience to the Father converts it back to him. He grows up in wisdom and knowledge of God, replacing the disobedience of Adam with his own human life of perfect righteousness. And in a life of increasing solidarity with sinners, Jesus enters more and more into their condition, taking their sin and sickness on himself in order to undo them by his purity and offer in exchange his own life and righteousness. Like Calvin, Torrance emphasises the whole human life of Jesus as being one of saving significance.

iii) ***Jesus sanctifies fallen flesh in the very act of assuming it*** – Torrance emphasises that Jesus' assumption of fallen flesh has to be understood dynamically and cannot be separated from his sanctification of it. Jesus assumes fallen flesh but does not sin and that can only be understood dynamically – in the very act of assuming fallen flesh Jesus wrestles with it and sanctifies it. The whole life of Jesus is a dynamic one of wrestling, of learning obedience, of publicly identifying himself with sinners in baptism, but also of growing up in righteousness and intimate communion with the Father. In the midst of his increasing oneness with sinners, climaxed on the cross, Jesus is forging a life of perfect human righteousness and it is that positive human righteousness which lies at the heart of the doctrine of our justification and of union with him through the Spirit.

(2) The humanity of Jesus means that what he does is the act of man

If the deity of Jesus means that what he does is the act of God, his humanity means that it is also the full act of man. In his humanity, Jesus is the genuine act of man, not autonomously or apart from his act as God, but in and through his act as God everything that he does is at the same time the full act of man.

The humanity of Jesus is the guarantee of human knowledge of God

The humanity of Jesus is the guarantee that in Jesus man knows God, that not only is revelation genuinely of God but that in Jesus man has received, grasped and understood revelation. Jesus is the one who knows God from within the heart of God but who has become man in order to translate his knowledge into the heart, mind, speech and act of man. Jesus is not only God revealing himself to humanity, but man coming to accept divine revelation and know God. He is the God who is known and the man who knows, the one true human knower of God. As God, he knew God already but became man in order *as man* to know God and for us. In his knowing of God and in his bringing us to share in his knowledge through the Spirit, he is the guarantee of our knowing.

The humanity of Jesus is the guarantee of human reconciliation and forgiveness

The humanity of Jesus means that in him the love of God has reached down to embrace human life, to reconcile man to himself in forgiveness and to draw the human heart into fellowship with him. The humanity of Jesus means that not only is he God coming down to reconcile man to himself, but that he is the man in whom the divine reconciliation is worked out for all humanity, the man who receives and knows and who indeed is the divine forgiveness. This is something that began with the incarnation but is worked out above all at the cross and in the resurrection. The risen humanity of Jesus is the guarantee of human reconciliation and forgiveness.

(c) The 'hypostatic union' of God and man in the one person of Christ

For Torrance, the union of God and man in Christ is the basic fact of the Christian faith. The 'hypostatic union' (from *hypostasis*, the Greek word used for 'person') is the union of God and man in the one person of Christ, or the doctrine of 'two natures (divine and human) in one person'. The hypostatic union established in the incarnation means that there is now a permanent union of God and man in the person of Christ. In him, in his living person, God and man are now united for all time. That means that Jesus, in his one person, is the living bond between God and man, the living heart of revelation and reconciliation and indeed himself the fact of revelation and reconciliation.

In these Christology lectures, Torrance devotes considerable space to explaining the origin and details of the doctrine of the hypostatic union in the early church and its development in Reformation theology. Technical as some of its details are, the doctrine provides the church with a fundamental guide and key to understanding not only the person of Christ but other doctrines as well.

(1) The nature of the hypostatic union

i) ***two natures in one person*** – the hypostatic union means that in the incarnation God became man in such a way that without giving up his divinity or ceasing to be God, he was now also man in the person of Jesus. There are not two persons, a divine Jesus and a human Jesus, but only one who is both. He who is the eternal Son of the Father, the second person of the Trinity, is now also man. He who as God always had a divine nature, now has also a human nature.

ii) ***'without confusion, change, division or separation'*** – according to the Council of Chalcedon, the divine and human natures of Christ are united 'without confusion, change, division or separation'. His divine nature is not changed into human nature, but remains what it was and his human nature is not divinised but remains human. That means also that there can be no confusion between them, since each remains distinctly what it was. They are united 'without change or confusion'.

The fact that they are united however in the one person of Christ means that we cannot divide Christ in his divinity from Christ in his humanity or make any separation between his divine and human nature. They are united 'without division or separation'.

(2) The importance of the hypostatic union

i) ***it guards the full reality of Christ*** – the doctrine of the hypostatic union guards the full reality of Christ for the church in two ways: a) it recognises two fundamental features of Christ, the fact that he is one Christ and the reality of both his divinity and his humanity. It thus outlines *positively* the nature of Christ in his wholeness. b) It states *negatively* how the union of divine and human natures in Christ is *not* to be understood. There is to be no change, confusion, division or separation between the natures. It does not attempt to define *how* Christ is one person in two natures, for in the nature of the case that cannot be done. Just as we cannot say how God created the universe out of nothing, so we cannot say how he became man. We can recognise his reality once it has come into being but we cannot say how it came into being.

The doctrine of the hypostatic union thus recognises the fundamental features of the reality of Jesus and without trying to explain them guards them by saying how they are *not* to be understood. It allows the one whole Christ in his positive reality to keep on disclosing himself to us by delineating and marking off wrong ways of understanding. It sets the boundaries within which Jesus in his wholeness can be known without distortion. For Torrance, the doctrine of the 'hypostatic union', ever since its definitive formulation in the Creed of Chalcedon of 451, has been of fundamental significance in guiding the thinking of the church.

ii) ***it is the heart of the gospel*** – the doctrine of the union of God and man in Christ is the absolute heart of the gospel. It tells us that the full reality of God in his love has come all the way to suffering and sinful humanity and has united himself with us. It tells us that we have been accepted in the fullness of our humanity and brought as we are into union with him in Christ. It tells that because Christ is the permanent union of God and man, his person is the indivisible and living centre of our salvation for all time. The doctrine of the hypostatic union is a theological way of putting what Jesus is saying in his 'I am' statements in the gospel of John, 'I am the resurrection and the life', 'I am the bread of life', etc, and what Paul means when he speaks about 'our [your] life in Christ Jesus, whom God made our wisdom, our righteousness and sanctification and redemption'. Jesus *is* all these things in himself. He does not just give them to us, he *is* them. The hypostatic union is a theological way of saying the same thing which also gives us the ground for why Jesus *is* all this in himself, namely that he is the living union of God and man in his person. Torrance calls the hypostatic union 'the heart' and 'the mainstay of the doctrine of atoning reconciliation'.

(3) The hypostatic union needs to be understood dynamically

Torrance emphasises that the hypostatic union cannot be understood statically. It is the union, begun at Bethlehem, of God and man in the person of Christ but it needs to be carried through the whole life of Jesus and worked out on the cross in atonement and then on into resurrection. It needs to be understood dynamically in terms of Jesus' growth in wisdom and in terms of his battle with evil. Torrance writes of how the bond of prayer between Jesus and the Father, the innermost heart of his life of atoning obedience, came under fearful attack by the powers of evil, seeking to separate him from the Father and destroy the bond between God and man in him. The hypostatic union, forged at Bethlehem, had to be maintained and lived out throughout the life of Jesus, in the teeth of the attack of evil and in the face of the divine judgement on sin. Throughout it all, the hypostatic union held fast as Jesus clung to the Father in utter and obedient dependence in prayer. And so the hypostatic union emerged victorious and unscathed in the resurrection as the eternal union of God and man in Christ Jesus.

(4) The use of 'anhypostasis' and 'enhypostasis' in understanding the hypostatic union

Torrance also emphasised the importance of 'anhypostasis' and 'enhypostasis' in understanding the hypostatic union and clarifying its nature.

i) ***anhypostasis*** says that the humanity of Jesus had no reality of its own apart from the incarnation of the Son (from the Greek, *an-hypostasis*, 'not-person' or 'not-reality'). In other words, Jesus as man would not have existed if the eternal Son had not become man. The humanity of Jesus only came into existence in the incarnation. It was entirely the act of God and had no independent reality.

ii) ***enhypostasis*** says that the humanity of Jesus did have full reality in the incarnation of the Son (from the Greek, *en-hypostasis*, 'in-person', ie. having reality *in*-the-person of the Son). Although entirely the act of God, the humanity of Jesus had full, individual and personal reality *in* the person of the eternal Son.

Taken together anhypostasis and enhypostasis help to clarify more precisely the nature of the person of Jesus. His humanity has no existence apart from the incarnation of the Son, but does have real, full and personal existence in the person of the Son. The incarnation for Torrance is a model of grace, as he brings out in his discussion of the virgin birth. Our salvation is entirely the act of God and not a human act, but an act of God in which we have full personal reality.

(d) As Word and Son become flesh, Christ is the truth of God

The biblical concept of truth, word becoming event, the Word become flesh

The concept of Christ as the truth of God brings together and amplifies some of the points which have already appeared as leading features of Torrance's theology. For Torrance, the biblical concept of truth is that of word becoming event. Truth is what happens when the word of God becomes event. It is not simply the intellectual concept of the correspondence of statements to reality, but the much more dynamic one of action that corresponds to word. It is doing the truth. As an example, Torrance would quote the story of how when Elijah revived the widow of Zarephath's son, she said to him, 'Now I know that the word of the Lord in your mouth is truth.' For Torrance, the word of God which was lodged in the tabernacle and which the Israelites failed to allow to become flesh in their hearts and lives, has himself become flesh in order to do the word in their midst. 'And the Word became flesh and dwelt among us, full of grace and truth.' Jesus is the utter and complete truth of God because he is the Word of God who has actualised in human flesh and event what he is in God.

The significance of Christ as the Word and Son in God become event in human history

To speak of Christ as the Word and Son of God is to translate the theological language of 'hypostatic union' and of the deity and humanity of Christ back into biblical language. It is to use biblical categories to say many of the same things from a different angle and to make clear, through interpretation of biblical passages on the Word and Son, the basis for theological language in biblical language. Torrance's order of exposition in his lectures is, in fact, to begin with the bible, with theological interpretation of biblical passages on the Word and Son and on Jesus' whole life of faithfulness to God and man which led to the cross. The doctrine of the union of God and man in Christ emerges from the biblical passages and guides the whole interpretation, but it is only near the end of his lectures on Christology that the doctrine is expounded in its details as a whole.

The different elements of *Christ as the Word and Son in God become event* can be looked at briefly in turn before putting them together to see their significance as a whole:

i) ***the being of Christ in God*** – the significance of Christ having his being in the heart of God is that he is with God and is God. He is, to use biblical language, the Word who was in the beginning with God and is God, the Son who dwells in the bosom of the Father. When he becomes flesh and in human form speaks and acts, that is the presence of God himself face to face with people in the midst of human history.

ii) ***Jesus the eternal Son, the image of the Father*** – as the eternal Son Jesus is the image of the Father and the perfect reflection of his glory. To know him is to know the Father. To see him is to see the Father, as Jesus said in John. Torrance points out how the categories of Word and Son are used together of Jesus and in similar ways to speak of the incarnation but adds that the category of Son is the fuller. The Son knows the Father, hears his word and speaks it in human language. By word and deed together and by being himself the image of the Father the Son makes him known.

iii) ***Jesus the eternal Word that is in God*** – in the very heart of God, Torrance used to say, there is Word, the Word which Jesus is. From all eternity there is a Word in God, a speaking in the heart of the Trinity and Torrance used to quote Anselm's famous phrase about the *intimate speaking in the highest being* (*intima locutio apud summam substantiam*). The Word of God, in other words, did not begin to exist when God spoke to his creation. It, or rather he, is eternally part of the being of the Trinity. To know God in Christ, therefore, is not just to know the

Son of the Father, it is to know the Word of the Father, and just as the Son is the image of the Father so the Word can be thought of as the mind and rationality (understood personally) of the Father, as Torrance calls him.

iv) ***the becoming flesh and deed of the Word and Son*** – the Word and Son of God become flesh in history in revelation and reconciliation. The Word becomes event and throughout the course of his life speaks and does the word of God in utter faithfulness. The Son becomes 'the son of the house' that is Israel, living as the obedient Son who makes known the Father and fulfils his reconciling and atoning will even in death. In the life, mind, heart and soul of Jesus, the Word of God becomes personal event in human history and is the very truth of God. Jesus the eternal Son becomes 'son of man' and as the faithful son who knows the Father and does his will in truth he is the perfect reflection of the Father, 'the image of the invisible God'.

The identity of knowledge of Christ and knowledge of God

As the eternal Word and Son within God, Jesus is the Word and image of the Father. When he becomes man, he becomes in man what he was in God. Or to put it the other way round, what he is in God he becomes in man, so that as man he is the very truth of God, Word become event, the Word of God become human speech, the image of the Father become a human person. To know and hear Christ is to know the Word and mind of God, to know and see him is to know and see the Father. The absolute identity of knowledge of Christ with knowledge of God is one of the cardinal points of the Torrancian theology and applies equally to Christ as Word and as Son.

i) ***to apprehend Jesus the Word is to apprehend the mind and rationality of God*** – to know and apprehend the word of Jesus on earth is to apprehend the very mind and rationality of God in heaven. In knowing Jesus we are knowing the Word in the Trinity, God himself in the basic structure of his personal being, if we can stretch words to put it like that. Torrance will have nothing to do with a 'non-cognitive' knowledge of God, as if we could know God only with our hearts rather than with the minds of our hearts.

Torrance used to make a distinction between apprehend and comprehend. We can apprehend an object, he used to say, such as a football with our hands, but we cannot comprehend it in the sense of getting our hands right round it. We can grip something even if we cannot get our hand round it. Similarly, he said, we can apprehend God but we cannot comprehend him. For Torrance, faith involved an intellectual component in which through grace and in the Spirit our minds can genuinely apprehend God in his personal being, even if his reality far outstrips our comprehension.

ii) ***to know Jesus the Son is to know the Father and see his face*** – the point need not be laboured here, save to strengthen if possible what has already been said and reiterate it by adapting Torrance's quote from H.R. Mackintosh: there can be no knowledge of God other than in Jesus and when we look in his face we see the very face of God and then we know that we do not need to see the face of the Father, because we have already seen it in Jesus and could not see it elsewhere or elsehow.

The salvation of Christ is the salvation of God

As Word and Son of the Father, Jesus is the love, the compassion, the righteousness, the judgement, the mercy of God become event in history. In Jesus the love and faithfulness of God have become event and been actualised in history. The righteousness of the Father has become incarnate in the human righteousness of Jesus. The whole life of Jesus, in his teaching and creative word of forgiveness, in his ministry of compassion and healing and in his cross, resurrection and ascension is the salvation of God become event. It is the truth of God, the salvation of the Father become event in Jesus.

Knowledge of Christ in time is knowledge of the mind and will of God in eternity

The identity between knowledge of Christ and knowledge of God means that what we come to know in Christ of the will of God, is the will of God in eternity and from all eternity. What is made known to us in Jesus in time is the eternal will of God, or as Calvin put it, Jesus makes known to us the will of God as it was from the beginning. For Torrance there can be absolutely no distinction between the will of God in eternity and the will of God as we know it in Christ in time. Any such distinction is a false dualism, which leads to a false way of understanding predestination. We can know nothing of God other than what he makes known to us in time in Christ. The incarnation means that there is no God apart from Jesus the man, because he has become man in Jesus. There is therefore no will of God apart from Jesus, for in him his will has become man. The incarnation means that there is no dualism between a God in eternity and a God in time. The God in eternity *is* the God in time in Jesus. Without ceasing to be the eternal God, God in eternity has become flesh, has become God in time in Jesus. What therefore we know of the mind and will of God in Christ, is the mind and will of God in eternity. For Torrance, 'Pre-destination means that what God is toward us in Jesus Christ on earth and in time, he is antecedently and eternally in himself, and that everything that God is in himself he is toward us in Jesus Christ.'

For Torrance, the event and time conditioned character of all knowledge of God (indeed of all knowledge in general) is a point of major importance. There is no spaceless and timeless knowledge of God. We cannot therefore think of a static eternal God apart from the living God who actively makes himself known to us in time and space in the history of Israel and above all in Christ. Abstract western or eastern philosophical views of God are very different from the God who makes himself personally known in word and action in the biblical history.

(e) The person of Christ in relation to humanity and the individual

In his dogmatics Torrance endeavours to be true to the logic of scripture and Christ. As mentioned already, he tries to understand it as faithfully as possible out of itself without distortion through the use of preconceived structures of understanding which fail to hold it together in its wholeness. He presents the central elements of biblical doctrine embedded in the teaching of their scriptural whole and held together in Christ.

i) ***Christ is the agent and key to creation*** – in biblical language, Christ is the Word and Son through whom everything was created, who upholds the universe by the word of his power and in whom it all hangs together. He is the one in whom all men and women find the secret of their life and in whose image they were created. In his classic *On the Incarnation of the Word* (one of Torrance's honours seminar texts), Athanasius argues that because Christ is the one in whom all human life was created and finds its life, it is he and he alone who can come to restore men and women to his image.

ii) ***the person of Christ with his work is a whole*** – for Torrance, the person and work of Christ cannot be separated or understood apart from each other. The person of Christ includes his work as one whole Christ and he is only known 'clothed with his gospel', clothed with his whole work of salvation. His whole saving life, his work of atonement begun in the incarnation and completed in the cross and resurrection, is part of his person. Jesus in his person is one whole living salvation.

iii) ***salvation is complete in the person of Christ*** – Torrance teaches emphatically that the salvation of all is complete in the person of Christ. The operative words here are *in Christ* or *in the person of Christ,* not outside him but *in his person.* He points to the many biblical passages which use the indicative past tense to speak of salvation, 'while we were enemies we were reconciled to God', 'God was in Christ reconciling the world to himself', 'but God, even when we were dead through our trespasses, made us alive together with Christ', etc. In Christ, we have been saved, past tense, and for Torrance that is the good news of the gospel which brings us to faith.

iv) ***the concept of the one and the many*** – fundamental to Torrance's theology of Christ is the biblical concept of *the one and the many.* He points out how the high priest in Israel wore on the breastpiece and shoulder-pieces of his robes the names of the twelve tribes of Israel engraved on precious stones, symbolising the fact that he represented all Israel and that when he went in to meet God on the Day of Atonement all Israel went in with him in his person. He was 'the one' representing 'the many'. Torrance also points out how 'the many' means 'all' and is clearly interpreted as such in passages of the New Testament. Jesus' words, for example, about his giving 'his life as a ransom for many' are interpreted by Paul as 'as ransom for all' and Paul can say, 'one has died for all; therefore all have died'. Jesus is the one who represents the many, the one who acts in the place of the all.

In the person of Jesus, the salvation of the whole of humanity and indeed of the whole universe is already encompassed and completed. One of Torrance's strongest emphases, which runs all the way through his teaching, is the cosmic hope and understanding of the New Testament. The birth, death and resurrection of Jesus is the beginning of the new creation which reaches out through the gospel to renew and recreate all things.

v) ***anhypostasis and enhypostasis*** – Torrance uses the concepts of *anhypostasis* and *enhypostasis* to help show how the salvation of the whole human race is complete in Christ but is not automatic and comes to us personally.

Anhypostasis – the doctrine of *anhypostasis* says that Jesus' humanity only came into being with the incarnation of the Son. He assumed human nature into oneness with his deity, not a pre-existing individual human person. In so doing, he assumed the human nature of every human person and in that human nature worked out the salvation of all. In his human nature in which he the Judge bore in himself the divine judgement on sin, in which he undid its corruption and which he presented renewed and restored in him to the Father, Jesus has accomplished the salvation of the whole of humanity. Taken by itself the anhypostatic nature of Jesus' humanity could mean an ontological solidarity with all humanity which meant that their salvation was automatic as they were all of necessity saved.

Enhypostasis – the doctrine of *enhypostasis* says that in the incarnate Son, Jesus is fully an individual person. He is man and a man. He wears the human nature of all, but through the act of God he does so as fully individual and fully personal in the person of the Son. He bears the humanity of all in the shape of a single person. He is the salvation of all in his own individual person and his salvation is identical with his individual person. That means that the salvation of all is not automatic but comes to us personally in personal relations of encounter and response in faith. Calvin put it somewhat similarly when he said that all the parts of our salvation have been completed in Christ but that that remains of no use to us until we are brought into union with him by the Spirit through faith.

Anhypostasis and *enhypostasis* need to be taken together. Separated they distort our understanding of the person of Christ and of our salvation in him. By itself, *anhypostasis* could lead to a doctrine of universalism or limited atonement, while *enhypostasis* could imply Arminianism. Together, they help express the New Testament perception of the completeness of our salvation in Jesus with the need for faith.

(f) The nature of faith and reason

For Torrance, faith may be defined as what happens to our reason when it encounters the nature and reality of God. It encounters a personal reality it has not met before, which it cannot fit into its predefined categories, which far outstrips its powers of comprehension but which makes itself intelligible in terms of its own unique reality. Reason must either reject such a reality or recognise it and learn to reshape its whole way of perception in accordance with the nature of this new reality. If it does the latter, reason becomes faith. It becomes in Torrance's language the mode of apprehension appropriate to the eternal God. Faith may be defined as the obedience of reason to the nature and reality of God. It is the appropriate response to the Person-Word-event it encounters in Christ, the Son and Word of the Father become man for us in historical event.

The nature of faith may therefore be outlined as having the following characteristics:

i) ***faith is personal*** – faith involves becoming personal as Christ is personal. As the Son of the Father who lives eternally in the communion of the Trinity and who became a human person, Jesus meets and transforms us personally, drawing us into a relation with him of trust and love and of union and communion which reaches back and takes us into the eternal love and communion in God. Faith involves being taken out of our individualistic and self-enclosed modes of existence into genuine personal relation with God and with all others in the new creation of Christ.

ii) ***faith involves hearing and understanding*** – as personal knowledge of the Word of God, faith inevitably involves an element of hearing and of understanding. For Torrance, all knowledge of God is through his word and in listening to it we learn to hear and understand and know him without the use of any pictures or images of him. Faith is auditive knowledge in which our minds and hearts learn to recognise and hear the living Word through the written word and rest on it in trust and understanding. Although understanding is never complete, all faith from the beginning involves a degree of understanding in which God in his being is apprehended as love and truth and inherently to be trusted.

iii) ***faith involves event and historical memory*** – Torrance stresses that our knowledge of God in inseparable from the event in which he has made himself known to us. We cannot know him except through his will to make himself known to us and through the way that he chooses to do so. In the long history of Israel culminating in Jesus, God was making himself known in space and time, within creation, in the concrete events of Israel's history and the lives of her people. He made himself known in his word to Abraham, Isaac and Jacob, to Samuel and the prophets. His word came to them in the midst of their ordinary existence and embedded itself in their history, shaping it and fulfilling itself in event. God's whole revelation is inseparable from the whole event of Israel's history and of the life of Jesus. Torrance therefore in his lectures spends considerable time recounting and narrating the thread of the biblical history in the light of its goal in Christ.

When we know God, we know him through the events of biblical history as the God who endures in it and behind it, 'I am the God of Abraham and Isaac and Jacob . . .' We know God as the same God who spoke to Abraham and guided Israel and we know him as those who are the living successors of their history, who have been incorporated into it through the coming of Jesus. Knowledge of God thus involves a kind of historical memory in which we know him in his word and actions in time and through time. When we know the risen, ascended Christ we know him through the events of his word and life on earth.

For Torrance, the actual involvement of the living God in the real events of space and time is an essential component of faith. Faith does not just believe in God, it believes that he acts for us in space and time and that in Jesus he has decisively saved us and inaugurated a new creation which is waiting to be unveiled. The incarnation, as the actual becoming man of God, the death of Jesus on the cross and the empty tomb are all fundamental to faith.

The fact that God comes into time as historical happening means something else for Torrance. It means that we in the midst of our history are confronted by a living event we cannot ignore, God in the person of Jesus meeting us personally. It means the need for decision and faith and that is the element of truth in existentialism. But whereas in existentialism the emphasis goes on us and the need for authentic existence and living in the present, in Christian faith the emphasis is on Christ and life lived in encounter with him and out of him.

iv) ***faith involves living by the faith of Christ*** – Torrance points out the significance of the Greek wording of Galatians 2.20, 'I have been crucified with Christ; it is no longer I who live, but Christ who lives in me; and the life I now live in the flesh I live by ***the faith of*** the Son of God, who loved me and gave himself for me.' We have been brought to know God. Our old way of living in which we did not know God has been put to death with Christ. We now live, we have faith, we interpret the scriptures and do theology, and yet it is not us but Christ who lives in us. The real believer is Christ and we live by and out of the human faith of Christ.

v) ***faith is living by the 'vicarious humanity' of Christ*** – a key part of Torrance's theology is the fact that everything that Jesus did in his humanity he did for us and everything that Jesus is he is for us. It is all ours through union with him in faith. What we could not do for ourselves God has come to do for us as man. The person of Christ is not just God acting for our salvation, it is God acting as man for us. Christ's life of 'passive obedience', in which he suffered the judgement of God and atoned for our sins on the cross, means that we are freed from them. Christ's life of 'active obedience', in which he positively fulfilled the Father's will, means that his human righteousness is ours and is a fundamental part of our justification. Jesus has completed all the parts of our salvation in the whole course of his life. His human life he lived for us and in our place.

The relation between our faith and Christ's, our life now and his vicarious humanity for us, is exactly that described in Galatians 2.20 and described elsewhere in Paul as life in union with Christ.

vi) ***faith is union with Christ through the Spirit*** – for Torrance, the Christian life is one of union with Christ in which in faith we live out of his faith and his righteousness. Having no righteousness in ourselves, we are united to him so that we may live out of his. Our faith is the knowledge, given to us in the Spirit, that he has accomplished our salvation in his person and work and that we are saved purely by his unconditional grace.

This does not mean that we do nothing although it does mean that we do nothing for our salvation. For Torrance, there is an analogy here with the person of Christ. The fact that the humanity of Christ owes its being entirely to the action of God in the incarnation, does not mean it is not real. The fact that Christ is all of God, or that all of God is in Christ, does not mean that there is nothing of man in him, but the opposite, that all of man is in him. Torrance used to explain that in the logic of grace, 'All of grace does not mean nothing of man. All of grace means all of man.' The knowledge that forgiveness and salvation is all of grace liberates us out of ourselves into union with Christ, freeing us to live fully and freely out of him. All of grace means all of man, just as the action of God in Christ means all of man in Christ.

Acknowledgements

It is a pleasure to thank the several people, members of Torrance's own family and others who have contributed so much in various ways to the publication of these lectures. It has been a privilege to collaborate with Jock Stein of Handsel Press and latterly with Robin Parry of Paternoster Press in the preparation of these lectures for publication. Jock's publishing expertise has been invaluable throughout. The typesetting is his as is the labour behind the bulk of the index as well as its final compilation. To Robin fell the task of collaborating with Inter Varsity Press in the USA and overseeing the final publication. To both are due thanks for their unfailing helpfulness.

My brothers James and Donald Walker lent their copies of Torrance's lecture handouts. Several people, Donald and Judith Walker, Marion Foggin, Clare Parsons and Jennifer Floether, have commented on elements of the text and made useful suggestions. Professor David Fergusson of New College has from the beginning been warmly supportive and encouraging. Dr Tom Noble recalled how Torrance used to recommend reading his introduction to *The School of Faith* as preparatory reading for his lectures, while Dr Nathan McDonald gave help with points relating to the Hebrew of the lectures. Particular thanks are due to Dr Elmer Colyer and Professor John Webster for their careful reading of the whole text and their judicious comments.

Any points of difficulty in interpreting the text were discussed with Torrance's brother, the Rev David Torrance, who knows his thought well and was also able to contribute valuable historical information. He and my brother James, who heard the lectures, have both read all or much of the edited text and made many helpful and perceptive comments. Professor Alan Torrance assisted on a number of points of difficulty. The help of all three of them has been invaluable and their time and support very much appreciated. Thomas S. Torrance supplied useful background information on both his father and the lectures as well as keenly supporting and ably assisting their final publication on his father's behalf.

I would also like to thank my parents, family and friends for their support and encouragement throughout as well as colleagues at the Edinburgh University Field Centre at Firbush Point, Loch Tay, for their patience with me as I absented myself from their company in the evenings and days off to work on the lectures. It has been an inspiration to be able to do much of the work in such a congenial and beautiful setting. Finally it is an enormous privilege to have been asked to edit Torrance's lectures and to come back to them in such a way after thirty years.

The text of the lectures

For general interest, but more for the sake of scholars, particularly those of Torrance's theology, the following is a brief account of the editing process and the differences between the lectures as here presented and the original manuscript of the lectures.

The initial manuscript

When the initial manuscript was handed over to Jock Stein of Handsel Press to be edited for publication, it had already been transcribed on to computer disc. It consisted almost exclusively of the handouts of his lectures which Torrance had had duplicated for students. By the mid 1960s at the latest, Torrance was in the process of producing full handouts of his lectures, typed out by the New College secretarial staff. By the mid 1970s if not earlier, and certainly by the time he retired in 1979, it would seem that almost all if not all of his lectures on Christology and Soteriology had been duplicated for students.

The lectures had never been intended for publication and there was a covering letter stating, 'the text is not publishable in its present state'. In general, however, the material was very readable as it was, if in need of extensive polishing and minor editing in preparation for publication. Some sections were not as polished as others and on occasions the English read awkwardly, while a few sentences were expressed so tersely as to make the meaning hard to follow. Headings were not always consistently numbered and occasionally combined numerical with alphabetical numbering in the same series of headings. Torrance assumed a background knowledge in his students which allowed him to make numerous allusions to biblical passages with no reference and to use technical terms or Latin expressions without explanation. Some typing errors had also occurred naturally enough in the transcription process and occasionally references would have a misplaced page or chapter and verse number. The manuscript of the lectures on Soteriology was missing a lecture on redemption in the Old Testament which the present editor remembered as having been part of the dogmatics course.

Guiding principles behind the editing process

There were three main guiding principles:

i) ***fidelity to the author's thought*** – fidelity to the text and the author's own thought was naturally the overriding principle at all times and on the occasions when the text did require editing, fidelity to the author's thought remained paramount.

ii) ***readability and accessibility of the text*** – the second main principle was to make the text as readable and accessible to as wide a range of readers as possible and in particular to those with no knowledge of technical theological or philosophical terms. This involved the following: the addition of headings, the subdivision of paragraphs and sentences and of one very long chapter, minor editing of the English, the addition of biblical references and explanatory footnotes and the provision of a glossary of terms for those unfamiliar with theological language.

iii) ***comprehensiveness of the text*** – the third principle was to make the text as comprehensive an account as possible of Torrance's lectures and theology on Christology and Soteriology. This entailed the addition of a missing lecture, of handouts on Dogmatics, on the Resurrection and Ascension and on the doctrine of the Church, and of two excerpts from *Conflict and Agreement in the Church.*

iv) ***consistency of format*** – a fourth principle, of minor importance as far as the text was concerned, but important for publication, was simply the consistency of the material in terms of numbering of headings, format and layout, etc.

The main changes

Headings

Torrance's existing headings and their divisions of the text have naturally been retained but the numbering and frequency of headings has been standardised. In addition, a substantial number of headings have been added to make the text more readable and accessible. As a general rule, headings without numbers have all been added, while numbered headings are the author's, but here too some numbered headings have also been added.

Addition, division and transposition of material

Several handouts, on 'Scientific Dogmatics', 'Redemption in the Early Church' (the missing lecture on redemption in the Old Testament), the 'Resurrection and Ascension of Jesus' and on the doctrine of the Church were typed in. The two excerpts from *Conflict and Agreement* were of a sufficient quality to be scanned in. With the exception of the first handout, the additional material now forms the latter part of the lectures on Soteriology.

There are several changes, mostly in the way of division and transposition of material, to the layout of the Christology lectures:

i) the division of one originally very long chapter into four. In Torrance's original manuscript, 'Chapter 3: The incarnate life of the Son in the union of his divine and human natures' consisted of four sections totaling 115 pages in A4 format! The beginning of section 4 of the chapter refers to previous sections as 'chapters', indicating that they may have originally been so. For the sake of readability, those divisions have been restored and the four sections each with their own original headings now appear as the separate chapters 3, 4, 5 and 6 in the present book.

ii) the transfer of sections 4 and 5 (on Bultmann and mythology) and of the other more technical passages of chapter one to the endnotes. This is material of theological significance dealing with controversies of the early and mid twentieth century of interest to the specialist rather than to the general reader.

iii) the transfer of the bulk of chapter two, 'The Biblical Witness to Jesus Christ' to chapter ten of the Soteriology lectures, where it appropriately follows the chapter on the ascension of Jesus and the sending of the Spirit on the apostles. Section 1 only, 'Encounter with Christ in the witness of the New Testament', is retained here and becomes the final section, section 4, of chapter one.

iv) Torrance's Eschatology Addendum to his Soteriology lectures is transposed to become the Addendum to the Christology lectures, where it sits alongside the related and similarly technical material of the endnotes to chapter one.

v) the inclusion in chapter one of a handout on 'Scientific Dogmatics'.

Subdivision of the text

Apart from the one chapter mentioned above, subdivision involved paragraphs and sentences. Long paragraphs, sometimes well over a page, were broken into shorter paragraphs based on the natural division of thought in the text. Sentences also were sometimes rather long, making it hard to follow the meaning at the first reading. Torrance's style of holding and balancing together different concepts meant that he could often express himself in long sentences. Unnecessarily long sentences were always subdivided. Otherwise long sentences were divided where it made them easier to read and where the meaning was not affected. Sometimes it was not possible to divide a sentence without some loss of meaning and then it was left as it was.

Inclusive language

While the use of 'man' in conjunction with male pronouns such as 'he', 'him' or 'his' has been replaced by a variety of expressions, particularly mankind, humanity, men and women, and occasionally humankind, in order to make its use appear less gender specific, the use of 'man' as such has been retained. As Torrance emphasised in the preface to his last major work, "the word 'man' is used throughout in the *inclusive biblical sense* and not in a sexist way". The biblical 'man', while linguistically male, refers to man and woman together, to man generically as humanity and its retention has a number of advantages. 'Man' remains closer to biblical thought and usage: it is more personal and less abstract than mankind, humanity or humankind. In its use as a singular noun which is also used generically, 'man' expresses the biblical concept of the unity of the human race and of 'the one and the many' in a way which is closer to the biblical concreteness of expression.

References

The text had no footnotes and indeed not many references other than biblical ones. References have been transferred from the main body of the text to footnotes and extensive biblical referencing added to biblical passages quoted or alluded to, but not directly cited. In all but one or two cases where it has not been possible to trace the source, Torrance's references have been verified and occasionally amended. Several cross-references to other works of his have also been added in order to enable the reader to follow up and compare the discussion in the lectures with that elsewhere in the Torrancian corpus.

Explanatory footnotes

Wherever there were technical theological or philosophical terms, or Latin, Greek, Hebrew and occasionally German words, explanatory footnotes have been added for the general reader. Such footnotes are all editorial, as are footnotes providing explanation and amplification of points of special interest or importance in the text.

Minor editing

A major part of the editing task was editing which was 'minor' in nature but cumulatively considerable. Minor editing involved such things as amendments to punctuation, for example, the addition or deletion of commas or of other punctuation marks, in order to make a passage read better or its meaning clearer. It also involved, in keeping with modern style, the extensive deletion of the capitals used throughout the text for divine pronouns and words like Creator, Saviour, Redeemer, but also for words such as Revelation, Incarnation, Prophet, New Covenant, Resurrection, etc.

In the main, however, the task of minor editing involved little changes or alterations of the English to make it flow better, sometimes the use of different words and sometimes simply the transposition of words or phrases. Although 'minor', little changes to the English or to the punctuation could make a significant difference to the way a passage reads. Occasionally where the text was difficult it was a matter of finding ways of expressing the same thought more simply. While the need for minor editing was extensive, it was balanced against fidelity to the author's own wording, allowing the integrity of the author's thought and style to remain unchanged.

The example of Torrance's own editing of his lecture material

It was fortunate that in the process of editing, examples of Torrance's own editing of his lecture material came to light, both confirming the process already underway and acting as a guide. It became apparent that two of the Soteriology chapters, with their own headings, duplicated a major portion of two of the other chapters. For example, in chapter one ('The Atonement in the New Testament'), the third section headed, 'Atonement as Redemption', appeared as 'Chapter 2 Atonement as Redemption'. In chapter four ('The Priestly Aspect of Atonement'), the major section, headed 'Reconciliation', appeared as 'Chapter 6 Reconciliation'. A word-for-word comparison of the relevant material revealed that it was identical except for minor variations. It was clear that at some stage Torrance had edited the material since there were numerous minor differences between the versions, small changes to the English or punctuation to make it read better. When twenty or so years later he went back to the material, it naturally appeared to be different chapters with no overlap of content.

A second example was the word-for-word comparison between Torrance's book *Space, Time and Resurrection* and the Resurrection and Ascension handouts typed into the Soteriology lectures. The comparison revealed the handouts had undergone a very similar process of minor emendation. The examples supplied a very useful guide as to how Torrance would himself have edited his lectures for publication. Needless to say, it was always the more polished of the identical Soteriology chapters which was selected as the basic text.

Chapter One

INTRODUCTION TO CHRISTOLOGY

The task of christology[1]

Our task in christology is to yield the obedience of our mind to what is given, which is God's self-revelation in its objective reality, Jesus Christ. A primary and basic fact which we discover here is this: that the object of our knowledge gives *itself* to us to be apprehended. It does that within our mundane existence, within our worldly history and all its contingency, but it does that also beyond the limits of previous experience and ordinary thought, beyond the range of what is regarded by human standards as empirically possible. Thus when we encounter God in Jesus Christ, the truth comes to us in its own authority and self-sufficiency. It comes into our experience and into the midst of our knowledge as a *novum*, a new reality which we cannot incorporate into the series of other objects, or simply assimilate to what we already know.

We cannot compare the fact of Christ with other facts, nor can we deduce the fact of Christ from our knowledge of other facts. The fact of Christ comes breaking into the continuity of our human knowledge as an utterly distinctive and unique fact, which we cannot understand in terms of other facts, which we cannot reduce to what we already know. It is a new and unique fact without analogy anywhere in human experience or knowledge.

And yet Jesus Christ gives himself to be known as the object of our experience and knowledge, within our history and within our human existence – but when we know him there, we know him in terms of *himself*. We know him out of pure grace as one who gives himself to us

---

[1] As an introduction to his class, Torrance used to recommend the introduction to his book of Catechisms officially approved and used by the Church of Scotland: see T.F. Torrance, *The School of Faith* (London: James Clarke 1959), particularly here the sections 'The Method of Instruction: 1. General Principles, 2. Particular Principles' and 'The Nature of Theology', pp. xxi-lxix.

and freely discloses himself to us. We cannot earn knowledge of Christ, we cannot achieve it, or build up to it. We have no capacity or power in ourselves giving us the ability to have mastery over this fact. In the very act of our knowing Christ he is the master, we are the mastered. He manifests himself and gives himself to us by his own power and agency, by his Holy Spirit, and in the very act of knowing him we ascribe all the possibility of our knowing him to Christ alone, and none of it to ourselves.

But let us note: it is only when we actually know Christ, know him as our personal saviour and Lord, that we know that we have not chosen him but that he has chosen us; that it is not in our own capacity to give ourselves the power to know him; that it is not in virtue of our own power or our own capacity that he gives us to know him, but in virtue of his power to reveal himself to us and to enable us to know him; that is, faith itself is the gift of God. Or let me put that in another way: when we know God in Christ, we do not congratulate ourselves on our own powers of intuition or discovery, and pat ourselves on the back because we have been able to see that there is more in Jesus than meets the eye, that God is there himself. No, we do the exact opposite: we acknowledge that in knowing God in Christ, we do so not by our own power, but by the power of God.

The starting point of christology

In other words, in knowing God in Christ, we acknowledge that we are up against a fundamental *mystery*. How we know Christ, we cannot say in terms of our capacities or abilities or any *a priori* understanding,[2] or what you will. We only know that we know Christ, and that is the act of Christ himself, the miracle of his Holy Spirit. Here, then, in Christ is a knowledge that is not possible anywhere else, and that is inconceivable elsewhere. By our own experience and thought all we can arrive at here is the realisation that here is a fact beyond our natural powers to grasp. Here is a mystery that baffles us. We cannot penetrate into it by our apparatus of thinking or perception, nor can we get behind it to see and describe just how it came about. In knowing Christ we acknowledge the fact that confronts us as a lordly act from above and beyond us, which we can only acknowledge.

---

2 From first principles.

Thus we know Christ by acknowledging him, by confessing him as Lord and God. In other words, in knowing Christ, we acknowledge that what confronts us is *revelation,* revelation that tells us that here is true man and true God. The very mystery we acknowledge in knowing him, that we human beings know God, we see to repose in the mystery of the person of Christ, the mystery that in some indescribable and inconceivable way which we cannot explain or understand out of our own knowledge, he is God, and very God, and yet man and very man: God and man become one person. We know Christ in the mystery of that duality in unity.

That is the starting point for a true christology – and that is precisely where the witness of the New Testament faces us, face to face with Christ in his wholeness as God and man. We begin right there, with that witness to Christ, and with the fact that Jesus Christ himself confronts us in that witness as God and man in one person. Our theological task is to begin with awareness and acknowledgement of that mystery as the actual object which we seek to know theologically. That is, we seek to clarify our knowledge of this mystery – but if we are to be true and faithful to it, if we are to be scientific and rational, that is, behave in terms of the nature of this mystery that confronts us, we must not begin by denying its mystery character or by transmuting it into something non-mysterious. We have to stand by it and acknowledge that though the very nature of the object of our knowing defies complete solution or explanation, we cannot drop the problem or run away from it. We must wrestle with it, inquire of it, be obedient to it, and seek in every way to let it *declare itself* to us, so that we may grow in understanding of it. Whatever we do, we must be faithful to the actual facts, and never allow preconceived notions or theories to cut away some of the facts at the start because we cannot understand them in terms of what we already know or hold to be possible. The ultimate fact that confronts us, embedded in history and in the historical witness and proclamation of the New Testament, is the mysterious duality in unity of Jesus Christ, God without reserve, man without reserve, the eternal truth in time, the Word of God made flesh.

A number of preliminary questions are raised at this stage, at the very approach to the doctrine of Christ, questions which require clarification and certain affirmations if we are to proceed in our christology in such a way as to behave rationally in terms of the nature of the object, that is, the Christ presented to us through the biblical testimony. Before we do that, however, it is worth pausing to consider what we mean by 'science' and by 'rational',[3] and what we mean by 'scientific dogmatics'.[4]

The nature of 'scientific dogmatics'

John Macmurray has said that modern science and the scientific spirit are the creative achievement of the Reformation.[5] That claim is not without its justification. The reformers had a passionate belief in the truth, and a readiness to sacrifice pleasant illusions and traditional preconceptions for the sake of the truth. They were determined to let the truth declare itself to them, the whole truth and nothing but the truth. Out of this there grew a way of knowing in which people were determined to be real in their thinking, that is, to think in the way the facts compelled them to think, or to think in accordance with the nature of the given reality. That way of knowing, which now dominates the modern world, is what we call science.

Many people, of course, use the word 'science' in a narrow sense, to refer only to the kind of knowledge we require in order to use things – and so they restrict 'science' almost entirely to natural science. But in the European tradition we have used the term 'science' in a wider and more basic way to speak of the kind of knowledge we get when we seek to know something strictly *in accordance with its own nature and activity*. In this basic sense it is used of the social sciences as well as the natural sciences, and more properly of the pure sciences than the applied sciences.

In the basic sense, then, science refers to the kind of knowledge which is forced upon us when we are *true* to the facts we are up against. Here we do not think in the way we want to think, but in the way we *have to* think, if we are to do justice to the 'object' we are investigating. If a man in a restaurant insists that he sees pink elephants sitting at the

---

[3] See the discussion, T.F. Torrance, *Theological Science* (London: OUP 1969), p. 11f.

[4] The section which follows, The nature of 'scientific dogmatics', is the text of a handout given out to students. It has been added to help readers grasp the importance of understanding what Torrance means by 'science' and 'rational'. The latter part of the handout, which is of a slightly more technical nature, has been transferred to the endnotes where it can be read in full. For an extended discussion on the nature of science, rationality and of theology as a science, see *Theological Science*.

[5] *Reason and Emotion* (London: Faber 1935), p. 172.

other tables, you know that he has become temporarily irrational for he is not thinking in accordance with what is 'out there'. The rational person, free though he or she is, thinks as they are compelled to think by the external world. Science is a rigorous extension of that rationality in which we distinguish what is 'out there' from our own subjective 'images'. In science we ask questions and answer them under the compulsion of what is 'over against us', and so let our thoughts take shape *in accordance with the nature of what we experience* and under its pressure upon us.

Scientific thinking is not 'free thinking', but *thinking bound to its chosen object*, thinking which develops special modes of inquiry and proof appropriate to the nature of that object. Because each particular science is bound to its own field in that way, it will not allow another department of knowledge working in quite a different field to dictate to it on its own ground, either in prescribing its methods or in predetermining its results. Rather, each science allows its own subject matter to determine how knowledge of it is to be developed and tested, for method and subject matter are not to be separated. Edmund Husserl, the great philosopher, used to speak of a positive science of this kind (for example, physics) as a 'dogmatic science'.[6] In a dogmatic science scientists hold to be true only what they are compelled to think, as they let the pattern and nature of what they are investigating impose themselves on their own mind. They are not being dogmatical[7] when they do that; they are humbly submitting their mind to the facts and their own inner logic. Thus physicists are not free to think what they like. They are bound to their proper object and compelled to think of it in accordance with its nature, as it becomes revealed under their questioning.

In the same sense, and in the same modern tradition that gave rise to modern science, Reformed theology has developed the science of dogmatic theology. In the set of theological disciplines, dogmatics is the 'pure science' in which we are concerned to penetrate down to the basic realities about which we must give an account, and which we are compelled to think out in accordance with their own nature and the basic principles we derive from them. In dogmatics, then,

---

[6] See *Theological Science*, pp. 2-3 for the reference and the quotation from Husserl.

[7] Torrance uses 'dogmatical' here rather than 'dogmatic' in the popular sense in order to preserve the use of 'dogmatic' in its original meaning (of being concerned with positive investigation of reality) and avoid confusion with the popular meaning.

theology is bound to its given object, God's Word addressed to us in Jesus Christ, and develops its understanding of it in accordance with its nature and with the way in which it is actually disclosed to us in history. In dogmatics we do not engage in free thinking or in arbitrary speculation, or in the invention of our own images, but in a thinking that is controlled and tested in accordance with the given facts and their own basic forms. The 'facts' of course are of a different kind from those which we have for example, in astrophysics, as different as the nature of God is from the nature of a star. Hence the way of knowing and the way of demonstration employed by theology is very different from that of astrophysics. In its own field, dogmatics insists that reason must behave in accordance with the nature of its divine 'object', God in his self-revelation, and attempts to be true to that – to allow anything else would be irrational and arbitrary, and hence unscientific.[8] [E1]

We now resume our study of the preliminary questions which require clarification before we proceed further in our christology. We begin with the inescapable relation between Christ and history or time.[E2]

1 The relation of Christ to history[9]

The mystery of Christ is presented to us within history – that historical involvement is not an accidental characteristic of the mystery but essential to it. That is the problem.

Let us first put it this way, recalling the bi-polarity of our theological knowledge. If God has become man in the historical Jesus, that is an historical event that comes under our historical examination so far as the humanity of Jesus is concerned, but the fact that *God* became man is an event that cannot be appreciated by ordinary historical science, for here we are concerned with more than simply an historical event, namely, with the act of the eternal God. So far as this event is a fact of nature it can be observed, and

---

8 Note: for [E1] etc. see the endnotes. Endnotes contain lengthier, more technical discussions and are distinguished from footnotes by a preceding [E].

9 Although the lectures here are substantially revised and fuller in content, see Torrance's 'Auburn Lectures' (given in Auburn Seminary, New York, 1938/39): T.F. Torrance, *The Doctrine of Jesus Christ* (Eugene: Wipf and Stock 2002), pp. 2-13, for striking similarities at points with what follows in this chapter.

so far as it is historical in the sense that other natural events are historical, it can be appreciated as such; but the essential *becoming* behind it cannot be directly perceived except by an act of perception appropriate to the eternal event. That act of perception appropriate to the eternal event is *faith*, which is an enabling of reason given to it in the very act of receiving revelation.

But now have we not said too much? The act of perception appropriate to an eternal act, or divine act, would surely be the pure vision of God, which we do not have in history. Here on earth and in time we do not see directly, face to face, but see only in part, as through a glass enigmatically, in a mystery.[10] We see the eternal or divine act within history, within our fallen world where historical observation is essential. Faith would be better described then as the kind of perception appropriate to perceiving a divine act in history, an eternal act in time. So that faith is appropriate both to the true perception of historical facts, and also to the true perception of God's action in history. Faith is not the perception of revelation divorced from history. Nor is it the perception of history by itself, divorced from revelation, but it is the way we are given within history to perceive God's acts in history, and that means that faith is the obedience of our minds to the mystery of Christ, who is God and man in the historical Jesus. What is clearly of paramount importance here is the holding together of the historical and the theological in our relation to Christ.

If the two are not held together, we have broken up the given unity in Christ into the historical on the one hand, and the theological on the other, refracting it into elements which we can no longer put together again. We then find that we cannot start from the historical and move to the theological, or from the theological and move to the historical without distortion, and nor can we rediscover the original unity. We can only start from the given, where the historical and the theological are in indissoluble union in Christ.[11] [E3]

The inseparability of the historical from the theological in Christ

Here we must insist that a proper christology be scientific: that is, it must be faithful to the whole fact of the mystery of Christ. It can never start from one aspect of that mystery such as the historical or the

---

10 See 1 Cor 13.9-12.

11 Following the transfer of the section which follows to the endnotes, this paragraph has been inserted to fill the resultant gap in the text and facilitate a more fluent connection of thought.

eschatological, or the transcendental – but from the dual fact, the whole mystery of true God and true man. That fact calls into radical question the basic assumption (of both idealism and liberalism) that no fact in the time series can have absolute and decisive significance, for the Christian faith pivots upon the fact that here in time we are confronted by the eternal in union with time. Here in our human flesh in Jesus Christ we are confronted with the eternal Word of God which has assumed our human nature and existence into oneness with God. That is the whole unalterable, stubborn fact that we encounter, which cannot be reduced to anything else without falsification. We must wrestle with it and seek to understand it – *God in time, God as man, God active in history.* Apart from that historical act of God in history, there is no knowledge of God, no real experience of God's help and redemption. Christianity has to do with men and women, with contingent history, with our involvement in relativity, in the reality of events as they happen. Redemption that is not actualised in *our* history is no redemption for us at all. It does not touch us and would not be intelligible.

Everything in Christianity centres on the incarnation[12] of the Son of God, an invasion of God among men and women in time, bringing and working out a salvation not only understandable by them in their own historical and human life and existence, but historically and concretely accessible to them on earth and in time, in the midst of their frailty, contingency, relativity and sin. Whatever christology does it cannot depreciate or minimise historical existence with its stark factuality. It stands or falls with the fact that here in our actual history and existence is the saviour God. The historical element is absolutely essential, for apart from it the whole mystery of Christ is dissolved into thin air, and the incarnation means nothing at all.

Going on then from the fact of the mystery of Christ – of God and man in union, of eternity and time in unity, of God's act and historical event in inseparable relation – we may make several positive affirmations of prime importance.

(a) It is the once and for all unity of God and man in Jesus Christ that preserves his humanity

The unity of God and man in Jesus Christ means that true unimpaired humanity does not vanish like smoke in the presence

---

[12] God's becoming man, from the Latin '*in carne*','in flesh'.

of eternal majesty. *Nec tamen consumebatur*![13] As Cyril of Alexandria used to point out with reference to the burning bush, just as the bush was not consumed by the fiery presence of God, so the humanity of Christ is not consumed by his deity. The unity of eternity and time in the incarnation means that true time in all its finite reality is not swallowed up by eternity but eternally affirmed as reality even for God. The unity of God's action and historical event in Jesus Christ means that far from being destroyed or depreciated, history is conserved and preserved by this mystery. Only in such a union of true God and true man can the historical element be maintained unreservedly because it is brought into essential relation with God. Human nature and historical existence are assumed by the eternal God into oneness with himself so that without ceasing to be human nature and historical existence they are eternally affirmed and preserved. In other words, it is only when we are true to the mystery of true God and true man in Jesus Christ that justice is done to the historical Jesus, and all docetic violence[14] is repudiated.

(b) The unity of God and man in Christ is accomplished from the side of God

If this mystery, the unity of God and man in Jesus Christ is God's own act, then, 'what God has joined together, let not man put asunder'. The very fact that it takes God almighty – and even he at such desperate cost – to join God and man in Jesus Christ, tells us in unmistakable language that this is not what we can do. *We cannot* join God and man together. We are unable to bridge the gap between God and man, nor can we ascend up to heaven and bring God down from there. But it is here face to face with the incarnation in space and time, the union of God and humanity in Christ, that we learn that properly for the first time. Only when we see this union actualised in Jesus Christ do we know that we could never join man and God together.

Here is an act of pure grace, the stupendous and absolutely free act of God almighty, and it carries with it the irresistible inference that what God has done here for us, we cannot do for ourselves. In fact the incarnation tells us plainly that all our efforts to go from humanity to God are useless and false – all our efforts to join man to God are judged and disqualified, and by this *fait accompli* in Jesus

---

13 Lat, 'And it was nevertheless not consumed'.

14 Violence to the full humanity of Jesus.

Christ they are completely set aside and revealed to be utterly wrong. God has done the impossible, the incredible thing in Jesus Christ, but it is only now that he has done it that we see how utterly impossible it actually is, impossible for us to accomplish from the side of humanity.

(c) It is impossible to move from the historical Jesus to God

All this means that any christological approach that starts from the man Jesus, from the historical Jesus, and tries to pass over to God, and so to link human nature to God, is utterly impossible. In fact it is essentially a wrong act: for it runs directly counter to God's act of grace which has joined God to humanity in Christ. All attempts to understand Jesus Christ by starting off with the historical Jesus utterly fail; they are unable to pass over from man to God and moreover to pass from man to God in such a way as not to leave man behind altogether, and in so doing they deny the humanity of Jesus. Thus though Ebionite christologies[15] all seek to go from the historical Jesus to God, they can make that movement only by denying the humanity of Jesus, that is by cutting off their starting point, and so they reveal themselves as illusion, and the possibility of going from man to God is revealed as likewise illusory.[E4]

No, it is quite clear that unless we are to falsify the facts from the very start, we must face with utter and candid honesty the New Testament presentation of Christ to us, not as a purely historical figure, nor as a purely transcendental theophany,[16] but as God and man. Only if we start from that duality in which God himself has already joined God and man, can we think God and humanity together, can we pass from man to God and from God to man, and all the time be strictly scientific in allowing ourselves to be determined by the nature of the object.

2 Jesus Christ and the New Testament *kērygma*

If we are to be faithful to Jesus Christ as he is presented to us in the biblical witness, the Christ whom we encounter in the tradition of the church, we cannot take up a so called neutral or impartial attitude to

---

[15] Christologies that view Jesus as essentially an ordinary man, even if unique.

[16] 'Divine manifestation'.

Christ. We can behave only in terms of the given object, and allow ourselves to be unconditionally determined by it, if we are to let it declare itself to us. But this encounter of faith with Christ entails conformity with him: it entails a relation between us and him in which we are reconciled and adapted to him. In that adaptation there is set up an analogical relation of repentance and likeness to Christ within which we are able to know him as he gives himself to be known as Lord and saviour. In other words, our approach to Christ can be only from the standpoint of sinners whose sins have been forgiven, and for whom Christ is the Son of the living God become flesh in order to reconcile the world to God.

H.R. Mackintosh used to remind his students that 'Jesus was not a Christian'.[17] A Christian is a sinner whose sins have been forgiven, who knows himself or herself to have been saved by Christ. But Christ was not a sinner who needed forgiveness. Our approach to Christ must be a Christian approach: we must not try to look at Jesus in such a way as to gain entry into his religion, that is into his own private relation to God the Father. We can approach Jesus only as sinners who need the mediation of Christ in order to go to the Father, so that in the analogical relation set up between us and Christ, we can approach Christ only in acknowledging his uniqueness and sinlessness on the one hand, but on the other hand, only in yielding ourselves to him, in obedient conformity to his saving grace and as sinners desperately in need of him. Christ is utterly unique, but what corresponds to him on our part, is a Christian attitude, the attitude of forgiven and reconciled sinners.

Now, is that not the way in which the New Testament presents Christ, through witnesses who acknowledge from the start that he is saviour and mediator between God and man? Is it not the case that it is from the point of view of forgiven sinners that Jesus is presented by Matthew, Mark, Luke, John, Paul and Peter? Even in the synoptic presentation, we do not have a Jesus presented as he is in himself (whatever that means), who was later interpreted by the church as the Christ, and turned into a theological figure, a dogmatic Christ. What we have presented in the Gospels is certainly the historical Jesus, but no merely historical Jesus; rather is he the Christ, the dogmatic Christ, the Christ of faith. That is, he is Jesus Christ seen through the eyes of sinners who have found in him the redeeming presence of God, who have encountered him as true God and true man in one historical person

---

[17] Cf. T.F. Torrance, *Theology in Reconstruction* (London: SCM Press 1965), p. 135f.

living and working among men and women. What they say about him is that *Jesus* (that is the anointed historical Jesus) is the Christ, the Messiah (that is the saviour sent from God). That is how he is presented in all the Gospels, in the synoptic Gospels as well as the fourth Gospel. Or to put the same thing in another way: from first to last in the Gospels as well as in the Epistles, the presentation of Jesus Christ is based on the certainty and seen in the light of the fact that he rose again from the dead and is ever present to his church through the Spirit. They bear witness to his majesty: 'We have seen the Lord'.[18] 'He has poured out this which you see and hear',[19] that is, his Spirit at Pentecost. The whole account of Jesus Christ is illuminated, shaped and permeated with the glory and revelation that break out clearly in the resurrection.

The New Testament presentation of the Jesus of history as the Christ of faith

What has happened in the New Testament presentation of the historical Jesus Christ was precisely what happened on the mount of transfiguration[20] – the historical Jesus Christ, without in the slightest ceasing to be historical, and in the context of the Old Testament (Moses and Elijah), is transfigured in the light of his death and resurrection, and in the light of the divine revelation acknowledging him as God's beloved Son. Without ceasing to be the historical Jesus Christ, he is presented to us throughout the New Testament as God and saviour, true God and true man. That is the Christ of faith, that is, he who is at once the historical and the theological Christ. It is the glorified Christ who illumines the Jesus of history and casts over him the halo of the light of revelation. It is his own divine light. We do not see Jesus of Nazareth apart from that light anywhere in the New Testament. The only place where, it is sometimes claimed, we may get a glimpse of Jesus apart from that light is in Tacitus or Josephus or Suetonius,[21] but none of them were eye witnesses, and there was no Jesus apart from that light.

If we approach Jesus Christ in the way in which he is actually presented to us in the New Testament, if we allow Jesus Christ really to confront us as God and saviour, then that *fact* determines not only the fundamental attitude of the inquirer, but basically influences his

---

18 See John 20.18; cf. Luke 24.10, 34-35 & Matt 28.10.

19 Acts 2.33.

20 Matt 17.1-9; Mark 9.2-9; Luke 9.28-36.

21 Contemporary Roman and Jewish historians.

or her apprehension of Christ. If Jesus Christ is really the Son of God then it must be clear that a quite different approach must be adopted toward understanding him from that required for any other figure in history – although even on a purely historical level, we cannot help but grant that we are confronted with something that is without parallel anywhere else in all history. If, however, Jesus Christ stands before me as true man and true God, God who created this unity of man and God, then my whole knowing of him will be determined by his act, and will be made real and possible only through his act upon me. If God comes to me in Jesus Christ as my saviour then all my thought about Jesus Christ will take its rise from that act of salvation.

A fact-in-interpretation, Christ clothed with his own gospel

Our approach to knowledge of Christ is therefore from a fact that acts upon us, a fact that attests itself as saving action. Christianity does not start from a bare historical fact as such, but, so to speak, from a *fact-in-meaning*, a *fact-in-interpretation* – not a fact in *my* interpretation, though it must be one that I appropriate as my own, but a fact in the light which God himself gives us through his Holy Spirit. In other language, we do not begin with only a bare historical fact in the New Testament presentation, but a fact that has become a word, a fact that assaults us as the living Word of God, the Word made flesh. The Word of God has taken historical form and is now never without that historical form. It takes its form from our human language and our human reason, but it is all that as the medium of divine revelation, and permeated with the message of God. Here the Word of God become flesh is no mere message from outside of, or alongside of, the historical event of Jesus, but is Word of God to man as essentially human word and essentially historical event, and yet without ceasing to be the transcendent and eternal Word of God. That Word of God become event, that message of God active in history, is the New Testament *kērygma* or proclamation,[22] and in the very heart of that *kērygma*, as its content, is the person of Christ. Or to put it the other way round, the Christ that is presented to us in the Gospels, the Christ who comes to us himself, is the kerygmatic Christ, the Christ clothed with his own gospel, the Christ who is himself active within history through his gospel, the Christ who is inseparable from his own active life of revelation and reconciliation.

However, let us pause here a moment and consider the situation carefully. We have noted that in the Gospels we do not start from a bare historical fact, and then later put a meaning or interpretation on

22 *Kērygma*, Gk, proclamation, message, that which is preached.

it; we start from a fact-in-meaning, a fact-in-interpretation – *but* it is not our interpretation with which the fact is clothed, but an interpretation which the fact of Christ brings with it. It is not an interpretation which we put upon the fact as we experience it, but an interpretation which the fact imposes upon us out of itself. It is Christ clothed in his own gospel.[E5]

Here, it is the objective content of the *kērygma*, Christ himself as act of God and as historical deed, what Christ was and what Christ did, that controls both presentation and response. Thus even though Christ is presented from the point of view of those who have experienced his divine and saving power, the presentation is strictly controlled from beyond the faith of the primitive church by objective fact rooted and grounded in the historical Jesus Christ. In other words, it is ultimately Christ himself who is in control throughout the presentation of him in the witness and proclamation of the primitive church – and that is precisely the meaning of the New Testament *kērygma*, in all the various strata of the New Testament tradition reaching back to the primary source material even of the synoptic Gospels. To see how this is so, we must examine the structural bed of the New Testament presentation of the kerygmatic Christ.

When we turn to this New Testament material we find several major factors controlling the witness, all of them making it indubitably clear that what is presented is not a reinterpreted and distorted Christ, but the authentically historical Jesus Christ confronting and imposing himself upon that witness.

(a) Controlling factors in the New Testament witness

(i) The historical factuality of Jesus

All the witness of the New Testament rests upon the objective and ontological *actuality of the historical Christ* – what it says is that Jesus is the Christ. Jesus is the Lord. That is, it attests a very definite historical fact, Jesus of Nazareth crucified under Pontius Pilate, but it also involves the believing confession that Jesus is Lord and saviour. The witness to the fact and the witness to the truth coincide in such a way that the witness to the truth depends entirely on the fact that these specific events did actually happen. Therefore the truth or the meaning of these words cannot in any way be detached from their historical reality. Jesus is Lord, Jesus is the Christ.

Take two examples. Look first at the synoptic account of Jesus Christ. Whether we look at it in its final character as the result of the editing of the evangelists, Mark's own editing of his source material, the editing of Matthew and Luke, or of their own common source ('Q'), or we look at proto-Mark, we find that stubborn enigmatic fact of the so called 'messianic secret'. All the evangelists and their original sources clearly hold that Jesus is the Christ, and the Son of God, and yet in spite of that they allow the actual dramatic existence and history of Jesus to declare it, and take great pains not to put into the mouth of Jesus their own affirmations to the effect that he is the Son of God. In other words, they *allow the actual objective history to tell its own secret*, but in this way they make it clear that what is of paramount importance in the gospel is what Christ actually was and what he did in Judaism; and that what he did, he did with an intention that was inextricably embedded in the actual course of his historical life. All that they needed to do was to be faithful witnesses to the historical drama of his life and work. In the language of Hoskyns and Davey,[23] what they present is the *opus operatum*[24] of Jesus Christ intentionally and carefully isolated from mere opinions about him, and it is that *opus operatum* which with a compelling force arising out of its own historical factuality imposes upon the witnesses its own message and theological significance. That is equally true of the theologians of the New Testament, John, or Paul, or the author of the epistle to the Hebrews.

For all of them, all that they have to say rests upon a very particular history to which they are seeking to be faithful and obedient, and apart from that historical factuality of Jesus, all that they have to say would have no real meaning whatsoever. They do not claim anywhere that what is historical is the tradition itself, but that the tradition is historical because it conforms to the actual history of the existence, words, and deeds of Jesus. The last thing they would dream of implying is that their own experience or theologising has created the history to which they bear witness, or is superimposed upon it, and that they are really moving in a world of spirituality and piety which is not essentially tied down to historical fact. Moreover, according to their witness, it is not only their experience of Christ which is tied down to the historical factuality of what he was, but that what Jesus did himself was governed and determined by what he was in actual history.

All this can be summed up by saying that the main burden of the New Testament witness is that Jesus is the Lord, the saviour, the Christ sent of God. A very clear example of that is to be seen in the choice of Matthias[25] to take the place of Judas in the circle of the twelve

---

23 Hoskyns and Davey, *The Riddle of the New Testament* (London: Faber 1931).

24 Lat, 'work worked'.

disciples – he had to be one of those who had been an eye-witness of the historical Jesus from the day he was baptised by John to the day when he ascended into heaven. It is the actual history of Jesus, who he actually was and what he actually did, that is the controlling factor throughout. That is why that *historical* ontology is so paramount in the Apostles' creed. When the centre of gravity shifts from the historical factuality of Jesus to the spiritual experience of men and women, then the historical Jesus is demoted to a purely secondary place as of only parabolic or perhaps of only mythological significance. But that is exactly what cannot be said of the New Testament witness anywhere. No amount of juggling with the New Testament witness can make it yield the alleged fact that it makes an existential statement which is then attached to a mythological framework.

(ii) The historical context of Israel

The second controlling factor follows from this. If it is the historical factuality of Jesus that is of controlling importance, then that Jesus must be presented as really *embedded in history*, embedded therefore in the hard stubborn history of Israel. That is precisely the case with Jesus. Even if it is the historical factuality of Jesus that is the controlling factor, how did it come to exercise that control over the minds of the witnesses and the church? How did it interpret itself, and with what categories and conceptions did it operate? The answer to this question is clear all over the pages of the New Testament, evident not only in the face value of the witness itself, but from the most exhaustive lexicological examination of its language and concepts. The historical fact of Christ is embedded in the history of Israel, and it imposes itself upon the witnesses with controlling power because it belongs to the inner compulsion of historical Israel, and is the actual fulfilment of the purpose embedded in its long history. Thus the interpretative categories and conceptions through which the fact of the historical Jesus imposes itself upon the witnesses, and by which it controls their witness are not their creation and are not imported by them from outside this historical context, say from the mystery religions of Greece, but derive from the actual history of Israel in which Jesus is embedded and from which he emerges.

---

[25] Acts 1.15-26.

The compulsive Old Testament purpose behind the New Testament witness
Take for example the New Testament witness to the suffering of Jesus and its understanding. This is firmly set (i) in the context of the history of Israel, so that the movement of Israel in time, apparent throughout her historical existence, is regarded as that which occasioned the passion of Christ, and (ii) in the context of the Old Testament scriptures, so that the revelation of God mediated through them is allowed to interpret the passion of Christ as the fulfilment of the divine purpose embodied in Israel. Thus once the particular history of Jesus appears on the scene of Palestinian Judaism, the whole history of Israel is seen to advance irresistibly to its end in him. That is why Jesus had to suffer, for his particular history was the fulfilment of the historical and redemptive purpose embodied in Israel. Moreover, the New Testament bears witness to this in such a way as to show how its own witness came to be controlled by this compulsive purpose, for the New Testament witnesses bear witness to something admittedly against their own inclinations and satisfactions, aspirations and desires. Just as Judaism had consistently avoided the whole notion of a suffering Messiah, so the New Testament witnesses themselves reveal that they too shrank from it but were forced to acknowledge it by the historical interweaving of the particular history of Jesus and the whole history of Israel. It was therefore against their own piety that they were forced to interpret the passion of Jesus in terms of the suffering servant. History would not allow them to do anything else.

Thus the passion of Jesus is not presented in the pages of the New Testament as symbolic of a spiritual notion of sacrifice, but as the direct outcome of all that went before it in Israel, as the obedient fulfilment of God's saving intervention in all the long story of this stubborn people gathered by God into covenant with himself. This is of supreme importance, for it means that the interpretative witness of the New Testament to Christ is subordinated to and controlled by the Old Testament scriptures, and that basic fact will not allow us to say that the New Testament gospel was the product of the creative spirituality of the primitive church, and that the Old Testament scriptures were only brought in to illustrate it. Through its setting in the context of historical Israel and its setting in the Old Testament scriptures, the New Testament witness to Christ is presented in a way that is objectively and authoritatively controlled from beyond the subjective experience of the primitive church. The New Testament witness is a faithful and obedient witness to Christ wrested from its writers by an authority and a compulsion to which they could only submit. That is very evident for example in the slowness and unwillingness of the

New Testament witnesses to acknowledge deliberate divine purpose in the humiliating weakness and passion of Christ.

Jesus himself is under obedience to the will of God and the Old Testament scriptures

But now we must go further: this compulsive obedience to a divine and historical purpose embodied in Israel characterised not only the consciousness of the New Testament witnesses but the consciousness of Jesus himself, and of Jesus above all. Nowhere have we any evidence in the pages of the New Testament for the idea that the gospel was the product of the creative genius of Jesus. Even in the fourth Gospel where the most profound theological teaching is found on the lips of Jesus, we have the strongest emphasis on the fact that Christ can do nothing of himself, and can say nothing of himself – he is entirely at one with, and obedient to, the Father who sent him. In the Gospels and in the Epistles it is the obedience of Jesus to the God of Israel which is unflaggingly stressed. He knows himself to be under compulsion. He had come to do God's will; he had come to suffer, and all that was written of him he had to fulfil – and though he shrank from it, or rather from the terrible cross and passion it entailed, he set his face like a flint toward it and was obedient unto death, even the death of the cross. This fact cannot be stressed too much, for Jesus is portrayed in the New Testament witness not only as the one sent from God to man in fulfilment of the purpose embodied in Israel, but also as the man who perfectly and obediently fulfils God's will. In other words, the historical Jesus is not only identical with God's saving action toward man, but the fulfilled response of man toward that saving action. He is not only God's Word become flesh, but he is that Word received, appropriated, assimilated in the whole course of his obedience alike in word and deed – his life of teaching and action is the fulfilled human response to God's revelation of himself.

It is therefore the obedience of Christ in his word and action which supplies the final and authoritative interpretation of God's purpose of redemption embodied in the covenant people. It is the obedient and authoritative response of Jesus in mind and word to the will of God which supplies the concrete basis and the normative pattern for the whole of the New Testament witness to him as God's word and deed of salvation. Thus whatever a critical handling of the synoptic and Johannine problem reveals about the details of the dependence of the New Testament interpretation of Christ upon Christ's own self interpretation, the principle is clearly laid down and assumed by all, that the obedient witness of the New Testament presentation of Christ is grounded upon his own obedience in word and deed to God the Father. Thus the compulsive obedience of the New Testament witness to the Old Testament scriptures in their interpretative presentation of Christ is inextricably interwoven with, and utterly dependent upon, *the compulsive obedience of Jesus himself to the will and word of God revealed through the Old Testament scriptures*. It is this combination which exercises the objective control of the New Testament witness to Christ, and makes impossible the idea that the gospel derives not from Jesus himself but from the spiritual experience of the primitive church.

(iii) The self-proclamation of Jesus

We come now to a third principal factor directly connected with this, *the deliberate witness of Jesus to himself*, his own self-proclamation. In other words, the kerygmatic presentation of Christ rests upon the fact that ***by word and deed together he proclaimed himself as the Christ***. This has often been put in the past by saying that the witness of the evangelists and the other New Testament authors reposes ultimately upon Jesus' own self-consciousness, or upon his messianic consciousness. But that I believe to be a wrong way of putting it, for two reasons. First it isolates his consciousness from his concrete witness to himself in word and deed, and inevitably psychologises it; and secondly, its direct exclusion of the historical and ontological[26] from their place in the basic fact upon which our interpretation rests, inevitably makes it impossible to reach any understanding of the ontological significance of Jesus. Moreover, if we begin with the self-consciousness of Christ and rest our own interpretation of Christ upon it, we will never be able to disentangle Christ's self-consciousness from our own, or our own from what is alleged to be Christ's, so that in the end it will be our own spiritual experience and consciousness which will be dominant. It is not surprising therefore that this way has again and again led to the conclusion that we cannot penetrate behind the spirituality and religious consciousness of the first Christians to Christ himself.

It is better to begin here with the fact that Jesus is presented in some of the oldest strata of the New Testament as a *prophet* – that is to say, as one who under divine compulsion in his involvement in Israel, brings a divine message to God's people.

According to Mark, the gospel begins with John the Baptist, and according to Luke it was John's task to prepare a people for the Lord, to prepare the way for Christ. Moreover, according to Christ himself,

---

[26] Ontology is the study of being, or the nature of being or reality; hence ontological means to do with being, or concerning ultimate reality.

John was not only a prophet but more than a prophet, one whose word was charged with eschatological power, who brought a word of God that is itself also an act of God in the fulfilment of his word. Thus John was a herald announcing the coming of the kingdom, but this was an announcement which took effect once it was made. Just as a royal decree becomes law and is operative as soon as it is proclaimed, so the very *kērygma* or proclamation of the kingdom meant that in and with that *kērygma* the kingdom impinged upon the present and was operative among men and women. So, for example, in a Jewish law court, when the herald called out the decisions of the court, the act of proclamation was considered as putting the decisions into effect, and making them formally and actually binding.[27] Jesus began his ministry by stepping straight into that situation, and continued the *kērygma* of the kingdom, declaring that what he proclaimed was *actually being fulfilled as current reality in and through his proclamation of it*. In Jesus himself the kingdom had come and was actively and effectively intervening among men and women in the unity of word and deed. Now there is a significant difference here between the proclamation of John the Baptist and the proclamation of Jesus, for John the Baptist points away from himself to the coming one, who is mightier than he, and before whom he can only decrease, whereas Jesus not only announces the good news of the kingdom but is himself the good news, so that in his case the *kērygma* is absolutely determined by who Jesus was.[E6]

The simple truth is, that in the *kērygma* of Jesus it is the fact of Jesus himself, the historical and ontological fact of who he was and is, that is all important. Thus in the *kērygma* of Jesus, the breaking in of the eschatological kingdom of God coincides not only with the event of its proclamation on his lips, but also with his own advent. In his own *kērygma* Jesus proclaims himself as bringing in the kingdom, and that as having reality and effect in and through his person. That belongs to the earliest stratum in the synoptic material, the basic fact that in proclaiming the kingdom Jesus proclaims himself. On this *kērygma* of Jesus, the whole of the New Testament presentation of the gospel is based.

(b) The self-presentation of Jesus in the apostolic kērygma

The whole nature of the *kērygma* of Christ as his self-presentation involves four further factors that need to be noted.

---

[27] See Friedrich on *kērygma* in Gerhard Kittel, *Theological Dictionary of the New Testament*, Eng. trans. (Grand Rapids: Eerdmans 1966), vol. 3, p. 714.

(i) Inseparability of the word and deed and presence of Jesus

Because the content of the *kērygma* (that the kingdom of God breaks in) is identical with the act of proclamation (as itself the operative reality of the kingdom) and with the advent of the person of Christ (the king of the kingdom), the self-presentation or self-proclamation of Jesus can only be made in a movement in which ***the word and deed and presence of Jesus are all intertwined***. In this movement, the self-revelation of Jesus is given as much through the unfolding drama of his life in obedience to the divine compulsion embodied in Israel, as by word – indeed he deliberately holds back revelation by word so that it may *keep pace* with revelation through the dynamic movement of his advance to the hour of eschatological completion on the cross. He refuses to proclaim himself in word apart from the historical drama of his ministry, and makes both dependent upon the direct confrontation of his person.

(ii) Inseparability of the kērygma *from the rabbinic teaching of Jesus*

Even so Jesus imparted a good deal of *teaching* in his *kērygma*,[E7] and here there can be *no sharp separation between didachē*[28] and *kērygma*. All the Gospels, and the oldest strata of the Gospels, set forth Jesus as teacher as well as prophet and preacher. Unlike John the Baptist, Jesus was also a rabbi , that is one who concerned himself with expounding and passing on to his pupils, in studied discourses and parables and aphorisms, the divine law. A rabbi was an authorised and authoritative transmitter of the sacred tradition – but as a rabbi Jesus was unlike the rabbis and scribes of the Jews for he taught with unique authority. Through discourses and aphorisms and parables, the teaching of Jesus transmitted the word of God in a way characterised with the direct authority of a divine oracle like the Old Testament scriptures. Moreover, this transmission of oracular teaching was accompanied with miraculous deeds as direct divine attestation of his *logia*.[29] His teaching was recognised as *word of God*, and this teaching formed an essential part of the content of his *kērygma*. It was inevitable, therefore, that the blending of these oracular utterances with his own self-proclamation in the *kērygma*, entailed an identification between his own word and the very word of God – and it was precisely that very fact that played such a compulsive force in bringing him to the cross. The important point for us to note here, however, is that the *kērygma* of Jesus carried

[28] Gk, 'teaching'.

[29] Gk, 'sayings'.

with it considerable instruction prepared in the rabbinic way for careful and reverent memorisation and repetition. But this was committed not to the multitudes, like the parables, but to duly authorised disciples that they might in turn be authorised and authoritative transmitters of the *kērygma* and the *didachē* of the kingdom.

Considerable work has been done on this whole question by Professor Harald Riesenfeld with a group of scholars in Uppsala[30] which enables us with great ease to break through the net drawn over the historical Jesus by the form-critical scholars who insist that we cannot get behind the subjective improvisations of the primitive community to the teaching of the original Jesus. But in order to maintain that case they have to cut out of the oldest strata of the New Testament this insistent emphasis on Jesus as teacher, teacher not in the Greek sense which we find later on in the early church, at Alexandria for example, but in the sense of Palestinian Judaism. We are thus driven to the conclusion that the kerygmatic presentation of Christ by the New Testament witnesses derives directly from and reposes essentially upon the *kērygma* of Jesus himself and the considerable transmission of *didachē* which it entailed.

(iii) Jesus' transmission and extension of his own kērygma *to the apostles*

But there is still a third factor to be noted which is well summed up in the words of Jesus himself, 'He who hears you, hears me'.[31] The kerygmatic presentation of Christ by the apostles is *regarded by Christ as his own kērygma* in effective operation. In order to understand this we may begin again with the fact of Christ as embodied in Israel, and as the actual fulfilment of the historical ordeal and divine mission of Israel. As we have seen, the New Testament witnesses, as well as Jesus himself, saw themselves as being under that compulsive purpose working itself out in Israel, so that they too had a part to play in that fulfilment of the role of Israel. That is the specific function of the twelve disciples whom Jesus gathered round him as the pillars of the new Israel in this new era of messianic fulfilment.[32] As such, the disciples are apostles or authorised ambassadors or plenipotentiaries of Christ, specially trained in order to be authoritative transmitters of his own *kērygma*, so that whoever hears them, hears Christ himself. But this

---

[30] Harald Riesenfeld, *The Gospel Tradition and its Beginnings* (London: Mowbray 1957).

[31] Luke 10.16.

[32] Luke 22.28-30; Matt 19.28.

training of the apostles entailed a training both in word and deed; they were therefore chosen to be with Christ in his tribulation, to accompany him throughout his ministry from the Jordan to the cross, and to participate in their own way in the unfolding drama of his self-presentation, and in the revealing of his messianic secret and purpose that was unrolled by his encounter with Israel, and his advance to the cross; but they were also chosen as those who in their participation in this unfolding drama of Christ's life, should be instructed in the mysteries of the kingdom. Thus while the parables were spoken to those without, to the disciples it was given to know the mysteries of the kingdom, and to them Jesus carefully imparted his teaching and sacred tradition after the manner of the Palestinian rabbis, but with a new authority.

It is important to see that in his instruction of the disciple-apostles, the instruction involved the intertwining of word and deed, parable and miracle, teaching and action in the kingdom. It was not a teaching that involved simply statements about general or revealed truths, but a teaching that had, as an essential part of its content, the dramatic events in the ministry of Christ in his encounter with Israel and encounter with the powers of darkness, and above all the actual event of his own *kērygma* of the kingdom which was itself supreme historical and eschatological event, for with it the kingdom had broken into the midst of Israel in decisive power leading straight to the cross. Owing to their special nature, these events in the life and work of Jesus required to be understood, reported and handed on in a special way through which others could be rightly instructed in them. The apostles were thus brought within the inner movement of the life of Christ that they might be trained by him in word and deed to be authoritative witnesses of the kingdom and of the breaking in of Christ himself in word and deed. As such the apostles were constituted by Christ as specially authorised and competent witnesses and proclaimers of the kingdom.

The Jewish concept of the apostle-shaliach

But here Jesus takes over in a special way the Jewish Palestinian notion of the apostle-*shaliach*,[33] and sends out from himself apostolic messengers to carry his own *kērygma* in word and deed, so that when people hear their word it was Christ's own authoritative *kērygma* that

---

[33] See the article by Rengstorf on '*Apostolos*' in Kittel, *op. cit.* vol. 1, 1964, esp. p. 413ff. See also the Soteriology volume of these lectures, *Atonement*, chap. 10, sec. 1 on 'The apostolate', and the discussion of '*shaliach*' there.

they encountered. When the apostles proclaimed Christ, it was Christ himself who remained the real active subject in the *kērygma*, as well as its real content. That is the meaning of the apostolic *kērygma*. It is so objectively bound up with Christ that he continues to be the operative agent in the witness of others to him. *Kērygma*, therefore, does not simply mean missionary preaching of the gospel of Christ, but the special and solemn proclamation of Christ through authorised and competent witnesses who have themselves been instructed in Christ's own self-proclamation. *Kērygma* refers, then, to authoritative *kērygma* which not only transmits Christ's own *kērygma* but derives from and reposes upon direct embassage from himself, for as Christ was sent by the Father, so he sent the apostles, and sent them out with the mighty word of the gospel, which he entrusted to them: 'If you forgive the sins of any, they are forgiven; if you retain the sins of any, they are retained.'[34] It is in and through this apostolic *kērygma*, that the authoritative teaching and preaching of Jesus himself is transmitted, and is the content of what we have in the Gospels.

It is this conception of transmission of *kērygma* and *didachē* through authorised and competent ambassadors that attests and guarantees the fact that the proclamation of the gospel in the apostolic church is not the creation or distilled result of the spiritual experience of the first Christians, and it is upon that apostolic transmission of the faith that the church is founded. 'I received from the Lord what I also delivered to you'.[35] Paul's words here regarding the authoritative warrant for the Lord's supper apply equally to the transmission of the *kērygma* of Christ. Compare Paul's, 'my gospel and the preaching of Jesus Christ, *to euangelion mou kai to kērygma Iēsou Christou*'[36] where Paul stresses the identity between his gospel and the *kērygma* which Jesus announced himself.[E8] Here we have an essential factor in the earliest New Testament witness, namely the relation of the *kērygma* to the authorised apostles and transmitters of it selected and trained by Jesus, and if we follow the New Testament's own conception of the *kērygma*, we find that it involves the peculiar relation of the herald to Christ himself described in his words, 'He who hears you hears me, and he who rejects you rejects me'[37] – that is *kērygma* in which Christ himself continues to retain control of the *kērygma* even when it is found on the lips of others. In this way the reality or object proclaimed in the *kērygma*

---

[34] John 20.23.

[35] 1 Cor 11.23.

[36] Rom 16.25.

[37] Luke 10.16; cf. Matt 10.40; John 13.20.

continues to give the *kērygma* its objectivity in the historical fact of Jesus Christ himself.

(iv) The relation between faith and the kērygma *– the relation of the church's faith and understanding to the faith and obedience of Jesus himself*

We now come to the fourth factor in the relation of the *kērygma* to Christ which requires our consideration. According to the Gospels Jesus bore witness to himself not only, and perhaps not even chiefly, in his words, but *in his actions*. That witness, that self-witness of Christ in his actions required to be transmitted, and transmitted appropriately, but how can that be done? Surely it was only right that this unique preaching in which Jesus proclaimed himself demanded a *corresponding form of transmission*. That kind of preaching cannot be handed on by mere reporters of history, for they cannot see the decisive factor in it all, namely, that this Jesus discloses and authenticates himself as the Christ. Thus in the oldest strata of the synoptic material we find that we do not have mere historical reports, but a reproducing of the *kērygma* of Christ himself, with witness to his self-disclosure in and through it, all in the form of new *kērygma*. This reproducing and transmitting of the *kērygma* is of such a nature that in and through the *kērygma* of the apostles it is Christ's own proclamation of himself that is operative. That is the meaning of the gospel, *euangelion*, which refers primarily to Christ's own proclamation, but set forth, transmitted, and now actually operative through the *kērygma* of the apostolic church.

The nature of faith: Kierkegaard on the apprehension of God in time

Now let us turn for a moment to the teaching of Kierkegaard that if we are to apprehend a historical fact we must apprehend not simply what has actually taken place and is now a static fact of history, but apprehend the *happening* itself, and indeed how it happened. But in apprehending a movement, the coming into being of a historical event, we must behave in terms of it. This apprehension involves an act of decision or an act of faith. Thus the New Testament witnesses report the events or happenings in the life of the historical Jesus, but they also bear witness to their belief that Jesus disclosed and authenticated himself to them as the Christ, the Son of the living God. Yet in the nature of the case they cannot transmit in ideas or factual reports that to which they bear witness in their belief. Their witness and belief challenge us to decision and belief with them, and only by an act of decision or belief can we enter into the situation that confronted them, and apprehend what they apprehended. Our way of apprehending Christ's self-presentation in his actions must involve on our part a way of action corresponding to his action. Our mode of knowing Christ must be analogous to the mode of Christ's coming into being in history. This entails on our part a movement of reason which Kierkegaard called the 'leap of faith', or a resolution, or a decision.

There is no doubt that this is important. Unless in some real sense we share here in the life of Christ, we really cannot apprehend him; unless in some real sense what took place in his crucifixion and resurrection takes place also in an analogous way in our own experience, it can finally mean nothing to us. That is a very strong emphasis, for example, in the fourth Gospel. The truth conveyed to us by Christ is not simply a truth revealed by word, but a truth embodied in his person, so that to apprehend it we must personally have an experience of Christ himself as the one sent by the Father. Only by going through Christ to the Father can we come to know Christ as the Son of the Father. Only by an act of decision in obedience to the challenge of Christ can this come about.[E9] In Kierkegaard, the important element is not found in the decision of faith itself, but in the fact of Christ behind the decision. In encounter with Christ, decision derived its importance from the person of Christ himself, and therefore the decision cannot be abstracted from what Christ himself was and did.[E10]

Faith is an act of appropriation and trust which is wholly based on Christ and his decision for us

However, what according to the gospel is the decision required of me? In the *kērygma* I am certainly challenged to make a decision, but the gospel announces to me that in Jesus Christ God has already taken a decision about me; it announces that my existence has already been invaded and brought under the sovereign rule of God's grace in the life, death, and resurrection of Christ; it announces that the kingdom of God has overtaken me in Christ, and that my destiny has been laid hold of by Christ and determined by his crucifixion. Therefore the gospel challenges me to appropriate the decision which God has already made about me in Christ; it challenges me to cast my lot in with Christ and share in the history of Christ who has given himself in sacrifice to be my saviour. The *kērygma* certainly challenges me to take a decision, but that is a decision to appropriate and trust in a decision which God has already made about me in the life, death, and resurrection of the historical Jesus Christ. Thus the decision about which the New Testament gospel speaks has its whole focus and content in the decisive action of God in the historical Jesus – that is the objective reality of my decision in faith, and apart from that objective reality my so called decision simply rests in mid-air.[E11]

Let us try to understand that by looking at it from the other way round. If Jesus Christ is the Son of God become man, then the historical humanity of this particular man, Jesus, cannot be fully appreciated or understood apart from the fact that he is Son of God as well as Son of Man. We must therefore interpret Jesus in the light of the origin from which he came and without which he would not be. We must interpret Christ as who he really is, not as what he appears to be merely on the horizontal plane of history. What he appears to be on the horizontal plane of history is determined by what he is on the vertical dimension in his relation to the eternal God. It is futile to try and interpret a predicate in abstraction from its subject; so it is futile to try and interpret Jesus as he appears to outward observation in abstraction from the fact that he, the Son of God, became this Jesus, for the historical appearance of this Jesus is a predicate of the Son or Word of God who became this man. The historian can only try to place Jesus on the horizontal plane in a time series, or in the midst of a historical movement: he cannot deal at all with the vertical movement in and through which Jesus came into being in history. In this movement from God to man, from above to below, Jesus presents himself as a fact of revelation, as Word of God – yet this movement of his cannot be represented simply and purely on the horizontal plane or in merely historical terms. Both its presentation to, and its reception by men and women in history require a divine act, a transcendent act.

Thus the reception of Christ's self-presentation requires a divine transcendent act within man corresponding to the divine transcendent act by which the Son of God became man. In other words, it requires the *Holy Spirit.* No one says that Jesus is Lord except by the Holy Spirit.[38] [E12] The New Testament teaching is that through the power of the Holy Spirit I am able to encounter God in Christ and through a personal decision appropriate him as my saviour, but in such a way that my decision is an act of obedience to Christ who has already made a decision on my behalf in his obedience to God on the cross.

The early church's piety and kērygma *controlled by Christ and his obedience*

In other words, whereas for existentialist theology[39] [E13] I am saved by my own act of faith or decision, according to the New Testament gospel what saves me is the obedience of Christ upon which I am summoned to cast all my reliance, for it is his obedience which saves me and it is

---

[38] 1 Cor 12.3.

[39] Existentialist philosophy or theology emphasises existence, courageous personal decision, and action.

Christ through his Spirit who gives me to share in his obedience. Thus my decision rests upon his decision for me: my faith is my reliance upon his faithfulness and a sharing in his faith.[40] In the New Testament gospel Christ's faith, his obedience, his knowledge are the foundation of my faith, obedience and knowledge, so that my faith, obedience and knowledge are objectively controlled by his. Similarly, in the preaching of the early church, in the *kērygma*, it is Jesus Christ and his obedience which shapes and controls the presentation and preaching of the church. Thus instead of the piety and spirituality of the earliest church controlling the presentation of Christ, and even forming and creating much of it, that church in all its piety and spirituality was by its very nature controlled by the obedience of Jesus Christ to the Father.[E14]

Arising out of our discussion of Jesus Christ and the New Testament *kērygma* here we may now make several affirmations about our procedure in christology.

3 Procedure in christology

(a) Knowledge of Christ by revelation through the Spirit

In christology we know the person of Christ as he is presented to us in the New Testament in the same way as he is presented to us in the *kērygma*. The object of our knowledge in the doctrine of Christ is 'Christ clothed with his own gospel' (as Calvin expressed it), Christ disclosing

---

[40] See Gal 2.20 in the King James Version, the most faithful of all the versions to the original Greek at this point which has, 'the life I now live in the flesh I live by the faith of the Son of God', i.e. by Christ's own faith, as Torrance used to point out in his lectures. See further T.F. Torrance, *Conflict and Agreement in the Church*, vol. 2 (London: Lutterworth 1960), 'An aspect of the biblical concept of faith', pp. 74-82, esp. p. 80; *The Mediation of Christ*, revised edition (Edinburgh: T & T Clark 1992), pp. 81-84, 98; and also *A Passion for Christ*, ed. Gerrit Dawson & Jock Stein (Edinburgh: Handsel 1999 & Lenoir: PLC Publications 1999), p. 24ff. 'Preaching the Faith of the Son of God'. Since Torrance's advocacy of the King James translation, the whole question of the 'subjective genitive' as it is known (the faith of Christ) as opposed to the 'objective genitive' (faith in Christ) has become an ongoing debate in modern scholarship following the publication of R.B. Hays' book, *The Faith of Jesus Christ: The Narrative Substructure of Galatians 3.1 – 4.11* (Chico: Scholars Press 1983, republished Grand Rapids: Eerdmans 2002).

himself in and through the *kērygma*. That is made very clear in the teaching of St Paul. He is not interested in bare historical facts about Jesus as such, that is, he is not interested in a reconstruction of historical facts which are demonstrated like other historical facts on the mere plane of profane history. But on the other hand, he is not indifferent to the truth of the earthly historical Jesus, for everything depends upon it – for example, in 1 Corinthians 15 where Paul points out that if Jesus Christ is not actually risen from the dead, then we are yet in our sins,[41] and in that case the bottom would fall out of the whole gospel. What Paul is interested in is this historical Jesus Christ clothed with the gospel of reconciliation, a Jesus who as such is Word of God and salvation. In Paul's own language it is not Christ 'after the flesh'[42] that we are concerned with, but Christ 'after the Spirit', or 'according to the Spirit'.[43]

That does not mean that Paul is indifferent to the historical Jesus – but that a Jesus who is known only in a carnal manner, as by the mere historian, the reporter of historical events, can be of no interest to us. That Jesus, observed and reported according to ordinary historical criteria, was a rabbi, a carpenter, an exorcist who apparently failed in his mission and was executed for alleged blasphemy and treason. That is all that the mere historian can see, and that is not worth reporting. But what we are concerned with is not that merely historical and therefore falsely historical presentation of Jesus, but the historical Jesus presented after the manner of who he really was, Christ 'after the Spirit'. Granted that we cannot prove that Christ was the Son of God by the canons of criticism the scientific historian uses, nevertheless we do claim for Christ a 'demonstration of the Spirit'[44] as Paul called it. Now it is this Jesus Christ, spiritually discerned, by a transcendent mode of apprehension corresponding to his own transcendent mode of becoming flesh, who is the object of our theological knowledge.

Here then, we have in christology an object of knowledge presented to us in a complex of historical fact and spiritual event, and our knowledge of that object must be appropriate to its nature. All this is already made clear in the Synoptics. It is not the flesh and blood of Jesus as such that reveal him, not the merely historical humanity of Christ, but the Father in heaven who reveals Christ to us in a

---

41 1 Cor 15.17.

42 2 Cor 5.16, 'Christ after the flesh (*kata sarka*)' KJV.

43 See Rom 1.4, 'according to the Spirit (*kata pneuma*)'; cf. 1 Cor 2.4ff.; 2 Cor 3.6ff.; Rom 8.1ff.; Gal 3.2ff.

44 1 Cor 2.4 (*apodeixei Pneumatos*).

transcendent way – that is by way of *revelation* from above. That is how we know that Jesus Christ is the Son of the living God.[45] At the same time we must acknowledge that Christ after the flesh is open to historical investigation by all and sundry whether they believe or not. That is the aspect of the gospel which is subject to general knowledge and to secular interpretation. But the *mystery* of the kingdom, the Christ as true God and true man, is known only to those who respond to him 'after the Spirit'. Only they, when they look at Christ in the flesh, see more in Christ than the Christ 'after the flesh'.

(b) Knowledge of the historical Jesus according to the Spirit

It is only by being true and faithful to the mystery of Christ, knowing him the way he presents himself to us, kerygmatically *kata Pneuma* (in the *kērygma* according to the Spirit), that we can go back and interpret the Jesus of history. But as we shall see later, the Jesus of history has no independent existence or being apart from the fact that the Word was made flesh.

If the Son of God had not been born of woman, had not become incarnate, there would have been no Jesus of Nazareth. If our knowing of Jesus is to correspond to the order of his existence and coming into being in history, then we can only start with that dual fact of Jesus Christ as true God and true man. It is that dual fact that conserves the historical humanity of Jesus in any investigation of the historical Jesus. Then and only then do we see the historical Jesus in his true perspective, and need not be worried by the problem of how to transmute historical facts into matters of faith, and need not therefore be tempted to falsify 'the historical Jesus' in order to get faith out of him. Only then can and does the Jesus of history become intelligible, and only then can and does his historical existence remain unimpaired as historical existence.

Think of what the historian as historian is faced with. Historians are presented with a complex of historical reports and beliefs in a way encountered nowhere else – even as historians they will have to face the strangeness and uniqueness of this material. Their first duty as historians will be to enquire how the presentation of the gospel story here arose on its own view. Here the historian will find that the normal historical categories break down, for again and again the story is historically apprehensible only at the extreme edges of the account, as at the resurrection (which cannot of course come within the normal canons of historical criticism). Here too the crucified and risen Word is

---

[45] Matt 16.16-17.

regarded by the New Testament presentation not only as the object of its proclamation but as the subject of it.

What are historians to do in the face of that? They must either reject what they cannot demonstrate on the ground of the normal criteria employed by historians, or they must be forced to question the adequacy of the criteria to interpret this particular and unique history. If they adopt the former course, they fail to behave in terms of what is actually presented to them, and so fail to deal with the Jesus Christ who in this proclamation proclaims himself. If they adopt the latter course, then they are forced to find a new set of criteria appropriate to the peculiar nature of the object that is presented to them – that is to say, they will be forced to adopt the standpoint of faith, but that means apprehending Jesus not only on the plane of mere history but as the Son of God who has come from beyond into history, as *act of God in time*. In other words, they apprehend him in a way which allows them to leave intact the historical Jesus as he is presented, without having to cut and hack at the material in order to reduce it to something like what is historically reasonable and apprehensible according to the normal canons of historical credibility and interpretation. Thus either we believe in Jesus according to the New Testament witness, or we are forced to carve out of the evidence a Jesus according to the demands of our own preconceptions, but the result of that always proves to be illusory and futile, as the centuries of criticism have shown.

(c) The relation of dogma to **kērygma**

The third observation we must make, however, is that although we can truly apprehend the historical Jesus Christ only according to the Spirit (*kata Pneuma*), that is, in a way appropriate to his own nature as Son of God, this apprehension *kata Pneuma* takes place only on the ground of authorised and authoritative witness that derives directly from Jesus himself. Christology is concerned with that duality, with understanding Christ theologically through his self-revelation in the Spirit, but also with understanding that has its objective basis in the historical Jesus, for it is Jesus alone, who is presented historically in the *kērygma*, who reveals himself to us after the Spirit (*kata Pneuma*). Thus while christology is concerned with the *kērygma* of Christ in the power of the Spirit, it is concerned with that only in its essential relation to the transmission of teaching or *didachē* from the historical Jesus. Christology is concerned not simply with the preached Christ, nor is it concerned simply with the recital of the words and acts of the historical Jesus, but with both of these in their essential interrelation, that is with *didagma*. *Didagma* is the doctrine of Christ which is objectively imposed upon the church when it is obedient to the mystery of Christ according to its didactic content and kerygmatic presentation. When that *didagma* is carefully and authoritatively articulated in the church, it is known as dogma. Dogma is the church's formulation of its knowledge of Christ within the sphere of the authorised transmission of *kērygma* and *didachē*, but a formulation that is articulated in direct obedience to Christ himself, who imposes himself objectively upon the mind of the church through its witness. Because dogma results from *didagma*, it also partakes of the authoritative character of the apostolic transmission of the *kērygma* and *didachē*. In dogma the authoritative teaching of the apostles is met by responsible and authoritative understanding and formulation.[E15]

Let us not forget, however,[E16] that all our human language as such is inadequate to express divine and eternal truth. All theological speech about God is to a degree 'improper' as Calvin once expressed it, for our knowledge is in part only, as Paul said, and it is through a glass darkly that we see, not yet face to face. But if the Word of God has assumed our human speech and clothed himself with our humanity with its human ways of thinking, in physical dimensions for example, we must seek to understand the Word in the mode in which he, the incarnate Son of God, communicates himself to us, and so seek to understand the relation of the word, *logos*, to human speech, *lalia*, a relation in which there is no diminishing of the nature of the *logos*, but also no diminishing of the nature of the *lalia*.[46] But that we can do only by seeking to know Christ in his wholeness as true God and true man. That is the task of christology.[47]

---

[46] Cf. John 8.43 KJV, 'Why do you (ye) not understand my speech (*lalian*)? Even because you (ye) cannot hear my word (*logon*)' .

[47] On the task and place of christology in the church, the function of the apostolic witness and the nature of dogmatics, see further, T.F. Torrance, *Theology in Reconstruction*, chap. 8, 'The Place of Christology in Biblical and Dogmatic Theology', pp. 128-49.

This point in the text marked the end of the introductory chapter of the lectures manuscript. The section which follows here is the beginning of the original second chapter ('Chapter Two – The biblical witness to Jesus Christ'). We have here only the first section of that (**1 Encounter with Christ in the witness of the New Testament**) which now forms a new section 4 here (**4 The biblical witness to Jesus Christ**). The remaining sections of chapter two are now the final chapter of the Soteriology volume of these lectures,

4 The biblical witness to Jesus Christ

Encounter with Christ in the witness of the New Testament

When we turn to the holy scriptures to find what they have to say about Jesus Christ we are aware that something happens: the one to whom the New Testament bears witness, Jesus Christ, himself acts upon us. In other words, the witness to Christ in the New Testament is more than witness: it is Christ's own word to us about himself. It is his own self-witness. Jesus Christ, so to speak, steps out of the pages of the New Testament and confronts us face to face and reveals himself personally to us. It is God who comes to us in this Christ, God who comes to be his own mediator, God who comes to authenticate himself to us. Now *what* God reveals to us in Jesus Christ and the *manner* of his revealing, the content and the mode of revelation, are inseparable. These two questions belong together, '*what* do the scriptures have to say of Jesus Christ?' and '*how* is it that here in these scriptures Jesus Christ speaks to us himself?' Therefore as we proceed now to ask *what* is it that the New Testament scriptures tell us of Christ, we have also to face the question of *how* Christ is related to the scriptures, to the apostolic witness which they record.[48] It is in answering this question that we begin to learn something of the content of that witness. Let us remember, however, that here we do not start or operate with some distinctive epistemology or theory of knowledge before christology, for there is no distinct *how*, apart from *what*.

Knowing Christ through knowing his salvation: the words of Melanchthon[49]

Let us begin here with some famous words of Melanchthon, from the beginning of his 1521 *Loci Communes*, '*Hoc est Christum cognoscere, beneficia eius cognoscere*, This is to know Christ, to know his benefits'. That is, the knowledge of Christ arises in the knowledge of his salvation. *How* we know Christ and *what* we know of him belong inseparably together. Through his saving action upon us we come to know him and know who he is. That is what happens when we read the New Testament and listen to its witness.

Atonement. (The original numbering of sections 4 and 5 of chapter one which are now in the endnotes **[4 The relation of the *kērygma* to history: the problem of eschatology & 5 The relation of the *kērygma* to history: the problem of mythology and christology]** has been left unchanged.)

48 See *Atonement*, chap. 10, for a much fuller treatment of this question.

49 See further, T.F. Torrance, *The Doctrine of Jesus Christ*, pp. 15-18ff.

These words of Melanchthon, however, are ambivalent, and have been differently interpreted. The danger lies in a subjective and pragmatic approach to Christ in which it is not Christ himself, but the human subject who holds the focus of attention. Let us take someone, for example, who knows Christ because they value Christ for what he has done for them, because Christ satisfies their needs, and their christological knowledge is built up in that way, by value-judgements (A. Ritschl) or by judgements of experience (F. Schleiermacher, W. Herrmann). But if our knowledge of Christ is built up on the fact that we experience or value Christ as our redeemer, that we pass a judgement about Christ, that we make an existential decision in which we come to know and find ourselves, then our christology is essentially anthropocentric in character. Such a knowledge of Christ requires a prior store of human principles or tenets, categories or values, with which to measure out, in this or that coin, the market value of Christ. But true Christian faith can have nothing to do with such thirty pieces of silver, for they mean Christ's coming under human standards, the betrayal of the Son of God to a self-righteous humanity. Mankind and the human self are here set up as critics and evaluators of Christ and his work, and the judgements passed on Christ will naturally vary with the scale of values that mankind possesses. But all this presupposes that humanity is in possession of values capable of measuring or judging Christ and estimating his person: or to put it the other way round, it starts off by presupposing that Christ can be brought under our normal standards and criteria. It means in fact that Jesus Christ is little enough to be domesticated or subordinated to our own ideas and satisfactions.

But who is man to make such a presumption? What value-judgements can we sinners set upon Christ arising out of our own estimation of him? None at all. The opposite is the case. It is not my judgement or examination of Christ that gives me knowledge of him, but the examination he makes of me. When we are confronted with Christ as saviour and Lord, we are confronted with one who defies valuation. With a gentle but holy majesty he smites our estimation, the attributes we give him to the ground. 'Why do you call me good?'[50] 'I receive not honour from men.'[51]

---

[50] Mark 10.18; Luke 18.19.

[51] John 5.41 KJV (cf. RSV, 'glory').

Christ can only be understood in the light which his own person creates for himself

If we are to approach Christ truly, we must approach him in his own light and in the understanding which his own person creates for himself. His person is his own self-authentication. He never appeals to external authority, and refuses to be brought under the judgement of man. Judgement concerning him, said Jesus, was a supernatural act. Nobody but the Father knows the Son, and those to whom it is revealed by the Father.[52] Only those who share the Holy Spirit with whom the Father has anointed the Son can share in authentic knowledge of Christ.

But to return to the words of Melanchthon, 'This is to know Christ, to know his benefits'. His famous words are part of a wider sentence that reads, 'to know Christ means to know his benefits, and not as *they* [the scholastics] teach, to reflect upon his natures and the modes of his incarnation'.[53] It is clear from the context here that Melancthon was not focussing simply on what Christ does in us, as though it was what he did in us that was important and not also what he was in himself, but was rather contrasting scholastic arguments as to the nature of the incarnation with living knowledge of the saving Christ. Melanchthon thus meant the words not as Ritschl and others interpreted them, for whereas what they made central was the fact that Christ acts upon us, and so reveals himself to us in giving us his benefits, Melanchthon's primary emphasis is the other way round, on the glory of God. It is not because Christ brings us benefits, that he is the Son of God, but the reverse. He is the Son, and it is because he is the Son who reveals God to us in and of himself that he heals us, gives us his benefits, and we know ourselves to be sheltered and healed in him. Melancthon's emphasis is on the living Christ and on what it is to know Christ. For him faith is a living knowledge of a living and saving Christ.

Obedient acknowledgement of the whole Christ as true God and true man

We must learn here to think with God always in the centre. God speaks in such a way as not to be brought under our rubrics and estimates.

---

52 Matt 11.27; Luke 10.22.

53 *Loci Communes*, 1521, in Melancthon and Bucer, Library of Christian Classics, vol. XIX (London: SCM Press, and Philadelphia: Westminster Press 1969), p. 21-22. (Also in Melanchthon's *Werke in Auswahl*, student edition, ed. R. Stupperich, vol. II.1, Gütersloh 1952, '*hoc est Christum cognoscere beneficia eius cognoscere, non, quod isti docent, eius naturas, modos incarnationis contueri.*')

He meets us as the Lord. He saves us and we know we are in his presence. Here our knowledge of God, our theological judgements are not self-centred, but are called out of us as matters of acknowledgement and obedience. We are confronted with the majesty of God and surrender ourselves to him in adoration and devotion. That is why faith insists that what believers do is to let themselves be told by the Word, by Christ himself, allow themselves to be determined by Christ who confronts us in his word, and acts upon us – so that the judgements of faith are not those which believers make according to what they already know, but those which are formed in them as they are obedient to what is presented to them. God summons us, and we obey. He authenticates himself to us and we acknowledge him. He confronts us with a divine act of majesty which creates and forms in us a perception appropriate to what he is, and we are controlled by it. He establishes himself in our human knowing in a way according to his nature, and does not allow our knowing of him to be halted by our normal limitations and capacities – for he upholds us from below and enables us to know what is beyond our natural capacities, and what we acknowledge is an act of adoration and glorification of God.

But it is as sinners that we encounter Christ, and as sinners that we are summoned to hear his word and to yield to it the obedience of our minds, so that when we know and obey him, that is a reversal of our disobedience, and involves a decision we take against ourselves, contrary to our own self-will. That is why Christ comes with a sword, and not to send peace on earth, and why it is a devastating experience to really in all earnestness acknowledge Jesus Christ as Lord and God; for us to know him involves a denial of self and a crucifixion on our part.

Moreover, in this encounter we are aware that we meet with God, very God, and none other than God. If in this immediate confrontation with Jesus we do not see that we are immediately confronted by the very person of God, then we cannot come to that conclusion otherwise or later. The confession of the deity of Christ arises out of the immediate confrontation with Christ and his immediate self-revelation in his word – it is not reached by a process of reflection or inference. We cannot think of the deity of Christ as a sort of addendum to be tagged on later, or as a sort of predicate which *we* attribute to him on certain grounds. Jesus Christ confronts us in the *whole fact*, as true God and true man. The Word of God comes to us in Jesus Christ, and so personally and with such authority and majesty, that we are given to know Jesus Christ as God himself, and here we know that we know God only by God.

Chapter Two

THE INCARNATION

Christian faith starts with the knowledge of God in Jesus Christ. In that knowledge we are concerned not only with the duality of God and man in the unity of one person, but with the unity of Christ's person and his act in the one work of salvation. Jesus Christ is one person whose word is wholly involved in his act and whose act is wholly involved in his person. We cannot therefore think of his person apart from his atoning work, or of his atoning work in abstraction from his person. We begin with the person of Christ, but it is his person who carries out the work of salvation, and in the strict sense it is Jesus Christ himself, the mediator, who is the atonement. It is Christ atoning who concerns us here. Therefore even when we begin with his incarnation, and with his birth at Bethlehem, we are beginning right away with the atonement, for his birth, as the beginning of his incarnate person, is one end of the atoning work, with the resurrection and ascension as the other end. But when we begin with the person of Christ, it is the Christ who has revealed himself to us that we are concerned with, the Christ whom we know through his own word, as well as through his own work. We are concerned with the Christ who *is* the word, who utters the word and whose word is identical with his saving work. Revelation and atonement are thus inseparable, Christ revealing and Christ reconciling, for the speaking of the word and the working out of the atoning deed are done within the one person of Christ, and partake of the unity of his deity and humanity in that one person. At every point it is in that perspective of Christ's *wholeness* that we are to consider christology and soteriology.

1 The incarnation and the old Israel

The incarnation of the Son of God has a prehistory, a background or hinterground of preparation and significance which we must not overlook. If in the divine purpose, the incarnation came at a particular point in time, in the history of Israel, it was clearly of design: it is at that point in the context of the history of Israel that Jesus is to be understood. If we are to be faithful to the witness of scripture we cannot but start in the same way. That does not mean that we are simply to interpret Jesus in terms of his background in Israel. The background for Christ the Son of God can only be the background which the fact of the incarnation creates for itself out of our world. No doubt from the secular point of view there is a long prehistory to Jesus, but theologically we must say that when the Son of God breaks into that historical development, he throws it all into critical reorientation. The prehistory is critically and creatively reinterpreted by the incarnate Word, and it is only in that light that we must look at the prehistory of the incarnation in Israel.

(a) The Old Testament background

(i) Prelude to the theology of Heilsgeschichte *or salvation history*

We begin by going right back to Genesis to examine its theological account of the divine purpose of creation and redemption.[1] God made man, male and female, and placed man in a perfect environment. As man and woman they are made to have fellowship with God, and in themselves they are essentially social beings, in harmony with God, and in harmony with their environment. It is as male and female, in the unity of man, that they are made in communion with God, and as male and female, one man, they reflect the glory of God. Man is in the image of God.[2]

Then we discover that the bond of fellowship between God and man is broken by rebellion and sin.[3] It belongs to the nature of sin to divide, to create disorder, to disrupt, to destroy fellowship. What are the consequences of sin? Not only is the bond of communion between God and man broken, issuing in man's guilty fear of God, but the bond between man and woman is impaired: guilt and shame come in between them, and even the symbol of wearing clothes is interpreted in terms of the hiddenness of man from woman and of woman from man. The man-woman relationship is involved in the broken relation with God. With the bond between them broken, man and woman are individualised, and each is turned in upon himself or herself. But even the unity of man as male, and the unity of woman as female, within the individual heart is disrupted, in the knowledge of good and evil. Each knows that he or she is no longer what he or she ought to be.

---

1 Gen 1 – 2.

2 Gen 1.26ff.; 2.7ff.; 2.18ff.

3 Gen 3.1ff.

Thus the rupture in the relation between God and man, and man and woman, entails a rupture within each between what a person *is* and what the person *ought* to be. Once the constitutive bond between God and man is broken, every other relation suffers irreparable damage. And so we find the relation between man and the environment broken. Adam and Eve are thrust out of the garden of Eden, and the way back to utopia is barred by divine judgement.[4] Moreover, man now exists in a state of tension with nature. Man must earn his living by the sweat of his brow among thorns and thistles,[5] and woman has pain in childbirth.[6] Mankind is out of gear with nature, and anxiety characterises their life. But the consequences of broken fellowship with God extend deep into human life and keep spreading. The first brothers fall out with each other, and one slays the other.[7] And so the story of the theological narrative goes on. It is a double story. On one side it is the story of the atomisation of mankind, for the internal rupture results in individualisation and conflict. On the other it is the story of human attempts at re-socialisation, great attempts to mend the broken relations, to heal the internal rupture, to bind divided humanity together again, as at Babel.[8] But all the attempts to heal man partake of our fallen nature and cannot but give new orientation in sin to the broken relationship with God, so that all attempts break themselves on the divine judgement and result in further disintegration. Mankind is unable to re-socialise itself, unable to heal its internal rupture for that which really makes man man is the bond between man and God.

That is the theological prelude to the Old Testament *Heilsgeschichte*,[9] the prehistory of incarnation, atonement and recreation.

(ii) Second prelude: God's personal intervention in the plight of humanity

Right from the start, the promise is made that the seed of the woman shall bruise the head of the serpent.[10] The only answer to man's predicament is the destruction of the power of evil, and a recreation of the bond between God and man. But if the first creation was the creation of man in the image of God, the recreation is through an act in which

4 Gen 3.23-24.

5 Gen 3.17-19.

6 Gen 3.16.

7 Gen 4.1ff.

8 Gen 11.1-9.

9 German theological term, 'salvation history'.

10 Gen 3.15.

God condescends to take on himself the image of man. The whole movement of redemption adumbrated from the start is a movement of God coming to man in order to restore man to God, of God taking man's place in order to give man God's place – the principle of substitution and the principle of incarnation. And at the start it is made clear in the story of Cain and Abel that this is the way of grace.[11] It is a story that has its explanation in the sacrifice of Isaac.[12]

How is mankind to be reconciled to God? There are two possible ways. The way of Cain in which man offers of the fruits of personal labour to God, the way of man from man to God. Man provides a personal offering, a personal sacrifice. The way of Abel is one in which God provides the sacrifice, the sacrifice of another. Abel followed God in his sacrifice of animals to cover – in Old Testament language to atone for – Adam and Eve's sin and shame. Abel let God provide the sacrifice and offered it to God. So in Abraham, who would offer his best, his only son, we see that his offering is displaced by God who himself provides the lamb.[13] Substitution and free grace are identical. Cain's way of approaching God runs against God's grace, even though it uses God's gifts. It is rejected. Abel's way is accepted, because it is God's gracious provision. That adumbration of God's way of redemption is worked out more fully with Abraham, Isaac, and Jacob. It is the way in which God comes in pure grace to gather frail humanity into covenant and communion with himself, and even provides for man a covenanted way of response to God's grace.[14] Man responds by faith, but in faith relies upon a divinely provided way of approach and response to God in the covenant.

That is the second theological prelude, interwoven with the first. The one is analytical, the other positive. Then the Old Testament goes on to unfold the way which this redeeming purpose of God took in the world, in the history of Israel, in and through whom that purpose began to assume flesh and blood in history.

(iii) The sacred history of Israel: theology of salvation history

In order, so to speak, to get a foothold within humanity God selects one particular people, the Jews,[15] and in that people he works within

---

[11] Gen 4.1ff.

[12] Gen 22.1ff.

[13] Gen 22.10-14.

[14] On 'a covenanted way of response', see also T.F. Torrance, *The Mediation of Christ*, revised edition (Edinburgh: T & T Clark 1992), p. 74ff.

[15] Gen 12.1f.

humanity, preparing for the incarnation of the beloved Son of God. Thus the story of Israel is *the prehistory of the incarnation* of the Son of God. Jesus is born through the womb of Israel and within Israel through the womb of the virgin Mary, of the seed of Israel, of the seed of man. How are we to interpret that story from the perspective of the incarnation?

Look at it like this. If you are going to make something you need to have tools in order to make it and give it shape. If you are to understand something you must have the *conceptual tools* with which to grasp it and shape knowledge of it in your mind. The tools of the mind are categories, concepts, truths, beliefs, etc. What tools do we humans have for knowing the living God?[16] What are our mortal instruments for receiving his revelation, indeed for receiving his Son into our human existence? Even if we were to be confronted with God, how could we know him, how could we grasp him, and assimilate his majesty to our knowing? Would he not transcend us so utterly that we would simply pass him by as a stranger? Would he not be quite incomprehensible? How can the finite grasp the infinite? How can mere mortals grasp and assimilate in their knowing the transcendent majesty of the holy and living creator?

(1) The election of Israel as the instrument of salvation

In his purpose to reveal himself to mankind, and to enter healingly within human existence, God refused to allow our limitations and weaknesses to inhibit his purpose of love and redemption. He condescended in incredible humility to find a way of entering within our beggarly weakness and poverty, to find a mode of divine entry into our finite and mortal existence, in order from within as creator and saviour to restore us to complete fellowship with himself, both in knowing and in being. Hence God selected one race from among all the races of mankind, one of the smallest, and, as Moses said, most beggarly and contemptible of all races, in order to make that race the very instrument of his redemptive purpose to reveal himself to every people and to save all humanity. God chose and fashioned the people of Israel, but they were the most stubborn and stiff-necked people under the sun.[17] They disobeyed God at every movement in his saving purpose. They knew well they were chosen by God for the special purpose of salvation yet

16 See further Torrance, *op. cit.* pp. 5-9.

17 Cf. Exod 34.9.

all through their history they fought against God. They stoned and attacked and abused his messengers. They killed the prophets. They contradicted God to his face, and resisted him, proving themselves utterly unworthy of his love, and they broke themselves again and again upon the word of God, dashing themselves against the covenant in which he had laid hold of them and held them in unswerving love, and so in their sheer resistance to God they were smitten down in suffering and agony and judgement. And yet the constant miracle of the whole redemption story is that in spite of all, God's purpose of love remained unchanged. He refused to be rebuffed or thwarted, and it was the very steadfastness of his covenant will that meant Israel's judgement as they broke themselves against it.

Had any other nation been chosen, said Jesus, Nineveh or Sodom or Gomorrah, they would have repented in dust and ashes long ago, but the Jews, it seems, were chosen in spite of it all and indeed because of their unworthy and very recalcitrant and rebellious nature, for God was determined even with the most difficult human material to fulfil his purpose, in order to best show his grace and love in covenant relation and purpose, in order to prepare for the new covenant or testament in Jesus Christ.

And so God took this stubborn people, as a potter might take the worst and lumpiest and most resistant and intractable clay, in order to put it upon the wheel for moulding and shaping into an earthen vessel designed to contain heavenly treasure. God chose Israel, then, with all its recalcitrance and intractability, with all its resentment against his love, and subjected them to ordeal by history and judgement. He used their very stubbornness and the judgement they brought upon themselves in order to train them. By elaborate religious ritual and carefully framed laws, by rivers of blood from millions of animal sacrifices, by the broken hearts of psalmists and the profoundest agony of the prophets, by the tragic story of Israelite politics and the shattering of this people again and again and again, God taught the Jews, through centuries and centuries of existence yoked to his word and covenant, until the truth was imprinted upon their conscience and there was burned into their souls the meaning of holiness and righteousness, of sin and uncleanness, of love and mercy and grace, of faithfulness and forgiveness, of justification, atonement, and salvation; the meaning of creation, the kingdom of God, of judgement, death, and at last resurrection; the concept of the Messiah, the suffering servant, and yet prophet, priest and king, and so to the very brink of the gospel.

(2) The birth of Jesus out of the womb of Israel: the incarnation

And then at the last in the fullness of time, when God had prepared in the heart and soul and religion of Israel a womb for the birth of Jesus, a cradle for the child of Bethlehem, the saviour of the world was born, the very Son of God – born of God right into the midst of Israel with all its suffering contradiction of God, into the midst of the Old Testament faith and all that reached out in it to fulfilment in this very hour of incarnation. And so when the hour came in the fullness of time, there were actually some who, when they saw him, recognised him as the Son of God come in the flesh, the redeemer of Israel, and the light to lighten the Gentiles – Zechariah, Anna, Simeon, and John the Baptist, and who more than the blessed virgin Mary, and then, one after another, the twelve disciples, and many others who acknowledged that this was indeed the Christ, the Son of the living God, the saviour of the world.

But this also is clear, that many of the Jews, even of the scribes and priests, knew that Jesus was the Messiah, and yet wilfully blinded themselves because he was not the kind of Messiah they wanted, and they still insisted in trying to bend the will of God to their ideas and desires. And so to the very last, they resisted the purpose of God's wonderful love and actually crucified the Messiah, the Son of God. But throughout all that, the faithfulness and love of God never wavered, and even the crucifixion of Jesus, which gathered up in itself all the tragic story of the Jews into final and ultimate intensity, was purposed, as St Peter said, according to the definite plan and foreknowledge of God,[18] and used as the mightiest instrument of all for salvation and the supreme revelation of God's eternal love. Through Israel, and through Calvary, Jesus was launched upon the world as the saviour of all, and in and through Jesus the Jew it was none other than God himself come among men and women in incredible condescension and humiliation, to become one with them in all their bitter and stubborn hatred of God's grace, in order to heal and gather mankind in spite of all into the fellowship and communion of the divine life.

Thus the knowledge of God, of Christ, and of the Jews are *all bound up inseparably together,* so that when at last God came into the world he came as a Jew. And to this very day Jesus remains a Jew while still the eternal Son of God. It is still through the story of Israel, through the Jewish soul shaped by the hand of God, through the Jewish scriptures of the Old Testament and the Jewish scriptures of the New Testament church, that the gospel comes to us, and that Jesus Christ is set

---

18 Acts 2.23.

before us face to face as Lord and saviour. Apart from this Old Testament prehistory and all the biblical revelation through Israel, we would not have the tools to grasp the knowledge of God; apart from the long history of the Jews we would not be able to recognise Jesus as the Son of God; apart from the suffering and agony of Israel we would not understand the cross of Calvary as God's instrument to atone for sin and to enact once and for all his word of love and pardon and grace. Apart from the covenant forged in sheer grace with undeserving and rebellious Israel, and the unswerving faithfulness of the divine love, we would not be able to understand the mystery of our restoration to union with God in Jesus Christ. Apart from the context of Israel we could not even begin to understand the bewildering miracle of Jesus. The supreme instrument of God for the salvation of the world is Israel, and out of the womb of Israel, Jesus, the Jew from Nazareth – yet he was no mere instrument in the hands of God, but very God himself, come in person in the form of a servant, to work out from within our limitations and recalcitrance, and to bring to its triumphant completion, the redemption of mankind, and our restoration to fellowship with the very life of God himself.

That is the proper perspective from which we are to understand and interpret the person and work of the Son of God in the whole of his incarnation. All that we have said is remarkably summed up in the words of Jesus himself to the woman of Samaria: 'You worship what you do not know; we worship what we know, for salvation is of the Jews.'[19] 'You worship what you do not know' – that is Jesus' firm verdict upon all natural theology, and all religion adulterated with natural theology. It is in the history of Israel, in the Old Testament revelation with its covenant and liturgy and law that the lineaments of the face of God begin to be seen, until the face of God is fully seen in the face of Jesus Christ himself in whom God and man meet face to face.

(b) The New Testament perspective – the Christian doctrine of Israel[20]

(i) One movement of salvation

The whole historico-redemptive movement in the Old and New Testaments is to be regarded as essentially one. The Old Testament

---

19 John 4.22.

20 The following twelve sections are to be found, with minor changes, and without the headings added here, in T.F. Torrance, *Conflict and Agreement in the Church*, vol. 1 (London: Lutterworth 1959), pp. 287-98.

speaks of the coming one, the coming of the kingdom; the New Testament speaks of the one who has come, and of the kingdom as having arrived in Christ Jesus himself. The Old Testament is the revelation of the *verbum incarnandum*,[21] and the New Testament is the revelation of the *verbum incarnatum*:[22] the centre of gravity in both is in the incarnation itself, to which the Old Testament is stretched out in expectation, and the New Testament looks back in fulfilment. This one movement throughout the Old Testament and New Testament is the movement of God's grace in which he renews the bond between himself and humanity broken and perverted at the fall, and restores man to communion with himself. God does that by giving himself to man in such a way as to assume human nature and existence into oneness with himself. He condescends to enter into our human nature and so elevates it into union with his own divine nature. That is what took place in the incarnation of the Word, in the midst of Israel, in the midst of mankind.

(ii) The pre-movement of the incarnation

Throughout the prehistory of the incarnation, which was itself in a profound sense part of the movement of the incarnation, God prepared a *way*, manifested his *truth*, and assumed man into a *life*-relation with himself. In Israel he prepared a *way* of covenant love in which he established a union between himself and Israel; within that covenant relation of love God manifested himself as the *truth*, bringing Israel into communion with himself; through union and communion God bound Israel to himself as the Lord, the giver of *life*, and so set up his kingdom in the midst of estranged humanity. He began to open up through Israel a new and living way for the redemption of all mankind that was to find its fulfilment in Jesus Christ, *the way, the truth, and the life*.

(iii) Prophet, priest and king

The activity of grace within the covenanted people of God involved the self-giving of God and the assuming of Israel into oneness with God through prophet, priest, and king. According to the Old Testament's understanding of itself, the covenant was established in the once and for all events at Mt Sinai[23] in which God decisively

---

21 Lat, 'word requiring to be incarnate'.

22 Lat, 'word incarnate'.

23 Exod 19.1ff.

revealed himself and enacted his revelation in the midst of Israel. He gave himself to the people of Israel to be their God and he took Israel to be his people. What God did he give to Israel? The God who proclaimed his name to Israel in these words, 'The Lord, the Lord, a God merciful and gracious, slow to anger, and abounding in steadfast love and faithfulness, keeping steadfast love for thousands, forgiving iniquity and transgression and sin, but who will by no means clear the guilty, visiting the iniquity of the fathers upon the children and upon the children's children, to the third and the fourth generation.'[24] God gave himself in sheer grace and love to Israel without any diminishment in his nature as holiness and love – that is why Sinai occupied a position of such unsurpassable significance in the history of Israel. Such a self-giving of God which is the self-giving of the self-affirming God, the '*I am who I am*',[25] was made in the unity of law and cult, that is, the unity of word and mediation, of truth and reconciliation. And so the covenant came to rest upon the twin foundation of the Sinaitic law and the Levitical liturgy, as represented supremely by Moses and Aaron, prophet and priest in essential and complementary unity. Once this covenantal basis was consolidated in Jerusalem, God manifested his coming kingdom through the Davidic line of kings, and the messianic kingdom came to overarch the covenantal relation of word and pardon, prophet and priest. The Messiah was the king of the kingdom who provided in himself the way, the truth, and the life, and so provided the way of restoration of mankind to the Father.

(iv) The agony of Israel and the faithfulness of God

This triple activity of God's grace and self-revelation, in prophet, priest and king, was not static but was carried through the most harrowing and profound historical experience the world has ever known, in the whole life and agony of Israel. The three modes of divine activity and grace had to be worked into the innermost existence and being of this people, if it was to become the instrument of God's ultimate self-giving to mankind. This nation was a beggarly and despised people, as Moses told them, and it proved itself to be the most stiff-necked and rebellious of peoples, but it was chosen out of pure love and on that basis alone was brought into covenant relation with God. The keeping of the covenant did not depend on Israel's worth, but on the contrary, was conditioned by the pure unstinted outflowing love of God in the continuous act of grace, of grace for grace. What a magnificent account

24 Exod 34.6f.

25 Exod 3.14.

of that covenant love is given by the prophet Hosea! But it became very clear that God could keep faith and truth with this rebellious people only by judgement, by punishment, as well as by mercy. He held on to his purpose of love, binding the covenant-people to himself, refusing to divorce it in spite of persistent rebuffs. The covenant grounded in mercy (*hesed*) and truth (*'emeth*) was maintained by God in utter faithfulness, that is, in the consistency of truth and in the utter steadfastness of love. In that covenant relation of truth and love Israel had to suffer, for it shattered itself on the unswerving persistence of the divine purpose of love. Israel suffered inevitably from God, for God would not let his people go, even when they rebelled against him and kicked at his way of righteousness, truth and mercy.

(v) Intensification of the covenant: the suffering servant

God used the historical experience of Israel to reveal himself more and more profoundly and to give himself more completely to Israel. He used the suffering and judgement of Israel to reveal the terrible nature of sin as contradiction to God's love and grace, to uncover the deep enmity of humanity in its persistent self-will before God in his divine self-giving. But transcending all, God used this nation in the ordeal of history and suffering to reveal his own infinite love and the undeflected persistence of his holy will to bring forgiveness and reconciliation, until his love achieved its purpose of final union and communion of man with God in Jesus Christ. In that ordeal, the word and the cult were not mere letter and liturgy, but were worked out into the very existence of Israel; that was surely the great prophetic burden of Deutero-Isaiah[26] and Jeremiah. Law and cult have no place in God's will merely as such; they have their place only as they are kneaded into the very existence and understanding and life of Israel. That was the reason for the suffering of Israel, for word and truth and love had to be wrought out in the breaking and making of Israel as the servant of the Lord.

The whole conception of the *suffering servant* represents the activity of God whereby he begins to draw together the cords of the covenant in which he had bound Israel to himself as his chosen partner in redemption-history; it represents the saving activity of God in which he began to narrow down his assumption of Israel into union with himself toward the point of the incarnation where, in the midst of Israel, he was to assume man into oneness with himself in the ultimate act of incarnation and reconciliation. The great sign of the covenant made

---

[26] Isaiah 40 – 55.

with Abraham and Isaac was circumcision, for in it the covenant was cut into the flesh of this people, and remained throughout the generations as the sign that the promises of God would be fulfilled in the life of this people only as the word of God was translated into its flesh, into its very existence. It was the sign that at last the covenant had to be written into the heart, in the 'crucifixion' of self-will, in the putting off of 'the enmity of the flesh'.[27] But once the covenant came to be enacted so deeply into the existence of Israel that it was written into the 'inner man', its whole form would change. It would be a new covenant. Such a total 'circumcision' was fulfilled at last in the flesh of Jesus Christ, for through his crucifixion, the new covenant was inaugurated, and the new and living way was opened up in the humanity of the Son of Man.

(vi) Intensification of the contradiction

Israel suffered most throughout its history as bearer in its existence and life of the divine revelation. It suffered from the mighty arm of the Lord, that is, at the hands of the word of God, because it had to be broken and remade, reshaped, and realigned with the covenant-will of God. Thus the very covenant relation of Israel to God through which it became *laos*, God's people, and *klēros*, God's inheritance, entailed political and national disaster for Israel in its will to be *ethnos*, a nation like the other nations of the earth.[28] That was part of the deepest agony of Jeremiah. The astonishing thing here is that the more God gave himself to this people, the more he forced it to be what it was in its sin and self-will, to be in truth what it actually was, a rebel. The very self-giving of God in holy love not only revealed Israel's sin, but intensified it: it intensified the enmity between Israel and Yahweh[29] and intensified the contradiction between Yahweh and Israel – hence the 'suffering servant'. God insisted on giving himself to Israel in spite of its enmity to him, and insisted on assuming Israel in its sinful contradiction into partnership with himself – hence the profoundest agony of psalmist and prophet alike, and hence also 'the identity by assumption' of the suffering of Israel with the suffering of the Messiah so poignantly described in Isaiah 53.

---

27 Cf. Rom 8.7f.; Eph 2.15-16 KJV (RSV 'hostility').

28 Cf. the discussion on *laos* and *ethnos* in *The Mediation of Christ*, p. 14f.

29 Heb, '*YHWH*', the name of the Lord, literally, 'I am who I am', or 'I will be who I will be'.

Moreover, in the intensification of the relationship between Israel and God, God's self-revelation had to blind Israel in a profound sense, and his self-manifestation had to hide himself from Israel: *Eli, Eli, lama sabachthani?* (My God, my God, why have you forsaken me?)[30] How could it be otherwise when God entered into the heart of Israel's estrangement in order to make atonement, when the assumption of refractory Israel into oneness with God intensified judgement upon Israel's self-will as well as fulfilled the self-giving of God to Israel in love? To us, no doubt, as we look back from the incarnation, the experience for Israel becomes clearer and clearer, but Israel itself became blinder and blinder – 'Who is blind but my servant?'[31] – as God's self-giving pressed toward the ultimate act of incarnation and atonement. That is what we see so clearly and tragically in the resistance of Jesus' contemporaries, even of the high priests.

(vii) Ultimate rejection, ultimate union

In the ultimate act of union between God and Israel, and in the ultimate conflict which that entailed, in Israel's refusal of the Messiah, the rejection of Israel had to take place. God gave himself to Israel and assumed Israel into covenant partnership with himself – and that covenant provided in the midst of humanity a revelation of God's will to be man's God in spite of human sin. It was therefore with Israel in its sinful existence and indeed in its refusal of God that God bound himself in the covenant of love, while Israel, on its part, was unable to escape from the decision of God's love that had overtaken it in the covenant of grace gathering it into partnership with God. Israel suffered from that covenant, but suffered because of its persistent refusal of grace, suffering more and more until, in the ultimate act of God's self-giving in the incarnation, Israel rejected it in the crucifixion of the Messiah, and in so doing shattered itself on the cross – 'His blood be on us and on our children.'[32] Theologically, therefore, the complete destruction of Jerusalem and the temple in AD 70 had to follow upon the crucifixion of the Son of Man.

But at the very heart of that great darkness it was supremely revealed that God had given himself to humanity at its very worst in its ultimate rejection of grace, and in spite of man's ultimate rejection of grace God

---

30 Matt 27.46 & Mark 15.34, the words of Jesus on the cross quoting Psalm 22.1.

31 Isaiah 42.19.

32 Matt 27.25.

had joined himself to mankind for ever. The ultimate refusal of God which took place in Israel was the very means whereby the holy love of God achieved its final victory over sin, for by the crucifixion of Christ man was brought into reconciliation with God. That took place in the mediator, who as true God and true man had chosen Israel as the people in whose midst he penetrated into the innermost existence of mankind in estrangement from God, and in the heart of that estrangement consummated an eternal union between God and man in himself. This man was himself the *way*, the *truth*, and the *life*, the *mediator*: henceforth all humanity come to the Father by him.

The miracle was that just when mankind shattered itself against the judgement of God, it was called out of death into resurrection, out of destruction into life, out of darkness into light, out of bondage into freedom; just when Israel destroyed itself in the crucifixion of the son of David, just when the vine of God's choosing and planting was cut away down to the ground, there sprang up out of the earth a new shoot, a new vine, for he who had willed to be Israel and was crucified, rose again as a root out of the dry ground to be the true vine.[33] That meant also the resurrection of Israel, the Israel of the covenant, as Paul insisted so powerfully, but here we must note that the crucifixion and resurrection of Jesus revealed the pattern of experience adumbrated all through the long ordeal of Israel's suffering. In its completion the pattern is seen to be essentially cruciform, but now in the light of its full manifestation, it is not difficult to see how the pattern of the recurring death and renascence, or rebirth of Israel throughout its history was bent forward by the finger of God to point to the crucifixion and resurrection of Jesus, the Israelite in whom there is no guile[34] but the Israelite who took upon himself the role of Israel, recapitulating in himself the ordeal of the servant in order 'to stand in the gap', to be made a curse for the atonement of Israel, and in the midst of Israel, for all humanity.

(viii) Particularisation and universalisation

Now, however, it is possible to look back and see something else – that the activity of grace which selected one people, and one particular course of history in its human and historical particularity, enacted a covenantal relation of union and communion with God that was essentially universalistic from the very beginning. It was essentially

---

33 Cf. Isaiah 53.2.

34 Cf. John 1.47.

dual in its nature: particular and universal. That was apparent in the choice of Abraham, one particular man, yet the covenant promise was that in him and his seed all nations would be blessed.[35] In the enactment of the covenant between one particular people and Yahweh at Sinai, the bond of the covenant was the decalogue[36] which was essentially universalistic. The movement was paradoxical in character – the more particular it became, the more universal it also became; the deeper the bond between God and man was driven in the human existence of Israel, the closer redemption made contact with creation; the more intimately Israel was tied to the one and only God, the God of all, the more the activity of grace broke through the limitations of national Israel and reached out to all the world. That was particularly apparent in the election of Israel to be God's *laos*, people, upon which Israel's aspirations to be *ethnos*, nation, were shattered again and again, for to be bound to God as Israel was, was essentially to become the *qahal*[37] or the *ekklēsia*[38] of God and so to transcend the sociological and political husk of Israel to become the one people of the living God. It was characteristic of the whole activity of God's grace that it should suborn the very refusal of Israel to be *laos* to minister to its purpose of universal blessing and redemption. And so the more like a single particular *ethnos* Israel became the more it had to be scattered in *diaspora*[39] over the face of the whole earth.

At last in the acute personalisation of the covenantal bond between Israel and God in Jesus, it became absolutely universal for all mankind. That was already apparent in the suffering servant portrayed by the cult-prophets. The suffering servant was Israel assumed into oneness with the word of God, and it is in that duality that the 'servant songs' of Isaiah[40] as they are known are surely to be understood. But even there it is evident that as the word became one with Israel, it became more and more one Israelite, for that is the only way in which the word assumes human nature and existence into oneness with itself.

---

[35] Gen 12.1-3; cf. 17.1f.

[36] Gk, *deka logoi*, 'ten words', from the Hebrew equivalent, translated as the 'ten commandments'.

[37] Heb, assembly, congregation, covenant-community.

[38] Gk, church, literally the 'called out'. See the discussion on *qahal* and *ekklēsia* in *Conflict and Agreement*, vol. 1, pp. 285-87.

[39] Gk, 'dispersion, scattering'.

[40] Isaiah 42.1-7; 49.1-10; 50.4-10; 52.13 – 53.12.

Thus while in one sense, the suffering servant was Israel assumed into oneness with the word, it is primarily to be understood as the Word identifying himself with Israel, and becoming one particular Israelite, an individual person, the Messiah. Thus the ultimate self-giving of God to Israel in its historical particularity narrowing down to one particular Jew, meant the universalisation and transcendence of the Old Testament form of the covenant, and the setting of the relation of God and man on a wholly new basis in which redemption was more than the restoration of Israel, more than an event that penetrated back into the foundations of creation; it was a *new creation* in which the fullness of the eternal purpose of God was to be realised in an altogether transcendent way.

(ix) The election and rejection of one for all

Now it is also possible to see more clearly than anywhere in the Old Testament itself that the life and ordeal of Israel were the election of one people as the instrument of divine love for the redemption of all mankind and all creation. The election of one for the salvation of all characterised the whole story of God's dealings with Israel. But within Israel that activity of grace reached its climactic fulfilment in a singular event, in the incarnation. In Jesus Christ, the incarnate Lord, the election of one for all has become ultimate fact within our human existence; in him, election and substitution combined in the most unique, most intense and personal concentration, with a view to universal redemption. It is in Jesus Christ, who is the real meaning and substance of the life of Israel that we are to understand Israel's ordeal in history and place in the divine purpose.

In Jesus Christ, it is revealed that the *election* of one for all becomes salvation for all in the *rejection* of one for all. What took place on the cross revealed what was happening to Israel in the election of God: because it was an election of man in corporate enmity to God, an acceptance of mankind in its sinful existence, election involved the reprobation of man's will to isolation from God and reprobation of that refusal of God's grace. The election of Israel as an instrument of the divine reconciliation, an instrument which was to be used in its very refusal of grace so that in its midst the ultimate self-giving of God might take place, meant, then, not only that Israel was elected to be confronted with the ultimate events, the last things, before which its refractory self-will was to be exposed to the full judgement of God, but also that Israel was elected to act in a representative capacity for all peoples in its rejection of Christ. The consequent rejection of Israel is to be understood in the light of the substitution of Israel for all other peoples.

(x) Reaffirmation through judgement and rejection

How can we express this, for human words are too inadequate here? It is clear on the one hand, that the election of Israel to be the instrument of God and the sphere within which the Son of God should come, not only as the divine judge of humanity but as man judged by God, peculiarly involved Israel in the wrath of God. At the same time, we cannot but acknowledge on the other hand, that the election of Israel to be the sphere in which the Son of God let himself be condemned as a sinner and be put to death on the cross, meant that Israel could only fulfil the gracious purpose of God by rejecting Christ and condemning him to a sinner's death. The Jews carried that out in fearful wickedness, in the ultimate refusal of grace that sin involves, but throughout it all the Son of God remained in sovereign control. Surely that was a great part of his unspeakable agony, that he was in control: how could he, the incarnate love of God, let man become guilty of the ultimate wickedness of putting the Son of God to death? And yet he came in love to do this, to penetrate into the blackest heart of human evil and to take it all upon himself. And so to the last he pressed hard upon Israel with the finger of God, shutting it up to becoming utterly guilty of the rejection and murder of the Son of God.

It was not that he made the Jews more guilty but that he exposed the infinite guilt of man's hatred of grace, drawing it out in all its enmity that he might bear it and bear it away as the lamb of God in holy and awful atonement. As such he bore that infinite guilt, not only of Israel but of all mankind revealed in the guilt of Israel, that he might acquit and justify the ungodly, Jew and Gentile alike. Here, he bore the guilt of those who, standing in a representative relation to all others, carried out the crucifixion of Jesus. He bore to the full the guilt of Israel that he might acquit and justify Israel. 'Father, forgive them, for they know not what they do.'[41] 'Who is blind but my servant?'[42] – wilfully blind, no doubt, but blinded in the role for which Israel was chosen. It was chosen as the sphere of revelation and atonement, and as such, Israel was regarded by God as his firstborn son. It was too as such, as God's servant, God's beloved son, that Israel was involved by election in the rejection of the Messiah and therefore in the ultimate wrath of God.

But the wrath that has come upon Israel through the cross has to be understood as the chastening wrath of the heavenly Father. There is an outpouring of the wrath of God which is not the chastening of a

---

41 Luke 23.34.

42 Isaiah 42.19.

son but the banishing of the disowned and disinherited into the outer darkness upon which God has for ever turned his back, and Jews and Gentiles alike may bring themselves under that curse. But the judgement and wrath in which Israel as a people is involved means not the final casting out of mankind, but God's own descent within the existence between creator and creature perverted by the fall of man, and his negation of the contradiction we have introduced into it by our sin. God's wrath here means, therefore, in unmistakable terms that what he has created he still affirms as his own handiwork, and that he will not curse it or cast it off into nothingness. Even in wrath, God wills to remain man's creator and man's God.

His wrath against Israel does not mean that he banishes Israel from his covenant of love and truth but that he affirms that covenant, negating everything that threatens to dissolve it. God's wrath against Israel does not mean his abandonment either of his eternal purpose or of his covenant promises, but on the contrary is the act of his holy love within the covenant in which he asserts himself as holy and loving creator in the midst of human perversity, in the midst of humanity's refusal of grace. God's wrath is judgement of sin, reprobation of our refusal of God, but as such it is already part of atonement, part of re-creation, for his wrath is in fact his reaffirmation of his creatures in spite of their sin and rebellion. Certainly, it is reaffirmation in judgement against sin, but it is a reaffirmation that the creature belongs to God and that he wills to remain its God. God's wrath insists that we remain his children, that we belong to him body and soul, and it is within that belonging that judgement takes place.

(xi) The rejection of Israel as the reconciling of the world

It becomes clear, then, that the rejection of Israel is not its abandonment but the reaffirmation of Israel in the fullness of the covenant and its promises. The covenant remains. God keeps his promises, and his faithfulness is not made of none effect by the faithlessness of his ancient people. The rejection of Israel as a people is only to be understood in the light of the substitutionary nature of the cross, for Israel's rejection is bound up by God with the atoning rejection of the man on the cross, or rather in his acceptance of the sentence of our rejection – *Eli, Eli, lama sabachthani*? Paul did not hesitate therefore to speak of the rejection of Israel as the reconciling of the world in language almost identical with his assertion that by the death of his Son we were reconciled to God. But it is precisely on the same ground that Paul could speak of the restoration of God's people Israel. 'For if while we were enemies we were reconciled to God by the death of his Son, much more, now that we are reconciled, shall we be saved by his life.'[43] Similarly, 'For if their rejection (Israel's) means the reconciliation of the world, what will their acceptance mean but life from the dead?'[44]

(xii) Salvation through Israel's rejection and restoration

Three facts of supreme importance emerge here.[45]

(1) While Israel's fall, and blindness, and rejection, resulted from its refusal of grace, from its crucifixion of the Messiah, nevertheless its rejection was involved in the substitutionary work of the cross, for God used that very refusal and crucifixion in order to bring forth salvation for all. Thus the rejection of Israel worked out to the riches of the Gentiles. That must determine our whole outlook upon the Jews – they were blinded for us that we might see: they were stripped and deprived that we might become rich with the gospel. We can only see them where they are still held by God in the shadow of the cross. We are their debtors in Christ.

(2) But the very substitutionary nature of Christ's rejection means also the restoration of Israel, for it is already involved in the resurrection of Jesus of Nazareth, the rejected son of David. For as the rejection of Jesus meant his taking rejection in our place in order to restore us to life in his resurrection for us, so the rejection of Jesus by Israel in our place will mean their restoration to life in resurrection with momentous consequences for us all. Thus the restoration of God's ancient people will have a part in the eschatological events of the consummation, and even the full blessing of the Gentiles depends upon the fulfilment of the covenant promises to Israel. If the rejection of Israel brought reconciliation and riches to the world, what will the restoration of Israel involve but life from the dead?

(3) The restoration of Israel, however, takes a way as unique as Israel's instrumental place in the redemptive purpose of God, and is to be looked for along the line of the representative capacity which it still has in the election of God. The way to Israel's salvation therefore, lies somehow through rejection; the way to its enlightenment lies through its blindness; the way to its fullness lies through its impoverishment – these are ways of God past finding out, for they belong to his

---

43 Rom 5.10.

44 Rom 11.15.

45 See Romans 9 – 11 for the whole discussion here.

unsearchable judgement,[46] to the deepest mystery of the cross. But this much is revealed, that through darkness God's ancient people will come to the light of the resurrection, and all Israel will be saved. That does not simply mean that the Jewish people will eventually become Christians and members of the one holy catholic and apostolic church, but that within the one church of Christ, the Israel of God, there will be a special place for Israel as a people, and that even in its present blindness or rejection Israel has a unique mission in the world, for by his election of Israel God has once and for all bound up the salvation of mankind with Israel.

2 The incarnation and the new Israel

When we turn from the Old to the New Testament, we turn from the old form of God's covenant to its new form, where it is perfectly and finally fulfilled. In the Old Testament the covenant is described in this way: God out of sheer grace bestows himself upon his people as their God and gives them to himself as his people. In that covenant, he wills to be a father to his people, and desires his people to be his children. 'I will be your Father, and you will be my children. I am holy, therefore be you holy. Walk before me and be perfect.'[47] But God knows that his children in their sin and frailty are unable to fulfil his covenant, and so he provides for them a way of covenant response and fulfilment which was but a pointer ahead to the actualisation of the covenant in the very being and life of man. That would take place when God provided from within Israel, and from within man's actual existence and life, complete and final fulfilment of the covenant both *from the side of God* and *from the side of man*.

That is what takes place in the incarnation. God not only fulfils his promise of love in the covenant in giving himself to humanity in complete and utter grace, but he accomplishes for man, and from within man, man's fulfilment of the covenant, man's appropriation of God's gift of himself. But that fulfilment of the covenant will of God to give himself to man is also the fulfilment of the divine judgement upon sin, and the fulfilment from within mankind of man's obedient submission to that verdict of the divine love against sin. Thus in the incarnation God comes himself, freely condescending to enter into our lost and estranged humanity, taking our lost condition upon himself in order to effect, through judgement and mercy, reconciliation with himself.

---

46 Rom 11.33.

47 A mosaic of quotations summing up the form of the covenant. See Gen 17.1.

In this act of condescension God comes as God the Son and God the Word. He comes as God the Son to enter our rebellious estate in order to effect reconciliation by living out his life of filial obedience where we are disobedient, and he comes as God the Word to enter into our darkness and blindness in order to effect revelation by manifesting the love of God and by achieving from within humanity faithful appropriation of divine revelation. The act of God the Son and of God the Word are not two acts but one act, for revelation is part of reconciliation and reconciliation is part of revelation. In both, as one mighty act, God fulfils the covenant from the side of God, 'I will be your God, your Father', and fulfils the covenant from the side of man, 'I will be your obedient child'. This is the mighty act of the incarnation which is at once the act of God's humiliation and the act of man's exaltation, for he who in such amazing grace descended to make our lost cause his own, ascended in accomplishment of his task, elevating man into union and communion with the life of God.

We shall think of that whole movement in terms of the prophetic, priestly, and kingly ministry of Christ. His prophetic ministry was the descent of his word into the midst of our darkness to effect revelation, but that already overlaps throughout with his priestly ministry as the humiliation of Christ the Son who entered into our disobedient estate in order by his obedient sacrifice to effect reconciliation with God. But both in the ministry of the word and in the ministry of the priest, it is the king who has come, with the royal word of grace, to set us free from our bondage and to redeem us for a life in which in incredible grace God gives us to share in his own glory.

Christ the Word made flesh, the Son made servant

Jesus Christ was prophet, and he had a prophetic function to perform – but he was prophet in the unique sense of being identical with the word which he proclaimed. He *was* the Word of God. We have already seen that the function of the prophet in the Old Testament was not only to bring the word of God to the people but to criticise the law and the cult as such and to insist that they must be done into the very existence of Israel – and we saw that oneness of Israel with the word to belong to the very essence of the Isaianic notion of the suffering servant. The servant was Israel assumed into oneness with the Word of God, or the Word of God identifying himself with Israel. But the Word of God thus becomes one with Israel by becoming more and more one Israelite, the Messiah, for that alone is how the Word assumes human nature into oneness with himself. When we turn to the New

Testament we find that Messiah immediately. He is the Word made flesh in a particular Israelite, Jesus the son of David, the son of Mary. In the Gospels, in the early chapters of Acts, and especially in the epistle to the Hebrews, the concepts of the Son, the servant, and the Word or revelation of God are all brought together to describe the incarnate work of Christ as he steps forth to reveal the Father's will of love and reconciliation, and to effect it. We shall now examine first what the New Testament has to say about the incarnation of the Word, and then what it has to say about the incarnation of the Son.

(a) The Word made flesh

What did John mean by the 'Word'? There can be no doubt that it was the word of God in the Old Testament that he had in mind, the word that came to the prophets, the word that acted so mightily in Israel's history, the arm of the Lord in revelation. But the prologue to the fourth Gospel makes detailed use of the Old Testament meaning of 'word', the very word *dabar* itself which we must now examine.

(i) The meaning of 'word', dabar

Dabar comes from a semitic root meaning back or hinterside.[48] That is evident in the kindred word *midbar*, used to describe the backside of the desert, or in the word *debir*, the holy of holies, the back-side of the temple or tabernacle. Judging by the LXX[49] translations of *dabar*, *logos* (word), and *rēma* (thing), *dabar* has a twofold significance. On the one hand, *dabar* refers to the hinterground of a thing, that is word in the sense of meaning, and so it is translated by *logos*. On the other hand, it also means a thing, an event, or even a head of cattle, or as we would say a piece, where it is translated by *rēma*. *Dabar* refers then to word not so much as expression but as the inner reality of the word, but it also refers to event, not so much to event as such, but to event with a hinterground of meaning. Every event or thing has its *dabar* or hinterground of meaning, and so the plural *debarim* means history and is translated in Greek as *rēmata*. O. Procksch speaks of these two elements of *dabar* as i) the dianoetic element, where the meaning of an

---

[48] See the article on 'The Word of God in the Old Testament' by Procksch in Kittel, *Theological Dictionary of the New Testament*, vol.4, Eng. trans. (Grand Rapids: Eerdmans 1967), pp. 91-100, esp. pp. 92-93.

[49] The Greek translation of the Old Testament, called the 'Septuagint', or 'LXX' from the Roman numerals for 70 since it was originally translated by '70 scholars' (the actual number was 72).

event becomes evident (the person who understands the *dabar* of a thing understands it), and ii) the dynamic element, which is the outer aspect of *dabar* as event or action. This is apparent in the relation of *dabar* to *ruach*, breath or spirit. *Dabar* is uttered by *ruach* and is filled out with power, through which it becomes known, and eventuates.

It is in this way that the Old Testament speaks of the word of God as coming, as taking place, becoming event. This is especially clear in the Old Testament references to the word of the Lord where both elements come together. That is precisely the significance of the prophet who brings the word of God which is a mighty event, the word of God in action, a word that makes history. It should also be noted that where word and event coincide there, in the Hebrew idiom, is *truth*. God's word is truth, for his deed corresponds to his word.[50] The same applies to man's word. There must be a relation of faithfulness between the word, the speaking of it, and the doing of it, but also a relation of faithfulness between the speaking and the hearing of it. When a word is truth it is credited or believed, and then it is confirmed with *amen*.[51]

That is enough to help us grasp something of what John means when he speaks about Christ as the Word of God.[52] John is clearly thinking of the Old Testament tabernacle, the moving tent of meeting, as it was called, the place where God and man met and God revealed himself to man. That tent was lodged in the midst of Israel and when Israel moved it moved with it, and when Israel camped it was pitched in the midst of the camp[53] – and so all through Israel's pilgrimage. The tabernacle had an outer court and an inner court, but in the very back, behind the inner court there was the holy of holies, the *debir* and within the *debir* there was the ark and within the ark there was lodged the word of God, the law.[54] This was known as the ten words, the *debarim*. But *debarim* also means history. But this is history with a hinterground of meaning in the holy of holies, history as determined by the word of God. The tabernacle enshrined the word of God, the word that made Israel's history. But all through Israel's pilgrimage that word was hidden in the *debir*. Sometimes, however, it was made bare, when the word of God came to Israel through a prophet and God made bare his mighty arm, and acted upon Israel through his word.

---

50 See 2 Sam 7.28; 1 Kings 17.24.

51 Deut 27.15ff.; Num 5.22 – cf. 'The words of the Amen, the faithful and true witness', Rev 3.14.

52 John 1.1-18.

53 Num 1.50,53; 2.2ff.; 9.15-23; 10.1ff.

54 1 Kings 8.9; cf. Exod 24.12.

The meaning of 'word' in the gospel of John

With the Old Testament images and language in mind, John expounds the incarnation of the Word. The Word that was hidden in the bosom of God, the Word through which all things were made has become (*egeneto*) flesh, has tabernacled among men and women, and we see its grace and truth. It has become a man in Jesus Christ. All through the history of Israel that Word was behind the law and the cult, and the prophets came forward under the constraint of the Word to insist that the Word must become flesh, that is, must be allowed to enter into the very existence of Israel, in judgement and mercy. All through the history of Israel that becoming flesh of the Word impended, and cast its shadow before it in prophet, priest, and king, and above all in the suffering servant, but now at last the Word actually becomes flesh in the midst of Israel: it enters our very existence and becomes one with us. John is saying that Jesus Christ is himself the tabernacle of God among men and women, himself the Word of God enshrined in the flesh, and in him that the glory of God is to be seen.[55] John follows up this by recording two incidents in the second and the fourth chapters in which Jesus in his own words identifies himself with the temple.

Now let us note what John has to say about this Word. *The Word is God, the creator* – Word by whom all things are made. He is the eternal Word, but now that Word, without ceasing to be what it eternally is, becomes a creature. He enters within the creaturely existence he created and becomes one with his creatures. However, he enters into the creation in such a way as to dwell in it as a personal presence, who comes to his own, who is not received, but who effects personal meeting and faith with those who do receive him. It is a personal Word who becomes flesh and meets us as man. We recall how in Genesis the creating Word of God created by command, but in regard to man he addressed man and created him as the creature of direct personal address. Now the Word becomes such a man, addressed by the Word, and takes up his dwelling as man among humanity. He is both the Word of God who addresses man, and man addressed by and answering the Word. In all this the Word is the Lord God, the subject of the incarnation. He becomes creature in all his sovereign freedom as creator; and without ceasing to be that creator Word he becomes flesh, without any diminishment of his freedom or of his eternal nature. But as very Word of God and as remaining God's Word in all the fullness of his grace and truth he comes personally to man, light into darkness,

[55] John 1.14; cf. Exod 40.34-38; cf. also 2 Chron 5.13-14, 7.1-2.

declaring and manifesting God in the flesh in a fullness from which we can all receive.

(ii) The meaning of 'flesh'

'The Word was made flesh' – but what is meant by *flesh*? John means that the Word fully participates in human nature and existence, for he became man in becoming flesh, true man and real man.[56] He was so truly man in the midst of mankind that it was not easy to recognise him as other than man or to distinguish him from other men. He came to his own and his own received him not. He became a particular man, Jesus, who stands among other men unsurpassed but unrecognised. That is the way he became flesh, by becoming one particular man. And yet this is the creator of all mankind, now himself become a man.

The assumption of fallen flesh

But are we to think of this flesh which he became as *our* flesh? Are we to think of it as describing some neutral human nature and existence, or as describing our actual human nature and existence in the bondage and estrangement of humanity fallen from God and under the divine judgement? It was certainly into a state of enmity that the Word penetrated in becoming flesh, into darkness and blindness, that is, into the situation where light and darkness are in conflict and where his own receive him not. There can be no doubt that the New Testament speaks of the flesh of Jesus as the concrete form of our human nature marked by Adam's fall, the human nature which seen from the cross is at enmity with God and needs to be reconciled to God. In becoming flesh the Word penetrated into hostile territory, into our human alienation and estrangement from God. When the Word became flesh, he became all that we are in our opposition to God in our bondage under law – that is the amazing act of gracious condescension in the incarnation, that God the Son should assume our flesh, should enter a human existence under divine judgement, enter into the situation where the psalmist cried *Eli, Eli, lama sabachthani*,[57] so that the Word or Son of God himself gave out the same cry when overwhelmed with the divine judgement upon our flesh. St Paul declares quite plainly therefore that he was made under the law; he became a servant subject to the bondage of judgement and death; he was made in the likeness of sinful flesh, and was even made a curse for us. That is what we see

---

56 Cf. Gal 4.4; Rom 1.3; Phil 2.7; Heb 2.14f.

57 Psalm 22.1.

already in the baptism of Jesus – where he identifies himself with sinners, is baptised with the baptism of repentance, and immediately is driven by the Spirit into the wilderness where for forty days he fasts and is tempted in immediate fulfilment of his mission as made flesh of our flesh, and as identified with sinners from whom repentance is required, in complete solidarity with them.

Now when we listen to the witness of holy scripture here we know we are faced with something we can never fully understand, but it is something that we must seek to understand as far as we can. One thing should be abundantly clear, that if Jesus Christ did not assume our fallen flesh, our fallen humanity, then our fallen humanity is untouched by his work – for '*the unassumed is the unredeemed*',[58] as Gregory Nazianzen put it. Patristic theology, especially as we see it expounded in the great Athanasius, makes a great deal of the fact that he who knew no sin became sin for us, exchanging his riches for our poverty, his perfection for our imperfection, his incorruption for our corruption, his eternal life for our mortality. Thus Christ took from Mary a corruptible and mortal body in order that he might take our sin, judge and condemn it in the flesh, and so assume our human nature as we have it in the fallen world that he might heal, sanctify and redeem it. In that teaching the Greek fathers were closely following the New Testament. If the Word of God did not really come into our fallen existence, if the Son of God did not actually come where we are, and join himself to us and range himself with us where we are in sin and under judgement, how could it be said that Christ really took our place, took our cause upon himself in order to redeem us?

What could we then have to do with him? We stand before God as flesh of sin under God's judgement, and it is into this concrete form of our sin-laden, corruptible and mortal humanity in which we are damned and lost that Christ came, without ceasing to be the holy Son of God. He entered into complete solidarity with us in our sinful existence in order to save us, without becoming himself a sinner.

---

[58] Patristic theology, the theology of the early church fathers, argued that our whole flesh needed to be assumed by Christ in order to be healed (ie. body, mind and soul), for whatever was not assumed by him was unredeemed and unhealed.

For more on Nazianzen's argument and the patristic debate and its implications, see T.F. Torrance, *The Christian Frame of Mind*, new edition (Colorado Springs: Helmers & Howard 1989), chap. 1, 'The Greek Christian Mind', pp. 6-9, and T.F. Torrance, *The Trinitarian Faith* (Edinburgh: T & T Clark 1988), pp. 161-68.

The sanctification of fallen flesh

However, while we must say all that about the flesh that the Word assumed, we must also say that in the very act of assuming our flesh the Word sanctified and hallowed it, for the assumption of our sinful flesh is itself atoning and sanctifying action. How could it be otherwise when he, the Holy One took on himself our unholy flesh? Thus we must say that while he, the holy Son of God, became what we are, he became what we are in a different way from us. We become what we are and continue to become what we are as sinners. He, however, who knew no sin became what we are, yet not by sinning himself. Christ the Word did not sin. He did not become flesh of our flesh in a sinful way, by sinning in the flesh. If God the Word became flesh, God the Word is the subject of the incarnation, and how could God sin? How could God deny God, be against himself, divest himself of his holiness and purity? Thus his taking of our flesh of sin was a sinless action, which means that Jesus does not do in the flesh of sin what we do, namely, sin, but it also means that by remaining holy and sinless in our flesh, he condemned sin in the flesh he assumed and judged it by his very sinlessness.

It is St Paul here who opens up for us the profundity of this fact. God sent his Son in the concrete likeness of sinful flesh, *en homoiōmati sarkos hamartias*, an expression which is used in Romans, 'For God has done what the law, weakened by the flesh, could not do: sending his own Son in the likeness of sinful flesh and for sin, he condemned sin in the flesh'.[59] In the concrete likeness of the flesh of sin, he is unlike the sinner. The verse 'he made him to be sin who knew no sin'[60] does not mean that God made him a man who sins, or sins again, but that he was made that by way of exchange, *katallagē*, or substitution. That carries us right into the heart of the atonement. That atoning exchange begins right away with the incarnation, with its assumption of our flesh of sin, its condemnation of sin in the flesh, its sanctification of our humanity through the gift of divine righteousness and sanctification of man in Christ.

The New Testament teaches us, then, that though Jesus Christ assumed our fallen human existence, our fallen flesh under the dominion of sin and under the judgement of the law of God, he was yet without sin. He was wholly and perfectly obedient to God the Father. In the Hebrew idiom the Word became event in a way that

---

59 Rom 8.3.

60 2 Cor 5.21.

corresponds faithfully to the Word, and therefore the Word made flesh is God's truth. He is the faithful and the true, the perfect amen to God in the flesh. Although the Son enters into the resistance and hostility of our flesh against God, he does not resist God but throughout the whole course of his life is obedient and true and faithful. 'I am the truth', Jesus said and that applies not only to his bringing the truth of God to mankind but to his whole human life as truth done into the flesh, as truth enacted in the midst of our untruth, as truth fulfilled from within man and from the side of man, truth issuing out of human life in obedient response to the truth of God.[61]

That is the prophetic ministry of Christ, the Word made flesh to bring God's word to man, to incarnate that Word in himself, and so to be the word of God to us in our alienation and estrangement from God – not to be for us an alien word, for then he could not touch us or find us or communicate himself to us, and then his action would be neither reconciling nor revealing action. But within our alienation he is real word of God to us in such a way that he still remains eternal Word of God, word of God addressed to man, but word received, obeyed and lived out as word answering to God in perfect truth, in the concrete faithfulness to God of a life lived from beginning to end in holiness and love and obedience.

But the New Testament makes it very clear that this obedience of Jesus Christ in the flesh was not light or sham obedience. It was agonisingly real in our flesh of sin: 'he humbled himself and became obedient unto death, even death on a cross,'[62] and 'he learned obedience through what he suffered.'[63] So also the evangelists speak of the obedience of Christ. From the very start, Luke tells us, in an astonishing word about the growth of Jesus, *proekopten,* that he had to beat his way forward by blows.[64] His obedience was a battle. The temptations make that abundantly clear. It was in agony of blood, 'with strong cryings and tears'[65] in the things that he suffered that Jesus learned obedience, bringing his holy relation with sinners to its perfection and completion at last on the cross. We shall return to this when we come to consider the incarnation more specifically in relation to the sending of the Son into our humanity.

---

[61] Cf. John 14.6; 1.14.

[62] Phil 2.8.

[63] Heb 5.8.

[64] Luke 2.52, 'And Jesus *increased* (*proekopten*) in wisdom and in stature, and in favour with God and man.'

[65] Heb 5.7 KJV (RSV 'loud cries and tears').

But now let us ask what did St John mean by speaking of the fact that the Word *became, was made,* flesh – the word is *egeneto*. This term has proved a very difficult thing for Greek and Latin minds to understand, because it appears to conflict so strongly with the assumption of the impassibility and unchangeability of God. But let us look first at what is actually said and then at the problem it raises.

(iii) The meaning of 'became'

The Word *became* flesh in such a way as not to cease being the eternal Word of God. This 'become' is clearly unique and miraculous event, a pure act of God's wisdom and mercy which is ultimately unfathomable by us. 'The Word was in the beginning with God and was God, and all things were made, *egeneto*, by him.'[66] The Word is the subject of that action, of that becoming or happening in which all existence came into being through him. The creator did not always exist as a creature made out of nothing, but now having made the creature out of nothing, the creator himself becomes one of the creatures that he made. No wonder this is folly to the Greek, and an offence to the Jew! But John in his prologue goes on and uses the same word *egeneto* to describe the historical existence and appearance of John the Baptist. John deliberately inserts into the prologue which speaks of the *becoming* flesh of the eternal Word these verses about the historical existence and coming of John the Baptist, in order to make it clear how the word *egeneto* is to be understood. It is in all these senses of *egeneto* that the Word became flesh, became event, came as a historical man in a definite historical event. The Word who is the source and Lord of all existence now assumes existence within creaturely and historical existence without ceasing to be the eternal Word and Lord.

From very early times the church has used the expression the 'assumption of the flesh', *assumptio carnis,* to describe *egeneto* in this fullness. The *assumptio carnis* means that God willed to *coexist* with the creature, that he the creator willed to exist also as a creature for the reconciliation of the estranged world to himself. Thus he the Lord of the covenant willed also to be its human partner, in order to fulfil the covenant from its side. But this very condescension of God, in which he humbled himself to enter into our lowly creaturely and fallen existence, means also the elevation of our creaturely existence, by the very fact of God's will to unite himself to it and to bring the creature into coexistence with himself. Thus his very act of becoming man is itself an act of reconciliation.

---

66 See John 1.1-3.

But the *assumptio carnis* also means that the eternal God, without ceasing to be eternal, has taken *temporal form*, as well as creaturely existence. God has assumed our time into union with himself, without abrogating it. He the eternal has become temporal for us in the form of our own temporal and historical existence, not simply by embracing our time and historical existence and ruling it, but by permitting time and our historical existence to be the form of his eternal deity. Thus he is not only accessible to us in time and history, but we in time and history are free to approach the eternal and to live with him.

But further, the *assumptio carnis* means also that God has joined himself to us in our estranged human life in order to sanctify it, to gather it into union with his own holy life and so lift it up above and beyond all the downward drag of sin and decay, and that he already does simply by being one with man in all things. Thus the act of becoming incarnate is itself the *sanctification* of our human life in Jesus Christ, an elevating and fulfilling of it that far surpasses creation; it is a raising up of men and women to stand and have their being in the very life of God, but that raising up of man is achieved through his unutterable atoning self-humiliation and condescension.

A unique becoming in which God now also exists as true man in one person

At the same time the expression *assumptio carnis* serves to guard against the error that the 'becoming flesh' means that there arises a third entity who is a mixture of divine Word and flesh, an Arian Christ.[67] Jesus Christ who is true God and true man is not a third being, something between God and man. He is the one mediator between God and man, yet mediator in such a way that he is himself *God and man in one person*. The becoming flesh of the Word is therefore an act of the true God in the person of the Word.

This means that in the *egeneto sarx* (became flesh) we have something unique, a relation between God and man, the creator and the creature, which has no parallel anywhere in creation. We must speak of a personal presence of God in all created being, and in a certain sense therefore of a unity of all created being with God, but as such created being has an existence different from and parallel to God's existence, though absolutely dependent upon him and derived from him. But

---

[67] For Arius, Christ was not fully God, but as the highest being created by God was an intermediary between God and man.

here, in the Word *become* flesh in the unity of God and man in Jesus Christ, Jesus Christ *is* God. Jesus Christ has no existence apart from or different from or parallel to God's existence. He has his existence only in this divine act of condescension in which God gathers man into coexistence with himself. That means that here in the Word made flesh God and man are so related in Jesus Christ, that *Jesus exists as man only so far as he exists as God,* and yet as God he also has an existence as flesh or *sarx*. There would have been no Jesus apart from the incarnation, so that the existence of Jesus even as man is an existence only in the Word become flesh, but in that the Word became flesh, there now exists a man Jesus who is true man and exists as historical human beings exist. That is the patristic doctrine of the *anhypostasia* and *enhypostasia,* which we shall consider more fully later.

There is one further point about the *egeneto sarx* that we must note. The *egeneto* refers to a *completed event,* one that has taken place once and for all in the union of God and man in Jesus Christ; but it is also a historical event, a dynamic event, a real happening in the time of this world which is coincident with the whole historical life of Jesus. While therefore the incarnation refers in one sense to that unique event when the Word entered time and joined human existence, it also refers to the whole life and work of Jesus, from his birth at Bethlehem to his resurrection from the dead. But if this historical happening in the whole historical life of Jesus is happening that is also within the eternal Word, then that historical happening is one that does not simply fall within the limits and corruption and decay of mere historical happening. Unlike other historical happenings that flow away into the past and tumble down into the dust, this historical happening *remains eternally real* and alive happening, breaking through all the contingency and relativity of history in our fallen and decayed existence, historical happening that is still accessible to us on the plane of history as well as in communion with the eternal.

(b) The Son become servant

We are not now concerned with a different theme, but with precisely the same theme as that of the Word become flesh. In speaking of the incarnation in terms of the Son become 'servant', the New Testament tells us that the categories of *Word* and *flesh* are not adequate in themselves to describe the incarnation, and have to be used together with others, notably with those of *Son* and *servant.*

That is very apparent in the fourth Gospel. In its prologue it speaks of the *Word* made flesh, and in that light sets the whole gospel as the revelation, and reconciliation of God in Christ, but it then moves on from the prologue to speak all through of the *Son* in his obedience to the Father and in his fulfilment of the role of the servant. That belongs to the very nature of the case, for the incarnation of the Word means an incarnation in which the Word is not simply addressed to man from without but so enters into human existence that it becomes a word that is heard and appropriated by man, and a word that is answered for man by this man in the whole course of his obedient life. Thus within the incarnation, the Son is the fuller category, for the Son hears the word of the Father, and the Son answers the Father by word and life, and the revelation mediated through the Son is the revelation of the word (*logos*) which he has received from the Father and now speaks in the language (*lalia*) of man. Of all the books of the New Testament none more than the fourth Gospel presents Christ as the servant-Son obedient in everything to the Father, doing only those things that please him, and from beginning to end fulfilling his will. It is thus that he the Son declares, 'exegetes' the Father, and reveals him to and within human life on earth and in history.

Now in the fourth Gospel this relation between the incarnate Son and the Father has its source in a divine and eternal sending by the Father. The Son is sent by the Father, so that the 'became flesh', *egeneto sarx*, is here interpreted, in one of its aspects, in terms of a mission from the Father into the world, but within the incarnation, the *egeneto sarx* in its other sense as historical happening, is interpreted in terms of the obedience of the incarnate Son to the Father. That has nowhere been more succinctly put than by St Paul in his epistle to the Galatians, 'when we were children we were in bondage under the elements of the world: but when the fullness of time was come, God sent forth his Son, made of woman, made under the law, to redeem them that were under the law, that we might receive the adoption of sons'.[68]

The New Testament expounds the incarnation as the Son made servant by using three main Old Testament motifs which we must look at, for they contain the very heart of the New Testament Christology and Soteriology.

---

[68] Gal 4.3-5, quotation from the KJV which has, '*made* (*genomenon*) of a woman, *made* (*genomenon*) under the law', where the RSV has, '*born* of a woman, *born* under the law'. (See the note on Torrance's preference for this translation in his *Space, Time and Resurrection* (Edinburgh: Handsel 1976). Cf. John 1.11-18.

(i) The motif of the servant-son

Already in the Old Testament, in the servant songs of deutero-Isaiah,[69] the concepts of the son and the servant have been run together, that is, the concept of Israel as God's firstborn and chosen or beloved son, and the concept of Israel as God's servant. It is the New Testament term *pais* or 'son' which appears to bring together into one word those two aspects of the Old Testament thought as applied to the Messiah, the servant-son. All this clearly lies behind the baptism of Jesus when he is consecrated as the servant-son, the Son of the Father who is sent on his mission as the suffering servant in fulfilment of God's covenant will. Baptism is not only the occasion of his public acknowledgement by the Father as his beloved Son, but the occasion of his solemn anointing or consecration as the servant who in his obedience to God is to be led as a lamb to be the sacrifice for the sins of the world.[70]

Two of the principal teachings of the servant songs are here applied to Christ. He is sent by the Father to fulfil a vicarious mission in suffering: he, the Son of the Father, is sent as the suffering servant to suffer under the judgement of God in our place and in our stead. In fulfilment of this substitutionary work the Son also fulfils the covenant which God the Father has made with his people, and as such the Son is the mediator of the new covenant. It is in that very light that Jesus at last solemnly founded the new covenant in his body and blood at the last supper, as he who came not to be served but to serve and give his life as a ransom for many. Jesus' own term to describe this his servant-son function is '*Son of Man*'. The concept of the servant-son is derived in the first place from Israel as God's son and God's servant, and from Israel as the suffering servant, but in associating all that with his own chosen title of 'Son of Man' Jesus gives the whole concept of servant-son a wider and in fact a universalistic reference. Thus the semitism[71] 'ransom for many'[72] is rightly interpreted in the New Testament itself as 'ransom for all'.[73]

But let us note that this mission of the servant-son is regarded as being fulfilled not simply in Christ's final passion on the cross, but in the whole course of his obedience. We may refer here simply to one

---

69 Isaiah 42.1-7; 49.1-10; 50.4-10; 52.13 – 53.12. Chapters 40 – 55 of Isaiah are known as 'deutero' (second) Isaiah.

70 John 1.29f.

71 Semitic (Hebrew) word or saying.

72 Matt 20.28; Mark 10.45.

73 1 Tim 2.6.

very pregnant and significant passage in which Jesus speaks of the baptism with which he is being baptised,[74] that is, the passion which he was undergoing in the continuous present. It was into that passion that he was born, into that passion that he was solemnly and lawfully consecrated at his baptism, into that passion that he was thrust right away in his temptations when he was tempted to evade the cross but in which he chose the way of suffering and shame for our sakes. And so, all through his obedient life until the garden of Gethsemane and the prayer wrung out of him there with strong crying and tears, 'Not my will but thine be done',[75] it was finally in that passion that he fulfilled the role of the suffering servant and sealed it with his blood on the cross.

(ii) The motif of the ben-bayith, *'the son of the house'*

Ben-bayith is a peculiarly Hebraic conception which is applied equally to a small domestic scene or to the royal house of a whole kingdom. The interesting thing is that this expression can be used in two ways and in two senses. It may be used for the son or heir of a house, the one who is the lord of the house, the householder, but it may also be used of the servant of the house who is in charge of its affairs, its steward who has to give an account of his stewardship. This term is applied for example to Joseph in Egypt, but is applied also to Moses in God's house. Because of the double meaning of the 'son of the house' it is variously translated in the Septuagint (LXX). Sometimes it is translated naturally enough by *huios* (son), but frequently by *oikonomos* (manager of a household, steward), but *oikonomos* is used in two senses, either of the householder, the head or lord of the house, or of the steward, the servant of the house. Thus Moses is spoken of in Hebrew as the *ben-bayith*, the son of the house with reference to God's house and family in Israel, but that is translated sometimes by *oikonomos* where he is the chief steward, the householder on earth of God's household, while Aaron is subordinate to him. Yet the term *ben-bayith* is also translated by *doulos* (servant) where it is meant specifically to apply to a servant, and this term *doulos* is also applied to Moses, the servant of the Lord. The interesting thing is that Moses is thus spoken of as the son of God's house and as the faithful servant of the Lord, and to my mind it is he who supplies the main ingredient in the image of the suffering servant in the Isaianic songs.

---

[74] Luke 12.50.

[75] See Matt 26.39; Mark 14.36.

When we turn to the New Testament we find this language of the *ben-bayith* frequently on the lips of Jesus himself, and also in the epistles of Paul and the epistle to the Hebrews. We need only note the argument of the opening chapters of the epistle to the Hebrews. Christ is the revelation and the Word of God, God's own Son who reveals him, for he is identical with him whom he reveals. This Word or revelation of God the writer expounds in terms of Christ's sonship, but then when he wants to pass over from the concept of Christ's sonship to that of his priesthood which is to be his main theme he makes use of this concept of the *ben-bayith*, 'son of the house', and deliberately brings Jesus into likeness and yet into contrast with Moses. Moses is the *ben-bayith* faithful as a servant in God's House, but Christ is the *ben-bayith* faithful as the Son over God's house.[76] But even as the Son over God's house he is sent on a mission in which he enters into our bondage under the law, learns obedience and suffers, and only as the servant-son does he fulfil his solemn work of priesthood in the atoning oblation of himself in his obedient life and death on our behalf. Here too we have the concept of the servant-son but it is universalised, by aid of the *ben-bayith* concept as the work of God and of the Son, the creator of all who is Lord over all his house, all creation and all the church, but who enters into our estate of frailty and bondage in order to redeem mankind. The *ben-bayith* also carries with it from the Old Testament the nuance of the royal son, the son of God's universal kingdom. It is as that Son that Jesus is sent on his mission of suffering obedience, and in that mission he is utterly faithful.

The *ben-bayith* motif is found above all on the lips of Jesus himself in many of the parables of the householder and the king and owner of the vineyard who set his servants to work, who required them to be faithful stewards and whom he called to account. We need mention here, however, only that final parable in this series, the householder and his vineyard,[77] told after the cleansing of the temple in passion week, in which Christ revealed to the Jews that he knew that they intended to kill him, knew that they recognised him and yet wilfully blinded themselves to him, and were now deliberately going about to kill him in order that they might have the vineyard to themselves. It is in that act of startling revelation of his own mission now reaching its hour of eschatological destiny, and startling revelation to the Jews of their own innermost conflict of knowledge and deliberate disobedience,

---

76 Heb 3.1-6.

77 Matt 21.33-46; Mark 12.1-12; Luke 20.9-19.

that Jesus went straight forward to the cross, and fulfilled his mission as God's *ben-bayith*, himself the heir and the last in line of the servants, God's servant-son, now about to suffer and die in obedience to the Father. It is in this connection also that Jesus speaks of himself as the Son of Man.

(iii) The motif of Adam, the son of God

This is found in Paul but in the Gospels also, for example in the Lucan genealogy of Jesus which is traced back to Adam, the son of God, and followed immediately by the account of the great temptation of Jesus on the ground of 'If you are the Son of God', in which Jesus, unlike Adam, overcame temptation and remained obedient to the will of God. I cannot help but feel that the concept of Adam lies in Jesus' own name for himself, the 'Son of Man' (the Son of God as man) – certainly to the concept of the Son of Man there corresponds very closely what Paul particularly has to say of Christ the new man, the last Adam.

It is that contrast that is so revealing for our understanding of the incarnation of the Son. Unlike Adam, Jesus does not wish to be like God,[78] but in Adam's nature he confesses before God the adamic existence, the state of man as fallen, and bears the righteous wrath of God upon its sin. However, he bears that not as a fate to be resented or simply to be endured, but as a verdict in which he willingly acquiesced, and to which he gladly conformed. He does not avoid the burden of God's command, or of the state of man under the divine judgement, but he takes it all upon himself and bears all its consequences in his life and death.

That is just what we, the children of Adam, refuse to do. That is the rebellion of sin in which we hourly repeat the rebellion of Adam. Adam refused to preserve the order of paradise, refused to keep within the limits of creatureliness imposed upon him by the creator, refused to contain himself within the bounds of God's will, and now man, as Adam's child, refuses to fit into the order of restoration; mankind will not admit that they are flesh standing under judgement and can live only by grace. They will not admit that God is right in his verdict on them, and thus cling only to God's mercy manifest in his very judgement, cling only to God's forgiveness which carries in its heart the judgement of the sin of the forgiven. Humanity resents that utter reliance on God; men and women want at least to co-operate with God in saving their lives – but that is the very way to lose their lives for by that very process sin is not really acknowledged, and its judgement and condemnation in the flesh are not really accepted.

---

78 See Phil 2.5f.

The new Adam who undoes the sin of the first Adam

Jesus does the very opposite of all that and of Adam. He enters into Adam's rebellious existence and ranges himself among sinners wearing their flesh of sin, standing with them under the divine judgement, and there he, unlike them, acknowledges God's just judgement on sin and so condemns sin in our flesh. By his obedience he is the amen to God's word of truth against our flesh. He accepts the verdict upon sinful man, the limits of the creature under the law, and so is obedient, where Adam and all the adamic race are disobedient, obedient even unto the death of the cross. Within our flesh of sin Jesus is sinless, not in spite of being within the flesh of sin, but because he is within it the amen of obedience to God. He is sinless, not in spite of the fact that, but because he is the friend of publicans and sinners, and even at the end dies between malefactors under the sentence of death. In all of that Jesus Christ is the last Adam, the one who through his obedience brings to an end the bondage of Adam's sin, breaks its power and opens up a new and living way to God. By his obedience within adamic flesh and adamic existence he bursts through the continuity of adamic existence and opens up a new continuity in a new Adam, the new man, and so is the firstborn of the new creation, the pathfinder to God, 'I am the way, no man comes to the Father, but by me.'[79]

What is it that the servant-Son does here within our humanity? Here within our fallen and disobedient humanity, where we are less than human because of our sin, here where we have dehumanised ourselves in our rebellion, here where we, the sons and daughters of God, have become bastards and not true sons and daughters, he the Son of God becomes true Son of Man, true man for the first time in utter obedience, that is in true sonship toward God the Father. True man does not sin. True man is man answering in truth the word of God addressed to mankind. Men and women who commit sin, who disobey the word of God, have fallen from their humanity into inhumanity. The commission of sin is no attribute of true humanity, but the attribute of inhumanity. But within this human-inhuman existence of Adam, Jesus Christ has come as the Son of God, the Son of Man as Jesus called himself, to live out a truly obedient and filial, that is, a truly human life, in perfect and unbroken communion with God the Father. It is in that connection also that Jesus applies to himself the title, for it speaks of the lowly way his divine sonship took within our estranged humanity in order to restore us to fellowship with God and to integrity in union with the

---

[79] See John 14.6.

divine life. That lowly mission of the Son is wonderfully described by St Paul in these words: 'you know the grace of the Lord Jesus Christ, that though he was rich, yet for your sake he became poor, so that by his poverty you might become rich.'[80] The whole doctrine of the incarnation is summed up there.

But now we must turn to the *locus classicus*[81] on the servant Son in the New Testament, and give it some detailed attention, and then from our theological exegesis of it, go forward to definite theological affirmations about the incarnate sonship of Christ.

Philippians 2: the classic passage on the servant Son

> Have this mind among yourselves, which you have in Christ Jesus, who, though he was in the form (*morphē*) of God, did not count equality with God a thing to be grasped, but emptied himself (*heauton ekenōsen*), taking the form (*morphēn*) of a servant, being born in the likeness of men (*en homoiōmati anthrōpōn*). And being found in human form (*schēmati*) he humbled (*etapeinōsen*) himself and became obedient unto death, even death on a cross . . .[82]

Two preliminary notes regarding this passage.

(1) The term *form* or *morphē* cannot be taken in the strict Platonic or Aristotelian sense, a sense technical in the schools only, and not in current usage. *Morphē* just means form in the ordinary sense, but the sort of form, nevertheless, which corresponds to inner nature. Here it is not the so-called essential form or essence that is referred to.

(2) The verb *ekenōsen* can mean: (a) as the King James Version translates it, 'made himself of no reputation', that is, robbed himself of his glory. Paul uses the word elsewhere in this sense and it was in this sense of self-humiliation that it was always interpreted by the Greek fathers. (b) It may mean, quite literally, 'emptied', as many modern scholars have translated it.[83] But if so, the Greek does not say that he who was in the form of God emptied anything *out of* himself, but that he emptied *himself* out of a heavenly and glorious *morphē* into an earthly and inglorious *morphē*, that is, he made

---

[80] 2 Cor 8.9.

[81] Lat, 'classic passage', literally 'classic place'.

[82] Phil 2.5-11.

[83] This includes the RSV, the translation quoted above.

himself of no reputation, and humbled (*etapainōsen*) himself. He doffed his glorious form and veiled himself in the humble form of a servant. There is nothing here about any so called metaphysical change in God the Son such as an emptying out of God the Son of any divine attributes or powers. He emptied *himself* out of his divine form into a human form. We must note, however, that the 'form of the servant' corresponds to the real act of the Son, to his being in humanity. That human form was no outer garment, but a real existence in humanity assumed into oneness with the existence of the Son who here condescended to human estate.

The self-humbling of the Son to become servant, obedient unto death

The meaning of the passage must be construed, therefore, as follows: the Son of God humbled himself, laying aside his majesty and glory, and took upon himself the form of a servant (as opposed to that of a lord). But even as man, in the form of man, he humbled himself, submitting to the limitations of our creaturely estate under the judgement of the law, submitting, in his obedience to the Father, even to the point of death on the cross, all in fulfilment of his redeeming purpose. Thus the transcendent act of humiliation – the grace of the Son in becoming man – has its counterpart even within his earthly and human existence as Jesus bent to shoulder the cross and died in humiliation upon it. Thus the event of the crucifixion is grounded in the self-humbling of the Son in becoming man. The atonement begins in the will of the Son to become man – that is, in 'the lamb slain before the foundation of the world',[84] to use other New Testament language. Basically the same point was made by St Paul when he wrote to the Romans that God 'did not spare his own Son but delivered him up for us all'[85] – for the sacrifice of the Son on earth derives from and remains one with a transcendent sacrifice in God. The historical crucifixion is grounded in a transcendent act of pure grace, and it is that act eventuating itself, fulfilling itself, in our human existence and its death. But although the transcendent act of self-giving and self-humbling fulfils itself in our human estate, in the death of the cross, it does not cease to be transcendent act. Therefore it carries on through the cross and completes its movement in exaltation to the right hand of God the Father.[86]

---

84 See Rev 13.8 KJV. The RSV is not as close to the Greek here.

85 Rom 8.32 KJV.

86 Phil 2.9-11.

One further point must be noted about this passage. The whole movement of humiliation and incarnation is related to revelation as much as to reconciliation. Jesus veils his glory under the form of a servant, in order to get near man for revelation and reconciliation, but in this, the veiling of the Son is a necessary part of his future unveiling for it is a means to its fulfilment, and so to achieving a reconciliation that is not only from the side of God to man but from the side of man to God.

In this *locus classicus*, then, there is no ground for any theory of *kenōsis* or *emptying* as that has been expounded in the 'kenotic theories' of the incarnation. *Kenōsis* refers to the self-abnegating, redemptive descent of God into human life. *Kenōsis* and *tapeinōsis* (humbling) both refer to the self-sacrificial self-communication of God to mankind. That is to say, there is no ground for saying that in becoming man the eternal Son emptied himself of some of his divine properties or attributes in order to come within our human and historical existence. It is God himself, he who was in the form of God and equal to God, who *condescended* to be very man of very man. Nothing at all is said of *how* that takes place. All kenotic theories are attempts to explain the *how* of the incarnation in some measure: *how* God and man are united in one Jesus Christ, *how* the Word has become flesh. All that is said is that this union is a way of incredible humiliation and grace. The New Testament does have a great deal to tell us about the incarnation, in telling us what the Word and Son of God actually did, but refuses to explain the *mystery* that lies at the heart of it; that is *the miracle of the Holy Spirit*. Even in speaking of the birth of Jesus through the Spirit, and of his resurrection through the power of the Spirit, the New Testament at no point offers us an explanation, but refers the mystery to the direct act of the eternal God, to the will and love of the Father.

(c) The descent and ascent of the Son

Under this title we come to gather up what the New Testament has to say about the incarnational movement of the Word and Son of God. The language of *descent* and *ascent* which comes from the Old Testament liturgy is applied in the New Testament most clearly to baptism, in which we descend into the waters of death, are buried and ascend again in resurrection and life. But our baptism is a sign and seal of what Jesus Christ has done once and for all on our behalf on the cross, and of his ascent in resurrection out of death into newness of life. But that descent and ascent of Christ in death and resurrection represents the nadir, the turning point, of the whole incarnational movement, in which he the Son of God descended into our mortal humanity, into our fallen existence under the judgement and sentence of death. Making expiation through his obedient submission to God in life and death on our behalf, he then ascended wearing our redeemed humanity and presented it in himself before the face of the Father where he is set down at his right hand. Thus the whole incarnational act of humiliation and exaltation is a descent and ascent, but within that movement of descent and ascent at its lowest point there is his descent into our death, and then his ascent out of it in order as risen and new man to ascend back to God. It is in that whole movement of descent and ascent, *katabasis* and *anabasis*, that we are to understand the movement of the Word and Son of God into our human existence, gathering our human existence into oneness with himself, and then the movement of the Word and Son of God from within our humanity back to the heavenly Father, a movement which restores humanity to communion with God but far transcends the original creation in the nature of the union which that communion involves.

This whole movement of descent and ascent is twofold in that it is a movement of *revelation through the Word of God* and *reconciliation through the Son of God.*

(i) A movement of revelation

It is a movement of *revelation* through the Word of God, in which the Son of God came as Word of God, humbling himself to man's lowly estate, donning the beggar's garment, and assuming the beggar's existence as his own, in order to persuade the beggar that God the Father was in earnest about forgiving him, and in order at the same time to enact that word of revealed forgiveness in actual pardon and reconciliation. That is what the New Testament describes as the *poverty* (*ptōcheia*) of Jesus, in which he exchanged his riches for our poverty, or our poverty for his riches. That is the *tapeinōsis* or the *kenōsis* of Jesus in which the Word of God comes to us in a lowly way in the company of publicans and sinners, in the form a servant that we may know him. It means that he the eternal Word of God, the Lord of heaven, stooped down to our low estate stripped of the effulgence of his glory that our weak eyes might behold him in the meek and lowly Jesus, and in and through Jesus be lifted up to the divine glory. From seeing him in the form of a servant we are carried with the lowly Jesus up to his glory, accompanying him till he is raised up far above all and given the name that is above every name, the glory which he the Word and Son of God had before the world began. Thus to the descent and ascent of the Word in his movement of revelation here, there corresponds the movement of our repentance and faith and vision of God, for we may only share in that revelation through descent and ascent, through death and resurrection, through self-denial in ourselves and exaltation in Christ alone. That has nowhere been more wonderfully expressed than in the *Magnificat* of the blessed virgin Mary, in her *tapeinōsis* on the one hand, and in her exaltation on the other hand.[87]

(ii) A movement of reconciliation

It is a movement of *reconciliation* through the Son of God, in which the Word of God came as Son of God, bowing himself to enter our flesh of sin and bondage, in order that he the almighty God entering within the compass of our estrangement and death might destroy sin and death, and deliver us from our estrangement and captivity in sin and self-will. The Son of God become man is the strong man of Jesus' own parable who invades the tyrant's house and by his power subdues him, binds him, and spoils him of all that he has unjustly usurped.[88] But he enters the house of alienation and bondage under the power of evil and subdues the power of evil not by divine violence, but by obedience and steadfastness as the Son to the Father's holy will in the face of the contradiction of sin, and the attack of all the power of evil; and so he overcomes by patience and passion, and sheer faithfulness and holiness and love, by living out perfectly within all the conditions of our humanity the obedience of the Son to the Father.

That is what Christ does all through his life, and what he does on the cross. In it all he penetrates into the very heart of humanity where evil is enthroned, and guilt is entrenched under judgement, and defeats evil by expiating guilt, by judging it through his holiness, by casting it out through his love, and so he bursts even the bonds of death asunder. Thus by taking our flesh on himself the Son of God exposed himself to the fearful assault of Satan, and evil and sin; he advanced to meet it at the very summit of its wickedness in crucifying him, drew it all upon himself and slew it as he submitted to the divine judgement upon it; he destroyed it as it was doing its worst in seeking to destroy him. That is the poverty and weakness of the Son of God in the life and death of Jesus, but it was through that poverty and weakness, in which he submitted to all the assaults of evil upon him in order to bear them, that he broke all its power in expiation and triumphed over it all in the resurrection, so making an open show of all the powers

---

87 Luke 1.46-55.

88 Luke 11.21-22.

of evil and darkness in manifesting that even their ultimate assaults against him in death itself could not avail.[89]

Thus the Son who took the way into the far country in order to find us and restore us to the Father, returns in triumph bringing with him many sons and daughters to glory. Through the fulfilment of his filial obedience and love within the conditions of our alienation and hostility, he opened up a new and living way in himself for us to return to God as sons and daughters to their heavenly Father. Therefore just as 'God sent forth his Son, born of woman, born under the law, to redeem those who were under the law, so that we might receive adoption as sons', so 'God has sent the Spirit of his Son into our hearts, crying "Abba! Father!"'[90] Therefore we are no more servants but sons and daughters, and if so then heirs of God through Christ.[91] That is the work of reconciliation through the Son of God made servant, that we who are the servants of sin under the bondage of the law may enter into the freedom of the sons and daughters of God. But just as the movement of the Word in revelation entails a corresponding movement of humiliation and exaltation on our part, so in reconciliation we have a movement of renunciation and confession, but also of exaltation in the words of the parable of the prodigal son. Thus, 'I will arise and go to my father, and I will say to him, "Father, I have sinned against heaven and before you; I am no more worthy to be called your son; treat me as one of your hired servants." And he arose and came to his father . . . but the father said to his servants, "Bring quickly the best robe, and put it on him; and put a ring on his hand, and shoes on his feet; and bring the fatted calf and kill it, and let us eat and make merry; for this my son was dead, and is alive again; he was lost and is found." And they began to make merry.'[92]

(iii) Salvation through the whole course of Christ's obedience[93]

We are not concerned at the moment with the subjective appropriation of our salvation through the Spirit but with the work of the incarnate Son which he fulfilled through his obedience to the Father. This is very

---

[89] Col 2.15.

[90] Gal 4.4-6.

[91] See Gal 4.7.

[92] Luke 15.18-24.

[93] On the saving significance of the humanity of Christ, and of his active and passive obedience and union of human nature with his divine nature, see T.F. Torrance, *The School of Faith* (London: James Clarke 1959), pp. lxxx-lxxxvii.

clearly expounded by Calvin in the following words: 'When it is asked how, after abolishing sins, Christ removed the discord between us and God and acquired a righteousness, it may be replied generally that he provided us with this by *the whole course of his obedience*. From the moment he put on the person of a servant, he began to pay the price of liberation for our redemption. In order, however, to define the manner of salvation more surely, scripture ascribes it to Christ's death as its property and attribute. Yet the remainder of obedience which he performed in his life is not excluded; and in fact his willing submission occupies the primary place in discarding the thought of himself in order to consult our interests.'[94]

This is the doctrine of what Reformed theology has called *the active and passive obedience of Christ*, but it is the active and passive obedience of the incarnate Son, in whom our human nature is united to his divine nature in the unity of the one person of the Son of God. There are then four things to be considered here: the active obedience of Christ, his passive obedience, their mutual unity and importance, and the union of our human nature with his divine nature in the incarnation of the Son.[95]

(1) The active obedience of Jesus

By *active obedience* is meant the positive fulfilment of God's saving will in the whole life of Jesus in his sonship. From the very beginning to the very end, he maintained a perfect filial relation to the Father in which he yielded to him a life of utter love and faithfulness, and in which he received and laid hold of the love of the Father. This active obedience was therefore his own loving self-offering to the Father in our name and on our behalf, and also his own loving appropriation of the Father's word and will in our name and on our behalf.

(2) The passive obedience of Jesus

By *passive obedience* is meant the submission of Jesus Christ to the judgement of the Father upon the sin which he assumed in our

---

[94] *Institute of the Christian Religion,* 2.16.5. The quotation is a condensed compilation of at least three sentences from this section of the Institute. It appears also, in part at least, to be Torrance's own translation although the language is closest to that of Beveridge. Italics have been added.

[95] For the following (with some minor amplifications,) see T.F. Torrance, *Theology in Reconstruction* (London: SCM Press 1965), chap. 9, 'Justification: its radical nature and place in Reformed doctrine and life', pp. 154-56. (The wording of the material in *The School of Faith* is identical at points although slightly different in order.)

humanity in order to bear it in our name and on our behalf. This is the passion he endured in the expiation of our sins, but it is also his willing acceptance of the divine verdict upon our humanity.

This distinction between the active and passive obedience of Christ has been emphasised in Reformed theology not in order to distinguish or separate them, but in order to insist that the whole course of Christ's active obedience is absolutely integral to his work of reconciliation, and that atonement cannot be limited to his passive obedience, that is to his passive submission to the penalty for our sin inflicted upon him in his death. As Calvin put it, immediately the Son put on the person of the servant he began to pay the price of liberation for our salvation.[96] The active and the passive obedience thus do not differ in regard to time, for both extend to the very beginning of the incarnation, to the birth of Jesus and both reach out to its fulfilment in his death and resurrection. Nor do they differ in regard to their subject, for they are both manifestations of the one obedience of the Son of God in our humanity. They are set in mutual unity in the *whole life of Christ.* Since this is so we may speak of the active obedience as an *actio passiva* (passive action), and the passive obedience as a *passio activa* (active passion).

(3) The importance of both the passive and active righteousness of Christ

This mutuality of Christ's active and passive obedience is important for it means that in our justification we have imputed to us not only the passive righteousness of Christ in which, in suffering his *death* on the Cross, he satisfied and atoned for our sins, but the active righteousness of Christ in which he positively fulfilled the Father's will in an obedient *life*. In other words justification means not simply the non-imputation of our sins through the pardon of Christ, but positive sharing in his human righteousness. We are saved therefore not only by the death of Christ which he suffered for our sakes but by his vicarious life which he lived for our sakes. It is in that light that we must see his atoning and justifying life and that we must understand the incarnation of the Son in the whole course of his obedience. We shall come to expound that fully in due course.[97]

(4) The union of God and man in the life of the Son

At this point, however, we must stress the fact that we are concerned in the obedience of the Son, not only with his active and passive

---

96 *Inst*. 2.16.5.

97 See especially the Soteriology volume of these lectures, *Atonement*, chap. 7, section 2(a).

obedience, but with the *holy union* he wrought out in his birth, life, death, and resurrection between our fallen human nature and his divine nature, a union in which he, while assuming our fallen nature, sanctifies it in the very act of assumption, and so begins our redemption from his very birth. Thus incarnation in the narrower sense of the term is itself redeeming event. In his holy assumption of our unholy humanity, his purity wipes away our impurity, his holiness covers our corruption. Thus if we are to think of the active and passive obedience of Christ as dealing with our *actual sins*, we are to think of his incarnational union of our human nature with his divine nature as dealing with our *original sin*, or as our sanctifying union with his divine nature.

This is supremely important, for it is only through this union of our human nature with his divine nature that Jesus Christ gives us not only the *negative righteousness* of the remission of sins but also a share in the *positive righteousness of his obedient and loving life lived in perfect filial relation on earth to the heavenly Father*. If we neglect this essential element in the vicarious humanity and obedience of the Son, then not only do the active and passive obedience of Christ fall apart but we are unable to understand justification in Christ as anything more than a merely external forensic non-imputation of sin. Moreover, if we neglect this essential element we are unable to see the humanity of Jesus in its saving significance, that is, to give the whole life of the historical Jesus its rightful place in the doctrine of atonement. It is necessary for us then to give the fullest consideration to the place of *the union of the human and divine natures in the being and life of the incarnate Son*, for it is that saving and sanctifying union in which we are given to share that belongs to *the very substance of our faith*. In other words, what we are concerned with is the filial relation which the Son of God lived out vicariously in our humanity in perfect holiness and love. He achieved that in himself in assuming our human nature into oneness with himself, and on that ground gave us to share in it, so providing us with a fullness in his own obedient sonship from which we may all receive.

****

Before we go on to consider the birth and life of the Son on earth, it may be helpful now to give in outline the doctrine of the union of God and man in Jesus Christ. Then when we have fully considered the content of that union in the life of Jesus we must give a full account of the doctrine of his person. But at this stage we may give this outline in five short paragraphs.

OUTLINE OF THE DOCTRINE OF THE PERSON OF CHRIST

(1) The mystery of true God and man in one person

The doctrine of Christ is the doctrine of *the mystery of true divine nature and true human nature in one person*. This is the very heart of the Christian faith. In Christ something has taken place which is so new that it is related to our ordinary knowledge only at its extreme edges; if it is to be apprehended by us it must be apprehended from outside the limits of our ordinary human experience and thought. It is a new and unique reality which has certainly invaded our human life but which we can know only by refusing to categorise it in the sphere of what we already know, and by seeking to know it only out of itself. Even then, we know it remains a mystery. That is, in the midst of its disclosure, it remains something ultimately inconceivable and miraculous that we can never master and dominate and so express exactly in our own thought and speech. We only can acknowledge it in wonder and thankfulness, in adoration and praise. That doxological[98] approach to the person of Christ is the first step in the doctrine of Christ. That is the Nicene[99] doctrine of Christ.

(2) The mystery of Christ only capable of negative definition

The place of the mystery of Christ in our understanding can only be stated and guarded in *negative* terms. The mystery is that in Jesus Christ true God and true man are united in one person – that is the doctrine of the *hypostatic union*. But we must mark out, on either side of that mystery, what it is by saying what it is *not*. In this way we allow the mystery to declare itself to us, and to keep on declaring itself to us without hindering the depth and breadth of its self-disclosure by positive man-made definitions of what it actually is. This is the Chalcedonian[100] doctrine of Christ. In this statement we say that God and man are united in Jesus Christ, divine and human nature in one person, in such a way that (a) there is no impairing or diminishing of either deity or humanity in the union; and (b) there is neither separation of the natures nor confusion between them. That is given its expression in the four great negative terms:

inconfuse	without confusion	*immutabiliter*	without change
indivise	without division	*inseparabiliter*	without separation

[98] To do with 'worship' and 'praise', from the Greek, *doxos*, glory.

[99] The Council of Nicaea, AD 325. See chapter 6 for more details.

[100] The Council of Chalcedon, AD 451. See chapter 6.

(3) The inseparability of *anhypostasia* and *enhypostasia*

The union of the two natures in the person of Jesus Christ, as thus expressed, is stated in the light of the transcendent act of grace in the incarnation of the one eternal Son, on the one hand, and in the light of the obedient life of the incarnate Son on earth, on the other hand. This is the doctrine of the *anhypostasia* and *enhypostasia* regarded in their complementarity. The union of the divine and human natures in Christ is entirely the result of the transcendent act of God the Son in becoming man, in assuming human nature. But as a result of that pure act of God, the Son of God, without ceasing to be God, now exists as a man, Jesus, who is fully and truly man with his own individual life. On the other hand, apart from that pure act of God in the incarnation, there would have been no Jesus of Nazareth, so that the truly and fully human life of Jesus is grounded in the act of the Son or the Word in becoming flesh.

(a) *Anhypostasia* asserts: because of the assumption of humanity by the Son, Christ's human nature has its existence only in union with God, in God's existence or personal mode of being (*hypostasis*). It does *not* possess it in and for itself – hence *an-hypostasis* ('*not* person', *i.e.* no separate person).

(b) *Enhypostasia* asserts: because of the assumption of humanity by the Son, the human nature of Christ is given existence in the existence of God, and co-exists *in* the divine existence or mode of being (*hypostasis*) – hence *en-hypostasis* ('person *in*', that is, real human person *in* the person of the Son). This means that Jesus had a fully human mind, will, and body, and was in complete possession of all human faculties. This doctrine of the *anhypostasia* and *enhypostasia* is a very careful way of stating that we cannot think of the hypostatic union statically, but must think of it on the one hand, in terms of the great divine act of grace in the incarnation, and on the other hand, in terms of the dynamic personal union carried through the whole life of Jesus Christ. The ancient Catholic Church never really came to put *anhypostasia* and *enhypostasia* together in full complementarity in that way. We have had to wait till modern times to see it in this fullness, although it was set out by Robert Boyd in the early seventeenth century in his *Praelectiones in Ephesios* (Lectures on Ephesians),[101] but it actually goes back to Cyril of Alexandria, *Contra Theodoretum.*

---

[101] Robert Boyd, *In Epistolam Pauli Apostoli ad Ephesios Praelectiones*, Geneva 1661 (first published posthumously 1652), cc 485 et seq. On Robert Boyd (1578-1627), see further T.F. Torrance, *Scottish Theology: From John Knox to John McLeod Campbell* (Edinburgh: T & T Clark 1996), chap. 2 'The Older Scottish Tradition 1581-1647', pp. 66-74, esp. p. 71.

(4) The hypostatic union to be understood dynamically and soteriologically

The union of God and man in Jesus Christ cannot be understood *apart from the reconciling and atoning work* of God the Son in both his incarnation and in his life and death and resurrection. Thus the doctrine of the hypostatic union has to be stated in essentially *soteriological* terms in order to give it its full truth in accordance with the whole life of Christ. This is the contribution of Reformed theology especially to the doctrine of Christ as expressed in the concept of the *communicatio operationum* (*communication of acts* of the divine and human natures). It is in this way that we seek to deliver the Chalcedonian doctrine of Christ from the tendency involved in the Greek terms to state the doctrine of Christ statically and metaphysically. As we noted earlier, the incarnation involves a union of God and man in Christ accomplished once and for all, but it also involves a living union continuous throughout the life of the historical Jesus Christ moving from his birth to his resurrection. To this once and for all union corresponds the *anhypostasia,* and to the continuous personal union throughout the life of Christ corresponds the *enhypostasia.* It is that whole life of Christ in his birth and growth, and in his active ministry, that we will shortly turn to consider as the life of the Son of God in our humanity.

(5) Reconstruction of the classical doctrine of Christ: *integration of Patristic and Reformation Christology, and of Christology with Pneumatology and the doctrine of the Trinity*

There needs to be a reconstruction of the whole classical doctrine of Christ in such a way as to bring together the patristic emphasis on the *being*-of-God-in-his-acts and the Reformation emphasis on the *acts*-of-God-in-his-being. This involves a rethinking of the classical doctrine apart from the deistic and cosmological and epistemological dualisms that undermined doctrine in the post-patristic and in the post-reformation times, in the post-patristic when the emphasis on the being of God became detached from his acts, and in the post-reformation when the emphasis upon the acts of God became detached from his being.

This calls for and involves us in radical rethinking on the incarnation in its relation to the creation of space and time, and the development of relational (ontological and dynamic) concepts together with the formation of appropriate cognitive tools with which to carry this through. This is the task of christology in the era of objective ecumenism in which we seek to find a way of advancing forward after Karl Barth toward a scientific theology[102] in which the concepts of theology at work within space and time are closer to the concepts of our understanding of the universe as it unfolds to our inquiries within the same space-time.

How can we undertake this without a thorough reassessment of the whole doctrine of the Spirit, especially in relation to the humanity of Christ, but also in relation to the doctrine of the Trinity? It does not seem possible to undertake a very radical reconstruction of christology without a far deeper and more exacting pneumatology. The spectrum of thought runs, *from* the Father, *through* the Son and *in* the Spirit, so that *through* the Son must be thought out not only in respect of *from* the Father but in respect of *in* the Spirit.

---

[102] See the section *The nature of 'scientific dogmatics'* in chapter one for what is meant by 'scientific' here.

Chapter Three[1]

THE ONCE AND FOR ALL UNION OF GOD AND MAN:
Christ's Birth into our Humanity

Those who are justified by grace, by faith in Christ, are the only ones who really know that they are lost sinners, apart from Christ, but those who have not received Christ's forgiveness and the verdict it entails upon their humanity are the ones who regard themselves as able to justify themselves. Similarly, those who have come to know the mystery of Christ as true God and true man are the only ones who really know that they themselves are in ignorance, and that by themselves, by their own capacities, they cannot know the mystery. But those who have not received Jesus Christ, who have avoided the mystery and therefore have not come to know it, are those who think they can understand how God and man can come together. Both the sinner who is forgiven by Christ and the man or woman who has come to see the face of God in the face of Christ, know that they can never master or dominate the mystery of Christ in their hearts, but can only acknowledge it gladly with wonder and thankfulness, and seek to understand the mystery of Christ out of itself, that is, seek to let it declare itself to them, seek to let themselves be told by the mystery what it is. They will acknowledge that this is a mystery that is not conceivable in ordinary human thought – it is a miracle. And if they know something of this miracle they will know that even their knowing of it is a very wonderful thing, that it is an act of God. They

---

[1] As already mentioned in the general editorial introduction, chapters 3, 4, 5 and 6 were, in Torrance's manuscript, part of one long chapter entitled, 'Chapter 3: The incarnate life of the Son in the union of his divine and human natures'. According to evidence in Torrance's own text (see the beginning of chapter 6), the chapters in question appear to be separate chapters even though grouped together as sections under one chapter heading. The present arrangement, of division into separate chapters, reflects that and makes them more readable in times of size.

know the mystery by faith, in the power of the Spirit, but not by themselves alone. It is a gift of God. That belongs to the very content of the doctrine of the virgin birth and its significance for our knowing of Christ. To that we now turn.[2]

1 The biblical witness to the virgin birth

(a) The synoptic Gospels

Matthew and Luke both bear witness to the virgin birth of Jesus. Thus it is only the Gospels which speak of the human origin of Jesus, of his birth and childhood, which give us definite accounts of the virgin birth. The genealogies of Jesus differ in their accounts, and certainly present literary problems, but as K.L. Schmidt pointed out, the word begot, *egennēsen,* is not necessarily biological. It is used of fathers in the genealogy of Matthew with the meaning 'begot' where no natural begetting is involved: that is evidently good Jewish usage. Jesus is, according to Matthew, son of Joseph by an express direction of God assigning Jesus to Joseph the son of David. He is ingrafted into the house of David, as Schlatter put it. Thus while Matthew and Luke both speak of the birth of Jesus of the virgin Mary, they are also ready to speak of Jesus as the son of Joseph. That is no embarrassment to them – and so in both Gospels the genealogies end, or begin, with Joseph, not Mary, although they do not assert that Jesus was the bodily son of Joseph.[3] Nevertheless, while Joseph is mentioned by Matthew and Luke it is Mary who is mentioned prominently and persistently. Joseph is not significant. It is also worth noting that after Matthew and Luke have completed their accounts of the birth of Jesus, they do not mention the virgin birth again, and Luke who paid so much attention to it in his Gospel does not deem it appropriate to put it into the accounts of the early preaching in the book of Acts in the same way as he does the passion and the resurrection.

Mark does not speak of the human birth and childhood of Jesus, and in the rest of the Gospel the narrative of the ministry and passion follows the same line as that of Matthew and Luke who are also silent about the virgin birth in their narratives of the ministry and passion

---

[2] For further reference, see Karl Barth, *Church Dogmatics,* vol. 1.2, Eng. trans. (Edinburgh: T & T Clark 1956), sects. 15 (esp. pp. 172-202, The Miracle of Christmas), 19; and Douglas Edwards, *The Virgin Birth in History and Faith* (London: Faber 1943).

[3] Matt 1.16; Luke 3.23.

of Jesus. But while Matthew and Luke are ready to speak of Jesus as the son of Joseph, Mark never does. He makes no reference at all to Joseph, but pointedly mentions Mary.

Take the incident at Nazareth recorded in Mark 6.[4] There is no mention of Joseph in Mark, although there is mention of the brethren of Jesus. The people in the synagogue ask, 'Is not this the carpenter, the son of Mary?' In Matthew the question is, 'Is not this the carpenter's son?' and in Luke, 'Is not this Joseph's son?' Matthew and Luke can speak in this way without misunderstanding because they have already pointed out that Jesus is not strictly the son of Joseph, but only the son of Mary. But Mark could not have spoken in this way without being misunderstood, or without a long digression to explain why he was not really Joseph's son. Yet Mark's expression on the lips of the people of Nazareth, 'Mary's son' is most un-Jewish. To call a man by naming his mother is extremely strange in Jewish speech. All the evidence points to the fact that this is an intentional way of putting it, that is, to a deliberate avoidance of 'Joseph'.

We may note one other passage in Mark,[5] where Jesus says of the Messiah, 'David himself calls him Lord; so how is he his son?' How can Jesus be Lord and son of David – that is, how can a divine Christ be born of human stock? (The parallel incidents in Matthew and Luke[6] are virtually identical in language).

In both these passages, Mark's language fits in remarkably well with the virgin birth, better in fact in the first passage than the language used by Matthew and Luke at the same point.

What is the significance of all this? Mark makes no explicit reference to the virgin birth, but then neither do Matthew and Luke from the same point in their narrative where Mark begins. But far from providing evidence against the virgin birth by his silence about it, Mark's language definitely leans the other way, toward a witness to the virgin birth, and in stronger ways than Matthew or Luke at one point. In Mark, there are, I feel, distinct allusions to the supernatural birth of Jesus of Mary.

(b) John – the Gospel and the Johannine writings

Here we have a verse, not recognised often enough, where explicit mention is made of the virgin birth of Jesus.[7] The whole passage reads, 'But to all who received him, who believed in his name, he gave power

---

4 Mark 6.3; compare the parallel passages, Matt 13.55 & Luke 4.22.

5 Mark 12.35-37.

6 Matt 22.41-45; Luke 20.41-44.

7 John 1.13.

to become children of God; who were born, not of blood, nor of the will of the flesh, nor of the will of man, but of God.'[8] 'Who were born' – singular or plural? In other words, should it be the singular, 'who was born', in which case the reference is to Jesus, or the plural, 'who were born', where the reference would be to all those who believed in him? If it is plural, there is a difficult connection in the Greek, but even so there is clearly an extended reference to the virgin birth – 'born not of *bloods*, nor of the will of the flesh, nor of a *husband*, but of God.' The word translated in the KJV and RSV here as 'man' should be more accurately translated as 'husband' – the Greek is not *anthrōpou* (man generically, male or female) but *andros* (a male person, a husband).[9]

What about the MSS (manuscript) evidence? All the main MSS give the plural reading except the Verona Old Latin (a MSS significantly of Ephesian origin) which gives the singular. These are all 5th century MSS. But there is considerable patristic evidence going back to the second and third centuries, Tertullian, Irenaeus, Justin Martyr, *Epistola Apostolorum*, and Hippolytus, Clement of Alexandria – that is, all the available patristic evidence has John 1.13-14 in the singular at that date. Nowhere to my knowledge is there evidence at that date for the plural (unless it is in the gnostic documents not yet available to me). But evidence for the singular is also given by Ambrose and Augustine, and ambiguously by Leo the Great (who uses the plural as well as the singular), and many codices, such as 10, 14, 36, 37, etc. It is worth noting that most of these sources have at least a connection common with the Ephesian text.

Tertullian, however, gives us explicit comments upon the text at this point,[10] where he remarks that the Valentinians had corrupted their text making the singular into a plural (they did not like the idea of the virgin birth), whereas all other texts were in the singular. That is a most impressive weight of evidence for the singular reading, all twice as old as the oldest of our main codices. According to Harnack,[11] the singular is the true text, a judgement which is being increasingly followed by scholars, and which seems to me to be undoubtedly

---

[8] John 1.12f.

[9] Cf. REB (REV), 'born not of human stock, by the physical desire of a human father, but of God'; NIV, 'born not of natural descent (Gk of bloods), nor of human decision or a husband's will, but born of God'.

[10] On the flesh of Christ (*De Carne Christi*), chaps. 19 & 24, in Ante-Nicene Fathers (Grand Rapids: Eerdmans repr. 1976), vol. 3, p. 537-8, 541-2.

[11] A. Harnack, *The Date of the Acts and of the Synoptic Gospels*, Eng. trans. J.R. Wilkinson (London, Williams & Norgate 1911), p. 148.

demanded. If the text is to be read in the singular, then we have here in the fourth Gospel quite explicit direct reference to the virgin birth of Jesus. It must be in line with this too that the Johannine 'only-begotten Son' is to be understood, as well as the references in John 3 to being 'born from above' (*anōthen*) which has primary objective reference to Christ himself. This was certainly the way in which Irenaeus understood it.[12]

But now let us take a Johannine passage from the first epistle, 'We know that any one born of God does not sin, but he who was born of God keeps him.'[13] Here John uses the perfect tense of the Christian, but the one spoken of in the aorist tense as 'he who was born of God' is certainly Christ himself, the one whom the fourth Gospel calls the only-begotten (*monogenēs*)[14] of the Father. It is upon Christ's unique birth once and for all that our birth depends and in his birth that we are given to share. That again strengthens our understanding of the relation of John 3 (which speaks of being 'born from above' and of he who 'descends from above') to John 1 (the only-begotten, 'who was born not of bloods, nor of the will of the flesh, nor of a husband but of God').

It should be pointed out that the expression 'not of bloods (*ouk ex haimatōn*)' comes from Ezekiel 16, 'I said to you in your bloods, "Live",'[15] which was incorporated into the Jewish rite of circumcision. St John distinguishes the new birth in Christ from that of the Jewish rite whereby a Gentile was incorporated into the covenant through circumcision and baptism.

Think of the significance of John 1.13 for the Johannine doctrine of baptism. Christ's birth was the one unique event, and our birth in Christ is a participation in his birth. That is the very heart of Christian baptism. In Christian baptism we are born from above because in baptism we are incorporated into the one who was born of the Spirit from above, whose birth was marked by miracle as the new beginning for mankind. St Paul says, when Christ died, I died, and when Christ rose again, I rose again. St John teaches likewise, when Christ was born of the Spirit, I was born of the Spirit. Baptism thus reposes upon the virgin birth of Christ as well as upon his death and resurrection. Now that is precisely

---

12 See my essay 'Ein vernachlässigter Gesichtspunkt der Tauflehre' in Evangelische Theologie, 1956, 10-11, pp. 433-57 & 481-92.

13 1 John 5.18.

14 John 1.14,18; 3.16 KJV.

15 Ezek 16.6, 'in your bloods' (*be-damaik*, plural), translated (as is the plural 'bloods', *haimatōn*, of John 1.13), by the singular, KJV & RSV.

the way in which it is expounded by Irenaeus who uses John 1.13 in the singular, where, incidentally, he gives us the earliest doctrinal understanding of infant baptism. This relation of our baptism to the baptism of Christ, our new birth to Christ's birth from above, was indeed the conviction of all the great fathers in the first five centuries, and even when the text in John 1.13 began to become plural (sometimes with a singular verb, and sometimes with a singular subject and a plural verb!). Thus even in the works of Augustine and Leo the Great (where we find John 1.13 cited in both plural and singular forms), they nevertheless continued to expound baptism as our sharing in Christ's virgin birth, and constantly cite this very passage in support.[16]

(c) St Paul

We have much the same teaching (the derivation of our sonship from Christ's) in St Paul.[17] The pattern of his thought runs thus: Christ is the second man, the last Adam. Adam owed his origin to a creative act of God, and he was a type of Christ.[18] Christ as the new man comes likewise from God. His likeness to Adam was not in sin, but in coming into existence and in representative capacity. 'As in Adam all die, so in Christ shall all be made alive.'[19] The first Adam then was not born of human parentage, not humanly generated. He came into existence at the hands of God, and the LXX[20] here uses *ginesthai*.[21] Compare Luke who speaks of Adam as the son of God,[22] and Matthew who speaks of the 'genesis' (*genesis*) of Jesus Christ.[23] Now the word for normal human birth in the New Testament, *gennan*, is not used of Adam, and Paul never uses it of Christ. Paul never says that Jesus was generated, only that he came into existence like Adam. But whereas the first Adam came into existence from the earth, was earthly, this last Adam came into existence from heaven – sent from God, he came

---

16 NB: Wolfgang Harnisch of Marburg (who has Bultmann's old chair) tells me that the text of John 1.13-14 has recently been shown to have been in the singular by P.L. Hofrichter, in an article in FZB 31, 1978, pp.155f; and in a monograph about the prologue of John's Gospel, entitled *Das Urchristliche Logosbekenntnis*, 1986.

17 E.g. Gal 3.26, 4.4-7.

18 Rom 5.14f.

19 1 Cor 15.22.

20 The Greek translation of the Old Testament.

21 Gen 2.7.

22 Luke 3.38.

23 Matt 1.18.

into existence of woman, but 'from heaven'. ('The first man was from the earth, a man of dust; the second man is from heaven.')[24] That does not mean that Jesus descended in his humanity from heaven, or that his humanity was pre-existent. His humanity was formed on earth but it came into being through divine initiative. But short of actually saying that Jesus was born of a virgin, what could be more explicit in speech about the virgin birth? Christ came down from heaven, the new man, the new Adam? That falls into line with the Pauline doctrine of the descent and ascent of Christ.

Now consider Galatians 4. Three times[25] Paul uses the verb *gennan* of human generation, but when in that very context he speaks of Jesus he avoids the word *gennan* and uses the word *ginesthai*.[26] In other words, in reference to Jesus' birth he refuses to use the only word the New Testament uses of human generation. Every time Paul speaks of human birth he uses *gennan*, but not once when he speaks of Jesus. Every time Paul wants to refer to the earthly origin of Jesus he uses the word *ginesthai*.[27] That is the strongest disavowal of birth by ordinary human generation in regard to the birth of Jesus. 'God sent forth his Son made (*genomenon*) of a woman, made (*genomenon*) under the law . . . that we might receive the adoption of sons',[28] referring back to Galatians 3: 'for in Christ Jesus you are all sons of God, through faith. For as many of you as were baptised into Christ have put on Christ.'[29] Because Christ came into existence under the law, he can redeem those that are under the law. Those who are baptised into Christ and put on Christ are given the Spirit of Christ and like him cry, 'Abba Father'.[30] To be incorporated by baptism into Christ is to partake of his Spirit of sonship which he is able to bestow on us men and women because of his own coming into existence of a woman, as a real man. So Paul can also say, like John, when Christ was born I was born a son of God, for in baptism I partake of Christ and his Spirit of sonship.

Thus Paul's theology is not only consonant with the virgin birth of Christ, but, like John's, implies it in his doctrine of sonship and baptism. But Paul's allusions to the virgin birth are as strong as Mark's and are

---

24 1 Cor 15.47.

25 Gal 4.23,24,29.

26 Gal 4.4 (*genomenon*).

27 Rom 1.3; Phil 2.7; Gal 4.4 (*genomen-/ou/os/on*).

28 Gal 4.4-5 KJV. The RSV translates genomenon as '*born* of woman, *born* under the law', which does not reflect Paul's preference for *ginesthai* over *gennan*.

29 Gal 3.26-27.

30 Gal 4.6; cf. Rom 8.15f.

quite explicit of Jesus' heavenly origin. The new Adam comes from heaven. He is not of the earth, though he comes into existence of woman. That is precisely the doctrine of the virgin birth. In St John and St Paul it is evident that the doctrine of the virgin birth is woven into the very texture of their theology which shows its inner importance: but that is just what we would expect. For us to know Jesus Christ truly means that our way of knowing him corresponds to his way of coming into being, our *ordo cognoscendi* (order of knowing) corresponds to his *ordo essendi* (order of being), as it were. That is important: only if we can see the inner truth of the virgin birth in the texture of saving doctrine, see its proper place in the doctrine of Christ, can we understand the biblical evidence and evaluate it properly. That will be the deciding factor.

2 The doctrine of the virgin birth

We have already noted that in a profound sense the incarnation begins with Israel as it is brought into covenantal union with the Word of God. It is only in Jesus Christ, however, that the Word or Son really becomes flesh, but in becoming flesh of our flesh he entered into our adamic existence as a man made of a woman, made under the law. Within that continuity of adamic existence, fallen existence, he is nevertheless true man, and true Son of God in true union with the Father. In his truth and obedience Jesus Christ breaks through the continuity of adamic existence and opens up a new continuity in a new Adam, in a new humanity. As such Jesus Christ is the firstborn of the new creation, the head of a new race in perfect union with God.[31] He was therefore both in continuity and in discontinuity with our fallen humanity. For the first time there is true man in the midst of our inhumanity, for in the midst of our fallen humanity Jesus is true man. In and through him, therefore, humanity which has been dehumanised through sin, finds its true being and true human nature in union with God. Jesus Christ is not only mediator between God and man, but as such opens up a new way from the old humanity into the new. It is in that light that we must approach the account of the virgin birth.

(a) Preliminary observations

(i) The virgin birth not a theory of explanation

The virgin birth must not be understood as a theory explaining how the Son of God became man. It is rather an indication of what happened

---

[31] Col 1.18; Rom 8.29.

within humanity when the Son of God became man. That act of becoming man was a transcendent act in the freedom of divine grace involving a miraculous creative act within our human existence; but in the nature of the case it is apprehensible by us only at its extreme edges, where the creative act, in its overlap with the creation we already know, is an event with two sides to it, an outward visible act in nature and another invisible supernatural act, *born of the virgin Mary* and *conceived by the Holy Spirit*. In understanding any act in nature we have to ask two questions, *What is it*? and *How is it*? And these two questions belong together. But here in answer to the question *what* we are confronted with an answer which has no natural *how* attached to it, but rather a *how* that transcends the natural event altogether. That transcendent *how* is described as an act of the Spirit, as a creative act from above which breaks into our humanity and into our nature. It assumes form and process within our humanity, and therefore its *what* can be spoken of, but its *how* recedes into the divine nature of the Son of God and is beyond our observation and understanding.

In other words, in the virgin birth the incarnation has taken a meaningful form which tells us that here in the midst of our nature and humanity God is recreating our humanity, that here God is at work in an act of pure grace. It is an act within our humanity and its creaturely continuity, for he who is no creature became creature. He came breaking freely into our creaturely continuity and partook of it though he was not a product of it. Therefore the virgin birth cannot be understood *biologically*. If you ask biological questions of the virgin birth you will only get biological answers, and to ask biological questions only is to presuppose from the start that there is nothing more here than normal biological process. Biological questions are all questions about the *what* and the *how* within the observable processes of nature. But even apart from the fact that here we are confronted with a *how* which is beyond biological process, what about the other questions we must ask, *why* and *whence*? To these questions we can only answer that here God acts as creator. God begins with himself alone as creator, working this time not out of nothing but within our human existence. Of that act in which God begins with himself alone, the virgin birth is the outward sign, the sign that here in the midst of our humanity, in the midst of true and normal humanity, God is creatively at work in a new way – the sign, in fact, that he who is born of Mary is the creator himself.

(ii) The virgin birth not to be separated from the whole mystery of Christ

The virgin birth cannot be understood apart from the whole mystery of Christ, apart from the union of divine and human nature in the one person of Jesus Christ. The virgin birth is the outward sign, the signitive form in humanity which the creative entry of the Son of God takes, when he assumes our human nature into union with his divine nature. The sign points to the mystery of Christ and bears witness to it, but the sign is not itself the reality. The reality is the hypostatic union of true God and true man. But if the virgin birth is a true and appropriate sign, the outward sign and the inward reality belong together as form and content of the incarnation. The outward sign has in it something which it signifies; it is the analogical form of the thing signified. Thus the virgin birth must correspond as sign to the nature of what it signifies, it must correspond to the nature of the mystery of Christ. Thus the mystery of the birth and the mystery of the person of Christ cannot be separated, and the mystery of the birth has to be understood in the light of the mystery of his person, the sign in the light of the thing signified, not the thing signified in the light of the sign. And yet, although we cannot understand the mystery of Christ out of his birth, the mystery of his birth does have much to tell us about the way that the mystery of his person has taken in its insertion into our fallen human existence at the very beginning of the earthly life of Jesus.

(iii) The virgin birth not to be separated from the resurrection

The virgin birth can also not be considered in abstraction from the triumphant consummation of Christ's life in his resurrection, for it is there that the mystery of his person is revealed. In fact the birth of Jesus of the virgin Mary and the resurrection of Jesus from the virgin tomb ('where no one had ever yet been laid'[32]) are the twin signs which mark out the mystery of Christ, testifying to the continuity and the discontinuity between Jesus Christ and our fallen humanity. The incarnation is not only a once and for all act of assumption of our flesh, but the continuous personal union of divine and human nature in the one person of the incarnate Son, a personal union which he carried all the way through our estranged estate under bondage into the freedom and triumph of the resurrection. Thus it is in the resurrection that we see the real meaning of the virgin birth, while the virgin birth has much to tell us about the resurrection. These are then the twin signs testifying to the miraculous life of the Son of God within our humanity, the one at the beginning and the other at the consummation of the earthly life of Jesus.

Both these acts were sovereign creative acts of God's grace in and upon and out of our fallen humanity, and they are, in the full sense, one continuous act including the whole historical life and work of the incarnate

---

32 Luke 23.53.

Son. Both these miraculous signs point to the single historical existence within the whole of historical existence which God has assumed into unique oneness with himself. They tell us that here within our fallen existence God has acted creatively and redemptively in such continuity with us that we may share in it, but in such discontinuity with our fallen humanity that we may all through sharing in him be liberated from our bondage and decay, and corruption and sin to a new life in the new humanity. The birth of Jesus tells us that God acts in Jesus Christ in such a way that his birth does not fall under the power of man, under the arbitrary forces of human history, or under the causal determinisms of this world, but that in his birth God the Son freely and sovereignly enters into them from without. The resurrection tells us that the life and person of Jesus are not held under the tyrant forces of this world, that though he was born of woman and made under the law, Jesus Christ was not dominated and mastered by our fallen flesh and its judgement, but is triumphant over it all, in achieving his redeeming purpose of reconciling our humanity to fellowship with God.

(iv) The virgin birth and empty tomb as pointers to the mystery of Christ

Now look at it in this way. The virgin birth of Jesus Christ points to the mystery of God's self revelation, that God reveals himself within man's fallen life, and therefore that God's revelation also veils itself in our humanity. At the birth of Jesus, the mystery of Christ as true God and true man is inserted into our existence and is necessarily veiled, veiled because inserted into the flesh of sin, the *sarx hamartias,* as St Paul called it. The resurrection of Christ points to the fact that God unveils himself, reveals himself within man's life. Here the mystery of God is resurrected out of our flesh of sin, out of our death and corruption and is unveiled in its glory as true God and true man in perfect union. The empty tomb points to the revelation of the secret of Christ and as such is the authentication of the virgin birth; it is the unveiling of what was veiled, the resurrection out of our mortality of what was inserted into it and recreated within it. But such a resurrection of true man and true God points back to the virgin birth of Jesus as a union of true God and true man. The humiliation of Jesus began at Bethlehem and reached its climax on the cross, just before his glorification in the resurrection. The new life began at Bethlehem and reached its unveiling in the resurrection. Thus the mystery of the virgin birth is the basis of the mystery of the resurrection. By the mystery of the resurrection the mystery of the virgin birth becomes effective and understandable. Here we have a closed circle – to deny the virgin birth involves a denial of the resurrection, and vice versa.

(b) The positive teaching of the virgin birth

The virgin birth tells us that Jesus was really and genuinely the son of a human mother, that he was born as other men are, of woman, and yet in a *unique way* which corresponds to his *unique person* as the Son of the eternal God who has entered into our humanity. That Jesus was conceived by the Holy Spirit means that the Son of God took his earthly origin in the womb of Mary through a special act of the Holy Spirit in accordance with his nature as the Son of God become man. It means that the secret and origin of Jesus lie wholly in God and in his sovereign will and grace alone; it means that the life of Jesus from its very beginnings within our human existence was one which was consonant upon the entry of the Son into our creaturely flesh in a creative way. Thus the incarnation of the Son in our humanity has its source in the hidden creative act of God, but it also assumes a form in the entry of the Son into our humanity which is appropriate to and is required by the nature of the incarnate Son as creator as well as creature. The birth of Jesus of the virgin Mary through the creative operation of the Spirit corresponds to the whole secret of his person and life and work, for it reveals in the most remarkable manner the way which the saving grace of God takes with our fallen humanity. It reveals God as the creator and redeemer actually with us in our estranged human existence, and as God bringing out of our fallen and sinful existence a new humanity that is holy and perfect.

Let us now elucidate this in a number of paragraphs.

(i) The reality of the humanity of Jesus

That Jesus was born of the virgin Mary means that he was a genuine man, that his humanity was not docetic.[33] The witness of scripture is that Jesus was really born of Mary, born through all the embryonic processes of the womb just as other human beings. And yet while the flesh of Jesus was the same as our flesh, he was born not as other men are of the will of the flesh, or of the will of an earthly father. In the history of the church the virgin birth was first denied by Cerinthus the heretic and gnostic who held a docetic view of the humanity of Christ – and the doctrine of the virgin birth was inserted into the creed partly in order to combat Docetism. That is very clear from the way in which it is used in Ignatius, for example. But the virgin birth equally excludes Ebionism, that is, excludes the idea that the Son of God united himself with one who was already man, or that a human being, either

---

[33] 'Apparent', from the Greek dokeō, 'appear'. Docetism was the view that Jesus only appeared to be human but was not really fully human.

in embryo or as already born, was at some point adopted to be the Son of God. The virgin birth also excludes the idea that God and man are co-equal partners – that is why the virgin birth repudiates all synergism.[34] What took place in the birth of Jesus took place in an act under the sovereign will of God, in which God alone was Lord and master, so that the birth was grounded in the sovereign will of God alone. But that does not mean that the birth of Jesus was an act of God without man. On the contrary, man is fully involved, but he is the predicate, not the subject, not the lord of the event.

(ii) Disqualification of human capabilities

The birth of Jesus was a real advent, an act of God's grace, a coming into man, and as such it carries with it a disqualification of human capabilities and powers as rendering possible an approach of man to God. The virgin birth is the doctrine that the movement of the Son of God to become man is one directional, from God to man: it cannot be reversed. The advent was a coming from beyond into human life. It is a coming into the realm of human power and ability, a real advent to man, into human existence with all its rational processes, but it is an advent that is grounded in God himself and not in human powers and capabilities. And so the birth from the virgin Mary carries with it a real disqualification of human powers as capable of producing Jesus. Christ Jesus is not in any sense, even in a co-operative sense, a product of human activity – the initiative, and the sovereignty of the act are entirely in God's hands. To put that otherwise: Jesus is in no sense the product of the causal-historical process of this world. God entered into humanity and assumed flesh and took it to be one with himself in the person of Jesus Christ. As such it was a real entry of eternity into time. Can eternity enter into time in any way except in a unique way, analogous both to eternity and to time? Does not the fact that eternity acts here mean that the birth of Jesus is a supernatural event, one that is grounded in the eternal, unconditioned by anything outside of it such as a human father, and is essentially a matter of pure grace?

(iii) A recreation out of the old creation

The birth of Jesus does not mean that this was an entirely new act of creation on the part of God, but rather a recreation within our human existence, a recreation that involves our human existence again in the creative action of God. The virgin birth is thus a creating in Mary by the creator Spirit. It is as creator himself, not as Mary's partner, that

[34] Gk, 'working together', the view that God and man co-operate for salvation.

Jesus is born of her. This creation then was not a *creatio ex nihilo,*[35] but a *creatio ex virgine,*[36] presupposing the first creation and beginning the new creation. That is a large part of the doctrine of the incarnation: that Christ really comes to us, to our human flesh and assumes it out of our fallen condition in order to redeem and sanctify it. It is of the utmost importance to assert therefore the reality of the humanity of Jesus, and the solidarity of his humanity with our humanity, and that is done very clearly by the virgin birth, although it does it in such a way as to show clearly also that this is an event that breaks into our human processes and is not the product of them.

(iv) The setting aside of human autonomy

The virgin birth, then, represents a break in the sinful autonomy of man. That does not imply any stigma upon marriage, or on our natural birth, but on the contrary a sanctification of our humanity and of the way in which we come into the world. We cannot but acknowledge that all our human life is involved in sin, and that our very existence is involved in original sin – but the birth of Jesus was a birth of the holy Son into that condition which far from acquiescing in its sin, resists it, sanctifying what sin had corrupted, and uniting it again to the purity of God. The virgin birth does not mean that Mary was herself immaculately conceived and on that ground could be immaculately a mother; but it does mean that out of Mary a sinner, by pure act of God, Jesus is born, the holy Son of God, and that his very birth sanctifies Mary, for it is through her Son that she is redeemed and given to share in the purity and holiness of God. Pure act of God, however, means that the sinful autonomy of man, the sinful act of human assertion in self-will, is set aside and excluded. In human sovereignty and autonomy man is not free for God or for his Word, but the act of man as the father, the *kyrios,*[37] the head, epitomises the autonomy and sovereignty of man. That is the very sovereignty and assertion that is set aside here where God acts alone in such a way as to set aside the assertion of man's will. That is the significance of the fact that in the birth of Jesus, man in the person of Joseph is set aside – he has no say in this matter, he exercises no act of self-will or of the flesh in order to bring about this act of God.

(v) The virgin birth the pattern of grace, the model for faith

That brings us to the point that in the virgin birth we are given at the very beginning of Christ's life a revelatory sign, a *sēmeion,* which tells

[35] Lat, 'creation out of nothing'.

[36] Lat, 'creation out of a virgin'.

[37] Gk, 'lord' or 'master'.

us what the divine act of grace is. Grace takes a form in the birth of Jesus which we may take as a pattern or norm for all our understanding of grace. Here God takes the initiative and approaches Mary through the word of his angelic messenger – the word proclaimed to Mary is the word of election or grace: she is chosen and told of God's choice. She has nothing to do in this matter except what is done in her under the operation of the Spirit. What Mary does is simply to receive the word, to believe, which she does not in her own strength but in the strength given her by the Lord, and she is blessed because of that, not because of her virginity. John of Damascus remarked that Mary conceived through the ear: she heard the Word and the Word spoken by the Spirit in her ear begot himself in her and through her, and so the Word which Mary heard and received and obeyed became flesh of her flesh. That is the normative pattern for the believer in his or her attitude toward the Word announced in the gospel, which tells men and women of the divine act of grace and decision taken already on their behalf in Christ. Mary's attitude is beautifully expressed in the words: 'Behold, I am the handmaid of the Lord; let it be to me according to your word.'[38] It is an act of glad and thankful and humble submission and surrender to the will of God. And within her there takes place the incomprehensible act of God, the birth of the Son of God in human form.

By that we are guided to think and given to understand something of our own salvation and recreation. As in the annunciation of the word to Mary, Christ the Word himself became flesh, so in the enunciation of the gospel, we surrender in like manner to Christ the Word now made flesh, and there takes place in us the birth of Jesus, or rather, we are in a remarkable way given to share through grace in his birth and to share in the new creation in him. That is the Christian message – the Christmas message. It is not of our self-will or free-will that we are saved and born anew from above. 'But to all who received him, who believed in his name, he gave power to become children of God.'[39] Here there is a 'become' dependent on the 'become' of 'the Word become flesh', grounded in it and derivative from it. What happened once and for all, in utter uniqueness in Jesus Christ, happens in every instance of rebirth into Christ, when Christ enters into our hearts and recreates us. Just as he was born from above of the Holy Spirit, so we are born from above of the Holy Spirit through sharing in his birth. Just as in the birth of Jesus there was no preceding action on our part, or human co-operation, such as the co-operation between a human father and a human mother, just as there

---

[38] Luke 1.38.

[39] John 1.12.

was no prior human activity there, so in our salvation and in our knowledge of God there is no *a priori*, no human presupposition, no Pelagian,[40] semi-Pelagian or synergistic activity.

It is from first to last salvation by grace alone – even our faith is not of ourselves for it is a gift of God – salvation for humanity, among men and women and within them, but a salvation grounded on an immediate act of God himself, and not on both God and man. We are saved by faith, but faith is the empty vessel (as Calvin called it) that receives Christ, faith so to speak is the empty womb through which Christ comes to dwell in our hearts. Faith as our reception of Christ, our capacity for Christ is itself a gift of grace. It is not a creation out of nothing, however, but a creation out of man, out of the human sphere of our choices and decisions, capacities and possibilities, a creation out of our full humanity but a creation of God – and therefore faith is something that is far beyond all human possibilities and capacities. It is grounded beyond itself in the act of God. In faith we are opened up from above and given to receive what we ourselves are incapable of receiving in and by ourselves. Faith is not therefore the product of our human capacities or insights or abilities. The relation between faith and the Christ received by faith is the Holy Spirit: *conceptus de Spiritu Sancto*.[41] Just as Jesus was conceived by the Spirit so we cannot say that Jesus is Lord except by the Holy Spirit.[42] It is by the operation of the Spirit that we receive the Word of God which is ingrafted into our souls, and, as it were, conceive the truth in our hearts and minds. We do not bring Christ in by our own power, by our own decision or choice, nor do we make Christ real to ourselves or in ourselves. How could we do that? That is entirely the work of the Holy Spirit – our part in being addressed by the Word is to hear the gracious decision that God has already taken, hear the word of the gospel that God has set his love and favour upon us, although we do not in the least deserve it. Although we have done nothing and can do nothing to bring it about, yet when he works in us what he has been pleased to do, it is ours to work it out in obedient living and faith.

(vi) Demonstration of the virgin birth only through the Spirit

We cannot offer any independent demonstration of the virgin birth – that is to say, we cannot offer any demonstration of it in ways that are

---

40 Pelagius believed that we co-operate with God (synergism) in salvation, and hence the heresy known as Pelagianism is that we contribute to our own salvation.

41 Lat, 'conceived by the Holy Spirit'.

42 1 Cor 12.3.

not appropriate to the nature of that birth. We cannot demonstrate it by appealing to anything outside of it, to any external evidence, to any criterion or norm beyond it. That cannot be done with regard to any Christian doctrine. In the very nature of the case the only demonstration is a demonstration of the Spirit, for the demonstration of a truth must be analogical and appropriate to the nature of the truth itself. Consider the resurrection, the twin miraculous event with which the virgin birth is so closely bound. The resurrection, by its very nature as real event breaking into the framework of our historical constructions in the fallen world, is not demonstrable by the canons of credibility which we bring to it in the course of our normal scientific historiography. We are concerned with evidence offered by historical witnesses, but that evidence is taken together with the fact of the resurrection as creative event, for the two are inseparable as *lalia* and *logos*,[43] as historical and bodily sign and the reality of which it is the meaningful sign. So with the virgin birth of Jesus. It has to be investigated in terms of the nature of the one who is born, and of the nature of the activity of the one who is born, that is in terms of the activity of the Spirit, and only in a way that corresponds to that nature can an appropriate demonstration be offered. If the doctrine of the virgin birth is true then that can be demonstrated only by the Spirit, through what St Paul called the 'demonstration of the Spirit (*en apodeixei pneumatos*)'.[44]

Under the action of the Holy Spirit therefore, and within the demonstration of the Holy Spirit, all we can do is to expound the doctrine in its own light, to set forth its intrinsic significance in Christ, and to set forth its integration with the whole doctrine of Christ, and with all the doctrines which cohere round christology as the core of dogmatics. It is as we let the doctrine shine in its own light, in its own true significance, in the coherence of the whole truth of the gospel, that by the demonstration of the Spirit its authentication as truth is acknowledged.

Here then we see the virgin birth as an act of God grounded in himself alone, and in an act of grace which becomes as such the archetype of all other acts of grace. We cannot treat it lightly or give it a place of only minor importance in our dogmatic theology. It is precisely by setting forth its importance, its archetypal importance in and for other doctrines that its truth comes home to us. The virgin birth thus becomes more than a sign – it is a determinative act of God.

---

43 Gk, 'speech' and 'word'. See John 8.43 KJV.

44 1 Cor 2.4.

That does not mean that we think of Christ as the Son of God because he was born of a virgin; it was because he was the Son of God and was very God that he was born of a virgin into this world. But here we cannot separate the sign from the reality. The Word comes into the world as deed, and the thing signified is embodied in the sign – so that the sign, the very form of Christ's birth, proclaims Christ in the very mode of his entry into our world, and proclaims analogously the mode of his entry into all who believe in him. The virgin birth is thus the way which the true humanity of the Son of God took once for all in our sinful world in coming for our salvation, and is therefore also a sign of the manner of his continuous coming to us within the same world.

(vii) Necessity and importance of the virgin birth

It is just because of this close and inseparable association of sign and thing signified in the virgin birth that we can show from the history of theology its necessity for true faith in Christ. Can we conceive the resurrection of Jesus apart from the empty tomb? Can we hold the incarnation as the union of true God and true man apart from the virgin birth? Certainly the history of theology shows that where the outward sign or form of either the resurrection or the virgin birth has been repudiated or demythologised, the inner content has inevitably gone with it. Thus the virgin birth as an article of credal faith has played a very important role in the history of the church in rebutting Docetism and Ebionism, Eutychianism or Sabellianism and Nestorianism,[45] but here too we have a powerful force keeping the church faithful to the basic doctrine of salvation and justification by the grace of God alone. It proclaims that in Christ there is created in our humanity the possibility of salvation, a possibility which does not arise from man but which is anchored from the side of God. In Christ who is true man and true God we have the mediator and reconciler in whom God and man are not simply brought near each other but in whom God and man become one for all eternity. It is in him the Lord Jesus, born of the virgin Mary and risen from the dead, that we are born again through the Holy Spirit, given to share as members of his body, and we frail human beings are thus enfolded with him in the life of God.

---

[45] See the glossary for a definition of these different christologies.

Chapter Four

THE CONTINUOUS UNION
in the historical Life and Obedience of Jesus

If the doctrine of the virgin birth of Jesus comes appropriately under the rubric of *anhypostasia*, the doctrine of the incarnate life of Jesus comes appropriately under the rubric of *enhypostasia*.[1] Actually these cannot be separated in that way, but a relative stress does fall upon *enhypostasia* when we come to think of the incarnational union of God and man in Jesus Christ as a dynamic historical event carried through the whole earthly life and death of Jesus into the resurrection and ascension. Because it is *in the Son of God* that this whole life is hypostatic (has real human personhood) we have to see the life and work of Jesus on earth in relation to the Father, but because in the Son of God *it is hypostatic* (*does* have real human personhood), we have to consider the life and work of Jesus on earth in relation to his fellow men and women. However, before we look at it in that twofold way we must begin by considering it in the unity of his own person as mediator.

1 The one and the many – the mediator

(a) The union of God and man in the person of Christ

What happens in the incarnation is the union of God and man. At last in the midst of our fallen humanity, within and in spite of our estrangement from him, God comes in his love and binds us to himself

---

[1] *Anhypostasia*, the fact that the humanity of Jesus had no independent existence apart from the incarnation of the Son of God; *enhypostasia*, the fact that the humanity of Jesus had real existence in the person of the eternal Son. For an outline of these doctrines see the end of chapter 2 above, or the end of chapter 6 below for the Reformation doctrine.

The Gk, hypostasis, is used for 'reality' and also for 'person'. The word 'hypostatic', two sentences below, refers to the real personal humanity of Jesus and for clarity its meaning in the context has been added in brackets.

forever. God and man meet in Jesus Christ and a new covenant is eternally established and fulfilled.

That takes place in the union of man and God in the infant and maturing Jesus, in a growing in wisdom and stature both toward God and toward man.[2] It is a growing which reaches its first stage when Jesus is twelve years of age, when according to Jewish law a son passes from infancy to the state of adult responsibility, and when the child himself confesses with his own lips the word of God sealed in his flesh in circumcision.[3] Then Jesus is found in his Father's house, not only answering the required interrogations but proposing them himself to the doctors of the law. Brought up from his mother's knee in the Old Testament scriptures he has already entered into a wonderful fullness of divine wisdom. The second stage is reached when, after years of toil at the carpenter's bench as the *ben-bayith*, the son of the house, taking his place along with Joseph as bread winner in the family at Nazareth, Jesus at last reaches the age of thirty, the age when under the Old Testament regulations a man might enter upon the active life of the priesthood. At that point in the fullness of time, Jesus steps forth among mankind, deliberately entering into active and living solidarity with his fellow men and women, in order to bring the union between himself and sinners to its completion in the mission of mediation upon which he has been sent by the Father.

The early stages of Jesus' living union of God and man are hidden from us. They remain veiled and we are only allowed to see that throughout he remains in subjection,[4] as a son learning obedience, and is already about the business of his heavenly Father. But we are allowed to see that the growth within the union forged at Bethlehem is a strenuous forward movement, a real battle of blows, *proekopten*, as Luke recorded it, through which Jesus grew in wisdom and favour with God and man.[5] The final stage of this union of man and God running throughout the life and ministry of Jesus is unveiled only obliquely at first, and yet even when the veil is at last lifted on the cross and in the resurrection it remains holy mystery. Beginning with his baptism among sinners at the Jordan to fulfil all righteousness, and ending with his baptism in blood on the cross, again among malefactors when he died, the just for the unjust, we see the person of Christ at work in a movement of increasing solidarity with his fellow men and women, increasing solidarity with

---

[2] Luke 2.40; cf. 2.52.

[3] Luke 2.41ff.

[4] Luke 2.51.

[5] Luke 2.52.

sinners. Throughout that growing interpenetration of the Son of Man with sinful man, the intensity of battle within the person of Christ increases, reaching its culmination in Gethsemane. Throughout it all he was sublimely serene and tranquil in his repose in the Father, but as his life developed he entered more and more intensely into the contradiction of sin and of sinners against him, living out in the midst of humanity the oneness with God which he had and was in himself. Thus Jesus enacted in human flesh and human life, in his sinless solidarity with sinful man, the will of God to be one with man and to gather men and women into the heart of God.

The unity of the person and work of Christ

Here we see in finality and in utmost intensity what took place in the life and ordeal of Israel. We see it in the unity of the person and work of Christ. If Israel is the sacred story of the penetration of the word of God into the midst of a stubborn and rebellious people, into its very mind and flesh, gathering it into covenanted relation with God, it is here above all that we see the Word made flesh in the unity of person and word, truth and life, word and deed in Jesus Christ. That is the first and the last thing that he fulfils and completes, the utter integration of God's word and will with our humanity – and he fulfils it in his own incarnate person and existence among us. He so lives out his life that from beginning to end he is one person, and his work in the flesh is one with his being the Son of God. He so lives that from beginning to end his actions are not different from his innermost heart, or to put it the other way round, he so lives that the course of God's action towards man is identical with his own existence in the flesh. There is no gap between a realm of truth and a realm of event here. He is the truth; he does the truth; he speaks the truth; he enacts the truth in physical flesh, and what he does in the flesh he is in himself, in his own person. His action is his presence in act. His word is his life in his speaking and living of it. In this absolute unity in Christ, God steps among men and women and gives himself to be known in act which is identical with his own person, in activity in which he is fully present, bodily present, in action which issues out of his innermost being and heart. That act of the ever-living God is identical with Jesus.

Look at it in this way. In Christ, what God communicates to man is not something, but his very self. This is distinct from all other acts of God. This is God's unique act, his reality-in-the-act, and apart from this act there is no God at all. In the act of creation, God does not communicate himself, but creates a reality wholly distinct from himself, but here in Jesus Christ God acts in such a way that he is himself in his act, and what he acts he is, and what he is he acts. We can think that out only in the doctrine of the Trinity, and cannot do that now, but what we are concerned to do here is to see that Jesus Christ as act of God in humanity is identical with God's own person. Christ Jesus is identical in his human existence and life with the self-giving of God to and for men and women, and so in Jesus it is with the operation of God himself for our salvation that we have to do. Thus we must think of the person of Christ and the work of Christ as completely one, so that he is in himself what he reveals of the Father, and he is in himself what he does all through his life and on the cross in reconciliation. It is only because Jesus is that in himself, and lives it out in himself, that he reveals the Father and reconciles the world.

Thus after thirty years in which he grew up more and more into what he already was, one with God in person and word and act, Jesus stepped forth among men and women to reveal the Father in the identity of his person and word, and to reconcile them to God in the identity of his person and work as the incarnate saviour of mankind.

It is Christ in his person who reveals, atones and reconciles

This unity of person and word, and person and work, and therefore of word and work, means that we cannot in any sense think of the work of revelation and reconciliation as a kind of transaction objective to Christ, or simply as an act done by Christ. It is above all the person of Christ revealing so that revelation cannot be separated off from his person. Similarly, it is the person of Christ atoning, so that atonement cannot be divided from Christ's person. It is because revelation is the person of Christ revealing that it is revelation, and it is because atonement is the person of Christ atoning that it is atonement. Thus, for example, the significance of the cross does not lie simply in the death or in the blood of Christ shed in sacrifice, but it lies in the fact that the person of Christ is the one who sheds his blood for our sin – it lies in the identity of his person and work. The atonement is his person in action, not the action by itself. Thus what Christ is in his person, as the incarnate Son in whom God and man are joined in the form of a servant, Christ is on the cross. The cross is the outworking of a divine decision that constitutes the person of the mediator himself in the incarnation. The reconciliation wrought out on the cross is already at work in the person of Christ, and all his life is the visible working and working out of what took place when the Son of God became man in the midst of our flesh of sin.

This identity of person and word, person and work in Christ is one of the main interests of the fourth Gospel. In the Synoptics, Jesus calls men and women to his side, to follow him, and he leads them. In John's Gospel, Jesus speaks of himself as the way. In the Synoptics, Jesus teaches the truth. In John's Gospel, he says, 'I am the truth'. In the Synoptics, he is set forth as saving man's life. In John's Gospel, he says, 'I am the Life'. That is to say, the act of Christ is Christ, the work of Christ is Christ, the truth of Christ is Christ; he is the way, the truth and the life in himself. His being and life *are* redemption. That is why the New Testament sums up the whole gospel of revelation and reconciliation in the name *Immanuel, God with us.*

(b) The election of Christ – the one for the many

In Jesus Christ, we see taking place in finality and in utmost intensity something else that took place in Israel – the election of one as the instrument of the divine love for the redemption of all. The election of one for the salvation of all characterises the whole story of God's dealings with Israel. Now within Israel that reaches its complete fulfilment in a unique way, in such a unique way that immediately we see that all that happened before it was but shadow cast long ahead of it by this unique event which was even then on its way, and had finally to take place in the incarnation of the Son. Here in Jesus, the election of one for all becomes ultimate fact in our existence – and here, therefore, election and substitution combine in the most unique, most intense and personal concentration of the one and the many. It is in that light that we must see the whole incarnate life of the Son of God as Son of Man, and of Son of Man as Son of God, of God towards man, and man towards God in the person of Jesus Christ.

In himself, as God and man in union, Jesus Christ is the actualisation of the eternal purpose of God to give himself to humanity in pure love and grace. Here in Jesus Christ, divine election has moved into time, and here all through the life of Jesus there takes effect, in actual history, God's election of man to be God's man. He comes to be God for man in order to remake man for God. God has eternally willed himself for fellowship with mankind, and willed mankind for fellowship with himself. Jesus Christ is the reality of that will, for in him God turns towards men and women and wills to be one with them, and in him they are turned wholly towards God to be one with God. These are not two independent movements but one movement of redeeming love in which God gives himself unreservedly to man and in which he gathers up humanity into the life of God in Jesus Christ. Here where God has given himself to be man's God once and for all, nothing can undo that decision. But here too God gives man to himself once and for all, and nothing can undo that decision. It is an eternal election of love, an everlasting covenant.

Election and judgement[6]

But let us note that this means a covenant with humanity in its sin, an election of man in sinful existence. God binds himself in Jesus to sinful men and women and graciously accepts them. Even within this situation, the incarnation is an act of pure grace. It is above all the movement of God's eternal love to be one with men and women in spite of their unworthiness and sin. But for this very reason, election intensifies the situation created by sin, intensifies the enmity between man and God. God gives himself to sinners and sinners cannot escape that gracious decision which has finally overtaken them and gathered them into covenant relation with God. God's love wills that the sinner shall not escape, shall not elude the election of grace, and that means that the sinner who refuses this election of grace resists that grace and is resisted by it. In other words, the election which moves into history in Jesus Christ and creates union of man with God involves the meeting of God and man over human sin. The very will of God to give himself in love is the positive act here, but the situation of man's sin means that God's positive will of love calls mankind to account for their sin in eluding him and alienating themselves from him. It stands man face to face with the divine love which wills that mankind shall not isolate itself, shall not be without God by taking its own way. Because self-will is now the nature of man, the good news of Christmas becomes already the news of the contradiction of sinners and the passion of Christ – 'Behold, this child is set for the fall and rising of many in Israel, and for a sign that is spoken against . . . that thoughts out of many hearts may be revealed', and as Simeon had added, turning to Mary, 'a sword will pierce through your own soul also'.[7]

That is the way, the way of contradiction and passion, in which we have to think of the whole incarnate life of the Son of God right from the very beginning, but a way growing in intensity as he advances to undertake the fulfilment of his mission. Jesus is the suffering servant Son right from Bethlehem. We must think of the work of the cross, therefore, as beginning immediately with his birth, increasing in his growth into manhood, and deepening in intensity as he entered his public ministry. His whole life is his passion, for his very incarnation as union of God and man is an intervention into the enmity between God and mankind. Jesus Christ steps into the situation where God

---

6 Cf. T.F. Torrance, *The Christian Doctrine of God* (Edinburgh: T & T Clark 1996), p. 246.

7 Luke 2.34-35.

judges mankind and where mankind contradicts God. He steps in not as a third party but as the God who judges man, and steps into the place of man who sins against God and is judged by God. The very union of God and man, and the living out of that union from day to day in the realisation of God's gracious election, intensified that state of enmity, making it ultimate, that is, making it the *eschaton*.[8]

By uniting God to man the judgement of God is brought to bear on man as never before. By uniting man to God man is placed under the divine judgement as never before. This is final judgement. Not as a third party but as the one made in the likeness of the flesh of sin, Jesus Christ stands under the bondage of the law and under the wrath of God. Not as a third party but as very God, Jesus judges man and condemns sin in the flesh. And so the ultimate or final judgement takes place only when God and man are ultimately or finally one in Jesus Christ. The very forgiveness which he proclaims in word carries at its heart a judgement upon sin, but in that the Word is made flesh, the forgiveness enacted in the flesh involves the ultimate action of condemnation of sin in the flesh. That is the passion, the life of the Son of Man who is the one Son of God taking upon himself the life and sin of the many. That is the life of the Son of Man who grows up as the one and the many from cradle to manhood, and that is the life of the Son of Man as he presses toward the cross through all the years of his loving ministry of forgiveness and healing. If at last it was with joy that he endured the awful cross and all that it meant in the ultimate contradiction between God and humanity, then it was with joy too that he lived the life which in being lived carried him straight to the cross from the cradle. From beginning to end there is not a murmur upon his lips, not a shadow over his gladness, not a stain upon his serenity. If his agony is unspeakable, his life of joy and peace in the midst of it all is unbroken and inexpressible.

(c) Substitution – Christ in our place

The election of sinful man for God is achieved by an action of God *for* man. The election is actualised in Jesus as mediation or intervention taking a substitutionary form. For the Son of God to enter our flesh of sin means that he stands in our place in subjection to law and judgement. He does not do that for his own sake but *for* our sake – 'for' here translates the Greek *huper* (or *hyper*, on behalf of) and *anti* (instead of), not only *dia* (on account of). Jesus stepped into the heart

---

[8] Gk, 'the last thing', the final judgement.

of the inevitable conflict between the covenant faithfulness of God and the unfaithfulness of man, and he bore it in himself to the very end. He shared in it from both sides, from the side of God who is offended by man, and from the side of man threatened with judgement and death by God. Jesus really and fully entered into that solidarity with us sharing to the utmost our human life and status, the situation in which we resist God and are resisted by God. He entered into our mode of being where we have no justification at all before God, but only condemnation. Where we the unjust have to stand there stands Jesus Christ, the just for the unjust. Where we sinners stand, there now stands Jesus Christ, our judge. In him there now takes place what ought to take place in us, the condemnation of sin in the flesh.

That condemnation takes place supremely on the cross, but the cross reveals what was taking place all the time in the incarnate life of the Son. His whole life, particularly after his baptism among sinners, was a life of intervention in our conflict with God, in which he penetrated into the depths of our personal existence and human society in sin, taking the conflict into his own innermost being, and suffering it in his heart, from the wilderness of temptation right through to the garden of Gethsemane.

As the reality of the divine election of love, Jesus Christ was the mercy of God incarnate who saw the disobedience of man as the greatest need of mankind, and who hastened to meet that need by pouring himself out in compassion and self-giving to man. And yet the more he entered into man to gather human life into oneness with God, the more intensely he took this conflict into his own heart. In him who takes our place like that, God's heart beats for humanity, but in him who so joined himself to us, 'touched with the feeling of our own infirmities'[9] and 'in all things made like unto his brethren',[10] it is the judge who came to condemn sin in the flesh. In the ultimate self-giving of God in love to man in Jesus Christ, man is confronted with the ultimate things, the last things before which all the secrets and intentions of the heart are revealed.[11] Here in Jesus, as the very heart of God is laid bare in compassion and mercy for man, the human heart is laid bare before God, in such a way that men and women are plucked out of their isolation and estrangement and alienation, out of their hiding place in themselves, and are placed before the light of the

---

9 Heb 4.15 KJV (able 'to sympathize with our weaknesses' RSV).

10 Heb 2.17 KJV.

11 Heb 4.12-13.

majesty and love of God where they must acknowledge the divine judgement upon them. 'If any man would come after me', Jesus said, 'let him deny himself, and follow me.'[12]

Here then, is one who steps into our place, who claims to displace us, and demands that we renounce ourselves for him. Here is a substitution where the guilty do not simply shelter behind the innocent, but such a substitution that the guilty are faced with the light, that men and women are dragged out of their self-imprisonment and brought face to face with God in his compassion and love, for it is God himself who steps into their place and takes their status upon himself. Man is not sheltered from God but exposed to him and bound to him as never before in a bond of forgiveness and reconciliation. It is through this substitution that election is achieved, so that election means that Christ died for all in being judged before God for all. How is that worked out in the incarnate life of the Son?

The judge and the judged

Jesus intervenes in man's state of enmity both as the beloved Son, and as the loving God, that is, both as the elect one and as the electing one, as the chosen man and as the choosing God. It is as such that he binds humanity to himself for ever, and yet he intervenes as the judge who comes to condemn sin in the flesh by his own holy life, and so to also hallow and sanctify human life for God. But in this very binding of himself to man, that is, in the actualisation of the covenant of God in our human flesh and existence, he bears his own judgement of man in the flesh and in his own human existence – and so election and substitution are one and the same act. The atoning and electing and incorporating act are one and the same act. The agony of Jesus – and how he was constrained until it was accomplished[13] – was that he was the judging God and the judged man at the same time, the electing God and the elected man at the same time, and in this unspeakable tension he remained absolutely faithful as the Son of God and Son of Man.

His was a steadfastness from both sides. On God's side, it is the steadfastness of love and grace even in judgement, of electing love even in condemning sin. It is the affirming and consummating love of union with men and women even in the fire of the divine wrath that consumes them. On the side of man as elected and beloved, it is the steadfastness of obedience to God, of calling upon God in prayer and

---

12 See Mark 8.34.

13 Luke 12.50.

trust, of confidence in his righteous will and utter and absolute reliance upon him. It is in the unity of this steadfastness, both divine and human, that there is at once the glorifying of God and the salvation of mankind. In this steadfastness, Satan and all the powers of evil are resisted and put to flight, defied and defeated, both by the God against whom they revolted and by man against whom they triumphed. It is in this steadfastness that the word of God is uttered in the incarnate life of the Lord Jesus, and the word of truth is uttered in which the answer of man is given in perfect correspondence to the word spoken. Together that word and answer represent the divine decision and election of love, and the human decision and appropriation of faith actualised in the historical life of the Son of Man from his birth to his resurrection, and to his exaltation at God's right hand.

In the face of this it is utterly inconceivable to us that anyone, man or woman, should finally reject the saving love of God incarnated in Jesus and enacted in his vicarious and substitutionary death on the cross – yet that is incomprehensibly what can and does take place – an utterly irrational event which we can only leave to the Lord God himself in his infinite mercy and judgement.

Having begun by considering the life and work of Jesus in the light of the unity of his person as mediator, we now move on to consider it in terms of his obedience and faithfulness to God, and then in terms of his love and faithfulness to man. We will begin with his faithfulness to God.

2 The life and faithfulness of the Son towards the Father

Here we are concerned with the descent of the Son of God into our alienated world, a world which has broken the covenant of God with his creation, shattered the communion it entailed between God and his creatures, and disowned the fatherly love and care of God over it. Into our disobedience and covenant-breaking life, into our disinherited existence, there descends God the Son in order to live out from within it a life of pure obedience, fulfilling the covenant will of God, and bringing humanity back from estrangement to communion with the Father. We have to think of all this not only in terms of passive obedience but of active obedience also, not only in terms of forensic and judicial righteousness and obedience, but in terms of positive communion and filial love, and of worship. Here we recall that the cult was an essential part of the Old Testament covenant, for it represented the will of God for communion between his creation and himself, a communion of gladness and praise, a communion of thankfulness and worship. God made the creation for such a communion that it might sing his praises, and reflect in gladness and joy his loving kindness and glory. Hence the restoration of creation involves the restoration of creation to communion and fellowship with him in which the peace of God reigns over all, and joy and gladness in God the Father fills the whole of creation. Thus in reconciliation and atonement, it is not only with obedience and justice that we have to do, but with the worship and adoration of creation, in which it faithfully reflects the Father's glory and love.

That is the way in which we are now to look at the incarnate life of the Son in the midst of our disordered, sin shattered, and divided world, for in it and out of it he lived a life which was an oblation of all obedience and praise, of all thankfulness and adoration, of all faithfulness and devotion, a life of perfect sonship on earth toward the heavenly Father. In that life-act of the historical Jesus, the Son of God so clothed himself with our humanity and so subdued it in himself that he converted it back from its resentment and rebellion to glad surrender to the holy will of God. He thus lifted humanity up in himself to communion with the Father, setting it again within the divine peace, drawing it within the divine holiness and placing it within the direction of the divine love. But that in itself is already the reconciling and sanctifying of humanity, and its restoration to fellowship with the Father, its redemption into the kingdom of God's grace. That is the saving significance of the human and historical life of Jesus the Son of God.

The Son's faithful restoration of the image of God in alienated humanity

Let us look at it in another way. Man was made in the image of God, created after God's image as male and female. That is God's eternal purpose for man, but with the fall of man that image was defaced and man became inhuman, turning the image of God into its opposite. Instead of reflecting the glory of God in a life of obedient thankfulness, man did the opposite and was given over to a reprobate mind. In that situation, God's creative purpose became a redemptive purpose: the image of God unto which men and women had been created became an eschatological goal. In the fulfilment of that creative and redemptive purpose God sent his only begotten Son into the world, that through him mankind might be restored to divine sonship, that is restored to the image of God. In the language of Paul, man was predestined to be conformed to the image of his Son.[14]

---

[14] Rom 8.29.

And so the Son came into our world, and was made in the likeness of man, in the likeness of the flesh of sin – that is, he took upon himself our image, and his visage was 'marred more than any man'.[15] The teaching of the New Testament stresses the poverty of Jesus, his humiliation, the fact that he became a 'nobody', the one who was ignored by people and who was 'despised and rejected of men'.[16] Cast out as not esteemed, he shared to the full our human life and existence in our lack of worth, in our want of all justification, in our unworthiness, even in our existence under the curse of God, as Paul says – all in order that he might restore mankind to the image of God, restore us before God as male and female in his image, the men and women who reflect God's glory and with whom God is well pleased, God's beloved sons and daughters. And that is precisely what Jesus in his human life on earth does. From beginning to end, he lives out within our perverted existence, and from within our perverted humanity that distorts the image of God, the true life of man created after God and actualised in real righteousness and holiness.[17] In other words, in all that he thought, willed and did, Jesus lived out among humanity a life of utter obedience and faithfulness to the creator and Father. As such he was the perfect image of God on earth, for in him the will of God was done on earth as it is done in heaven. He was the perfect man and as such the perfect reflection of the glory and grace of God. Therefore in him our humanity is restored to its perfection in communion with God, and in him God's word and will is perfectly reflected and directed toward man.

Now let us consider that incarnate life of the Son in three ways:
(a) in his life of utter dependence upon God in prayer,
(b) in his life of obedience in his Father's house, and therefore,
(c) as the perfect life, perfectly faithful to the divine will and word, and therefore perfectly reflecting the divine glory.

(a) Jesus' life of utter dependence upon the Father in prayer

This has to be seen from the perspective of the covenant which God has made with his creatures, and within humanity, in its special instance, with Israel. In this covenant, God has turned to humanity in such a way that he wills to be their God, wills them to be his dear

---

15 Isaiah 52.14 KJV: cf. RSV, 'his appearance was so marred, beyond human semblance'.

16 See Isaiah 53 here.

17 Eph 4.24.

children, and wills to have humanity stand and live before him as his human partner and friend. To this covenanted fellowship or partnership, prayer belongs as an essential element in man's existence as child of God, for men and women are called not only to hear the word of God but to answer it, not only to adore God but to call upon him, not only to obey God's summons but to summon God in prayer. It is an essential part of the covenant that God is a God who hears prayer, and that the creature is one who prays and makes petitions to God as a child to its father, and so realises its filial relation to its heavenly Father. That covenant prayer relationship belongs to the inner purpose and ground of creation. As we have seen, with the fall of mankind and the breach of the covenant in which mankind fell under the divine judgement, the covenant took on a special form as God's redemptive economy – and here the prayer of mediation or intercession occupies an essential place in the fulfilling of the saving covenant, in the offering of obedient sacrifice as well as in the prayer for divine succour and help.

(i) The fulfilling and sealing of the covenant through the redemptive prayer of Jesus

In the incarnation, in which the Son descends to fulfil the covenant from the side of man, as well as to fulfil, from the side of God, his will and purpose in the covenant for man, prayer becomes essentially *redemptive activity.*[18] It is in that light that we are to see the prayer life of Jesus. Here is prayer, not only in adoring God and hearing God, but prayer in calling upon him in utter reliance and dependence upon him, and in asking succour and strength from him – and as we shall see, it is also priestly prayer, intercession with God.

It is in our place that Jesus prays, standing where we stand in our rebellion and alienation, existing where we exist in our refusal of divine grace and in our will to be independent, to live our own life in self-reliance. In that condition, Jesus prays against the whole trend of our existence and against all the self-willed movement of our life, for when Jesus prays it means that he casts himself in utter reliance upon God the Father, in utter dependence upon his will, and refuses to draw a single breath except in that reliance and dependence. In this way, Jesus prays as a creature fulfilling the covenant prayer of creation to the Father, but he prays it from within our alienation and in battle against

---

18 See the comment on Calvin's exposition of 'the saving efficacy of the prayer-life of Jesus', T.F. Torrance, *The School of Faith* (London: James Clarke 1959), p. lxxxi.

our self-will. That is the prayer we are given to overhear: 'Not my will (that is, not the will of the alienated humanity which Jesus has made his own), but thy will be done.'[19] Thus he offers from out of our disobedience, a prayer of obedience. But such a prayer is his very mode of life as the Son of the Father on earth – it was prayer without ceasing, lived prayer, in which he ceaselessly sought from his Father in heaven his life and being as man on earth, in absolute reliance upon him at every point. And so by prayer in which word and life corresponded perfectly with one another, he offered again to the Father the steadfast answer of perfect filial obedience, and engaged the covenant will of God for his creatures.

Thus in Christ, the covenant is fulfilled, the will of God to be a Father to man, his alienated child, and fulfilled also, from within man's alienated life, a truly childlike and filial obedience in prayer and petition to the heavenly Father. In this prayer life of the historical Jesus, there is achieved from within our creation and in spite of its fall and constant downward drag away from God, a restoration to fellowship with God, and an engagement with God in the fulfilment of his covenant which becomes the binding together of God and man and man and God. Jesus prays and the Father answers his prayer, and from out of the midst of human corruption and weakness and sin, and even death, there is forged a new covenant relation of prayer between God and his creation, into which Jesus leads all who believe in him and share in his vicarious obedience to the Father. But that new relation of prayer and fellowship with the Father is forged in the teeth of all evil, and in the midst of our rejection, and it is answered and sealed by God's response in love and deed as well as in word. And since the whole life of Jesus is his prayer, acted out even in the midst of our death, the answer of God the Father is an answer in life and deed in the raising up of his beloved Son from death.

(ii) The attack by the powers of evil on the bond of prayer between Jesus and the Father

But now let us look at the prayer life of Jesus from a slightly different point of view, from the point of view of the attack upon it by all the powers of evil. In Jesus Christ the perfect communion between God and man was actualised, not only through the incarnation of the Word of God in this man, but through the obedient reliance of this man upon God the Father. In that double movement of God's faithful seeking and assuming of man back again into fellowship, and of man's faithful

---

19 See Luke 22.42; cf. Matt 26.39 and Mark 14.36.

return in Christ to God and complete dependence upon him, the holy and loving will of God for humanity was realised in the midst of its isolation and estrangement. The bond between God and man is recreated and actualised in the midst of our humanity in the very life lived by Jesus and signalised so fully by his life of prayer. Therefore all the powers of evil launched their attack upon Jesus; fearful temptations and assaults fell upon him, all in order to isolate him from God, to break the bond of fellowship between them, to snap the life of prayer and obedient clinging to the heavenly Father; to destroy the life of obedience to God's will and word, and so to make impossible any meeting between God and man in Jesus; to destroy the ground of reconciliation, to disrupt the foundation for atonement being laid in the obedient and prayerful life of the Son of Man.

Against all that fearful temptation in which all the hosts of darkness were mustered against him, Jesus resorted to prayer and unswervingly held fast to God the Father throughout it all. That holding fast to God in prayer, that battle against the powers of darkness doing their utmost to isolate him from God, and so to isolate man from God for ever, the fearful struggles of prayer with strong crying and tears, 'not my will but thine be done', all that belongs to the innermost heart of the reconciling and atoning life of Jesus reaching from the very beginning to the very end, and increasing in its unbelievable intensity right up to the cross. 'Father into thy hands I commend my spirit.'[20]

(iii) Christ's human prayer is the innermost heart of his atoning obedience to the Father and of his conversion of humanity to God

All through there was an utterly unbroken life of fellowship in unsullied confidence and trust in the Father, and unrelenting prayer, in which he not only repelled the assaults of darkness but so presented himself before the Father in worship and adoration that he made and perfected the positive self offering of man to God. It is here in Jesus Christ, in this worshipping and praying obedience of the creature to the heavenly Father, that all creation is turned and brought back to God the creator and Father almighty. That is the great *palingennesia*,[21] the great conversion of humanity to God, which receives its ultimate and eternal answer in the divine satisfaction and good pleasure when God the Father raised Jesus Christ from the dead, and for ever affirmed the reconciliation and restored fellowship effected in the obedient life

---

20 Luke 23.46 KJV.

21 Gk, 'rebirth'. See Matt 19.28 and Titus 3.5.

and death of his Son, thus placing it eternally beyond all the assaults of evil and all possibility of undoing. Thus the covenant will of God for fellowship with man was translated into eternal actuality.

Now if Christ's human prayer is an essential part of his atoning obedience offered to the Father, then it is not only the prayer of the victim but of the priest made on our behalf. Just by being what it was, his own life of petition and clinging dependence upon the Father was a life of intercession to God for us. In his steadfast obedience and life of prayer, Jesus penetrated into our life and recreated the bond between man and God, and therefore also between human beings. It is on that ground, of the recreated bond that he prays for us, intercedes for us, and acts as our mediator, high priest and intercessor, our substitute and representative before God, praying, and offering himself in prayer, standing in for us as our advocate, and pledging us in himself before God – and so he opens up through his flesh a new way to prayer and worship of God.

Or to put it the other way round, as Calvin does so frequently: Christ in his intercession joined to the shedding of his blood prayers that our sins might be pardoned. In and through his passion he bore our word in our name before the Father and prayed for us in our unclean life. Therefore he also puts his own prayer in our unclean mouth that there, on the ground of his obedience and prayer, we may pray with him, 'Our Father who art in heaven'. As a sign of the recreated bond of the covenant between man and God, and as a sign of the special redemptive form that the covenant will of God took in Israel, Jesus formed round him, as one body with himself, the disciples as the twelve pillars of the new covenant, and it was into their mouths that he put this prayer, 'Our Father which art in heaven', teaching them to pray in his name.

Jesus draws us into his own prayer

Then at last, as the prayer life of Jesus pressed towards its climax in Gethsemane he gathered the twelve disciples together at the last supper and formally and solemnly established with them the new covenant in his body and blood. At that supper he interceded for the disciples and for us who would believe on him through their word, and we are allowed to overhear his prayer in John 17. In that prayer, added to his vicarious passion set forth in the supper, he presented himself before the face of the Father and presented us to the Father as included in himself who had come just for this purpose to stand in our place. Then he went forth to Gethsemane and to the cross, where in high priestly intercession and sacrifice he fulfilled in deed and in death the prayer of his whole incarnate life, the prayer of obedience, 'Not my will, but thine be done,' and so was obedient unto the death of the cross. Therefore it is that when we in his name celebrate the supper, we also are given to have in our mouth his own prayer, and to pray in echo of his prayer in life and death and eternal intercession, 'Our Father who art in heaven', and in that prayer we engage in the fellowship of the new covenant as sons and daughters of the heavenly Father.

It is on the ground of this fulfilled covenant from within our alienated will, on the ground of the reconciliation it achieved, that Christ's victory becomes ours, his payment does away with our debt, his life enables us to be well pleasing to the Father. But it is also on the ground of this bond recreated in him that we are given to share in his prayer of covenant obedience, and share in the new covenant inaugurated and established in himself. It is in the name of Jesus, that is, it is in this prayer which Jesus lived out, in sacrifice and petition to the Father, that we are allowed to pray, and so engage in the fulfilled reality and all the fruits of the new covenant as God's dear children. That is what we do when we pray 'in the name of Jesus', but it is above all in the heart of the Lord's supper that we do that when we pray 'Our Father who art in heaven'.

(b) Jesus' life of obedience in his Father's house

(i) From birth to death the Son's whole life of redeeming obedience

The little glimpse we have of the life of Jesus at the age of twelve is all important for our understanding of the gospel.[22] At that point, as Jesus steps into adult responsibility as far as his relations with God are concerned, that is, so far as he now takes the confession of God the Father upon his own lips, and lives in his own faith and dependence upon the Father, we have a revelation of what he is sent to do and be. He is found in his Father's house, about his Father's business, and yet, Son of God though he was, he remained in subjection as a son to his earthly parents, and through his earthly subjection and earthly obedience to Joseph and Mary he lived the life of the Son of God become Son of Man, thus making *humanity* itself the house of God the Father. In other words, in Jesus Christ the Son of God descended into our 'house of bondage', and by living out in it a life of perfect obedience to the Father he restored it as the house of God the Father. It was not by being a father that he restored the Father's house or revealed the Father, but by being a son, and by restoring true sonship to our humanity in his own perfect filial life. Thus into our house of bondage, Jesus brought

---

[22] Luke 2.41-52.

the freedom of God's sons and daughters through living a life that broke through the bondage and slavery of our sin into the liberty of a sinless humanity rejoicing in the love and faithfulness of God the Father.

But in so doing, through his obedience as a Son within our disobedience, he brought the fatherhood of God in all his holy love to bear upon every aspect of our human life, the fatherhood of God who chastises his beloved Son, and the fatherhood of God who is well pleased with his obedience. The house of humanity is a house of bondage not only because of its estrangement from God but because of the judgement of the Father upon it. Yet in that house of bondage under judgement Jesus lived the life of perfect sonship. He submitted gladly to the Father's judgement and offered a son's love and devotion to him, so that through the sacrificial obedience of his own life he redeemed the house of humanity from its bondage under judgement and made it again the house of God where God dwells, and where man offers a life of praise and thanksgiving for his unspeakable goodness. Just as a son of great promise who is born into a bankrupt house, may through his life and work redeem it from debt and mortgage and entirely restore its fortunes, so Jesus, the Son of God's love, has been born into our bankrupt humanity, in order through his life and work to redeem it from debt and mortgage in judgement and death, and restore it as a habitation of God filled with the riches of his grace and glory.

When we translate the house of the Father with the expression the 'kingdom of God' or the 'kingdom of heaven', we see immediately how much of Jesus' life and teaching is concerned directly with this life of the obedient Son restoring man to the Father's house. In his own parables, Jesus varies the expressions of householder and king, household and kingdom as exact equivalents. It is as Father that God wishes to reign over mankind, and it as the Son of the Father that Jesus is the heir and the king of the kingdom. His coming as the Son is therefore the coming of the kingdom, and his life and teaching means the bringing of the kingdom of God's holy will to bear upon the whole of our disordered, chaotic life in the world, in order that it may all be brought back to the peace and grace, the guidance and loving care, of the heavenly Father, and so be restored to its true and sanctified end in God's purpose of creation. All that is remarkably expressed in the opening of the Lord's prayer, 'Our Father who art in heaven, hallowed be thy name, thy kingdom come, thy will be done on earth as it is in heaven.' Christ's life of obedience is a hallowing of the Father's name and a fulfilling of his will on earth as it is in heaven, and that is the coming of God's kingdom, and also the redemption of mankind as the second half of the Lord's prayer makes clear, all to the eternal glory of God.

(ii) The last Adam undoing the disobedience of the first Adam

The life and faithfulness of Jesus as the Son is twofold and yet one single life of obedience. He has come to live out in our inhumanity the life of true humanity, in the midst of our disobedience a life of obedience, and so to live the perfect life in communion with the perfect God. 'You must be perfect, as your heavenly Father is perfect,'[23] said Jesus, recalling God's word to Abraham, 'I am the almighty God; walk before me, and be perfect.'[24] In the sheer perfection of his humanity, in all its absolute purity and sinlessness, he offered the amen of truth from within our humanity to the word and will of God's eternal truth. In that perfection of his human life, he was the last Adam undoing the sin of the first Adam. Standing in the place of Adam and all mankind, he stood in the gap created by man's rebellion and reconciled men and women to God by living the very life he lived in the perfection of obedience. But he was also perfect in the fulfilment of the *mission* on which he had been sent by the Father, so that the whole life of Jesus was his glad assent to the will of the Father in sending him as his beloved Son to be the saviour of the world.

He was sent by the Father to live the life of sonship among mankind, but to live it not simply as Son of God but as Son of God become *man*, as Son of Man, that is to live it out from beginning to end within the limitations of our creaturely humanity, and within the limitations of our humanity in the house of bondage. For Jesus, therefore, the life of the perfect and true man in the midst of our sinful humanity was the life of man in perfect and absolute fidelity to his vocation as Son of Man. Because those are both one obedience, he lived out his life of sonship among sinners, learning obedience in steadfastness to God's word and will, and in fulfilment of his Father's will bringing his relation with sinners to its perfection and completion in the sacrificial oblation of his own life in the weakness and obedience of the cross. His obedience as true man and perfect son took the form of obedience in which he laid aside his glory in order that within our frailty and weakness, where we are assaulted by all the attacks and temptations of the evil one, he might perfectly fulfil the Father's will of love and holiness.

The baptism into repentance – the temptation not to be man

That is what we see taking place in Jesus' baptism at the hands of John, as he is baptised among sinners with the baptism into

---

23 Matt 5.48.

24 Gen 17.1 KJV.

repentance,[25] fulfilling righteousness in their midst,[26] and then is immediately driven by the Spirit into the wilderness. There he fasted forty days and nights in fulfilment of the baptism unto repentance within which he set himself to offer in our place contrition for our sin, acceptance of the divine verdict upon our guilt, and a holy life in amendment of ours – but all that had to be worked out within our condition, within our weakness and frailty, within our house of bondage – and so though acknowledged by the Father as his beloved Son at baptism, he lived only as the Son of Man. With what force the temptations came as he exposed himself to our weakness and frailty after forty days of fasting, temptations to live after all as Son of God, and not as a Son of Man in all the weakness and frailty of humanity. 'If you are the Son of God, command these stones to become loaves of bread.'[27]

And so with one temptation after another, the devil assaulted him with the temptation simply to be what he was, and to live the life of who he was, the mighty omnipotent Son of God. But Jesus had been sent to live the life of man within man's bondage and under man's judgement, and he chose that way with unswerving fidelity to his divine mission. But in choosing that way he chose the cross with all its weakness under the assaults of evil and under the holy judgement of the Father upon our sin. For him to be true and perfect man meant to be this man whose visage was marred more than any man's, but who under all the assaults of evil lived as a faithful son calling upon his Father. Under all the judgement and chastisements of the divine wrath against our sin, he lived a life of unfaltering trust and confidence in the love of the Father. That was a life which hallowed the name of God the Father and fulfilled his will on earth as it is in heaven. That was the life of the beloved Son in which God the Father is well pleased.

(iii) Jesus as man is the perfect believer, receiving the Spirit in his humanity for us all[28]

But we must also see that in this life, Jesus achieved from within our estrangement a life of perfect and unbroken fellowship with the Father in which his whole life not only corresponded in the amen of truth to the Father's will, but in which he offered in our name a life of perfect faith and confidence and trust and love and thanksgiving and praise.

---

25 Matt 3.11 KJV, 'I baptize you with water unto repentance, *eis metanoian.*'

26 Matt 3.15.

27 Matt 4.3; Luke 4.3.

28 Cf. T.F. Torrance, *The School of Faith*, pp. cvi-cix.

We have seen the significance of his prayer life for that, but now we have to note that he lived the life of the perfect believer, who believed for us, who yielded to God's faithfulness the perfect response of trust and faith, and who brought to God his Father the perfect response of thankful reception and appropriation. It was for our sakes and in our place that Jesus lived that vicarious life in utter reliance upon God and in laying hold upon his mercy and goodness. Ninety percent of all that Jesus taught about prayer was concerned with petitionary prayer, the prayer of the child asking gifts of its Father.[29] But he was himself that child asking and receiving, seeking and finding, and knocking to find the door of heaven opened to him. It was not for himself that he did that, for what did he the Son of God need that he did not have? It was for ourselves that he lived that life of trust and faith in the Father's goodness, of believing and appropriating the Father's bounty, that in him our humanity might receive that which we blindly ask, find that which we unwittingly seek, and have opened to us the door of salvation beyond all our expectation.

In other words, by his perfect obedience, his response of faith to the Father, his life as the beloved Son of God among sinners, he opened the kingdom of heaven to all believers. That we see also immediately at his baptism, when he set out upon his mission as the obedient servant Son, acknowledged by the Father in heaven as his beloved Son, for it was then that the heavens were opened and God sent down his Spirit upon his incarnate Son. It was not that he needed that Spirit for he was already born of the Spirit. He was already the Son of God in perfect communion with the Father and the Spirit, and had been from all eternity, but now as the incarnate Son he received the anointing of the Spirit upon our humanity which he wore, so that upon him and through him the doors of heaven are opened and the divine blessings are poured out. Therefore God has given all things into the hands of his beloved Son, for God has given him the Spirit without measure.

The counterpart to that mighty act of salvation in the baptism of Jesus, as he ascended out of the waters of the vicarious baptism unto repentance, was his mighty act of salvation when he ascended out of the waters of death, and so opened the kingdom of heaven for us and our salvation that God the Father poured out his Spirit upon the church at Pentecost. Indeed God has poured it out now upon all flesh, for once and for all the Spirit has been poured out for all who come to the Father through the Son, that they with the Son may enter into the Father's house, and live as sons and daughters crying through his Spirit

---

[29] Luke 11.5-13; cf. Matt 7.7-11; 18.19; 21.22; Mark 11.24; Luke 18.1-8.

like him 'Abba Father'.[30] Hearing like him, the blessed words of the Father, 'Thou art my beloved Son; with thee I am well pleased',[31] men and women partake of his sonship and become God's beloved children. Such then was the saving obedience of the Son of Man who had turned our wayward humanity back to God, remade it as his Father's house and brought down upon it all the riches of divine grace and glory. It was in himself that he the Son accomplished that, but he did that for us, and so of his fullness have we all received.

(c) Jesus' life of perfect faithfulness to the divine word, and perfect reflection of the divine glory

Through the incarnation of the Son, the eternal relation of the Son to the Father and of the Father to the Son was inserted into and grounded in our humanity, while through the entire life of the incarnate Son it was translated into our sphere of historical existence and actuality on earth. He who was God and man in one person acted from the side of God in the faithfulness of the divine truth and love, and acted from the side of humanity in the faithfulness of a life wholly obedient to the Father. In that unity of the divine-human faithfulness, Jesus Christ was not only the complete embodiment of the faithfulness of God the Father toward humanity but the complete embodiment of the faithfulness of the Son as Man toward the Father. It was as such and only as such, in the entire solidarity between the Father and the incarnate Son and the incarnate Son and the Father, that Jesus Christ stepped forth as the divine-human mediator. As such, he was at once the complete revelation of God to man and the perfect correspondence on man's part to that revelation. He was at once the fulfilled act of reconciliation on the part of God toward man, but he was also the fulfilled appropriation of that reconciliation on the part of man toward God. In that whole movement, *the human obedience of Jesus was not simply an instrumental but an integral and essential part of that divine revelation and reconciliation.*[32] Thus in living out to the full in our humanity the relation of the Son to the Father, and therefore in bringing the Father into direct and immediate relation with the whole of our human life, Jesus Christ was the perfect man perfectly reflecting the glory of God, but as such and precisely as such, the whole course of Christ's perfect human life on earth was identical with the whole course of the Father's action toward mankind.

---

[30] Rom 8.15-16; Gal 4.6.

[31] Mark 1.11; Luke 3.22.

[32] Cf. T.F. Torrance, *The School of Faith*, pp. lxxx-lxxxiv.

Jesus' whole human life reposes in the Father and is the very revelation of the Father

In other words, because the human life of Jesus was in entire agreement with the mind and will of the Father, the man Jesus was the image and reflection of God himself, but more than that, he *was* the very God he imaged and reflected in his human life. Jesus is identical with the revelation of God the Father. Again, because the human life and work of Jesus was in entire agreement with the life and work of the Father, the human activity of Jesus exhibited a perfect parallelism to the saving activity of God himself, but more than that, his activity on earth *was itself* the saving activity of God at work among men and women. 'I and the Father are one,'[33] said Jesus, 'My Father is working still, and I am working.'[34]

This fact is one that all the Gospels are concerned to show, but none more fully than the fourth Gospel, from which these two *logia* or sayings of Jesus are taken. We may state the point in two ways, corresponding more or less to the two emphases in the fourth Gospel and in the synoptic Gospels.

On the one hand, we may put it this way, by saying that the perfect human life of Jesus in all his words and acts reposes entirely upon the mutual relation of the Son to the Father and the Father to the Son. That is the significance, for example, of such a juxtaposition of thought as we have in verses like these, 'I am the good shepherd; I know my own and my own know me, as the Father knows me and I know the Father; and I lay down my life for the sheep.'[35] The act of Jesus in laying down his life is grounded upon the entire solidarity and mutuality between the Father and the Son, so that all that he does in his human life is identical with the act of God himself, but also so that nothing is done in his human life except what issues out of the love of the Father for the Son and the Son for the Father. The fourth Gospel lays the strongest emphasis upon the flesh of Jesus, and the perfection of his actual life in the flesh, but behind that stands the closed circle of the intimate and private relation of loving and knowing, of speaking and doing, that exists between the Son and the Father. It is because of that relation that the perfect human life of Jesus on earth is identical with the saving truth and love of God the Father.

---

[33] John 10.30.

[34] John 5.17.

[35] John 10.14-15.

On the other hand, we can put it another way, recalling especially words of Jesus recorded by Matthew, 'All things have been delivered to me by my Father; and no man knows the Son except the Father, and no one knows the Father except the Son and any one to whom the Son chooses to reveal him.'[36] The relation between the Father and the Son, and the Son and the Father is a closed relation, but entry into it is given through the incarnation of the Son, for in the perfect human life of Jesus the love and truth of God are addressed to man in the concrete form of a historical relationship of man to fellow man, of this man to others. The faithfulness and salvation of God are actualised within mankind in the concrete form of a human life in relation to other human lives. Before the perfect human life of Jesus, in his historical words and acts, men and women are confronted with the effective and active revelation and reconciliation of God the Father.

The majesty and authority of God in Jesus

The human life of Jesus on earth is the concrete embodiment of the revelation and reconciliation of God, the actual place on earth and in history, the one man, where God and man meet. In this man, this *new man*, God the Creator and Father, God the Judge and Saviour, is face to face with man. In this new man, mankind is placed, whether they will or no, face to face with the saving majesty and power of the living God. That is why, when we turn over the pages of the Gospels, especially the synoptic Gospels, we find that again and again the words used to describe the reaction of men and women to this man are the words that are used to describe an earthquake *ethaumazon, ethambēthēsan, exeplēssonto, ephobēthēsan,* etc. The very presence of Jesus, his very existence in the midst, the historical and human encounter his life itself afforded, struck men and women with amazement, astonishment, wonder, awe, fear. Here was a human life unlike all other human lives in its relation to them, for here they were confronted in what was undoubtedly human and historical, with something ultimate and final; they were face to face with the majesty and *exousia* or authority of God in a man on earth. His very existence among mankind, as we shall see, created upheaval and judgement, for it confronted them with the last things, the *eschata,* and turned them inside out. But at this point what we are concerned to see is that the perfection of the human life of Jesus at which men and women were so thunderstruck, reposed entirely upon the fulfilling, within the conditions and limitations of our humanity on earth,

---

[36] Matt 11.27.

of the mutual relation and fellowship of the Father and the Son. His human life was itself identical with God's final act of revelation and reconciliation. The embodiment of that relation of the Son to the Father in a perfect human life on earth was, therefore, a fact of volcanic significance for salvation and judgement, for revelation and reconciliation.

We have considered, then, the life and faithfulness of the incarnate Son toward the Father. Now we consider the same fact toward man.

3 The life and faithfulness of the Son toward man

As we turn to consider the life and faithfulness of the Son toward man, we cannot leave behind for a single moment what we have just been considering, for here all that Jesus Christ was as the Son toward the Father is turned out toward man, so that his relation to mankind is identical with the relation of the Father toward them, or to put it otherwise, in the turning of Jesus toward men and women, it is God himself who turns to them in revelation and reconciliation.

We have already seen that the Son is sent on his mission by the Father as his servant, the Son learning obedience as a servant, in order to fulfil his mission. But what *form* does that service or ministry take? How is the human life of Jesus employed in this mission of revelation and reconciliation? The New Testament employs many images to speak of this, but there are two outstanding ones found on the lips of Jesus himself which we shall use to describe his life and work toward man, that of 'shepherd' and 'king'. They are not separable, but clearly they employ different emphases, and together they give us a full account of his saving life and work toward mankind.

(a) Jesus the shepherd of the sheep

Here we may take as our primary text, the evangelists' record of Jesus' compassionate feeling for the lost multitudes. 'As he landed he saw a great throng, and he *had compassion* on them, because they were like sheep without a shepherd; and he began to teach them many things.'[37] In the Markan narrative, that is followed by the feeding of the five thousand which is clearly regarded as a great act of messianic shepherding or feeding the flock of God. In Matthew, the context is somewhat different, but equally significant. 'When he saw the crowds, he *had compassion* for them, because they were harassed and helpless, like

---

[37] Mark 6.34.

sheep without a shepherd.'[38] That is in the context of Jesus' preaching and teaching in the synagogues and of his healing the sick and casting out devils, and then of his appointment of the disciples to act as under-shepherds of the flock in preaching and healing. Along with those passages, we have to take the great parables of the shepherd and the sheep in the Synoptics and in the fourth Gospel,[39] parables which refer to his seeking and saving the lost sheep, shepherding them in the fold through calling them by name, laying down his life for them, and parables also of the final judgement in the dividing of the sheep from the goats.[40] All these, together with many other sayings on the same general theme, make it clear that this was one of the major ways in which Jesus regarded his own ministry to lost and damned humanity.

(i) The shepherd-kingship of Yahweh and the promise of the messianic shepherd

Behind this of course lies the Old Testament concept of the shepherd king applied to *Yahweh* in his relation to Israel, and the promise of the messianic shepherd when God will set up his servant David over the forsaken and oppressed sheep of his people. The Psalms are full of this concept but also the prophets, and several of the prophetic passages are clearly in the mind of Jesus and the evangelists, especially Ezekiel 13 and 34; Jeremiah 23 and 31; Isaiah 40; Micah 4 and 5; Zephaniah 3 and Zechariah 10 – 13. In these passages we find the divine judgement spoken against the false shepherds who do not feed the flock and are no shepherds, and who reject the true shepherds. We also find the picture of the true shepherd whom God will raise up to gather his sheep together as a whole and individually, giving great care to the hurt and weak, and the young and the lost. We see also a picture of the sheep scattered because there is no true shepherd, so that they become a prey to the beasts of the field; and then we see the picture also of a future shepherd whose life will be violently taken away, for the shepherd and the sheep will be smitten and many will perish, though a remnant will be saved by the word of the Lord. All that is undoubtedly in our Lord's mind, and the evangelists see it clearly and draw it out, for example in Matthew's emphasis upon the thirty pieces of silver for which Judas betrayed Jesus,[41] and which has reference to the betrayal and rejection of the good shepherd in Zechariah 11.

---

[38] Matt 9.36.

[39] Luke 15.1-7; Matt 18.12-14; John 10.1-16.

[40] Matt 25.31-46.

[41] Matt 26.14-16: cf. 27.3-10.

That is how Jesus regarded his life and faithfulness toward mankind, as the shepherd of the sheep, the shepherd who calls his sheep by name and leads them into the fold of salvation, the shepherd who does not run away when the wolf comes, and who lays down his life for the sheep. As such, Jesus looks upon the multitudes of men and women as the disinherited and lost, and he pours out his life in compassionate service for them, standing in the gap where there is no shepherd, and taking their hurt and their troubles to himself. He lays all their guilt and need upon himself, bearing it in his mercy, shepherding the flock in spite of all that they do to him, even when they turn round and smite the shepherd and cry 'crucify him, crucify him'. He lays down his life for the sheep, suffering in their place in order to save them and shepherd them at last into the fold of salvation. In spite of all that they did to him, the good shepherd did not reject the sheep or despise them, but sought in utter compassion and mercy to win them, to feed them with the bread of life, and to call each by name, spending himself to the utmost even for the hundredth that was lost until he found it.

That is the general picture of Jesus' saving ministry toward the lost and needy multitudes, but it is most clearly represented by his special attention to what he called the lost sheep of the house of Israel, the disinherited, and excommunicated publicans and sinners, who were excluded from the synagogues and the temple, and debarred from the communion and worship of God's people. Jesus deliberately associated himself with them, breaking down the barriers erected against them, deliberately eating and drinking with them, and enacting dramatic parables of the great messianic meal[42] which he spoke about in his teaching when the children would come from the east and the west and sit down with Abraham, Isaac and Jacob in the kingdom of God.[43] This brought upon him the wrath and resentment of the rulers (the false shepherds of Israel) but Jesus, in breaking down the wall of partition, sought the outcast beyond the boundaries of communion,[44] and by his unprejudiced communion with them sought to reintegrate the lost with the people of God. Such, for example, were Matthew and Zacchaeus and Mary Magdalene, drawn out of disinherited and excommunicated existence right into the inner fellowship of the messianic community; they were the lost sheep who heard the voice of the good shepherd and followed him.[45]

---

[42] Matt 22.1f; Luke 14.16f.

[43] Luke 13.28-29; cf. Matt 8.11-12.

[44] Cf. Eph 2.14; Luke 14.23; Matt 22.9-10.

[45] John 10.3-4; cf. Matt 9.9-13; Luke 19.1-10; Luke 8.2; Matt 27.55ff.

(ii) The compassion of God in Jesus

Now let us try to penetrate more deeply into what Jesus did as a shepherd, for it is then that we shall really understand his life and faithfulness as the Son sent by the Father to shepherd the lost sheep of mankind and gather them into the fellowship and life of God. We return to the words of Mark and Matthew describing the fact that when Jesus looked out upon the multitudes he had *compassion* on them for they were faint and scattered as sheep without a shepherd. The word translated 'had compassion' is one of the most pregnant and profound in the whole of the New Testament – *esplagchnisthē.*[46] The Hebrew word for mercy or compassion is *rahamim*, the plural for 'womb'. God's mercy or compassion is described in terms of the compassion of a mother for her unborn or newly born baby. Hence compassion is a good translation for the feeling which a mother has for her baby for they are both within one body or of one body. The nearest expression in Greek to the Hebrew is the word *splagchnizesthai* coming from *splagchna* meaning viscera. A clear instance of its meaning is to be seen in Luke from the prophecy of Zechariah, the father of John the Baptist, 'for you will go before the Lord to prepare his ways, to give knowledge of salvation to his people in the forgiveness of their sins, through the tender mercy of our God (*dia splagchna eleous theou hēmōn*)'.[47] Literally that means 'the bowels of the mercy of God', which is as good a rendering of the Hebrew *rahamim* as you could get.

The first thing to note here is that divine mercy and compassion are specifically attributed to Jesus in his relation to the multitudes: that is, his compassionate relation to the lost sheep of humanity is identically the same as God's and is identical with God's. When Jesus pours out his heart in compassion upon mankind, that is nothing else than God's own act of love and mercy. Thus the teaching and preaching, the healing of the sick and the driving out of the demons, the feeding of the multitudes,[48] are all acts of the pure compassion of God himself. In and through them all God is pouring himself out upon men and women. What Jesus does then is described by this word, *splagchnizesthai*. He has made himself one body with sinners and feels for them as a mother toward her unborn baby, and he pours himself out in love for them; his whole inner self is poured out for men and women in their weakness and need and sin. That is what is meant here.

---

[46] Mark 6.34; Matt 9.36, cf. 14.14.

[47] Luke 1.76-78.

[48] Mark 8.2f; Matt 15.32f.

The sympathy of the shepherd priest

In order to fill out that account of Jesus' shepherdly compassion let us turn to a similar account given in the epistle to the Hebrews where the image of the shepherd is replaced by that of the high priest (allied to the shepherd in the Old Testament tradition): 'For we have not a high priest who is unable to sympathise with our weaknesses (*sympathēsai tais astheneiais hēmōn*), but who in every respect has been tempted as we are, yet without sinning.'[49] 'In the days of his flesh, Jesus offered up prayers and supplications, with loud cries and tears, to him who was able to save him from death, and he was heard for his godly fear. Although he was a Son, he learned obedience through what he suffered; and being made perfect became the source of eternal salvation to all who obey him, being designated by God a high priest after the order of Melchizedek.'[50] Behind this lies the idea of the high priest in the Old Testament liturgy who bore on his shoulders and breast the names of the twelve tribes of Israel,[51] who had them written on his heart, as he entered within the veil of the holy of holies with the blood of sacrifice in order to intercede for them. As such he bore the iniquities of Israel before God, as Leviticus puts it, a concept that is applied to the suffering servant in Isaiah 53 and applied from there to Jesus himself in the New Testament. Of course Jesus' high priesthood was not a temporary measure like Aaron's, nor was it in symbol or ceremony that he fulfilled his liturgy. He fulfilled it in his very existence and flesh. In him we have the divine mercy or compassion translated into flesh and blood in our midst. The term the epistle to the Hebrews used here is *sympathēsai*, sym-pathy, com-passion, feeling-with. It is another term, but essentially the same idea is conveyed, for Jesus is spoken of as gathering up our weakness and sins upon himself and bearing them before God in compassion and sympathy and solidarity with us sinners.

Now let us return to the *splagchnizesthai* of the Gospels – that does not simply describe the emotions of Jesus; it describes his act, the act in which the whole person and existence and life of Jesus is involved. In him the divine mercy and love has become bone of our bone and flesh of our flesh. Here at last in Jesus, the divine *rahamim* has become actual fact, not metaphor but literal fact in our flesh and blood. In Jesus Christ, God has bound himself with our flesh, and as such, one body with us, he penetrates into our weakness and need with his

---

49 Heb 4.15.

50 Heb 5.7-10.

51 Exod 28.1-30.

indescribable compassion. In this way, as the epistle to the Hebrews puts it, Jesus learned how to be our high priest, by the things he suffered as flesh of our flesh and bone of our bone, in sheer sym-pathy and com-passion. That sympathy and compassion reached their utmost fulfilment on the cross where he poured out his very lifeblood in compassion and love for the sheep, but long before the cross, in all his relations with sinners, that active sympathy in dynamic intervening compassion was operative among men and women. In it he stooped to shoulder our weakness, *astheneia,* and to bear it as our high priest, as our shepherd priest before God, so that by his stripes we are healed.[52] The term *astheneia* on the pages of the New Testament is a profound term speaking of disease of the body and of the soul, and so his compassion met the double need of the sick and the sinful.

The cost and anguish of Jesus' compassion

We must now take a step further. This act of compassion in which Jesus became one body with us, poured himself out in love, and took upon himself our iniquities and diseases was *an awful act,* which he could only undertake 'with strong crying and tears', as the epistle to the Hebrews puts it.[53] That was evident in the way in which Jesus *groaned in agony* as he forgave and healed. It cost him infinite anguish. It was only by that kind of *splagchnizesthai* that he could heal and forgive, by bearing the awful burden of our *astheneia* upon himself.

Let us glance at some of these passages for they reveal just how Jesus fulfilled his daily ministry toward people. 'And Jesus moved with compassion, stretched out his hand and touched him and said, "I will, be clean". And as soon as he had spoken, the leprosy left him and he was cleansed. And he at once charged him with groans (*embrimēsamenos*) not to say anything about it, and sent him away.'[54] The same term is used of Jesus at the grave of Lazarus where it is said that 'he groaned (*enebrimēsato*) in the spirit, and was troubled', and then 'again groaning (*embrimōmenos*) in himself he came to the grave' – where quite clearly much more than ordinary grief is meant.[55] The Gospels also use another word, *stenazein,* to speak of the same thing, as in Mark, 'and looking up to heaven, Jesus groaned, and said to him, "*Eph-phatha*", that is, "Be opened." And at once his ears were opened, his tongue was

---

[52] Matt 8.17, 'He took our infirmities, *astheneias,* and bore our diseases.'

[53] Heb 5.7 KJV.

[54] Mark 1.40f. (Torrance translation — cf. KJV/RSV).

[55] John 11.33,38 KJV.

released, and he spoke plainly. And he charged them to tell no one'.[56] Again Jesus insisted that what they saw and heard in his groaning and healing was unspeakable. What is this that the disciples are not to speak about? In the ninth chapter of Mark it becomes clear, after the transfiguration. There, as Jesus prayed and discussed with Moses and Elijah the departure[57] he would accomplish at Jerusalem, he was transfigured and the disciples were stricken with fear. Afterwards Jesus charged the disciples to say nothing about it – they had been given to see into his unspeakable mystery, of which they had already had an inkling in his anguish of spirit as he healed diseases and forgave sins: it was the secret of the cross in his heart. It was with that secret in his heart that Jesus descended from the mount of transfiguration to heal the demoniac child in awesome circumstances, in which the Evangelists see adumbrations of the passion.

That then is the Jesus we see all through the years of his ministry as he seeks and saves the lost, heals those who are sick, and shepherds the sheep into the fold of salvation. That is the Jesus who says, 'Come to me, all who labour and are heavy-laden, and I will give you rest. Take my yoke upon you, and learn from me; for I am gentle and lowly in heart, and you will find rest for your souls.'[58] In other words, Jesus seeks to be yoked together with people in their awful burdens of sin and guilt that he may bear them. In the language of the fourth Gospel, he goes forth from his baptism as the lamb of God to bear and bear away the sins of the world.[59]

(iii) The role of the Spirit in the compassionate ministry of Jesus

There is still another line of New Testament teaching we must look at and bring to throw light upon the compassionate ministry of Jesus. We recall that Jesus was born of the Spirit in our flesh of sin, baptised by the Spirit in the waters of baptism among sinners, and anointed by the Spirit to preach the gospel of good tidings, to bind up the broken hearted, etc. Through the eternal Spirit he offered himself without spot to the Father,[60] and according to the Spirit of holiness he was raised from the dead.[61] That is the Spirit which Christ poured out upon the

---

56 Mark 7.34f. Where the RSV has 'sighed', Torrance has translated *estenaxen* as 'groaned'.

57 Gk, *exodon*, exodus, Luke 9.31.

58 Matt 11.28-29.

59 John 1.29f.

60 Heb 9.14.

church at Pentecost making it one body with himself. But that is the Spirit in which Jesus emitted his cries of anguish as he healed the sick and groaned as he raised Lazarus from the dead, for it was already an offering of himself through the Spirit in atonement for Lazarus – it was only in anticipation of Calvary that Jesus wrought those miracles, in which he healed the sick, drove out demons, forgave sins and raised the dead. All through his life and ministry, from the baptism to the cross, he was at work in holy atonement, bearing the sins of the world on his spirit, and through the Spirit offering himself in sacrifice to God: that is forgiving and healing only as he bowed himself to receive the just judgement upon our human sin and guilt, the just for the unjust. In this way we see that the whole of his life was an atoning sacrifice, although it is on the cross that at last all the sin of humanity is finally laid upon him, and there that through the eternal Spirit he offered himself once and for all in complete and final expiation for the sin of mankind.

The Spirit echoes the intercession of Christ[62]

In line with this we must look at another passage, this time from St Paul, 'Likewise the Spirit helps us in our weakness, for we do not know what to pray for as we ought; but the Spirit makes intercession for us with groanings that cannot be uttered. And he that searches the hearts knows what is the mind of the Spirit, because he makes intercession for the saints according to the will of God.'[63] That is the Spirit of Jesus Christ in which he was born, and baptised, in which he groaned in unspeakable fashion in his work of salvation, the Spirit in which he prayed with strong crying and tears in his flesh, the Spirit through whom he offered himself without spot to the Father. That Spirit of intercession and agony, who echoes the intercession of Christ, is poured out upon his church so that the church becoming one body with Christ is given to echo in its prayers the intercession of Christ himself. Let us note too that in this passage the Spirit is said to bear our weakness or infirmity (*astheneia*), taking it upon himself, and to intercede or intervene (*hyperentugchanei*) with unspeakable groans (*stenagmois*), in language that reminds us of Mark.[64] In Romans,[65] the same term (*entugchanei*) is used of Jesus' intercession at the right hand of the Father,

---

61 Rom 1.4.

62 Cf. T.F. Torrance, *The School of Faith*, pp. ciii-civ.

63 Rom 8.26-27. The quote is a combination of the KJV and the RSV.

64 Mark 7.34 (*estenaxen*).

65 Rom 8.34.

the same word as used of the heavenly intercession of Christ our high priest in Hebrews.[66]

Here we have clearly a common tradition in the church going back to the first witnesses of Jesus' own life and ministry on earth. We are justified therefore in using this to help us understand what happened in Jesus' earthly ministry not only on the cross, but before it in his ministry of healing and forgiving when he interpenetrated the lives of others to bear their burdens on himself. But the same language as used of the ministry of Jesus on earth is also used of the heavenly Christ who ever lives to intercede for us, not that he now cries with strong crying and tears as in the days of his flesh, but that he who eternally stands in for us as our advocate and intercessor has poured out upon us his Spirit. It is that Spirit who continues to echo in our stammering prayers on earth the compassionate intercession, the sympathetic intervention of Christ when he came to shoulder the whole burden of our sin, and bear it upon his own heart before God that we might be forgiven and healed. Therefore we are also justified in looking back to this ministry of Christ before the cross to provide us with our understanding of how even now (*mutatis mutandis*)[67] he ever lives to intercede for us, bearing upon his own heart before God all our needs and burdens.

The perfecting and completion of Christ's incarnational solidarity with sinners

We sum up this consideration of Christ's compassionate ministry as the shepherd priest by saying that he came to enter into complete solidarity with sinners in order to redeem them by taking their burdens upon himself. That is what the epistle to the Hebrews describes by the words which speak of Christ as made perfect through suffering and so qualified to be our high priest and the author of our salvation. The 'making perfect'[68] refers to his ordeal of consecration when before the cross he entered more and more into compassionate and sympathetic solidarity with lost and guilty sinners, bringing his relation of solidarity with them to its purposed end or completion on the cross. 'Making perfect' does not mean some process of moral perfecting in Jesus, but the completing or perfecting of a process into which he solemnly

---

66 Heb 7.25.

67 Lat, 'given the changes', or 'allowing for the differences', literally 'the things that need to be changed having been changed'.

68 Heb 2.10.

entered at his baptismal consecration and which continued in his relations with those he came to save. That he learned obedience does not mean his act of perfecting obedience to the Father so far as he himself was concerned, but his entering more and more fully into the actual practice and experience of what his obedience was as Son of God among sinners until his obedience was crowned in his suffering and death on the cross. Then he became at once the author and perfecter of faith[69] – that is, he carried through to its very end the whole course of faith, his life of faithfulness toward God and his life of faithfulness toward man. Thus the whole movement of entering into solidarity with sinners, and his obedience within that to the Father, reached its end or completion on the cross.

(b) Jesus the king of the kingdom

All the Gospels bear the strongest witness to the fact that with the presence of Jesus in the world the kingdom of God was present, directly impinging upon the lives of people wherever Jesus went. He came proclaiming that the kingdom of God had overtaken people, that it had come upon them beyond expectation and beyond all deserving – but when he proclaimed the kingdom that was the kingdom actually in effective operation among men and women. It was active among them as Jesus himself was among them in word and in deed.

To be sure Jesus was a man, but he was such a man that everywhere he was the Lord, not that he exhibited great lordly power – and everywhere he was a king, not that he displayed great kingly power as the world looks for it. His lordship and his kingdom were identical with himself as the Son of Man, who even in his human existence, existed in royal freedom toward and among all around him. That was the astonishing fact about him, his royal, lordly freedom, his majestic *exousia*, authority, in which he was perfectly free to be what he was, and to do what he had come to do. He was wholly free to do the Father's will. He was not bound by man, by any power of nature or history, by any of the fetters and shackles which all other men and women know only too well. He did not stand or fall with anything outside of him – he did not receive honour from man, nor did he accredit himself to any by any recognisable sanction or authority. He just was what he was with a royal presence and freedom in which he came and went with absolute superiority over everything, always and entirely the lord and master of everything. It was that royal presence and freedom that

---

[69] Heb 12.2 KJV/RSV.

made him unique and unforgettable – the presence of this man meant the presence of the divine kingdom, the kingdom of heaven among mankind.

(i) The cataclysmic impact of the royal freedom and authority of Jesus

Now that was precisely the terrifying thing about Jesus. He confronted man with an *exousia* and freedom that could be brought under no known standard or rubric. He towered above them all, and therefore there were no authorities or sanctions or places of security into which people could flee to escape him. In his presence there could be no neutrality, no escape, no avoidance of the ultimate things. Therefore the presence of this royal man threw men and women into upheaval and created a volcanic disturbance that shook humanity to its foundations – that is why so many words which are used to describe reactions to him are normally used to describe earthquakes or some stupendous earthshaking event. The presence of the king, of the ultimate authority, meant the presence of the judge of all the earth, walking about among humanity as another man, the kingdom and majesty of God addressing men and women, encountering and claiming them in the form of a human life among human lives, in the concrete form of a historical and personal relationship. Therefore in him, wherever he went, the kingdom impinged directly and sharply upon people's personal existence drawing everything into the sovereign light of his royal presence.

Now the presence of this kingdom in the royal presence of the man Jesus was the great positive good news of the gospel, that at last the light of the world had broken out; that in him there had overtaken a weary world in conflict with evil the ineffable peace of God, with peace and goodwill toward mankind, all men and women alike. In him the pure undeserved grace of God, royal grace, princely in its pardon and uninhibited in its lavish goodness, had overtaken man – that is the constant theme of the teaching and preaching of Jesus, just as it was the continuous fact enacted in all his gracious shepherding of the lost sheep of humanity. But it was the sheer freedom and royalty of this grace, its towering sovereignty that admitted no sanctions beyond or other than itself, that acknowledged no other authority than that of the majestic love of God the Father, that set the world in uproar and turbulent division. Under that divine light all darkness was revealed and exposed; under that royal grace and love all division and conflict stood revealed, and under that majestic freedom all bondage and tyranny were relentlessly exposed.

Thus the very presence of Jesus in the midst of mankind meant that the axe was laid to the root of the whole tree of humanity, that the judge of the world was among them with his fan in his hand to sift the chaff from the wheat and burn up the chaff in unquenchable fire.[70] In fact the presence of Jesus in all his royal freedom and lordly *exousia* meant the presence of the sword. It meant that the time had been fulfilled, and the time was at hand, had even now overtaken the world, when the kingdom of God was present, threatening to uproot every earthly dominion, every human power, and all their entrenched authorities and sanctions. The final judgement had begun, the last days had suddenly overtaken mankind, so that in the presence of Jesus hidden things were revealed, the first things were made last and the last things first, and all things were laid open and naked before his eyes. That is what the perfect humanity of Jesus meant for the men and women around him – the bringing of the light of the divine majesty to bear upon them in such a way that there was no escaping it, the bringing of the royal freedom of his love to bear upon all human and earthly dominion and power so that nothing could stand against it. Before the royal presence of this man, there was no neutrality, all was thrown into critical tension and final decision. That critical situation into which the presence of the kingdom threw man was precisely what Jesus used as his instrument to penetrate into the very heart of humanity and the evil entrenched within it in order to accomplish the royal work of his grace.

Let us now examine that situation created by the royal presence of Jesus in the world, looking at some of the concrete situations as they are recorded in the Gospels, in order to allow them to disclose to us what actually took place in Jesus' relation toward men and women.

The birth of the king – the upheaval created by the sign that is spoken against

We must note right away that with his birth as king at Bethlehem and the announcement of the glad tidings, his coming brought not peace but a sword, for it was his birth that provoked the fearful savagery of Herod against the infants of Bethlehem – and that was but the initial sign of the upheaval which the coming of the king and his kingdom meant for the kingdoms of this world. But it is to the prophetic utterances of Simeon and Mary that we must turn for our insight into what began to take place. Simeon's utterance was made as the infant

[70] Matt 3.9,12; Luke 3.9,17.

Jesus was brought into the temple, 'Behold, this child is set for the falling and rising (*keitai eis ptōsin kai anastasin*) of many in Israel, and for a sign that is spoken against (*kai eis sēmeion antilegomenon*) and a sword will pierce through your own soul also, that the thoughts of many hearts may be revealed (*apokaluphthōsin ek pollōn kardiōn dialogismoi*).'[71] Right from the start it is noted that this child is set for the falling and rising of many. Precisely the same thought is found in Mary's *Magnificat*, 'He has scattered the proud in the imagination of their hearts, he has filled the hungry with good things, and the rich he has sent empty away.'[72] But the same concept runs throughout the teaching of Jesus himself – coming out most startlingly perhaps in the parable of the labourers in the vineyard which is sandwiched in Matthew's record between the words: 'But many that are first will be last, and the last first' and 'So the last will be first, and the first last' – for many are called but few are chosen.[73] That is how we are to look upon the life of this man born to be king at Bethlehem – he had come to set our life on a wholly new basis, the basis of pure grace, but that involved a complete revolution, a radical inversion of status for mankind, a critical re-orientation of all things.

But what did Simeon mean by 'the sign that is spoken against', 'the sign that is contradicted'? Luke only uses this term *sēmeion* of the birth of Jesus and of the eschatological import of his death of which Jesus himself spoke in the 'little apocalypse'.[74] That is also the significance of the sign of Jonah,[75] and that is Jesus' answer, as Matthew and Mark see it, to the request for a sign. The sign, the *sēmeion*, is the cross. In the fourth Gospel, *sēmeion* is used of the miraculous deeds that point forward to the cross, beginning with the miracle of Cana,[76] when Jesus says that his 'hour is not yet come' using language repeated six other times in the Gospel, all making it clear that the *sēmeion* in question points forward to the eschatological hour of ultimate decision and passion on the cross. The miraculous events are thus drawn into the onward march of Jesus toward his supreme hour, and are made to be proleptic and sacramental signs or pointers of the supreme *sēmeion* when Jesus will die and rise again, and so refer to the whole of our

---

71 Luke 2.34-35 RSV/KJV.

72 Luke 1.51,53.

73 Matt 19.30 – 20.16; cf. Mark 10.31; Luke 13.30.

74 Matt 24; Mark 13; Luke 21 (*sēmeion*, v.7).

75 Luke 11.29f.; Matt 12.38f.; cf. Mark 8.11-12.

76 John 2.1-11.

human existence, spoken of already in the change of water into wine, the destruction and raising of the temple, etc. It is then that the cross and resurrection will set man's life on a wholly new basis and be the falling and rising again of many in Israel. Then the hungry will be filled with good things, the rich will be sent empty away, and the proud will be scattered in the imagination of their hearts, or as St Paul put it, the cross makes foolish the wisdom of this world.[77] That is why he speaks of the cross as a *skandalon* and a *mōria*, scandal and foolishness.

But that is why Simeon also speaks of this *sēmeion* as a *sēmeion antilegomenon*, a sign contradicted, or spoken against.[78] Again we may turn to the way in which this came to be understood in the theological tradition of the church, in which we find the same thoughts embedded and obviously going back to the original witness. See Hebrews 12,[79] where the writer summons the church to look away from themselves to Jesus the author and finisher of the course of faith who for the joy that was set before him endured the cross, despised the shame and is set down at the right hand of the throne of God. Then he adds, 'Consider him who endured such contradiction, *antilogian*, of sinners against himself, lest you also be weary and faint in your soul.'[80] What Jesus endured was the contradiction of sinners, the *antilogia* of the *hamartōlōn*, the word found so frequently in the Gospels to describe the very people whom Jesus sought to befriend and gather back into the fellowship of God but who turned against him at last and cried, 'Crucify him, crucify him'. There at the cross Jesus endured the full contradiction of sinners and of sin against him. But that was precisely what he came to do, as we shall see.

(ii) The uncovering of man and the unveiling of the human heart

There is still something else in Simeon's utterance that we must note. The sign that is spoken against, precisely by being spoken against, is the means by which the reasonings, *dialogismoi*, of the human heart are uncovered or revealed. That happened supremely at the cross, but it was happening all along throughout the life and ministry of Jesus – it is significant that the tense of the *antilegomenon* is in the continuous present, expressing the constancy and continuity of sin's attack upon Jesus.

---

77 1 Cor 1.18f.

78 Compare Luke's reference to the resurrection in Acts 28.22.

79 Heb 12.2.

80 See Heb 12.3 KJV.

Now this is the point where we penetrate right into the heart of Jesus' ministry toward sinners, in the fact that before his presence the secrets of people's hearts are all revealed. That comes out again and again in the Gospel records. Think of Luke's account of the healing of the paralytic where it is clear that Jesus manifests his divine *exousia* in discovering the secret reasoning of people's hearts[81] and in acts of forgiveness and healing. But note, as the evangelists point out, that on such an occasion some believed in Jesus, while others accused him of blasphemy.[82] In other words, as this *sēmeion* is spoken against there takes place a sharp division among people. The royal presence of Jesus had the effect of dividing them within themselves and among themselves; it cut into the differences already there and exposed them, but also brought other differences into the situation that cut across the old ones, but these were final differences which had already cast upon them the shadow of the final judgement at the last day. It is when the secret reasonings of the heart are revealed by the presence of Jesus that that begins to happen, and it can happen both to the unbelieving and recalcitrant Jews[83] and to the believing disciples.[84]

In the passages to which I have referred to so far we have the word *dialogismos*, reasoning, but other words are also used in this connection, such as *enthumēsis*, *ennoia*, *kardia*, thought, intention, heart, etc. All the evangelists bear steady testimony to the penetrating power of Jesus, before whose eyes all are open as a book for him to read. He encounters them in such a way that he gets inside their innermost thoughts and brings his divine majesty and grace to bear upon them there. Think of the way in which the scribes and pharisees reacted to Jesus when they brought to him a woman taken in the act of adultery.[85]

What is the significance of all this? In answer let us turn again to the theological tradition in the New Testament to see what they have made of this and other situations, and then in the light of it look back again at the ministry of Jesus before the cross to see how he fulfils it.

Romans 1.16 – 3.20: revelation of righteousness and judgement to Jew and Gentile

Our first passage concerns the exposure of the secret reasonings of the unbelieving. It begins, 'I am not ashamed of the gospel: it is the power

---

81 Luke 5.22.

82 Mark 2.1-12; Matt 9.1-8; Luke 5.17-26.

83 Luke 6.8f.

84 Luke 9.46-8, cf. 24.38.

85 John 8.3-11.

of God for salvation to every one who has faith, to the Jew first and also to the Greek. For in it the righteousness of God is revealed through faith for faith; as it is written, "He who through faith is righteous shall live".'[86] Here Paul is dealing first with what the gospel reveals to the believer, the apocalypse of righteousness from faith to faith. Recall the bipolarity inherent in the Hebraic conception of revelation which is carried over into *apokalyptein*, reveal, as an unveiling of God but also of the ear or eye of man that he or she may receive the divine revelation. Revelation involves the unveiling of God's end but it also involves unveiling at man's end. It is a revelation from God's faithfulness to man's responsive faithfulness, a revelation of divine faithfulness in the gospel that involves the believer in that righteousness. That Paul applies first to the Jew and then to the Gentile, but when he comes to the reverse truth, the revelation of the wrath of God out of the same gospel, he deals with the Gentile first, in Romans 1,[87] and then with the Jew, in Romans 2 and 3.

The passage from Romans 1.18 speaks of the revelation of judgement which is given by the gospel, under the light of the gospel. In other words, all mankind is placed under the x-ray light of the gospel and the secret reasonings of people's minds, their relations with the truth are revealed in a way that even they cannot know as they are involved in the very deception of sin. It is revealed by the gospel, and the judgement it brings to bear upon the innermost recesses of human being, that mankind 'became futile in their thinking and their senseless minds were darkened (*emataiōthēsan en tois dialogismois autōn, kai eskotisthē hē asunetos autōn kardia*)'[88] – note the words *dialogismos* and *kardia*, 'reasoning' and 'heart'. Already in verse 18 it is revealed by the x-ray light of the gospel that man 'holds down the truth in unrighteousness', but now in verse 25 it is revealed that they have 'changed the truth of God into a lie'.[89]

That unveiling of the innermost being of man happens to the Jew as well as to the Gentile, so that the Jew is clearly inexcusable too. Now that *apocalypse of the human heart* we see taking place in Jesus' relations with sinners, Jews and Gentiles, for in the light and majesty of his presence and the gospel he preaches, the hidden reasonings of the heart turning the truth into a lie are revealed and exposed as never

---

[86] Rom 1.16-17.

[87] Rom 1.18-32.

[88] Rom 1.21.

[89] KJV translation.

before, and man is placed before his eyes as inexcusable. Jesus Christ is the truth in grace, but also in judgement, penetrating into the innermost heart of man and laying it bare. In his presence men and women are turned inside out and his eyes search their souls – see again, for example, the pericope of John 8.[90] The reaction of the unbelieving, especially of the unbelieving Jew is *pōrōsis*, hardening as Paul called it,[91] again apparently following Jesus who grieved at the *pōrōsis* of the hearts of the Jews, the thickening and darkening of their spiritual understanding in the very light of the gospel, so that the light that was in them is turned into darkness, and how great then is that darkness! 'You say you see, therefore', said Jesus to the Jews, 'your guilt remains.'[92] It is for judgement that he has come that those who see may become blind! What does this uncovering of the heart lead to? What does the hardening of heart occasioned by the discovery of man's innermost thoughts lead to? It leads straight to the cross, to the crucifixion of Jesus.

Hebrews 4.12-16: the word of God that exposes all the thoughts of the heart

Our second passage from the theological tradition within the New Testament is from a passage in Hebrews concerned with believers. 'For the word of God is living and active, sharper than any two-edged sword (*zōn gar ho logos tou theou, kai energēs, kai tomōteros huper pasan machairan distomon*), piercing to the division of soul and spirit, of joints and marrow, and *discerning the thoughts and intentions of the heart* (*kritikos enthumēseōn kai ennoiōn kardias*). And before him no creature is hidden, but all are open and laid bare to the eyes of him with whom we have to do. Since then we have a great high priest who has passed through the heavens, Jesus, the Son of God, let us hold fast our confession. For we have not a high priest who is unable to sympathise with our weaknesses, but one who in every respect has been tempted as we are, yet without sinning. Let us then with confidence, *parrēsia*, draw near to the throne of grace, that we may receive mercy and find grace to help in time of need.'[93]

Here we have again a definite reflection of the gospel tradition. The sword that divides and cuts into the heart is the sword of which Jesus himself spoke when he said, 'Do not think that I have come to bring

---

[90] John 8.3-11.

[91] Rom 11.25; Eph 4.18.

[92] See John 9.41 KJV/RSV.

[93] Heb 4.12-16.

peace on earth; I have come not to bring peace, but a sword. For I have come to set a man against his father, and a daughter against her mother, and a daughter-in-law against her mother-in-law; and a man's foes will be those of his own household.'[94] Here Jesus speaks of his personal experience, for even his own family misunderstood and resisted him, and Mary herself was apparently involved in that misunderstanding.[95] The sword of the word had pierced into Jesus' own home at Nazareth, and was that not what Simeon meant when he said to Mary, 'and a sword will pierce your own heart also, that the thoughts of many hearts may be revealed'?[96] The presence of Jesus seems to have revealed that even in his own home there were some, including Mary herself, who if they did not doubt, appear, for a while at least, to have misunderstood his mission. The word divides even between the joints and the marrow, the soul and the spirit.

The high priest who uncovers and bears our sin, and answers for us to the Father

But let us note that this *logos* which is so critical of our innermost thoughts and intentions (*enthumēseōn kai ennoiōn*), is bi-polar in its operation like *apokalyptein*, reveal. To the *logos* that comes to us as a living thing there comes to meet it *our logos*, our reasoning and innermost thoughts. *Logos* involves a double relation, of our word with the Word of God. In that double relation there is revelation, everything is laid bare, but that is done by him who is our high priest. The critical word or *kritikos logos* who pierces into us like an incredibly sharp sword is none other than the one 'touched with the feeling of our infirmities',[97] who is full of compassion and sympathy – therefore we may come boldly to the throne of grace, even to be exposed, to be turned inside out, because it is his grace and mercy which does it, and that is his healing revelation and reconciliation. Here then on the ground of Christ's priestly intercession, on the ground of his substitutionary and atoning grace, the believer is searched through and through and utterly cleansed and forgiven, so that all his or her weakness or *astheneia* is born by Jesus, our high priest. That is precisely what we see on the pages of the Gospels when we find that the common people heard Christ gladly, and in their boldness pressed upon him and thronged

---

94 Matt 10.34-36.

95 See Mark 3.21f., 31f.; Matt 12.46f.; Luke 8.19-21.

96 See Luke 2.35.

97 Heb 4.15 KJV.

him, in order to get as near him as possible and even touch his clothes. His truth devastatingly exposed them, ruthlessly searched out their sins, but people threw themselves on him for forgiveness and healing, so much so that he was exhausted by it, and slipped away from them again and again, to recover his strength in prayer and reliance upon the heavenly Father. And we can understand what that meant when we learn what each act of healing cost him, and what the bearing of our *astheneia* meant for him in the agony of the cross.

But already this double activity of the word was taking place in the earthly ministry of Jesus as he worked out his priestly relation of solidarity with sinners, for he came not to judge the world but to save the world, and if his word of revelation revealed the secret reasonings of people's hearts and exposed them it also created and called forth from them an answering faith in him. Their *parrēsia* or boldness answered to the boldness of Christ himself, who from the side of man worked out the perfect answer of obedience to the Father and so opened up a new and living way to the Father. Because he, our high priest, goes boldly into the holy of holies with his answer of atonement, we also may go boldly in him, taking his answer on our lips, and so in his name humbly dare to go before the throne of grace. The whole incarnate life of Jesus is to be seen in terms of that answer of priestly representation and obedience from the side of man to God. Only as that answer is worked out in him, and in our humanity by him, does he go forward to the cross for the ultimate event, where man is called to account in the final judgement, and Jesus gives the final answer which is accepted by the Father and which satisfied him. 'This is my beloved Son, with whom I am well pleased.'[98] Or as the author of the epistle to the Hebrews puts it, 'He was heard for his godly fear. Although he was a Son, he learned obedience.'[99] On the ground then of that satisfaction, the good pleasure, the *eudokia* of the Father in his beloved Son, and his obedient response in word and life, we may come with boldness before God. That is precisely what we find people doing during the three years of his ministry, taking refuge under the wings of Jesus, flying from their own fear and unworthiness to find refuge in his answer to God on their behalf, and so finding shelter from the fierce accuser in being yoked together with the obedience and perfect life of the Son of Man.

---

98 Matt 3.17; cf. Mark 1.11; Luke 3.22.

99 Heb 5.7-8.

(iii) Christ's ministry as shepherd and king leads straight to the cross

In this section on the life and faithfulness of the Son toward man we have found in the earthly ministry of Jesus before the cross not only a shepherdly activity in which he sought and gathered lost humanity back into the fellowship of the divine life, but a royal activity in which with sovereign grace he so encountered people with his presence that he uncovered their innermost beings and exposed them to the light of his mercy and judgement. In that activity the kingdom of God impinged upon the lives of men and women in such a way that the twofold work of the cross was already revealed as active in the earthly ministry of Jesus: that is the divine exposure of and judgement upon our sin, and yet the divinely given provision in Jesus, within our humanity, of atonement for sin. Through that, taking shelter in the obedience of Jesus, we may go with boldness before the face of our Father in heaven, and find that we have place and acceptance in his fatherly heart.

We have considered this in terms of the basic relationship of Jesus towards men and women, and of his actual activity in relation to the lives of those whom he encountered during his ministry. That basic relationship and activity we have seen at every point to be proleptic to the cross, or to put it the other way round, to be the atoning mediation of Christ already at work long before the cross actually took place. We were able to understand the life and faithfulness of the Son toward man in that way because the shadow of the cross already fell upon his life and work, and because the evangelists record the incidents of his earthly teaching and healing from the perspective of the cross.

But now we have to do something else, in order to see in its depth and power the relation of the Son toward man: we have to see how what Jesus was and what Jesus did in his historical encounter with people inevitably led straight to the cross, and see that all through he lived and walked with such royal freedom and sovereign grace over it all that he controlled and directed it all so that it would lead to the cross when the hour was ripe, and when his relations with sinners had been brought to their destined moment in revelation and reconciliation. Then when his hour was come, he set his face like a flint towards Jerusalem, in order to gather up all that he had done and been, and bring it to its consummation in his death and resurrection in such a way that it availed not simply for those whom he actually encountered in historical and personal relationships, but in such a way that through the medium of that historical encounter he laid hold upon the very being of man, and in fulfilled solidarity with man wrought out atonement that avails for all men and women.

In order to do that we shall again take a basic text from Matthew and its parallel in Luke, paying particular attention to the fuller context given by Matthew.

The violence of the kingdom

Matthew: 'From the days of John the Baptist until now the kingdom of heaven has *suffered violence* (*biazetai*), and men of violence take it by force.'[100] Luke: 'The law and the prophets were until John; since then the good news of the kingdom of God is preached, and every one *enters it violently* (*biazetai*).'[101]

Where Matthew has 'the kingdom suffers violence', Luke has 'the gospel of the kingdom is preached' – does that mean that the *biazetai* in Matthew should be interpreted like the *biazetai* in the following clause in Luke, so that instead of translating it 'suffering violence', we would translate 'violently enters in'? There are pros and cons for both the active and passive translation of *biazetai* here, but theologically it is not necessary to come down on one side or the other. How does the kingdom of God press in, how does it storm into the hearts of men and women? *By the cross*. But the cross is the kingdom of God suffering violence, and there we see that the weakness of God is stronger than man, so that the preaching of this cross, where the kingdom suffers violence, is the power of God.

And that is precisely what we see in the life and ministry of Jesus before the cross: the preaching of the kingdom as gospel in the suffering patience of Jesus, in his compassion, is the very way in which the kingdom with divine *exousia*, divine majesty and truth, storms its way into the hearts of men and women and takes them under its sovereignty.

Look at the context of this saying in Matthew's Gospel, where Jesus speaks of John the Baptist as the Elijah of the New Testament. Recall the contrast between Elijah on Mount Carmel and Elijah under the juniper tree,[102] dejected and dispirited because the events of history after Mount Carmel have not taken the course he had hoped. God had certainly vindicated Elijah's faith, and the prophets of Baal had been overthrown, but the tyrant forces of evil were still in control defying God's sovereignty. Then Elijah is taught a supreme lesson on Mount Horeb. He is shown a terrific display of violence in wind, earthquake

---

100 Matt 11.12.

101 Luke 16.16.

102 1 Kings 18 – 19. The 'juniper tree' of the KJV (19.4-5) is translated by the RSV as 'broom tree'.

and fire, but God was not in the wind, or earthquake or fire. After the fire there came a still small voice, and immediately Elijah wrapped his face in his mantle: that was the *violence* of God. It is still the same story with John the Baptist. He expected the events of history after the baptism of Jesus to take quite a different course. He expected as Messiah a mighty deliverer coming in judgement and bringing upheaval and violence, who would redeem Israel from the New Testament Ahab and Jezebel, Herod and Herodias, and restore to God his sovereignty over his people. But instead of all that, he saw the meek and mild Jesus, preaching the gospel of grace and forgiveness to the poor and needy, and healing the sick. John sent messengers from prison, where he had been incarcerated by Herod, to ask Jesus, 'Are you he who is to come, or shall we look for another?'[103] And the answer came back, 'Go and tell John again what you see and hear . . . and blessed is he who takes no offence at me.' Like Elijah, John had misunderstood the violence of God and was offended at the weakness of Jesus, but in Jesus the still small voice of God had become flesh, and that was more powerful than all the imaginable forces of nature put together and unleashed in their fury.

The meekness of Jesus, his gospel of grace and vicarious suffering, is the most powerful deed the world has ever known

Jesus did not repudiate the preaching of John the Baptist, the proclamation of judgement: on the contrary he continued it, and as we have seen he searched the soul of man with the fire of divine judgement, but in Jesus that is subsidiary to – and only arises out of – the gospel of grace and vicarious suffering and atonement. In the incarnate life of Jesus, and above all in his death, God does not execute his judgement on evil simply by smiting it violently away by a stroke of his hand, but by entering into it from within, into the very heart of the blackest evil, and making its sorrow and guilt and suffering his own. And it is because it is God himself who enters in, in order to let the whole of human evil go over him, that his intervention in meekness has violent and explosive force. It is the very power of God. And so the cross with all its incredible meekness and patience and compassion is no deed of passive and beautiful heroism simply, but the most potent and aggressive deed that heaven and earth have ever known: the attack of God's holy love upon the inhumanity of man and the tyranny of evil, upon all the piled up contradiction of sin.

---

[103] Matt 11.3f.

To see how that is so, watch what happened when Jesus was arraigned before Pilate and the Jewish nation. Jesus had never lifted a violent finger against any one, and yet he became the centre of a violent disturbance that has shaken the world to its foundations. The incredible thing is this: the meeker and milder Jesus is, the more violent the crowd become in their resentment against him. The more like a lamb he is, the more like ravening wolves they become. By his very passion and suffering, by his meekness and grace and truth, Jesus imparted passion to his contemporaries and called forth violence from them until at last they laid violent hands upon him and dragged him off to the cross. Jesus is the embodiment of the still small voice of God: he is the Word made flesh, the Word that is able to divide soul and spirit asunder. That voice, that Word of God in Jesus penetrated as never before into the secrets of humanity and exposed them. The more he stood before them, the more the power of God broke its way into the citadel of the human soul. Before the weakness and mercy of Jesus, before this compassion, all barriers are broken down, all the thoughts and intents of the heart are revealed. What wind and earthquake and fire could not do, Jesus did: he penetrated into the proud heart of man and laid it bare, and in so doing he produced the most violent reaction that culminated in his crucifixion.

The agony of Jesus in bringing the truth to bear on humanity

That was not an accident. Jesus intended it all, and he controlled it all to the very end, although the very fact that he was in control meant unspeakable pain for him who was love – for how could he, the loving one, let humanity become guilty of the most wicked of all crimes, of putting the Son of God to death? How could Jesus who was in such perfect control of it all allow mankind, even provoke them, press them, to the ultimate point of becoming infinitely guilty of murdering the Son of God? That surely was a great part of the agony of Jesus in Gethsemane. But Jesus is indeed the loving one, the only one who is consistently loving, and therefore true love who resists all that is not love, love that is absolutely truthful and faithful within itself. He was therefore more than love, he was the truth of God. It was as such that Jesus stood before Pilate and before the whole nation of Israel, and as such that he was arraigned before humanity.

The more truth entered into the innermost centre of man's sin and guilt, the more it involved man in ultimate conflict with God who is truth and love. It was not that Jesus was making mankind more guilty, but that his absolute consistency as holy love, his truth, was exposing the infinite guilt of humanity as he drew it fully and completely upon himself in all its utter violence in order to bear it and bear it away as the lamb of God in atoning sacrifice. Here we have the ultimate compassion of Jesus Christ in which he so pours himself out upon mankind and for them that he enters into the innermost citadel of sin in order to take it upon himself. In exposing it he, the truth, drew out all its hate and enmity, revealing its true nature as sheer hatred of grace, and then he bowed beneath it and bore it all on his own body and soul on the tree in holy and awful atonement, and with groanings that cannot be uttered. But in that awful hour mercy and truth worked together and kissed each other, as the Old Testament would put it.[104] The cross is at once the absolute truth and absolute mercy. God is both just and the justifier of the ungodly, and what joins these together is the steadfastness or faithfulness of Jesus Christ both toward God and toward man.

From that cross we look back, and see what happened in the three years of Jesus' ministry, what lay on his heart as he healed the sick and forgave sins, what he was doing when he brought the truth of God to bear upon the lives of men and women in his teaching, what he meant as he deliberately scandalised them in order to put before them the decision of the cross and so expose their terrible secrets to the mercy of God.

(iv) Final judgement and salvation

The atoning work of Christ seen at work like that is no mechanical or merely forensic transaction; it is the activity of the divine person penetrating directly into the hearts of men and women and in an acutely personal way, by way of God's decision of love, opening up people in their decisions and gathering them into communion and union with God. That was the three years' ministry of Jesus. That is why he operated as he did with unheard of meekness and kindness, shrouding his divine majesty and even veiling the naked truth by parable, lest he should bluntly crush the bruised reed or quench the smoking flax.[105] He lived with publicans and sinners, and scribes and pharisees, and people of all sorts, gradually revealing himself, and as they were able to hear he spoke to them the truth, challenging them at every turn in their decisions before the majesty of the kingdom. Acting on their decisions and by means of them he penetrated into the innermost being of men and women as only he who is God and man could.

---

[104] Cf. Psalm 85 esp. vv. 10-11 KJV — cf. RSV.

[105] Matt 12.20; Isaiah 42.3.

And so all through those years of historical encounter and human living in the midst of people and their hurts and needs, he involved himself more and more, intertwined himself more and more completely with sinners, until in the fullest and most personal sense he was the representative of the divine judge to us, condemning by his truth our sin in the flesh, and was also our representative, representing us the judged as he wore our humanity. Because he was God's Son become man he could both incarnate God for us, and represent us before God, this one man on behalf of all men and women. In this authoritative representation, representation in truth and reality, of God to us and of all to God, Jesus Christ stood in the gap to work out to the bitter end in justice and mercy the conflict between God's holy love consistently true to itself, and man's persistent contradiction of God's love even when it was poured out in utter compassion and grace. In that, as the very heart of God beating within our humanity, he really suffered our distress, and bore also the whole of God's judgement upon the humanity with which, in all its guilt and rejection, he stood in complete solidarity. All the years of his earthly life, but especially during those three years of his public ministry, as he revealed the Father, and poured out the Father's compassion, he engaged himself more and more closely with the ultimate things, the very last things, until on the cross the *eschaton* took place, the final judgement and final salvation.

The nearer the cross came, the more Jesus pressed the people to decision

All through his life therefore, the face of Jesus was turned toward the cross. The nearer he approached to it, the more he pressed toward it, the more that final judgement with its final decision and ultimate division made itself apparent in his life and ministry. At first the Jews refused to make up their minds and he could do nothing with them – they were like children in the market place who would play neither at funerals nor marriages, who would accept neither the stern Baptist nor the gracious Jesus.[106] But Jesus continued to body forth in their midst the still small voice of God, the gospel of truth and grace, and so he continued to exert the pressure of his compassion and love upon people until reaction began to come and it came with violence. Some were so offended that they gnashed their teeth and took up stones to kill him, and even many of his disciples were scandalised and left him, while his very kinsfolk said he was beside himself.[107] But others believed

---

[106] Luke 7.31-35; Matt 11.16-19.

[107] John 8.59, 6.66; Mark 3.21.

and wondered at the gracious words that fell from his lips for never man spoke like this man. To some the still small voice, 'This is my beloved Son, hear him' was only thunder, while to others it was the music of angels, but always there was determined reaction, more and more determined reaction until the climax was reached. And it was through this determined reaction that the kingdom acted upon men and women but in such a way that many that were first became last, and many that were last became first, for many were called but few were chosen.

Our words and concepts ultimately fail us here, but even if we cannot state it with precision, it is clear in the Gospels that Jesus used the developing situation more and more to enable him to lay hold upon humanity and to shoulder the full load of the world's need and guilt – but to do that he had to exert constant pressure on men and women in order to force them to declare themselves to be toward him what they really were in their hearts, and all the time he was stooping to shoulder their full burden of sin and guilt. That is the way in which the Gospels give us the historical context of the crucifixion. Historically, Christ was crucified because he was bitterly resented. He did not fit in with the picture of God or of his Messiah that had been formed and built up in Judaism especially since Maccabean times.[108] The Jews did understand Jesus much more than they would have admitted. If Jesus had not been a divine figure, if he had not brought divine majesty to bear upon them in laying the axe to the root of the tree, they would not have bothered so much about him, especially when he was politically inoffensive, but to have his claims to be a suffering Messiah divinely confirmed with the *exousia* or authority which Jesus could not but manifest, was intolerable for the Jews. They were ready for a Messiah, *in abstracto*, in the abstract, but not for such a Messiah as Jesus was in reality. The great stumbling block to them was Christ's threat as Messiah to interpenetrate their very existence in such a way as to cut across their cherished ideas and desires and ambitions. They wanted Christ to subserve the notion of their own religiousness and were furious when he touched them at the point of their religious pride, and so by the pressure of his very presence as the incarnate truth he evoked from them the full movement of sin in undisguised contradiction. It was the coincidence of recognition and conviction of sin that galled them, and under the continued pressure of Christ they forced themselves to choose what in real measure they knew to be against the truth.

---

[108] 168-135 BC (from the beginning of the Maccabaean revolt to the death of Simon Maccabaeus).

Jesus' deliberate forcing of events to the climax on the cross and the hour of atonement

There can be no doubt about it that Jesus deliberately forced the issue. At last when the time drew near he marched straight upon Jerusalem and threw everything into the crisis, pressing the nation to come to an ultimate decision, pressing the people to the supreme point when as a whole people they would take a decision in the solidarity of their sin in resistance against the revealed grace of God. That was the Christ who came not to bring peace but a sword, who came to cast fire on the earth. And so Jesus kept his finger pressing hard upon the people, deliberately provoking evil to its final and complete reaction, and then he set himself to deal with it by the finger of God, in holy love. It was an act of aggression on his part for which he had long prepared. He invaded the realm of the strong man in order to bind him,[109] invaded by suffering and by love, in order to bind him by atonement. The cross was the culminating point of the struggle when he touched people at the very roots of their being, at the point where sin was most deeply entrenched, and did the tremendous deed that reversed all things.

The climax came in the last week, when Jesus entered Jerusalem openly as messianic king, and the crowds acclaimed him with unrestrained enthusiasm, still hoping that he would be their Messiah, their kind of Messiah, but when he cleansed the temple and indicated that his work was the work of sacrifice, the people, beginning with the authorities who had long been hostile, turned against him. It was then that Jesus told the parable of the vineyard which ends with the death of the son and heir, and it is clear that he had penetrated right into the very hearts of the priests and Pharisees who realised clearly that he meant the parable for them.[110] They knew that he was the Messiah but were wilfully ignorant, and were so enraged at the discovery of their innermost intentions to kill Jesus that they deliberately hastened the execution of their crime, doing their wickedest utmost to force the hand of the kingdom to serve their own desires.

Jesus refused to die until the right moment had come when he would lay down his life as the truth, that is, when the truth he brought had come home to the people, and when it was clear to them what he was about. The atonement must be made with full deliberation, and with full knowledge of the Jewish authorities although they blinded themselves at the same time, holding down the truth in

---

109 Luke 11.21-22; Mark 3.27; Matt 11.29.

110 Matt 21.33-46; Mark 12.1-12; Luke 20.9-19; cf. Isaiah 5.1-7.

unrighteousness and turning it into a lie in their own selves.[111] The hour had at last arrived for which Jesus had worked unceasingly in compassion for three years, when the people were ready to say deliberately – even when obstructed by Pilate – 'We will not have him to reign over us. Crucify him.'[112] 'His blood be on us and on our children',[113] all in face of his claim to be Son of God now at last openly revealed. At last the hour had come when Christ was to make atonement, at last the king of truth in vicarious suffering stormed into the ultimate stronghold of sin embattled and embittered by sheer resentment to grace, and expiated it in unutterable compassion and at unheard of cost.

That is the gospel story of the relation of the Son of Man toward man, and that covers the whole ministry of Jesus as the breaking in of the kingdom of God into the hearts of men and women in order to destroy sin from within its rooted and embittered contradiction of God. Jesus then gathers into the sovereign grace of the kingdom all the very worst that man can do, in order thus to break the power of guilt and set people free from being the rebels that they had become. But in the heart of all that, there is another account to be read, and another picture to be described.

(v) The building up of the messianic community and the creation of the church[114]

What about the reaction of the believing? What about the followers of Jesus? What about the disciples?[115] Right from the start of his ministry, Jesus began to build up the messianic community, the new Israel, as a fellowship of sinners within his revealing and reconciling work, sharing, in and through himself, in the life of the Son and the Father.

---

111 Cf. John 18.14.

112 See John 19.14-15.

113 Matt 27.25.

114 On the foundation of the church, from its foundation in Israel to its reconstitution and rooting in Christ, see further T.F. Torrance, *Theology in Reconstruction* (London: SCM Press 1965), chap. 11, pp. 192-208 'The foundation of the church: union with Christ through the Spirit', reprinted from Scottish Journal of Theology, 16.2, 1963. The article was also one of Torrance's student handouts, and merits careful study. Cf. T.F. Torrance, *The School of Faith*, pp. cxvii-cxxi.

115 See W. Manson, 'The Norm of the Christian Life in the Synoptic Gospels', *Scottish Journal of Theology*, vol. 3, no. 1, pp. 33-42.

That is the creation of the church as the community of the redeemed but it is gradually moulded and formed only as his own ministry takes shape and reaches its end or *telos* in the passion and resurrection. But in following the account that the Gospels give us of this little flock to whom it was the Father's good pleasure to give the kingdom, we see into the other and creative side of the ministry of Jesus as the creation of communion between man and God. The account is presented in three stages.

The three stages in the formation of the disciples

(1) In the first stage Jesus calls twelve men to himself to follow him as disciples, to form one body with him the Messiah, to form the reconstituted Israel. They are all from among those baptised and prepared for his coming by John the Baptist. Jesus himself steps into their midst as he who has shared that baptism and who now leads them on in the fulfilment of all that baptism had exhibited and declared. In this first stage, the disciples are learners, walking in the light with Christ as he is in the light, as he discloses the secrets of their hearts and they are wholly laid bare before him.

(2) The second stage is reached at Caesarea Philippi when the disciples learn that the ultimate obstacle to the kingdom is self, and there they very clearly reach a parting of the ways, where they must deny self and cast in their lot with Jesus pressing with him toward the cross, or walk no more with him.[116] This is the stage when many of the disciples were offended at Jesus, but the twelve cast their lot unreservedly with him, and immediately he begins to speak to them more openly of his messianic secret, of his crucifixion. In a profounder sense now, the disciples are one body with Christ, they have learned the secret of his name, the Christ the Son of the living God, and have the promise that they are to be the foundation of the church against which the gates of hell shall not prevail – yet they still misunderstand the nature of Christ's messiahship. But from now on Jesus summons them to share in his increasing tribulations and increasingly shares with them the mystery of the kingdom. In that fellowship of sharing in truth and suffering they are made to cohere more and more as the community on earth sharing in the relation of the Son to the Father, and in the mission of the servant who has come to give his life a ransom for many. This stage reaches its culmination at the last supper where Jesus solemnly founds the new covenant in his body and blood, and gives his disciples

---

116 Mark 8.27-38; Matt 16.13-28; cf. Luke 9.18-27.

to share in it through the giving of his body and shedding of his blood, binding them by that covenant into one body with himself to form the new Israel, the redeemed church of the new age.

(3) The third stage begins to arrive shortly after in Gethsemane, and is reached when Jesus is on the cross, absolutely alone, while the disciples are found among the sinners and in the crowd where there are those who mock and jeer at him. Jesus Christ is left utterly alone under the judgement of God upon the world's sin – he the Lord and master, he their representative and their very life – but in that agony of lonely substitution, he the lamb whom God had himself provided for atoning sacrifice. What an unending and unbridgeable chasm there is between the disciples and Jesus who dies for them alone, deserted, while they flee and are offended at him like the others and even deny him. The disciples could only stand afar off in sin and shame and fear, broken hearted that the bonds between him and them were utterly severed, by his crucifixion, and by their shameful fear and offence.

Then they remembered the last supper.[117] That was why he had appointed it, for he meant them to remember. And so they realised that within that awful separation and in spite of it and indeed because of it, he had effectuated his oneness with them in a way that nothing could ever break. For in the new covenant which he had inaugurated in his passion (as sacramentally set forth in the supper), that which bound them to him for ever was precisely their sin for which he atoned, precisely the fact that he had taken their sin upon himself and was crucified in sacrificial expiation of it. And so the disciples knew that their baptismal incorporation into one body with their Lord, renewed even at the last supper, had come to its stark reality in that atonement, and therefore in that supper which set it forth. The sacrament told them what no human words could, of oneness with God through the crucifixion of the Messiah, through his lonely substitutionary sacrifice, of a oneness so deep that they ate his body given for them and drank his blood shed for them. Being thus baptised with his baptism, and sharing with him his own cup they were constituted the community of the Messiah, the fellowship of the reconciled and redeemed.

---

[117] Cf. the Soteriology volume of these lectures, *Atonement*, chap. 10, sec. 5(f), the paragraphs headed 'The provision of the eucharist for the renewal of faith and recurring confirmation of baptism' and 'The last supper designed to form an unbreakable union with Christ cemented on the cross' – T.F. Torrance, *Conflict and Agreement in the Church*, vol. 2, (London: Lutterworth 1960), pp. 168ff.

All these three stages in their discipling were gathered up and crowned when Jesus returned to them in the same upper room on Easter evening granting them peace and reconciliation, breathing upon them his Spirit, and commissioning them as the apostles of the kingdom, the foundation of his church.[118]

The reconstitution of the disciples in the power of the resurrection and of the Spirit

But now look at St Luke's account of how that breaks into the faith of the disciples. Recall the third day after the crucifixion when Jesus has risen from the dead, joins the company of two disciples as a stranger and goes with them to Emmaus.[119] He talks with them gently, expounds to them the Old Testament scriptures and shows them that Christ *had to* suffer and die in atonement, that this was what he came to do and what he did do as Messiah, and all the time the still small voice of God caused their hearts to burn within them. At Emmaus, Jesus makes as if he would go further and only turns aside to abide with them when they constrain him, and St Luke uses the word *parebiasanto* – a strengthened form of the term *biazetai* we have been looking at – to emphasise the violent hands that the disciples laid on Jesus. It was then that the kingdom broke upon their vision in its full glory, and Jesus was made known to them in the breaking of bread. 'The kingdom of heaven suffers violence and the violent take it by force.' That is another kind of violence from that which crucified Jesus, but now because of the crucifixion it is a violence which corresponds to the violence of his compassion. Now on the ground of accomplished reconciliation, the pouring out of the love of God in compassion, the Son of Man creates and evokes a corresponding passion in the illumination and faith and appropriation of the reconciled and believing. The two disciples hastened back from Emmaus to Jerusalem, to the others in the upper room where they were together reconstituted in the power of the resurrection, fashioned into one body with Christ in the communion of the Spirit between Son and the Father, and the Father and the Son. Atonement is realised here in this nucleus of the church, the one body of Christ, where God and man are one in Jesus Christ.

We cannot understand the life and work of Jesus the Son of God toward man unless we put both those accounts *together*, the one within

---

118 John 20.19-23.

119 Luke 24.13ff.

the other. The large picture is that of Christ bringing in the kingdom of God's grace, bringing it to bear upon the innermost being and existence of mankind until it is made to yield all its secrets and to declare itself in all its fearful actuality as hostility to God, so that in that way sin might be judged and condemned in the flesh, but so that at the same time Christ might take it all upon himself, and through expiation of its guilt destroy its power. However, within that picture there is another of Jesus gathering around him a little flock centred in the disciples as a fellowship of reconciliation, creating in their midst real union and communion with God through their sharing in his own relation of sonship with the Father. That creative work in establishing *union and communion with the Father* forms the heart of his ministry, and of his great atoning work with its end or goal in the renewal of the whole of creation.

Chapter Five

THE MYSTERY OF CHRIST:
The mystery of the union of God and man in the person of Christ

In our consideration of the life of the incarnate Son in the union of his divine and human natures we move on to consider the 'mystery' of that union in the person of Christ. Hence we turn now to the more specifically theological tradition in the New Testament in order to see how already within the New Testament church the amazing fact of Christ in his person and work is discerned, and knowledge of him is unfolded in a way that was determined by the mystery of Christ as God and man, and by his work within humanity as mediator between God and man. Already within the New Testament, it is a theological Christ who is presented to us, for Christ the truth had so impressed himself upon the mind and thought of the church that there was immediately created within that church the theological mould out of which and from which the true and faithful doctrine of the person and work of Christ has always arisen.

The mystery of Christ's person unfolded only at the end of his mission

Jesus himself kept his messianic secret as God and man until the very end, unfolding it only in his actions as he advanced to the completion of his mission from the Father, but once his actions were complete, the Spirit was given in fullness and through him all that he had hitherto declared in a form necessarily veiled, shone out in its unveiled significance. Had Jesus spoken openly and directly about himself as very God and very man, as having divine nature and human nature in one person, there is no doubt that he would have been severely misunderstood, and his teaching could not have been heard or received aright, far less transmitted aright. He taught them only as they were able to hear, and able therefore to receive and transmit faithfully what he communicated to them, but what he communicated to them was in a form that immediately took on another dimension of depth when his mighty acts in death and resurrection were completed, and when the Holy Spirit was sent and given. To help us understand this we may take a simple analogy. We can draw a cube on a blackboard, and the cube is a representation in two dimensions, that is in the flat, of something which in point of fact exists in three dimensions. At first one sees it as just flat, but once the eye is adjusted to see it in a dimension of depth, then the representation appears to have a three dimensional significance. This is what happened with the self-witness and teaching of Jesus, which he impressed upon the minds of the apostles and disciples – they saw him in the flat, as it were, in two dimensions. But immediately the mighty acts were completed, and the Spirit was given, the whole focus of their vision changed, and they saw Jesus, identically the same Jesus, now in his own true dimension of glory, in a dimension of depth that receded back into his eternal deity and projected forward into his glorious advent.

John's apocalyptic vision of the glory of Christ[1]

We have a startling example of that in the first chapter of the Apocalypse, in which John describes the Jesus from out of whose mouth there came the same voice he had known and loved so much when Jesus was on earth. 'Then I turned to see the voice that was speaking to me, and on turning I saw one like a son of man'[2] – and John at that point uses Jesus' former familiar designation of himself, meaning us to see that he whom he now describes is one identical with the historical Jesus we know from the Gospel accounts. 'His head and his hair were white as white wool, white as snow; his eyes were like a flame of fire, his feet were like burnished bronze, refined as in a furnace, and his voice was like the sound of many waters; in his right hand he held seven stars, from his mouth issued a sharp two-edged sword, and his face was like the sun shining in full strength. When I saw him, I fell at his feet as though dead. But he laid his right hand upon me, saying, "Fear not, I am the first and the last, and the living one; I died, and behold I am alive for evermore, and I have the keys of Death and Hades".'[3]

That was what John saw, as he says, in the Spirit on the Lord's Day – and what an astonishing account of Jesus it is. It was the same Jesus, but now glorified with the glory which he, the Son of God, had before the world was, the glory of his transcendent deity, and yet in it and

1 See T.F. Torrance, *The Apocalypse Today – Sermons on Revelation* (London: James Clarke 1960).

2 Rev 1.12-13 (quotation condensed).

3 Rev 1.14-18.

unimpaired in the midst of that divine majesty there is the same beloved Jesus. That is how Jesus is known and apprehended according to his historical revelation and according to his own divine and human natures in one person. That is how he is to be seen and worshipped by the church as the exalted saviour and Lord who is yet identical with the meek and lowly Jesus of Galilee and Judaea, he who is full of grace and truth and in whom the fullness of the Godhead dwells bodily.

Now John's language is that of apocalyptic vision – truly theological none the less, and perhaps all the more expressive of the fact that here a true theological apprehension resists being encased in mere theological statements, or insists on overflowing those theological statements, for here is a glory and a divine mystery that reach beyond all human expression.

Paul's understanding of the mystery of Christ that goes back to eternity

Now when we turn to St Paul who more than any other, even more than the Johannine writer, gives us the full doctrine of Christ in his person and work, we find that he is absolutely convinced of the identity between his gospel and Christ's own *kērygma*. As he says in a doxological section at the end of his epistle to the Romans, 'Now to him who is able to strengthen you according to my gospel and the preaching (*kērygma*) of Jesus Christ, according to the revelation of the mystery which was kept secret for long ages but is now disclosed and through the prophetic writings is made known to all nations, according to the command of the eternal God, to bring about obedience to the faith – to the only wise God be glory for evermore through Jesus Christ.'[4] There at the end of the epistle, Paul refers directly back to the beginning of the epistle where he says, 'Paul, a servant of Jesus Christ, called to be an apostle, set apart for the gospel of God which he promised beforehand through his prophets in the holy scriptures, the gospel concerning his Son, who was descended from David according to the flesh and designated Son of God in power according to the Spirit of holiness by his resurrection from the dead, Jesus Christ our Lord, through whom we have received grace and apostleship to bring about obedience to the faith for the sake of his name among all the nations'.[5]

Paul is deeply conscious that as an apostle he is specially sent to expound and develop the gospel which is identical with the *kērygma* of Jesus Christ himself, but now Paul expounds it in the light of the resurrection and in the light of the scriptures of the Old Testament,

---

4 Rom 16.25-27.

5 Rom 1.1-5.

and what he thus expounds is *the mystery of Christ*. Here Paul is not only speaking of what Jesus did and taught, but speaking of *the being and person of Jesus Christ* in terms of his secret that goes back into eternity, but which is now revealed. To speak about *who Jesus Christ was and is*, to speak in *ontological* terms[6] of his being and his work, means to speak of Jesus Christ as Son of God the Lord, and as son of David; but to speak of Jesus as Son of God means, in the same breath, speech about the Father and the Holy Spirit. No doctrine of the person of Christ in his divine and human being is possible, except in that eternal mystery and in that trinitarian context. But when one begins to make ontological statements here about the being and work of Christ, the Son of God and Son of Man, one has already given the basis for a fully fledged christology.

It is to that biblical theological basis for the church's doctrine of Christ that we now turn, looking back upon all we have learned of the historical Jesus Christ to see his person and work in its dimension of depth receding into the eternal purpose and glory of God. By way of doing that, I want to select three very significant terms from the theological tradition within the New Testament, *mystērion, prothesis* and *koinōnia*, and show what they have to declare about Christ in this dimension of depth.

1 The mystery of Christ: *mystērion, prothesis, koinōnia*[7]

In its fullest and deepest sense, *mystērion* refers to the union of God and man eternally purposed in God, but now revealed and set forth in Jesus Christ as true God and true man in one person: a union which creates room for itself in the midst of our estranged humanity and through fellowship or communion gathers people, men and women and children, into one body with Jesus Christ. In these expressions, 'union' and 'one body with Jesus Christ', we have described the meaning of *koinōnia*. In the expressions 'eternally purposed' and 'set forth' we have the significance of *prothesis*. And in the expressions 'creates room for itself', 'fellowship' or 'communion', and 'gathering into one body with' Christ, we have the significance of *koinōnia*. All this has to be understood from beginning to end in terms of the incarnation, of the union of God and man brought about by the incarnation of the Word, the union of God and man in Jesus Christ.

---

[6] Terms that refer to 'being' or 'inner nature'.

[7] For what follows here on 'the mystery of Christ' see 'The Mystery of the Kingdom', T.F. Torrance, *Conflict and Agreement*, vol. 2 (London: Lutterworth 1960), pp. 82-91.

That union is one which recedes back into the mystery of the communion of the Father, Son and Holy Spirit, but it is set forth in the incarnate life of Jesus Christ in terms of the reconciliation of man and God, for through his atonement and through his Spirit, Jesus Christ who is God and man in himself, creates out of the world, a church concorporate with himself, or one body with him.

The mystery of the union in Christ, purposed, set forth and creating communion

Primarily, then, *mystērion* refers to the union of God and man in the one person of Jesus Christ. In him that union is thrust like an axis into the midst of our humanity, making everything to revolve round it and have significance only in relation to it. That axis recedes into eternity in the eternal election or *prothesis* of God, but it also manifests itself in history in the church of Jesus Christ. Jesus Christ is himself the manifestation, the setting forth (*prothesis*), of the eternal purpose (*prothesis*)[8] of God. And it is in communion with him, through participation in the divine *prothesis,* that the church of Christ is called into being and maintained from age to age as the sphere through which Christ continues to manifest himself, as the community or *koinōnia* in which he dwells by his Spirit. He who ascended to fill all things will bring that community to its fullness in his eternal purpose, for he, the first born of all creation, will return again to consummate his eternal purpose in the new creation. Then the mystery consummated already in Christ himself will be revealed and manifested in the new heaven and the new earth.

We may put that the other way round. Mystery is the secret that lies behind God's creation. In the heart of that creation, God created man, made in the union of male and female as one flesh, to reflect the image of God within their relation of union with God. But that union between man and God was sundered, and the union within mankind making mankind one flesh was sundered: the secret was lost to man, the mystery remained wholly recondite. But the eternal purpose of God remained, and so at last in Jesus Christ after long and patient preparation in God's purpose with Israel, the mystery of God's will became incarnate. It embodied itself in the midst of our humanity, begetting in Jesus Christ the one in whom all mankind is gathered back into communion with God. By the atonement in the God-man, through atonement and communion or *koinōnia* in him, humanity is restored to the lost relation with God, restored in Christ to union with

---

8 *Prothesis* is used both for 'setting forth' and for 'purpose'. See the section later on *prothesis*.

God. The church is the sphere of *koinōnia* in history, Christ's own body, where that mystery of the kingdom is proclaimed, revealed and actualised, and there is created a new humanity through participation in Jesus Christ the first-born among many brethren, the first-born of all creation.[9]

That in compendium or outline is the significance of *mystērion*, *prothesis* and *koinōnia*, but it needs to be controlled and modified by a more detailed exposition of the theological significance of these terms.

(a) The mystery of Christ – mystērion, *the union of God and man*

Mystērion has a twofold sense in the New Testament – and an opposite sense, the counterfeit *mystērion* of iniquity which we will not consider. Primarily, *mystērion* is the 'mystery of Christ' (*mystērion tou Christou*), as Paul calls it,[10] but it is also the *mystērion* that has become actualised among the apostles and prophets, and is to be described as the mystery of Christ and his church.[11] This mystery is *revelation* that is identical with Christ himself and here one thinks of the Johannine record of the majestic word of Jesus, 'I am the way, the truth and the life'.[12]

The mystery of Christ and his kingdom revealed to the disciples

In Timothy, the mystery is spoken of as 'the great mystery of godliness, God manifest in the flesh, justified in the Spirit'.[13] That is the mystery of the kingdom of which Jesus spoke in the synoptic Gospels, 'To you it is given to know the mystery, *mystērion*, or mysteries of the kingdom of God.'[14] It is significant that both singular and plural are used by the evangelists as if they wanted to emphasise the person of Christ as the full content of the mystery, and knowledge of this mystery. Christ in the midst is the real focus of the parable, so that in Johannine language the mystery is the 'I am', the *Egō eimi*, of him who is one with the Father, God with us in Christ. In synoptic language, he is '*Immanuēl*'.[15] Yet that Christ is the Son of the living God is not revealed by flesh and blood, but only by the Father. This mystery of the person of Christ, however, has the same doubleness as the word to 'reveal' in both Hebrew and Greek usage in

---

[9] Rom 8.29; Col 1.15,18.

[10] Eph 3.4.

[11] Eph 5.32.

[12] John 14.6.

[13] See 1 Tim 3.16 KJV.

[14] Mark 4.11; Luke 8.10; Matt 13.11 KJV – Mark has the singular, mystery, while the others have the plural.

[15] Matt 1.23.

the bible, where reveal means not only an unveiling or uncovering of God, but an uncovering of the ear or an unveiling of the heart of man. Thus the revelation of the mystery refers not only to the secret of the person of Christ as true God and true man, but also to the revealing of it to men and women. It is highly significant, therefore, that this mystery in the records of the synoptic Gospels, gathers round itself a conclave of twelve disciples to whom it is given to know the mystery as it is not given to those without. 'To you it is given to know the mystery of the kingdom, but to those without, all things are done in parables.'[16]

Several Old Testament passages are in view here and immediately leap into the mind of the reader, such as Deuteronomy 29 ('The secret things belong to the Lord our God; but the things that are revealed belong to us and to our children for ever, that we may do all the words of this law'),[17] Psalm 78,[18] and especially Isaiah 8 which speaks of the messianic testimony and instruction out of the Torah or law as sealed up among the disciples. 'Bind up the testimony, seal the teaching among my disciples . . . Behold, I and the children whom the Lord has given me are for signs and portents in Israel.'[19] This is recalled by an *agraphon* or unwritten saying of Jesus recorded by Clement of Alexandria, and the Clementine Homilies in which Jesus speaks of his *mystery* which he has between himself and the sons of his house.[20] Jesus and his disciples build together one temple or body in his mystery of the kingdom.

No doubt there is also in view here the twofold fact of the Danielic vision that the kingdom is given to the Son of Man and to the saints of the Most High.[21] The mystery of the kingdom is thus not only the mystery of the union between God and man in Christ himself, but the mystery of the union of the one and the many through atonement which Paul expounds in several of his epistles. Christ who died, the one for all, forms all who believe in him into one body with him, one new man,[22] with Christ himself, the union of God and man, enshrined at its heart. That is the mystery of Christ, God manifest in the flesh, and the mystery concerning Christ and his church.

---

16 Mark 4.11 — Torrance's translation.

17 Deut 29.29.

18 Psalm 78.2-4.

19 Isaiah 8.16-18.

20 *Stromata* 5.10.8; cf. *Clementine Homilies* 19.20, Ante-Nicene Fathers (Grand Rapids: Eerdmans repr. 1967), vol. 2, p. 459; cf. vol. 8, repr. 1974, p. 336.

21 Dan 7.13-14, 18, 22, 27. Cf. also 2.44.

22 Eph 2.15.

The unfolding of the mystery in the apostolic kerygma and the growth of the church

This same mystery is enshrined in the apostolic revelation and *kçrygma,* where through the Apostle-Spirit Christ himself dwells in the midst of the apostles, leading them into all truth, and making them in a unique sense, stewards of the mysteries of God, and able ministers of his Spirit.[23] It is on the foundation of this oneness between Christ and his apostles that the whole church is built up and grows up into Christ the head as one body with him. This mystery which was concealed from the ages but is now manifest in the *kērygma* of the apostles, is spoken of in a twofold way corresponding not only to the significance of revelation, but also to the significance and meaning of *oikonomia,* economy. The term *oikonomia*[24] refers either (or both) to the dispensation of the mystery on the part of God, or to the stewardship of the mysteries on the part of the apostles, which is given to them for the sake of the church.[25] That mystery is to be fulfilled in the *oikodomē* and *auxēsis,* the building and increase of the church,[26] and belongs in that fulfilment to the great gathering together into one of all things in Christ, things in heaven and earth, things visible and invisible, through the reconciliation of the cross.[27] In other words, the mystery concerning Christ and his church which reaches out in the redemption of the church and in cosmic significance will be brought to its complete consummation when, to use the language of the Apocalypse, 'the mystery of God will be finished (*etelesthē to mystērion tou Theou*)'.[28] That is the eternal purpose of God which he purposes in Jesus Christ, and which is now revealed and proclaimed in the church.

(b) The mystery of Christ – **prothesis,** *the election of Christ*

Like the word *mystērion, prothesis* has essentially a twofold sense:

---

[23] Cf. 1 Cor 4.1.

[24] Gk, literally 'household management', stewardship, administration, dispensation.

[25] For the use of *oikonomia,* variously translated by the RSV, see the following verses in their contexts, Eph 1.10 (plan), 3.2 (stewardship), 3.9 (plan); Col 1.25 (office); 1 Cor 9.17 (commission); 1 Tim 4.1 (training); cf. 1 Cor 4.1 (stewards, *oikonomous*).

[26] Eph 4.16.

[27] Eph 1.10; Col 1.15-20.

[28] See Rev 10.7 KJV.

(i) It refers to the purpose of God, and is used by Paul particularly of the eternal election which God has purposed in himself and brought about in Jesus Christ. It is the eternal purpose[29] which in Romans Paul speaks of as ranging from predestination on the one hand, to future glory on the other hand;[30] it is at once pre-destination and post-destination, as it were, but the emphasis is clearly on the purpose of God in Christ reaching out from and into the eternal and infinite mystery of God. In the fullness of time that eternal *prothesis* is incarnated in Jesus Christ, by whom all things were created, and through whom all things are restored to the purpose of the divine will. Thus *prothesis* is 'pre-destination', the eternal election moving into time in Christ the elect or beloved one, and reaching out to fulfilment and consummation in the church as Christ's body, 'the fullness of him who fills all in all', as Paul puts it in Ephesians.[31]

(ii) *Prothesis*, however, has another meaning as 'setting-forth', *pro-thesis*, where it appears primarily to have a liturgical significance. Thus in the famous passage in Romans,[32] Paul speaks of our justification freely by grace through the redemption that is in Christ Jesus, 'whom God set forth (*proetheto*) to be a propitiation (*hilastērion*) through faith in his blood to declare his righteousness . . .' The language of Paul recalls the language of the Old Testament in Exodus and Leviticus, and the thought that it is at the mercy-seat, *hilastērion*, where the blood of the covenant is set forth in atonement, that God communes with his covenant people.[33]

The eternal purpose is set forth in communion that reaches beyond the barriers

He holds communion with them on the basis of the atonement in which his covenant purpose is ever renewed in the midst of Israel. It is difficult also not to see here in the mind of St Paul, as in the Old Testament liturgy, the significance of the shewbread[34] associated with that communion in covenant with God. By eating this bread the priests

---

29 Eph 1.11, 'according to the eternal purpose which he has realized in Christ Jesus our Lord'.

30 Rom 8.28ff.

31 Eph 1.22-23.

32 See Rom 3.24-25 KJV.

33 Exod 25.17-22 (cf.37.13-16); Lev 16.2,13-16.

34 In the tabernacle, the shewbread lay on the table outside the holy of holies: see Exod 40.22-23; Lev 24.5-9.

participated sacramentally in the Word of life enshrined in the holy of holies: it was a kind of sacramental manna. In Hebrew this is spoken of as 'the bread of the face' or the 'presence' of God, and in Greek it is called the *artos tēs protheseōs*.[35] In Mark,[36] we have a significant passage where Jesus asserts the authority of the Son of Man over the Old Testament regulations and in particular over the barriers the Jews had created in worship in the house of God. Jesus deliberately broke down those barriers to inter-communion and gave as an example the act of Abiathar, the high priest, who took of 'the bread of the presence', the sacred shewbread of the priests, and gave it to common men in their hunger.[37] The thought here is that the Son of Man has authority to break down the *phragmos*, 'the middle wall of partition' as Paul called it,[38] dividing the Jews from the Gentiles, the inner from the outer court of the temple. Jesus himself spoke of this *phragmos* as the fence or hedge which God built round Israel, his tender vine,[39] which he cultivated with such care but which had to be destroyed while its inheritance was given to the nations of the earth.[40] The same word, *phragmos*, is used by Jesus in the parable of the wedding feast. God's servants are sent out to the highways and hedges or *phragmoi*, that is, to those from beyond the barrier of communion, to compel the people to come in and fill up God's house.[41] There they sit down to partake of the messianic meal, the heavenly manna, and drink of the water of life. That is in parabolic form the counterpart to the apocalyptic description of the great marriage supper of the lamb,[42] when the mystery will be completed and the church will become one with the Word of God. But until then the church is given the sacraments of baptism and holy communion in which the church as one body with Christ continues to feed upon the body and blood of Christ. There in this sacramental fellowship, corresponding surely to the priestly meal at the table of the shewbread before the face of God, the church holds

---

[35] Gk, 'bread of presentation'. Cf. Exod 39.36 (LXX 39.18) & Heb 9.2, 'the bread of the Presence' (RSV), or 'the shewbread' (KJV), literally, 'the presentation of the loaves'.

[36] Mark 2.23-28; cf Matt 12.3-4.

[37] 1 Sam 21.1-6.

[38] Eph 2.14 (*to mesotoichon tou phragmou*) KJV, ('dividing wall of hostility' RSV).

[39] Ps 80.8f.; cf. Isaiah 5.1-7 (*phragmon*, v. 5).

[40] Matt 21.33-43; cf. Mark 12.1ff.

[41] Luke 14.23.

[42] Rev 19.6-9ff.

communion with God, feeding upon the heavenly manna on the very threshold of the holy of holies, through the veil of which Christ our high priest has already entered.

Not all of this, of course, is immediately related to the actual word *prothesis* in its New Testament usage, but it belongs to the context of the word in the *koinōnia* of the church. We may sum up the significance of *prothesis* by saying that it refers both to the divine election or eternal purpose in Christ who is in himself God and man, and it refers to the fact that the eternal purpose is set forth in the incarnation,[43] and continues to be set forth in the midst of the church in its *koinōnia* through word and sacrament. Thus it is that we are given to have fellowship in the mystery of Christ.

(c) The mystery of Christ – koinōnia, *the communion of Christ*

Koinōnia: like *mystērion* and *prothesis*, *koinōnia* has a twofold sense, a primary sense and a secondary sense. Primarily, *koinōnia* means participation through the Spirit in Jesus Christ, participation in the union of God and man in him – in the Johannine record that is profoundly set forth in John 17. Secondarily, *koinōnia* refers to the fellowship which is the church, the communion which exists between members of the body of Christ on the ground of their participation in him.

Koinōnia *as participation in the mystery, and fellowship in the mystery*

Primarily, then, *koinōnia* means *participation* in the mystery of Christ. We have seen that *mystērion* is the union of God and man in Christ, for in the eternal purpose that union was incarnated and bodied forth among humanity in the Word made flesh. That is the mystery of the kingdom in its vertical dimension of *prothesis* as it is inserted into human life and history, the eternal axis of God's purpose of love. In Christ himself that mystery is fully realised and actualised. God and man are uniquely and finally one in him, and in him the kingdom has fully and finally come. Jesus Christ as true God and true man is the mystery of the kingdom in his own person. The whole work of atonement and reconciliation is already wrought out in him. It is a finished work. *Koinōnia* means our participation in that completed work of atonement and reconciliation. It is indeed only in that participation, in the *koinōnia* of the mystery of Christ, that we *know* the mystery of the kingdom.

Secondarily, however, *koinōnia* means *fellowship* in the mystery as well as participation, but fellowship only on the ground of participation. Through the eternal *prothesis* actualised in the incarnation

---

43 See also 2 Tim 1.9-10 and Eph 3.9-11.

of Christ, the mystery of the kingdom is inserted, so to speak, into our fallen humanity, into the midst of our life in the flesh, into the midst of our choices and decisions, into the midst of our knowledge. The penetration of that mystery of the kingdom, of the mystery of the union of God and man, into our humanity, means that it acts critically and creatively in the midst of our life and society, creating room for itself in the midst of our human life. That is, it creates the church, the circle of fellowship in which Christ himself dwells. We have already seen that to belong to the mystery of the kingdom in its secondary sense as mystery given to the saints of the Most High, and realised first of all in the apostolate – that is the nucleus of the *koinōnia*, the *communio sanctorum*, the communion of the saints. It is the *koinōnia* of those who all together have *koinōnia* in the mystery of Christ.

Those two senses of *koinōnia* are inseparable and are mutually related. There is no participation vertically in the mystery of Christ except through horizontal fellowship in the mystery, but there is no horizontal fellowship except by joint participation vertically through the Holy Spirit in the mystery of Christ who is true God and true man. Now it is supremely in the cross and resurrection, by atonement and reconciliation, that the union of God and man is inserted with power into our humanity, creating the church as the body of Christ, and giving it to participate in his relation with the Father. That insertion had already begun in the birth of Jesus, was continued throughout his whole incarnate life, and was enacted in the ministry of Christ where already, therefore, the church was founded as it was formed in the twelve disciples round the person of our Lord, one body with him.

The mystery is inserted as koinōnia *into the midst of our knowledge and our being*

In the incarnation, the mystery of the union of God and man, of the oneness of God and man in Christ, is inserted and enacted in our midst in a twofold way:

(a) it is inserted into the midst of our *knowledge* and that takes place in the teaching of Jesus and in the revelation of the Father through the Son to the disciples, giving them communion or participation in God's knowledge of himself. Thus Christ says in Matthew, 'I thank you, Father, Lord of heaven and earth, that you have hidden these things from the wise and understanding and revealed them to little children; yes, Father, for such was your gracious will. All things have been handed over to me by my Father, and no one knows the Son except the Father, and no one knows the Father except the Son and any one to whom the Son chooses to reveal him.'[44] Thus *koinōnia* is participation in the relation of the Father and the Son – that takes place through the Holy Spirit and is very clearly set out by the fourth Gospel in chapters 13 to 17. It was the insertion of that mystery into the midst of Israel that created at once the band of disciple learners and disciple receivers of revelation, and yet called forth the reaction of resentment which culminated in the cross. This is a *koinōnia* which cuts across the face of mankind's knowledge of God and calls it radically into question, and they resent it. But in spite of all the contradiction of sin, the oneness of God and man is inserted into the knowledge of sinners as an essential part of Christ's reconciliation. The teaching of Christ was an essential part of the atonement, and the atonement could not have taken place apart from it.

(b) On the cross, the oneness of God and man in Christ is inserted into the midst of our *being*, into the midst of our sinful existence and history, into the midst of our guilt and death. The inserting of the oneness of God and man into the deepest depths of human existence in its awful estrangement from God, and the enactment of it in the midst of its sin and in spite of all that sin can do against it, is atonement. In a profound sense, atonement is the insertion of the union into the very being of our alienated and fallen humanity. That insertion of oneness by atonement results in *koinōnia,* in the church as the communion in which Christ dwells, and in which we are made partakers of the divine nature. The *koinōnia* thus created by the atonement and resurrection of Christ is fully actualised in our midst by the outpouring of the Holy Spirit, and is maintained by the power of the Spirit as the church continues in the fellowship of word and sacrament. We cannot pursue here the doctrine of the church, but it is important to see that the church is founded not simply on the words of Jesus to Peter, 'you are Peter, and on this rock I will build my church',[45] but upon the oneness of God and man which in the birth of Jesus was inserted into our human existence, which reached throughout the whole course of his earthly life and particularly of his ministry, into the atonement and resurrection, and then into the ascension. The union of God and man which is the very life of the Son of Man is already of the essence of the atoning and reconciling work of Christ, and it is the same union which, after resurrection and ascension, gathers men and women through the Spirit into itself in and through the church. It

---

[44] Matt 11.25-27 ESV (English Standard Version); cf. Luke 10.21-22.

[45] Matt 16.18.

is in and through *koinōnia,* that the divine *prothesis* enshrining the eternal *mystērion* embodies itself horizontally in a community of those who are at one with God through the reconciliation of Christ.

A summary of mystērion, prothesis *and* koinōnia

We may now summarise the teaching enshrined in *mystērion, prothesis* and *koinōnia,* in traditional dogmatic language. The *mystery* of Christ is the hypostatic union of true God and true man in one person; and as that union is enacted in atonement and in resurrection it issues in the community of the reconciled, the community of the resurrection. The *prothesis* refers to the fact that what God is in Christ as God and man in union, God is antecedently and eternally in himself, and so the *prothesis* speaks of the recession of the hypostatic union into God and its grounding eternally in the communion of the Father and the Son and the Holy Spirit. But *prothesis* is also the setting forth of that union through Christ, through the atonement in such a way that men and women are given to participate in the communion of God the Father, the Son and the Holy Spirit. Thus *prothesis* is, as it were, the projection or the pro-thesis (putting forth) of that communion in and through Christ into humanity creating *koinōnia* as its counterpart through the communion of the Holy Spirit. Indeed it seems clear that these three terms imply the doctrine of the Trinity, *mystērion* more particularly the eternal Son, *prothesis* the eternal Father, and *koinōnia* the eternal Spirit. This trinity of action is grounded eternally in the holy Trinity of Father, Son and Holy Spirit.[46]

2 The mystery of Christ and the holy Trinity[47]

St Paul tells us that the mystery, which we have now seen to be the reality indicated by the doctrine of the hypostatic union, was hid with Christ from the beginning of the world, was not made known in the past ages,[48] but is now revealed by the Spirit. It is the mystery of the Father and of Christ.[49] That mystery, Paul also speaks of as God's eternal purpose which God purposed in himself, which he had purposed in

46 See further *Conflict and Agreement*, vol. 2, p. 92 where Torrance goes on to suggest that it might be more appropriate to use the term 'mystery' rather than the term 'sacrament' to speak of baptism and holy communion.

47 The following section has no equivalent in *Conflict and Agreement*.

48 Col 1.26; Eph 3.9.

49 Col 2.2.

Jesus Christ our Lord.[50] The mystery of Christ which is embodied and bodied forth in the incarnation and revealed to the saints is a mystery that recedes back into the eternal being of the Godhead. What God is in Jesus Christ in relation to man, he is antecedently and eternally in himself. If in Jesus Christ we encounter God and man in hypostatic union, then it is clear that hypostatic union involves a oneness between the incarnate Son and the Father which is eternal – it is a oneness that transcends all temporal and finite conditions, for it is a oneness in the eternal God himself. The hypostatic union is grounded in the eternal communion of Father, Son and Holy Spirit within the holy Trinity.

We cannot enter here into a discussion of the doctrine of the Trinity as such, but we must consider the relation between *prothesis* as the mystery hid eternally in God and as the mystery in its manifestation in the incarnation. That we now proceed to do in terms of (a) the 'pre-existence' of Christ, and (b) election.

(a) The 'pre-existence' of Christ

That is not a happy expression, but it is used to speak of the fact that the incarnate Son of God born of the virgin Mary is the eternally begotten Son of the Father. Jesus Christ spoke of himself as Son of the Father in a relation of exclusiveness and closed circularity, 'no one knows the Son except the Father, and no one knows the Father except the Son.'[51] That saying concerned the mutual relation of knowing between the Son and the Father, but in John's Gospel the Son also spoke in much the same way in regard to love and glory, life and authority, doing and working, and judgement.

Thus, for example, the words of Jesus' prayer in John 17, 'and now, Father, glorify thou me in thy own presence with the glory which I had with thee before the world was made'.[52] At the same time, Jesus prayed for the disciples and believers that they might be given to share in the oneness of the Father and the Son,[53] that is, that they might have fellowship (to use the Pauline term) in the mystery of the Father and Christ. In other words, the work of Christ on the cross, to which he was about to go forward, had its deepest significance in that it rested eternally in the oneness of the Father and the Son – and so, as the writer to the Hebrews expressed it, it was through the eternal Spirit

50 Eph 1.9; 3.11. Cf. KJV and RSV.

51 Matt 11.27; cf. Luke 10.22.

52 John 17.5.

53 John 17.20-23.

that Christ offered himself without spot to the Father.[54] The act of atonement was a trinitarian act, historical to be sure, but it rested ultimately on relations within the holy Trinity.

What Jesus is toward us he is antecedently and eternally in himself, in God[55]

The New Testament and the early church made a great deal of that point. If Jesus Christ is the Son of God for us, he must be Son of God for God. As the incarnate Son, his sonship reaches back to eternal sonship in the Godhead. If he is Son of God on earth, he is Son of God antecedently and eternally in himself.

Again, if Jesus Christ is the Word of God to us, he is the Word of God antecedently and eternally in the Godhead. Not only is he the Word of God uttered by God in the incarnation, but the Word eternally spoken by the Father in the communion of the Holy Spirit within the holy Trinity. Were that not so, the revelation we are given in Christ would not have eternal validity or ultimate reality. That is why the fourth Gospel begins with the wonderful prologue of the eternity of the Word in God, for it is from the eternal God that the Word proceeded, and all that follows in the Gospel – all that Jesus said and was in his dependence as the incarnate Son upon the Father – goes back to and is grounded in that eternal relation of Word to God within God. Similarly, the epistle to the Hebrews begins its exposition of the high priestly work of Christ by teaching that the Son came forth from the Godhead, the Son by whose word all things were created. It is that Son who came and manifested himself, and now in the incarnation stands forth as the divine servant Son to fulfil his work of atonement in entire solidarity with man, eternal Son of God though he was. But all that Jesus did has reality and validity just because it rests upon that eternal relation of the Son with the Father, and therefore reaches out through and beyond the span of years in his earthly ministry into God.

Again, what Christ is in all his life and action, in his love and compassion, he is antecedently and eternally in himself as the eternal Son of the Father. The act of reconciliation and oneness with man, the act of forgiveness in the earthly ministry of Jesus, that is not merely temporal event, but eternal event. Thus we must say that the whole course of Christ's human life and work has its ground in the action of the eternal God.

---

54 Heb 9.14.

55 On the oneness in being and act between Jesus and God, and its implications, see T.F. Torrance, 'The Christ who loves us', *A Passion for Christ*, ed. Gerrit Dawson & Jock Stein, (Edinburgh: Handsel 1999 and Lenoir: PLC Publications), chap. 1, pp. 9-20.

Unless there is this eternal and essential relation between the union of God and man on earth, and the eternal union of God the Father, the Son and the Holy Spirit in heaven, we are not assured either of real, or of eternal relations with God. Our salvation would have otherwise no ultimate ontological ground in reality. What God is toward us in Christ, and in him toward us, in his *opus ad extra*,[56] he is eternally in himself in his *opus ad intra*.

The person of Jesus is eternal, not his humanity

This does not mean that the humanity of Jesus is eternal, that it was eternally pre-existent. It does mean that his person is eternal, that his person is not human, but divine. But it also means that the humanity of Jesus was assumed into oneness with the eternal Son and shares eternally in the glory of the only begotten Son of God which he had before the world was created. The doctrine of the hypostatic union asserts a union of two natures in one person. It does not assert the pre-existence and in that sense the eternity of the human nature, for the human nature of Jesus was a creature of God, and in Jesus himself the human nature had no independent *hypostasis*[57] prior to the incarnation. But we must assert of the humanity of Jesus that it was given *hypostasis*, reality, real personal being, in the eternal Word, in the eternal Son, in the eternal *hypostasis* of God the Son.

On the one hand, therefore, we must say that in the incarnation something altogether *new* happened, even for God, for God the Son was not always man but he now became man, became a creature, though without ceasing to be God. On the other hand, the relation of the incarnate Son to the Father did not arise within time. The life of Christ on earth was the obverse of a heavenly deed, and the result of an eternal decision, an eternal *prothesis* which God had purposed in himself from all eternity.

(b) The eternal election of Jesus Christ

Prothesis understood in terms of the infinite recession of the mystery of Christ into eternity refers to the eternal abiding of the Son in the

---

56 Lat, 'work toward the outside'; *opus ad intra*, 'work toward the inside'.

57 Reality: literally, the Greek *hypostasis*, like the Latin *substantia* (sub-stantia) refers to what stands under (*hupo*, or *hypo*, under and *stasis*, standing) and therefore to the underlying essence or substance of something. It was the term used for the three persons (*hypostaseis*) in the one being (*ousia*) of God, and therefore depending on the use and context can mean reality, personal being, person. The explanatory definition, 'reality, real personal being', has been added to *hypostasis* in the following sentence – Ed.

Father, but *prothesis* understood as the setting forth of that eternal mystery in Christ, in God's oneness with man in Christ, and through Christ, is *election*. The language of the New Testament, especially of St Paul, about this appears to go back directly to second Isaiah, but also directly to the mind of our Lord himself.

To see this aspect of *prothesis* as election, let us turn to an important passage in Timothy where Paul speaks about 'God, who saved us and called us with a holy calling, not in virtue of our works but in virtue of his own *purpose* and the grace, (*kata idian prothesin kai charin*), which he gave us in Christ Jesus ages ago, (*pro chronōn aiōniōn* – before times eternal), and now has manifested through the appearing of our Saviour Christ Jesus, who abolished death and brought life and immortality to light through the Gospel.'[58] But put beside that passage the other important pronouncements on the same subject particularly from the eighth chapter of Romans and the first chapter of Ephesians, where Paul relates this *prothesis* to election in the love of God. Election rests on the relation of love between the Father and the Son, and election is the *prothesis*, the setting forth, the projection of that love in Christ the beloved Son of God, through whom we are adopted into Christ's eternal relation of sonship in love to the Father. Jesus Christ is identical with God's decision and man's election in the divine love. That *prothesis* is the great eternal presupposition of all God's relations with man, and of man's relations with God, and so St Paul speaks of election as the act of God which sums up the whole gospel in Christ.

Election is the eternal purpose of God that is identical with Jesus

Prothesis or election means, then, the eternal beginning of all the ways and works of God in Jesus Christ, in whom God in his free grace bestows himself in love upon sinful mankind and destines them for himself as children of God. That *prothesis* is manifested or set forth in the incarnation in which God himself has come to make our lot his own, to choose us and love us in our actual situation in spite of our sin and guilt. Election means, therefore, that Christ assumes our flesh, assumes our fallen estate, assumes our judgement, assumes our reprobation, in order that we may participate in his glory, and share in the union of the Son with the Father. That is the eternal mystery, the great secret hid from the ages but now revealed in the gospel.

In the supreme sense, Jesus Christ is himself the divine *prothesis*. He is identical with the eternal purpose of God: he is the will of God that has gone into action in choosing to live and die for all, and in his life

---

[58] 2 Tim 1.9-10. For 'ages ago' the KJV has 'before eternal times'.

and death to set his love upon all humanity, and therefore to choose all men and women for himself by pouring out his love for all. Here the twofold significance of *prothesis* means that our salvation in Christ does not rest upon any eternal hinterground in the will of God that is not identical with the foreground in the actual person of the incarnate Son, Jesus Christ. The *prothesis* does refer back to the eternal hinterground of the will of God, but *prothesis* tells us that that is absolutely identical with the existence and action, with the will of Christ for us which he carried out on the cross. If the pre-existence of Christ means that what God is in Christ he is antecedently and eternally in himself, election means that what God is in himself as love he is fully and entirely in Christ Jesus who died for us, for in Christ Jesus the grace of God has moved into time and completes in time the movement of his love toward man, gathering and involving humanity in that eternal movement between the Son and the Father, and the Father and the Son through the Holy Spirit. *Prothesis* means that not only in Christ the beloved are we eternally loved and elected, but that Christ is the *way* in which we are loved and elected. He is the way, the door, and there is no other way to the Father, no other door to salvation, than he.

How does this eternal *prothesis* operate as it moves into time and gathers man into the mystery of God, into the circle of the love of the Father and the Son? God's *prothesis* operates in a way true to himself, by way of communion or *koinōnia* analogous to and grounded in the communion which he has eternally in himself in the relation of the Father to the Son, and the Son to the Father. That is Christ's prayer in John 17 at the last supper. That is his prayer as he broke and distributed the *artos tēs protheseōs*, the bread of the presence, as he gave his disciples in *koinōnia* to share in his mystery and to be one with him as he was one with the Father. As the Apocalypse puts it, 'Behold, I stand at the door and knock; if any one hears my voice and opens the door, I will come in to him and eat with him, and he with me.'[59] The *prothesis* or election of grace goes into action through fellowship – that is what we actually see in the historical foreground, in the life of Jesus as he eats and drinks with publicans and sinners. But that is identical in the divine *prothesis* with the eternal hinterground in the divine will, in the communion of the Father, the Son and the Holy Spirit within the holy Trinity.

Eternal election becomes temporal event confronting people in Jesus

Once again, we cannot now pursue this further into the doctrine of the church, which is the doctrine of the corporate election moving into

---

[59] Rev 3.20.

history as the body of Christ. But at this point we must look back again at the incarnate life of Jesus Christ in the light of the threefold *mystērion, prothesis* and *koinōnia.* The eternal *prothesis* of God has become incarnate in Jesus Christ, has become history. In Jesus Christ, the *prothesis* became encounter, became decision in the living temporal relations with which we men and women have to do in our interactions with one another. Election is the person of Christ, true God and true man in one person, the union of the Father and the Son in eternal love incarnated in our flesh, and bodied forth among sinners. And so men and women in history, in their temporal actions and relations, in the midst of their temporal choices and decisions, are confronted by the Word made flesh, with the eternal decision of God's eternal love. In Jesus Christ, therefore, eternal election has become *temporal event.*

Election is thus not some static act in a still point of eternity. Election is eternal *pre*-destination, moving out of its eternal *prius*[60] into time as living act that from moment to moment confronts people in Jesus Christ. This is living act that cannot be abstracted from the person of Christ. On the contrary, here the person and act of Jesus Christ are one. Election is Christ the beloved Son of the Father, and the act of election in him is once and for all, a *perfectum praesens,*[61] an eternal decision that is ever present. God's eternal decision does not halt or come to rest at any particular point or result, but is dynamic, and ever takes the field in its identity with the living person of Christ. As such election is contemporary with us, acting upon us and acting upon us through our reactions in the personal relations of men and women which it invades and which it sets into crisis. It does that by facing them with the ultimate decision which God has already taken in his love on our behalf and now sets forth in Jesus Christ, but it confronts us with that ultimate decision in such a way that we are summoned in decision before it. What do you think of Christ? Who do people say that I, the Son of Man, am? Who do you say that I am? That is precisely what we see taking place in the whole ministry of Jesus as he penetrated into people's lives by his compassion, and revelation, and confronted them as the truth in the form of personal being, as election in the form of personal being.

That is the dimension of depth in which we are to see everything that Jesus did and said and was during the three years of his ministry as he pressed toward the cross, and the cross itself we see supremely in its setting in that context of the divine *mystērion, prothesis* and *koinōnia.*

---

60 Lat, literally, 'before, sooner', priority or beforeness.

61 Lat, literally, 'completed present', a finished action which is present.

Chapter Six

THE HYPOSTATIC UNION

With this chapter we conclude our section on 'the incarnate life of the Son in the union of his divine and human natures' which we began with chapter three, 'the once and for all union of God and man in Christ: his birth into our humanity'. In the last two chapters,[1] four and five, we considered the doctrine of Christ from two distinct aspects. We considered it from the aspect of the historical life and work of the Lord Jesus Christ the incarnate Son of God, and we considered that both in terms of his obedience to the Father, and in terms of his mission of reconciliation toward humanity. And we saw that at the heart of both was the relation between the Son and the Father which the incarnate Son translated into our flesh, and into which he sought to gather lost mankind, so that all who came to him might share in his sonship and be reconciled as sons and daughters of God. There we considered the doctrine of Christ dynamically in the whole course and movement of his incarnate life and mission.

We considered the doctrine of Christ from its aspect of mystery, from its source in the eternal decision of God, and from its aspect of revelation, the unveiling of the mystery to those who in the church are drawn by the Spirit into communion with Christ, and participate in the mystery hid from the ages, but now revealed and set forth in the gospel of the incarnate saviour. There we considered the doctrine of Christ *sub specie aeternitatis*,[2] in the light of his divine glory, in terms of his relation in being and person to the life of the Father, Son and Holy Spirit in the eternal communion of

---

1 As explained in the editorial introduction, chapters 3, 4, 5, and 6 were all part of a very long chapter 3 in Torrance's manuscript. The wording here of 'in the last two chapters' (the evidence referred to in the footnote at the beginning of chapter 3), indicates either that they were originally separate chapters put together to make one, or that even if sections of the same chapter they were of sufficient weight to be regarded by Torrance as different chapters. It is for this reason, as well as for the sake of readability and size, that they all have been treated here as separate chapters.

2 Lat, 'in the light of eternity' or 'from the point of view of eternity'.

the Trinity. And we saw that to be no less a dynamic account of Christ, for Christ is the only begotten and beloved Son moving into time and completing within time that movement of the eternal love of God.

Now in the third place, we act on that twofold biblical basis and offer a theological account of the doctrine of Christ, but in doing so we must be careful not to move away from either of these basic biblical aspects of the person and work of Christ which we have found to be the very essence of the New Testament revelation. We try to do this by penetrating into its inner logic – not by arguing logico-deductively from fixed premises, but by seeking to lay bare the precise relations embedded in the intrinsic nature of the subject matter. And here we are faced with a fundamental problem: how can we make careful theological statements about this amazing Christ without committing the sin of stripping him of his eternal glory in our account of him, or without converting the movement of his love and grace into a static relationship? Or to put the matter otherwise: how can we be faithful in our theological statements to the nature of the eternal being of the Son who became man and who yet remains God, and at the same time be faithful to the nature and person of the historical Jesus Christ?

That has been the constant problem of theology. We see it already in the early church, in the contrasting emphases between Antioch and Alexandria, in the tendency of the *logos* christology even before that to depreciate the historical Jesus. Then, after the battle with Arianism,[3] we see a tendency of post-Nicene christology,[4] while affirming the true humanity of Christ, to fail to give adequate account of the saving significance of the historical humanity of Christ, content apparently to give the historical Jesus a place only in the liturgical year, and not in the actual doctrine of Christ. By contrast the modern tendency, especially in the west has been to give an account of Christ solely in terms of what he did for man, rather than in terms of his person and being as the Son of God become man, with the result that the doctrine of Christ tended to be displaced by historicism on the one hand, or religious experience and spiritual values on the other hand.

The need to integrate the being and work of Christ, patristic and reformed theology

A study of the history of the doctrine of Christ makes it clear that if we try to state the doctrine of Christ purely in substantive or ontological terms, without adequate attention to his action and saving mission in

---

[3] Arius' teaching was that Jesus was the highest of creatures, subordinate to God and not himself God.

[4] The council of Nicaea AD 325.

history, then we fail to do justice to the New Testament revelation, and replace the understanding of the living Christ by a static dogma about him. But if, on the other hand, we try to state the doctrine of Christ in terms of action alone, in purely verbal terms, without adequate attention to the eternal being and person of Christ as God and man in one person, then we fail to do justice to the New Testament revelation, and replace the authentic Christ by a modern construction, in fact by a Jesus dressed up in the ideas and clothes of our own times.

The doctrine of Christ in the early church had at least this great advantage, that it sought to give its account of Christ in such a way as to leave Christ himself ample room for his own glory and self-revelation. It refused to encase the doctrine of Christ within the mind of man. It gave its account of him in such a way as to acknowledge the reality of his divine and human natures in their union in the one person of the Son, but declined to state *how* those two natures were united in Christ. It was content to declare that the difference of these two natures was not removed by their union, but rather that the propriety of both natures was preserved precisely in their concurrence and union in the one person of Christ the Lord. In other words, the early church sought to preserve the mystery of Christ, and sought to guard that mystery from errors that divided or separated the two natures of Christ on the one hand, or that confounded them or fused them into a higher or lower unity on the other hand. In so doing, the early church rendered theology magnificent service, and its account has ever since commanded the church's assent, although it is increasingly clear that it did not say enough – not that it could say one iota more about how the divine and human natures of Christ are united in the mystery of his person, but that it did not relate that mystery adequately to the historical obedience of Jesus Christ the incarnate Son, and to his atoning work, and so did not give sufficient attention to the *saving significance of the humanity of Christ*. That aspect was largely recovered by the Reformers who made the next major contribution to the historical doctrine of Christ.

Hypostatic union and atoning reconciliation cannot be properly expounded apart from each other

In our account we must try to give both the Patristic and the Reformation doctrines of Christ their full weight, and state the doctrine of the hypostatic union of two natures in the one person of Christ in such a way that we are faithful throughout to the whole biblical account of his person and work as the incarnate Son of the Father. This does not mean that at this point we have to recapitulate all that we have already said especially in chapter two, but it does mean that we must be careful not to state a doctrine of the person of Christ, or of the hypostatic union, and then go on to state the doctrine of the saving work of Christ as atoning reconciliation, as if atoning reconciliation were something that had to be added on to the doctrine of the hypostatic union. On the contrary, we have to see that reconciliation is the hypostatic union at work in expiation and atonement, and therefore that hypostatic union cannot be expounded aright except in terms of Christ's active ministry within our darkness and estrangement, bringing revelation and reconciliation to bear revealingly on one another.

If the mystery of Christ is the incarnation of the eternal purpose of God, then the doctrine of the person of Christ cannot be abstracted from the doctrine of the divine decision to bestow eternal love upon us, and to gather us back into eternal life. At the same time, it is important to see that the doctrine of Christ's work of atoning reconciliation presupposes the doctrine of the hypostatic union of two natures in his one person, for the whole work of reconciliation depends upon the fact that *one person acts both from the side of God, and from the side of man*, both in his divine acts and in his human acts, and that these acts are really and truly identical in the person of the mediator. But before we see fully that relation between the hypostatic union and atoning mediation or reconciliation, we have to consider the saving significance of Christ as truly divine and truly human.

1 The humanity and the deity of Christ

Let us first consider the humanity of Christ and then his deity.

(a) The humanity of Christ

The very fact that God became man in order to save us, declares in no uncertain way that the humanity of Christ is absolutely essential to our salvation. We may even say, and say reverently, that God had to become man for us and our salvation, if we hasten to add that this 'had to' is of *sheer grace*, and not necessity. In the language of the epistle to the Hebrews, 'he had to be made like his brethren'.[5]

(i) Christ's humanity is the guarantee of the coming of God

The humanity of Jesus Christ means that God has actually come among mankind to reveal himself and to reconcile men and women to himself.

---

[5] Heb 2.17.

Christ's humanity signifies the objective actuality of God's coming and presence in the very same sphere of reality and actuality to which we human beings belong. If Jesus Christ were not man as well as God, that would mean that God had not actually come all the way to man, that he had not really got a foothold in our creaturely world, as it were, within the time series in which we are. It would mean that God was still far away from us, as far as the heaven is from the earth, as far as creator is from creature. Any docetic[6] view of the humanity of Christ snaps the lifeline between God and man, and destroys the relevance of the divine acts in Jesus for men and women of flesh and blood.

The New Testament is at pains to make clear the full humanity of Christ. He comes as bone of our bone, and flesh of our flesh; he speaks with a human voice, is brought up in a human family, eats, drinks, thirsts and is hungry, grows weary and is pained, rejoices and sheds tears, and is encompassed with our frailty and infirmity. Here in Jesus the eternal God comes so near that he is a particular man among others, a particular historical individual, a frail human being, such a man in fact that people could easily pass him by as just another man, and easily fail to see anything else in him than ordinary humanity. All that means that in Jesus Christ, the eternal God has actually come to us, and is one of us in the same sphere of reality in which we exist, and with which we are so very familiar.

The stark actuality of Christ's humanity, his flesh and blood and bone, guarantees to us that we have *God* among us. If that humanity were in any sense unreal, God would be unreal for us in him. The full measure of Christ's humanity is the full measure of God's reality for us, God's actuality to us, in fact the measure of God's love for us. If Christ is not man, then God has not reached us, but has stopped short of our humanity – then God does not love us to the uttermost, for his love has stopped short of coming all the way to where we are, and becoming one of us in order to save us. But Christ's humanity means that God's love is now flesh of our flesh and bone of our bone, really one of us and with us.

(ii) The humanity of Christ essential for revelation

This humanity of Christ in its stark actuality is essential to God's *self-revelation*. In Jesus Christ, God's truth has become actual for us in space and time. Jesus Christ is the truth, the mystery in whom are hid all the treasures of wisdom and knowledge,[7] and from whose fullness we

---

6 Any view that Jesus' humanity was not fully and genuinely human, but only appeared to be so.

7 Col 2.3.

may all receive. The astounding thing is that the eternal Word by whom all things were created became a creature, became man, certainly without ceasing to be that eternal Word, and therefore his very creatureliness constitutes the act of revelation, and is the guarantee that revelation is here within creation and accessible to human creatures. It is the guarantee that God's revelation is revelation to creaturely humanity, in the language and life of man, man who is involved within the limitations of time and space, and who cannot escape from them, who can know only within them, within time and history. Because the eternal has become temporal, men and women can know the eternal truth in creaturely temporal form, the eternal truth in time. The historical humanity of Jesus is the guarantee that within the relativities and contingencies of our historical human existence, revelation is reality, and is actuality accessible to us at our level.

(iii) The humanity of Christ essential for reconciliation

The humanity of Christ is also essential to God's act of *reconciliation,* for the actuality of atonement is grounded upon the fact that in actual human nature it is God himself acting on our behalf. Thus any docetic view of the humanity of Christ would mean that God only appears to act within our human existence, or that his acts are only of tangential significance, that they do not really strike into the roots of our existence and condition, and have no relevance to our need. Atonement is real and actual only if and as the mediator acts fully from the side of man as man, as well as from the side of God as God. If the humanity of Christ is imperfect, atonement is imperfect, and we would then still be in our sins. If Jesus Christ is really and truly man, then his death for sin is an act of God himself in human nature, and not just an external act upon human nature. But if atonement is to fulfil its object, it must be not only act of God upon man, but act of man in response to God, man's sacrifice, man's oblation, satisfaction by man for sin before God. Apart from the human obedience and human life and death of Christ, apart from his human sacrifice, we have nothing at all to offer to God, nothing with which we can stand before God, but our sin and guilt. But here in the full humanity of Jesus, as it is joined eternally to his deity in incarnation and atonement, man's destiny as man is actually assured and restored to its place in God from which it has fallen; man's wrong has been set aside in and with the judgement accomplished upon the humanity of Christ, and now in his humanity our new right humanity has been established before God.

Now in the second place, let us consider the deity of Christ.

(b) The deity of Christ

(i) Christ's deity is the guarantee that salvation is the work of God

If the humanity of Christ is the guarantee of the action of God *among humanity*, revealing himself and reconciling sinners to himself, the deity of Christ is the guarantee that his work of revelation and reconciliation is not hollow and empty and unreal on its objective side; it is the guarantee that in Jesus Christ we have to do with the *full reality of God* himself. What Jesus does in forgiveness is not just the work of man, but the work of God, and is therefore of final and ultimate validity. Only God against whom we sin can forgive sin, but the deity of Christ is the guarantee that the action of Christ in the whole course of his life is identical with the action of God toward us. It is not something of God that we have in Christ, but God himself, very God of very God.

Let us note that strictly speaking, we cannot say that Jesus is divine, any more than we can say that God is human. We can say that God has become man, such that he is now also man in Christ, and so we can say that Jesus is man and also God, but to talk about divine humanity is confusion, and a form of monophysite[8] heresy: it is to deny his humanity. Christ is fully man, but while man, he himself in the whole course of his life is also God. Christ is God, true God as well as true man. The significance of his deity lies in the fact that it is God himself who acts in Jesus Christ, in his teaching and reconciliation. 'He who has seen me has seen the Father', he said.[9] We worship and adore Christ as very God of very God, for he *is* God, God incarnate. The relationship we have with Jesus is therefore identical to relationship with God. What Christ Jesus is to us in his person, in word and deed, what he is to us in all our knowledge of him in grace and forgiveness, he is eternally in God. The deity of Christ is thus the guarantee that the actions of Christ are not in time only, not just temporary or temporal actions, but the eternal action of God, eternally real in the Godhead.

When we say that Christ is the object of our faith and worship, we do not simply say that we believe through Christ, as we might believe through a prophet. We do believe through him, and only through him, but through him as mediator who is himself God as well as man, and so we believe through him, and directly *in* him, as God himself. The deity of Christ is not a derivative of our faith, not an inference from his consciousness or from his perfection, or from his work on our behalf.

---

[8] Monophysitism, the view that there is only one nature in Christ not two, from the Gk '*monos*' one, and '*physis*' nature.

[9] John 14.9.

Faith in Christ directly as God is the immediate statement of faith. It is such a primary statement that all other statements of faith have their source there, and are related directly to it. Christian faith starts from the fact that in laying hold of Christ, we lay hold of God himself, for what Christ is, God is.

If Christ is not God, if God is not fully and wholly present in Christ, and identical with Christ, then God does not reconcile the world to himself, and the work of Jesus is not eternally valid, but is only temporal and contingent and relative. If Christ is not God, then the love of Christ is not identical with God's love, and so we do not know that God is love. We may know that Christ is love, but if he is not really God in the complete sense, then all we have in Jesus Christ is a revelation of man, of humanity at its noblest reaching up into the clouds. If Christ is not God, then we do not have a descent of God to man. Thus as the obverse of the fact that Christ's real humanity means that God has actually come to *us* and dwells among us, Christ's deity means that God *himself* has come to save us. The dogma of the humanity of Christ asserts the actuality in our world of the coming of God, and the dogma of the deity of Christ asserts the divine content of our knowledge and salvation, the objective reality of our relation to God himself. The dogma of the deity of Christ means that our salvation in Christ is anchored in eternity: that it is more sure than the heavens.

(ii) The deity of Christ essential for revelation

The full reality of Christ's deity is essential to *revelation*, for the reality of revelation is grounded in the reality of Christ's deity. Certainly revelation would not actually be revelation to us unless it were in our human language and thought, but its reality as revelation of God is grounded on the reality of God's presence in it, the reality of God's act of self communication in and through it; that is, it is grounded on the identity between revelation and God the revealer. The humanity of Christ guarantees the actuality of revelation, but the deity of Christ guarantees its nature as revelation of *God*. Jesus Christ is the Son of the Father, and as such he *is* the revelation he brings. In Christ, God reveals himself in an act that is identical with his person. Were Christ not man, God's revelation would not actually be revelation to man, but were he not also God, it would not be valid, for only God can reveal God. To reveal God, the revealer must take the place of God, and only God can take his own place. This identity of Christ's revelation with God's self-revelation is the ground of our assurance and certainty that what we know and he whom we know in and through Jesus Christ, is none other than the Lord God himself, and that there is nothing in God essential to our knowledge of him which is hid from us. It is the guarantee that God as he is in himself has no reality other than that revealed to us in and through Jesus Christ.

Any weakening in the affirmation of the deity of Christ here results in indecision and uncertainty, and it is because of this weakness that people are engulfed in relativity, and are not sure about what they believe. How then can we know that they are not right and we are wrong? Such uncertainty is the inevitable outcome of doubts and clouded vision of the deity of Christ. When the deity of Christ is denied, his humanity is denied as well, for the bond between Jesus in his humanity and the Father is broken and then Jesus is made out to be a liar. But if Jesus is cut adrift from the truth, then we are all hopelessly at sea. Thus the full reality of Christ's deity is essential to revelation, and faith, for the reality of revelation is grounded in the reality of the action and presence of God in Christ, on the identity of his revelation with God's self-revelation.

(iii) The deity of Christ essential for salvation

The full reality of Christ's deity is essential for *salvation*, for the reality and validity of salvation are grounded upon the reality of Christ's deity. Man's salvation must be an act of *God*, else it is not salvation. The deity of Christ tells us that the action of Jesus in the incarnation and on the cross is identical with God's own action. How can man be saved? The answer is given in the words, 'You did not choose me, but I chose you'[10] – but if that 'I' is not God himself, it is ultimately an illusion. Everything depends on the fact that the whole course of Christ's life is identical with the course of God's action towards humanity. The whole of our salvation depends on the fact that it is God in Christ who suffers and bears the sin of the world, and reconciles the world to himself. The validity of our salvation depends on the fact that he who died on the cross under divine judgement is also God the judge, so that he who forgives is also he who judges. The reality of our salvation means that its reality is anchored on the divine side of reality, that the lamb is slain before the foundation of the world, that he has ascended to the right hand of God the Father almighty, and sits down with God on his own throne because he is God. Everything depends upon the fact that the cross is lodged in the heart of the Father.

It is important to see that if the deity of Christ is denied, then the cross becomes a terrible monstrosity. If Jesus Christ is man only and not also God, then we lose faith in God and man. We lose faith

---

10 John 15.16.

in God because how could we believe in a God who allows the best man that ever lived to be hounded to death on the cross – is that all that God cares about our humanity and its search after God, after truth and righteousness and peace? Put Jesus Christ a man on the cross, and put God in heaven, like some distant god imprisoned in his own lonely abstract deity, and you cannot believe in him, in a god such that he is monstrously unconcerned with our life, and who does not even lift a finger to help Jesus. But if you deny the deity of Christ you also lose faith in man, for that would mean that mankind is such that when they see the very best, the very highest and truest the world has ever known, they crucify that man in spite, and will have nothing to do with him except to hate him. Put God in heaven, and Jesus on the cross only as a man, and you destroy all hope and trust, and preach a doctrine of the blackest and most abysmal despair. Denial of the deity of Christ destroys faith in God and in man, and turns the cross into the bottomless pit of darkness. But put God on the cross, and the cross becomes the world's salvation. The whole gospel rests upon the fact that it is God who became incarnate, and it was God who in Christ has reconciled the world to himself.

We see then the significance of Christ's deity and humanity to lie in regard to his work of revelation and reconciliation. He who reveals God to man, and reconciles man to God, must be both God and man, truly and completely God, and truly and completely man. If the Son was to redeem the whole nature of man, he had to assume the whole nature of man; if in the Son man is to be gathered into the fellowship and life of God, it must be by one who is truly and completely God. Only he can be mediator who is himself the union of God and man, only he can be *pontifex*[11] who is himself the *pons*.

2 The hypostatic union in revelation and reconciliation

The divine and human natures and acts are truly and completely united in one person

When we take the essential significance of the humanity of Christ, and the essential significance of his deity, and put them together, as we must, for there is but one Christ, we are forced to acknowledge that the divine acts in the human nature of Christ, and the human acts in Christ, are *both acts of one and the same person*, and therefore that in that one person, the divine and human acts are united, and further, that the divine and human natures are *one and indivisibly united*. Moreover,

[11] Lat, *pontifex*, 'bridge-maker', and *pons*, 'bridge'.

here we acknowledge that in Christ, in all his acts in revelation and reconciliation, in mercy and holiness, God is as he is antecedently and eternally in himself; and that the love of Jesus and his decision to give himself a ransom for many, are a love and decision that repose upon and issue out of the eternal love and decision of God. We worship and acknowledge the person of Christ as the very person of God eternal, but this one person whom we worship and acknowledge as the person of God himself, is the one person in whom divine and human acts, divine and human natures are united, so that they are all *predicates of the one whole Christ*, the one and only Lord and saviour.

That worship and acknowledgement of Christ the Lord in his divine and human acts, his divine and human natures, is the doctrine of the 'hypostatic union', in which we assert of the mystery of Christ that *divine and human natures and acts are truly and completely united in one person or hypostasis.* That hypostatic union is also known as 'personal union', but personal union here means union in the *one person*. That is a personal union unlike any personal union we know even at its most intimate in marriage, which is union in one flesh, but union of two persons in one flesh. But this is such a union of natures and acts that they are united in one and only one person.

The deity and humanity of Christ have no revealing or saving significance for us apart from their hypostatic union in him

Another way of putting this is to say that when we examine the significance of Christ's humanity and the significance of his deity, we find that the humanity of Christ has no revealing or saving significance for us apart from his deity, and his deity has no revealing or saving significance for us apart from his humanity. The doctrine of Christ is the doctrine of true and complete humanity in full union with true and complete deity, and it is in that *union* that the significance of both revelation and reconciliation lies. It is such a union that the presence of full and perfect humanity does not impair or diminish or restrict the presence of full and perfect deity, and the presence of full and perfect deity does not impair or diminish or restrict the presence of full and perfect humanity. It is such a union that true Godhead and true humanity are joined together in Jesus Christ in such a way that they cannot be separated, and yet that they can never be confused, in such a way also that one does not absorb the other, nor do both combine to form a third entity which is neither divine nor human. In the hypostatic union, God remains God and man remains man, and yet in Christ, God who remains God is for ever joined to man, becomes man and remains man. In this union God has become man without ceasing to be God, and man is taken up into the very being of God without ceasing to be man. That is the mystery of Jesus Christ in whom we have communion through the Holy Spirit.

Now we must consider that hypostatic union in relation first to *revelation* and then to *reconciliation.*

(a) The hypostatic union of God and man in one person is the heart of revelation, and its full substance

The incarnation of the Word in human form and language

The incarnation of the Word means that the Word assumes human form and approaches us from within the actual forms of human life in the only way which we can understand. God's thoughts are not our thoughts and his ways are not our ways; he does not reveal himself to us, however, as he is in himself in his total otherness or difference from us, but comes down to us to reveal himself within the conditions of our human and creaturely nature. But the fact that God has become man, means that he is and can be free for us, so that it is possible for us to know him, not on the ground of any possibility or capacity that we have in ourselves or in human nature, but solely on the ground of the fact that God is free and able to meet us within our human nature, and to reveal himself there to us as very God. There, within human nature, God reveals himself as God in terms of what is not God, in terms of what is man. He speaks to us in a human voice, in human language, and in human thought forms. He assumes the humble form of a servant within the condition of our human nature. He did not assume a form unknown to us, but our actual human form under law, the form of servitude, and so speaks our creaturely and earthly language under all its limitations and imperfections.

The hypostatic union of God and human language is the basis of revelation

But all that would not make revelation, for the incarnation of the Word of God in a human form does not mean that if we think about human forms, we will automatically think about God, and that if we think correctly in our human forms, we will think correctly about God. No, not even in Jesus can we get across from man to God, unless in Jesus Christ there is hypostatic union between him and God, unless the human forms and speech and acts of Jesus are predicates of the one

---

[12] Cf. Hilary of Poitiers, *De Trinitate* (*On the Trinity*, Nicene and Post-Nicene Fathers, vol. 9, Grand Rapids: Eerdmans repr. 1955).

divine person.[12] It is only because Christ is himself personally God that his human speech and human actions, and his human forms of thought, are also divine revelation. The language of Jesus was creaturely language, and quite distinct from God's language, even his language about God, and creaturely language is only capable of speaking of creaturely things. If here God's language has become human and creaturely language, we would not hear God in Jesus' creaturely speech, unless there was a hypostatic relation between his creaturely language and God's own godly language. It is only in that union in which God's language condescends to take on creaturely form, and human language is joined to God's language, that there is real revelation.

Analogy and the hypostatic union

Hypostatic union involves two important factors here.

(i) It tells us that we can know God only in human terms, in terms of *analogy*. All knowledge of God and his relations with mankind are analogical, for in Christ, God has become like man, has taken on a human image, so that we may know God, and understand his revelation in terms of the image, likeness and analogies of man.

(ii) It tells us that it is not by human image, likeness, and analogies that we know God and understand his revelation, but rather through the *hypostatic union* of the human images, analogies and likenesses in Jesus Christ to God himself, that we know God. That means that only certain particular analogies are used, those which repose upon, and derive from, this one particular man, for he alone is in hypostatic union with God. All other analogies are empty, and contain nothing of God, but Jesus Christ is filled analogy, analogy where the content and substance lie in the hypostatic union of God and man in Christ. In the language of the epistle to the Hebrews, he is the effulgence of God's glory, but also the express image of God, the reality of the God he images in himself. All true knowledge of God is through Christ the Word, for there is only one Word, the only begotten Son who is in the bosom of the Father, who has declared him. But that Word has once and for all become man, assumed human form, and never divests himself of that human form. It is in this particular and unique human form for ever joined to the Word or Son of God, that we are given to share in the mystery of God. In Jesus Christ, in whom are hid all the treasures of wisdom and knowledge,[13] and in him alone, do we know God, and have communion with him.

---

[13] Col 2.3.

(b) The hypostatic union of God and man in one person is the heart of reconciliation and its full substance

In the humanity of Jesus, God veils himself to save us and draw us to faith

In Jesus Christ, God has come in the humble form of a servant, veiling his divine majesty, for we could not look on the face of God and live. If God came openly in his glory and majesty, we would be smitten to the ground in sin and death; the last judgement would be upon us, with no time to repent, no opportunity for personal decision in faith. The very humanity of Christ is the veiling of God; the flesh of sin, the humiliation and the form of a servant, the death of Christ all veil God – and so God draws near to us under that veil in order to reveal himself, and save us. It is sometimes asked if God could not reveal himself to us apart from or without Christ, without the humble form of a servant. But if revelation were to take place apart from the veiling of Christ, or in a form totally unknown to us, it would disrupt the conditions of our world and of our humanity, and instead of saving us, it would mean our disintegration. No, the very humanity of Jesus Christ makes salvation possible, for here in the man Jesus, God comes alongside us as man and within our historical existence with its temporal relations, choices and decisions, he acts there upon us personally through word and love, through challenge and decision.

God does not come to manipulate humanity, but to save people personally in personal reconciliation with the Father; and so he confronts them in such a way, that while he judges sin and exposes the human heart with all its evil, he forgives men and women and draws out their hearts in surrender and love to himself. And yet in all that, God has come in Jesus to be one with mankind, to act from within humanity, and as man to yield to the Father the obedience of a true and faithful Son, and so to lay hold of God for us from the side of humanity. It is within that union of the Son to the Father that the sinner is drawn, and given to share. In other words, the hypostatic union is enacted as reconciling event in the midst of human being and existence, and in it men and women are given to share by adoption and grace in Jesus Christ. We shall study that fully later under the doctrine of reconciliation, but here it is important to see that at its heart lies the hypostatic union of God and man in Christ. The humanity of Christ is the actuality of God's presence among man, but his humanity holds mankind at arms length from God, in order to give them breathing space, time, and possibility for surrender to God's challenge in grace, time for decision and faith in him. But it is humanity united to deity, and it is the action of God as man in Christ which delivers men and women from themselves and draws them out in surrender to God. That is the more subjective side of reconciliation.

The hypostatic union, worked out in atonement, is the objective heart of reconciliation

The hypostatic union is also the objective heart of reconciliation, in atonement. The unassumed is the unhealed, but in the hypostatic union God the Son has sinlessly assumed our flesh of sin into oneness with himself. In so doing he has judged sin in the flesh and made expiation for our sin in his own blood shed on the cross, and so has worked the hypostatic union right through our alienation into the resurrection where we have the new humanity in perfect union with God, and in that union we are given to share. The significance of that atonement lies not merely in that Jesus Christ as man offered a perfect sacrifice to God, nor does it lie merely in that God here descended into our bondage and destroyed the powers of darkness, sin, death and the devil, but that here in atonement God has brought about an act at once from the side of God as God, *and* from the side of man as man: an act of real and final union between God and man. Atonement means that God's action was translated into terms of human action, for only in so doing does it reach men and women and become relevant to them as saving act; but it remains God's action, for only so does it touch and lay hold of them, and raise them up to salvation in reconciliation with God.

The one action of the God-man, of God as man, is fulfilled in atoning reconciliation

There are not two actions in the life and death of Jesus Christ, but one action by the God-man, one action which is at once manward and Godward. It was act in our place, and yet act of God for us. Man cannot atone, cannot repair the past. Even Jesus as sinless man could not do that. If he were but man under the judgement of God, he would be annihilated in judgement – the cross would prove a fiasco. And yet atonement, if it is to take place, must take place in man's life, from man's side, but if it is to be saving and life giving atonement, it must be atonement for man, by God for man, for God alone can repair the past. Only the Word through whom man was made, by himself becoming man, can act in man's place and for man in such a way as to restore that which man lost, and recover what man lost in the creator Word of God.[14] The atonement is the work of the God-man, of God and man in hypostatic union, not simply an act of God in man, but an act of God *as* man. And so the hypostatic union and atonement belong together. Atonement is possible on the ground of the hypostatic union, and only on the ground of atoning reconciliation can the oneness of the Word and our flesh of sin be brought to its full *telos*[15] in the hypostatic union of God and man in the risen Jesus Christ.

---

[14] See the argument of Athanasius in *On the Incarnation of the Word.*

[15] Gk, 'end' or 'purpose'.

The hypostatic union is the mainstay of the doctrine of atoning reconciliation

What we have just said can be reinforced at two points by putting them differently. If we could divide the two natures of Christ, his divine and his human nature, into a nature of a divine person and a nature of a human person, then the human acts would not be acts of the divine person, and the divine acts would not be in the human person. In that event, the accomplishment of reconciliation would be illusory, for its ultimate achievement, the union of God and man, would not have been carried through. It is the doctrine of the union of two natures in one person which is thus the mainstay of a doctrine of atoning reconciliation. On the other hand, atonement is not an end in itself, any more than the judgement of sin and the expiation of guilt are ends in themselves. The purpose of atonement is to reconcile humanity back to God so that atonement issues in union between man and God, but it issues in union between man and God because the hypostatic union is that union already being worked out between estranged man and God, between man's will and God's will in the one person of Christ. It is the hypostatic union or hypostatic at-onement, therefore, which lies embedded in the very heart of atonement. All that is done in the judgement of sin, in expiation of guilt, in the oblation of obedience to the Father is in order to bring humanity back to union with God, and to anchor that union within the eternal union of the Son and the Father, and the Father and the Son, through the communion of the Holy Spirit.

(c) Outline of the main stages in the development of the doctrine of Christ and of the hypostatic union

Before we move on to consider the Patristic and then the Reformation doctrine of Christ let us outline the main stages in the history of the church's doctrine of Christ.

(i) *The Council of Nicaea* in AD 325, which affirmed that Jesus Christ is truly (*alēthōs*) God, in an affirmation of faith against the Arians.

(ii) *The Council of Constantinople* in AD 381, which affirmed that Jesus Christ was perfectly (*teleōs*) man, against the Apollinarians[16] whose teaching impaired the perfect humanity of Christ.

---

[16] Apollinarius taught that in Jesus the Word took the place of the rational spirit or mind (*nous*) in man. This was attacked on the ground that if Jesus did not possess a normal human mind and spirit then he was not fully human.

(iii) *The Council of Ephesus* in AD 431, which affirmed that Jesus Christ is one person, against the Nestorians[17] who divided Christ into two persons.

(iv) *The Council of Chalcedon* in AD 451, which affirmed that in Jesus Christ there are two distinct natures in one person, and that in the one person of Christ they were hypostatically united 'unconfusedly, inconvertibly, indivisibly, inseparably', or 'without confusion, change, division or separation'. This was affirmed against the Eutychians[18] and Monophysites.[19]

(v) *The Council of Constantinople* AD 680, which asserted that Jesus Christ possessed a human will as well as a divine will, against the Monothelites[20] who asserted that in Jesus Christ there was only one single will.

Those are the five main stages in the Patristic doctrine of Christ, but to them we must add two more from modern times, which we shall consider in due course.

(vi) *The Reformation*, which sought to state the whole historic doctrine of Christ in East and West more in terms of Christ's saving and reconciling mission, that is, in more dynamic terms.

(vii) *Early Scottish theology* (as in the teaching of Robert Boyd of Trochrig),[21] and *the theology of Karl Barth*[22] in our own day (after the assessment of the vast documentary study of the historical Jesus), where *anhypostasia* and *enhypostasia* are brought together to give full stress upon the historical Jesus Christ as the very Son of God.

---

17 Nestorius, who emphasised the full reality of both the divine and human in Christ, was accused of teaching a doctrine of two persons and so held to have compromised the unity of Christ.

18 Eutyches taught a doctrine of 'two natures before the incarnation and one after' which was condemned on the ground that Christ's human nature was no longer the same as ours but had been swallowed up by his divinity.

19 Monophysitism, the view that Christ only has 'one nature', *monos physis*.

20 Monothelitism, the view that Christ only has 'one will', from *monos* one, and the verb thelô (or ethelō) 'I will'.

21 See the section on 'Robert Boyd (1578-1627)' esp. p. 71, in chap. 2 'The Older Scottish Tradition 1581-1647' pp. 49-92, of T.F. Torrance, *Scottish Theology: From John Knox to John McLeod Campbell* (Edinburgh: T&T Clark 1996).

22 Karl Barth, *Church Dogmatics*, 4/2, Eng. trans. (Edinburgh: T & T Clark 1958), pp. 49ff., 91f.

3 The Patristic doctrine of Christ

(a) The differing strands in Patristic theology

As we have already had occasion to note, the attempts to formulate a doctrine of Christ in the early church tended to fall into two camps, according to the tendencies associated with Antioch and Alexandra, which involved in the Antiochene teaching, an ebionite[23] tendency, and in the Alexandrian teaching, a docetic tendency. But between those more extreme positions, there was a middle stream of development, running from Irenaeus to Athanasius and Cyril, which stressed equally the full humanity and the full deity of Christ, and it was out of that that there emerged the orthodox doctrine of Christ. It must also be added that with John Philoponos in the sixth century the theological terms used in christology were given a more dynamic form and interpretation.

In the teaching of Irenaeus and Athanasius, there was considerable stress upon the obedience of the incarnate Son, and consequently upon the saving significance of the humanity of Christ, both in regard to revelation and in regard to reconciliation. Also in their writings, notably in that of Athanasius, there is found a full and satisfying account of the atonement, in which incarnation and atonement are very closely associated, and are mutually involved.

(i) Defence of the deity and humanity of Christ

This association of incarnation and atonement was unfortunately not followed when the church councils came to offer their formulations of the doctrine of Christ, in which they had to affirm against heretical teaching, first the full deity of Christ, and then his full humanity. In the concern to assure the proper place in faith of the deity and humanity of Christ, they tended to lose sight of his atoning work, so far, that is, as credal formulations were concerned. However, it must be admitted that the lack in credal formulation corresponded to a lack in clarity and understanding among the fathers as to the significance of the death of Christ. When Chalcedonian christology came to be formulated, largely under the guidance of the Epistle of Leo, that is from the church in the West, the doctrine of the person of Christ was carefully and clearly formulated, but in such a way that the atoning work of Christ was not given its proper place. In the theology of the West there was an adequate doctrine of the incarnation, as in the teaching of Leo himself, but the doctrine of the death of Christ tended to be upheld in sacrificial

---

23 Ebionism, the view that Jesus was not God but an ordinary man, adopted to become Son of God.

terms of a forensic character, and these two, the incarnation and the death of Christ, were not properly or fully related together in doctrine.

But whenever incarnation and atonement are not properly and fully related, there is an inevitable tendency toward a conception of the two natures of Christ in which the two natures are not seen in their full unity in the one mediator. That duophysite tendency,[24] however, tended itself to be counter balanced or corrected by a tendency in the opposite direction, that is, toward monophysitism, both in the East and in the West. That was a tendency to allow the full humanity of Christ to be impaired through absorption into his divine nature, in spite of the rejection of monothelitism. That would appear to be a direct result of the failure to give the atoning work of Christ the mediator its full place in Chalcedonian and subsequent christology. Whenever the mediatorship of Christ is thrust into the background, as became increasingly apparent in the growth and development of the liturgy in East and West, it is very difficult to stem the tide of monophysite tendencies in christology.

The full humanity of Christ the ultimate danger point

As we look back upon the development of Patristic christology, we can see that the danger point lay ultimately in attacks not against the deity of Christ, but against his full humanity. The first great council did of course reckon with the dangerous attack of Arianism, and against it, in unmistakable terms, declared faith in the true and full deity of Christ – but in the post-Nicene period, where that emphasis was carried through, there grew up a shyness of speaking about the assumption by the Son of our flesh of sin, in case that would detract from the perfection of the incarnate Son. And again, when after Chalcedon attacks were launched against the fullness of Christ's human nature, there was no encouragement to take in all its seriousness the fact that he who knew no sin was made sin for us,[25] lest the assumption of 'flesh of sin' should detract from the perfect humanity of Christ.

(ii) The council of Chalcedon

That difficulty is already seen in the Chalcedonian christology itself, magnificent as it was so far as it went. The council of Chalcedon followed the councils of Constantinople and Ephesus, in which both Apollinarianism and Nestorianism were rejected. At Constantinople

---

[24] Duophysitism, from the Gk *duo* two and *physis* nature, is the doctrine that there are two natures, divine and human, co-existing in the incarnate Christ.

[25] 2 Cor 5.21.

the completeness of Christ's human nature had been affirmed, and at Ephesus the unity of the divine and human natures in the one person. Then came the important Chalcedonian statement:

> Following the holy fathers, we all teach with one accord one and the same Son, our Lord Jesus Christ perfect in Godhead and perfect also in humanity (*teleion ton auton en theotēti, kai teleion ton auton en anthrōpotēti*), truly God and also truly man, being of a reasonable soul and body (*theon alēthōs kai anthrōpon alēthōs, ton auton ek psychēs logikēs kai sōmatos*), of one being with the Father as touching his Godhead (*homoousion tō patri kata tēn theotēta*) and also of one being with us as touching his humanity (*kai homoousion ton auton hēmin kata tēn anthrōpotēta*), being like unto us in all things except sin (*kata panta homoion hēmin chōris hamartias*), begotten of the Father before all times according to his Godhead, and also in the last days born for our sake and for our salvation, of the virgin Mary the bearer of God according to his humanity, one and the same Christ, the Son, Lord, only begotten, of two natures, without confusion, without conversion, without division, and without separation (*en duo physesin asugchutōs, atreptōs, adiairetōs, achōristōs*); the difference of natures not being removed by their union, but rather the propriety of each being preserved and concurring in one *prosōpon* (*eis hen prosōpon*) and in one hypostasis (*kai mian hypostasin*) so that he is not divided or separated into two *prosōpa* (*eis duo prosōpa*) but in one and the same only begotten Son, God the Word, Lord Jesus Christ, even as the prophets of old and Jesus Christ himself taught us concerning him, and the creed of our fathers that has been handed on to us.

Strictly speaking *prosōpon*[26] and *hypostasis*[27] ought to be mentioned of Christ *together*: both are required to say what each by itself lacks.

It is worth noting right away that the only place where the saving work of Christ is mentioned is in connection with his birth 'for our sake and for our salvation'. That is important, for it means that the nativity of Christ was itself redeeming event, but it is not enough to say that, especially when it is silent about the saving work of Christ in his life and death, and when the statement about the human nature of Christ can be constructed in such a way as to play down the fact that he assumed our fallen humanity without of course sinning himself.

---

26 Gk, literally 'face', and hence external form as an individual.

27 Gk, literally 'standing under', and hence reality or concrete subsistence.

The difficulty behind the Chalcedonian concept of 'human nature' and 'divine nature'

The crucial factor here is the meaning of the 'human nature' of Christ. There is no doubt at all that by 'human nature' the fathers wanted to stress the actuality of Christ's union with us in our true humanity, that Christ was human in all points exactly like us, yet without sin. And that is right as far as it goes, for Christ was fully human like ourselves, coming into and living in our mode of existence, and sharing in it to the full within a span of temporal life on earth between birth and death, and in the unity of a rational soul and body. But the Chalcedonian statement does not say that this human nature of Christ was human nature 'under the servitude of sin' as Athanasius insisted; it does not say that it was corrupt human nature taken from our fallen creation, where human nature is determined and perverted by sin, and where it is under the accusation and judgement of holy God.

But that is all essential, for 'the unassumed is the unhealed', as Gregory Nazianzen expressed it, and it is with and within the humanity he assumed from us that the incarnate Son is one with the Father. Therefore the hypostatic union cannot be separated from the act of saving assumption of our fallen human nature, from the living sanctification of our humanity, through the condemnation of sin in the flesh, and through rendering from within it perfect obedience to the Father. In short, if we think of Christ as assuming neutral and perfect humanity, then the doctrine of the hypostatic union may well be stated *statically*. But if it is our fallen humanity that he sinlessly assumed, in order to heal and sanctify it, not only through the act of assumption, but through a life of perfect obedience and a death in sacrifice, then we cannot state the doctrine of the hypostatic union statically but must state it *dynamically*, in terms of the whole course of Christ's life and obedience, from his birth to his resurrection.

For many people the difficulty with Chalcedonian christology is this, that when it speaks of 'the human nature' of Christ, it seems to be speaking of some *neutral* human nature which we know in some way from our general knowledge of humanity, even though we nowhere have any actual experience of such neutral human nature. Here then, there appears to be a twofold difficulty. It appears to define the human nature of Jesus in terms of some general conception of human nature, and then to think of Christ's human nature as perfect, or at least neutral, and to that extent unlike our actual human nature. Now if Christ's human nature is perfect, and further, if Christ is the Word become man, the new Adam, then we cannot define Christ's human nature in terms of some general idea of human nature we have already conceived, for it is the human nature of Christ alone that is the norm and criterion of all true human nature. The same mistake appears to be present in the Chalcedonian concept of the divine nature of Christ, for it too is defined in terms of some general concept of divine nature, which somehow we have already formed in our minds, whereas if Christ is the Son of God become man, then it is the divine nature of Christ which must be our only norm and criterion for the understanding of divine nature. It is not surprising therefore that the Chalcedonian christology, in spite of its intention, should always tend towards a form of dyophysitism, tempting correction in the form of being counterbalanced by a new monophysitism.

(iii) The meaning of 'nature' and physis

It is possible, however, to interpret the term 'nature' or *physis* rather differently, by distinguishing it from the Latin *natura*. *Natura* refers originally to the state of being born and appears to have retained more of that in its Latin use (what we think of when we think of nature in general) than the Greek *physis*. *Physis* comes, similarly, from *phuō*, meaning to make to grow or to grow, but very early it came to have a distinctive sense. This appears best perhaps in the Greek phrase *kata physin*, according to the nature of something: for example, true knowing of something is to know it *kata physin*, according to its nature or reality, in terms of what it actually and really is, *kat' alētheian* or according to its truth. It was this sense of *physis* that Heidegger highlighted when he spoke of *physis* as referring to emergence, the realm of that which arises, which is not synonymous with the natural phenomena we think of in terms of 'nature' (in the sense of *natura*). *Physis* is rather *being itself*, that by virtue of which existents or essents[28] become and remain knowable, that which manifests itself in unfolding, and perseveres and endures in that manifestation of itself. Thus Heidegger could speak of *physis* as referring to the realm of things that emerge and linger on. *Physis* is also sometimes the process of emerging from the hidden, whereby the hidden is first made to stand out. In this sense *physis* can apply not only to earthly realities but also to heavenly realities, the world of God as well as the world of human beings and things.

'Physis' refers to the nature of things in their being – the parallel with 'alētheia', truth

That is to say, originally, *physis* was not narrowed down in its reference (as it was in Latin when it was translated *natura* or 'nature') to the

28 'Things that are', a neologism or new word derived from the Latin *esse*, to be.

realm of natural phenomena, for it referred to the nature of things in their own being and as they emerge before us out of their hiddenness. *Physis* is experienced, Heidegger maintained, primarily as the focusing of *being* upon our attention.

Now truth, *alētheia*, is the manifestation of the hidden, that which is what it is in the event of its disclosure. Thus in that sense *physis* and *alētheia* are more or less equivalents, for truth is the truth of being coming out of its hiddenness into manifestation, the revealing of *physis*. Truth means that the *physis* of something stands out before us and manifests itself before us in accordance with what it is in its own being, reality, or *physis*. Thus Heidegger could also say that the essence of being is *physis*, being that emerges and makes itself manifest, being coming out of concealment, while truth (*alētheia*) is the un-concealment (*al-ētheia*)[29] of being and of what inheres in being as it emerges to view. In view of this, we can understand why the Greeks could speak of knowledge of the truth as a knowing in the openness of being, knowledge that takes place in and with the emergence or disclosure of being, under the overmastering presence of being and under its power of *alētheia* or truth.

The use of 'physis' in the Greek fathers – alētheia, ousia *and* hypostasis

If, then, we take the term *physis* in this sense we can understand how the Greek fathers could use as equivalents thinking or knowing *kata physin* (according to the nature or reality of something) and thinking or knowing *kat' alētheian* (according to the truth of something), *alēthōs*, truly. In that sense the fathers could apply *physis* equally to God and to man, to Christ in his being as God, insofar as he is *homoousios*[30] with the Father, and to Christ in his being as man, insofar as he is *homoousios* with man. This does not mean that we are concerned here with some neutral nature, but with something that comes to view and imposes itself upon our minds from the side of the being that masters our attention.

Moreover, understood in this way, it is possible to see why some of the fathers could use the term *physis* as equivalent sometimes to being, *ousia*, and sometimes to *hypostasis*. Thus when some fathers spoke of Christ in terms of one nature, *mia physis*, they meant that in Christ we have the manifestation of one reality (*ousia*) not two realities; and when they spoke of *physis* as equivalent to *hypostasis* they meant that he was in himself the reality which became manifest

---

29 *Lēthē* in Gk means forgetting, oblivion, and hence the negative *a-lēthē* means un-concealment.

30 Gk, 'of the same being or nature'.

toward us, *physis* and *hypostasis* here being used to refer to the concrete objectivity of the one reality of Christ. In view of this, we can now see that some fathers who spoke of Christ as one *physis* were not necessarily monophysite (denying divine and human 'natures' in Christ, and letting the human 'nature' be swallowed up in the divine), but were consistent with Chalcedonian thought. Thus many traditional 'monophysites' to this day hold a 'Chalcedonian' christology – much of the difference that has been traditionally exploited here in debate is due to terminological differences rather than difference in actual meaning or intention.

Certainly after Cyril of Alexandria agreed to a formula which spoke of 'two natures', divine and human, in one person in regard to Christ, agreeing to drop his own expression '*mia physis*' (one nature), some sort of convention began to settle in. But even then the term *physis* (understood as the Latin 'nature') does not come to be used in the later sense of *physis-natura* until after Chalcedon. Others, who like Philoponos were closer to the thinking of Athanasius, came under the criticism of the Aristotelianising churchmen like John of Damascus.

(iv) The nature of Jesus' humanity – fallen humanity redeemed and perfected[31]

But now to return to our discussion: our immediate question is, How then are we to speak of 'the human nature of Christ' in the hypostatic union? We must surely begin with the fact that Christ is the new man, the perfect man, and the one man who represents all humanity. His human nature is true human nature (even if it was uniquely joined to divine nature, as we are not), and far from measuring its truth and fullness by our own human nature, we must judge the poverty of our human nature by the perfection and fullness of his human nature. But if we do that, we must also say clearly that he was made in the likeness of our flesh of sin; he assumed sinful flesh, that is, our adamic fallen human nature, and in sinlessly assuming it began its redemption and healing. He carried that redemption and healing throughout the whole of his life which he lived in perfect obedience, truth and holiness. Throughout, within the poor clay of our corrupt humanity, he showed forth perfect humanity, remaking ours and converting it in himself. Through his obedience unto death, and through his resurrection, in which he had power to lay down his life and to take it again, he raised

[31] See further T.F. Torrance, *The Trinitarian Faith* (Edinburgh: T & T Clark 1988), pp. 161-68.

our fallen nature as a perfect and incorruptible human nature, so that in the resurrection, the body which was raised from the dead was as perfect as his holy life and person all through his life from his birth to his death.

When we speak, therefore, of the 'human nature' of Christ in the hypostatic union, we have to say two things.

(1) On the one hand, we have to say that he was completely *like us,* in all things, in our frail, feeble and corrupt and temptable humanity, yet without being himself a sinner. Nevertheless, he did identify himself in complete and utter solidarity with us sinners in our fallen and guilty humanity, under God's wrath and judgement. He came to be one of us, and one with us in that condition, in order to save us and deliver us from the bondage and corruption of sin under the divine judgement. He was completely one with us vicariously.

(2) On the other hand, we must say that he was completely *unlike us* in that by taking our fallen human nature upon himself, he condemned sin in it; he overcame its temptations, resisted its downward drag in alienation from God, and converted it back in himself to obedience toward God, thus sanctifying it. From the beginning to the end of his life, he submitted our fallen humanity with our human will to the just and holy verdict of the Father, freely and gladly yielding it to the Father's judgement, and was therefore obedient unto the death of the cross. In all this the Son is wholly like us, in that he became what we are, but also wholly unlike us, in that he resisted our sin, and lived in entire and perfect obedience to the Father. And therefore in Christ's humanity there took place a vicarious[32] sanctification of our human nature and lifting of it up again into fellowship with God. There alone, in Christ, can human nature be true and perfect, for human nature was made for fellowship with God, and it is always less than human when it withdraws from or alienates itself from that divine fellowship, while in Christ it is restored to fellowship with God. Here Jesus was wholly unlike us in his actual human nature, for in his human nature he overcame the opposition and enmity of our fallen human nature to God, and restored it to peace with God first in glad and willing submission to God's judgement, and then in the resurrection from the dead.

---

[32] 'Standing in our place' (Lat, *vicarius,* substitute). Christ in his humanity stands in our place and represents us, and hence the term the '*vicarious humanity*' of Christ in which the humanity of Christ takes our place and represents us, so that what is true of him is true of us, and what he did in his (our) humanity is ours.

The Chalcedonian hypostatic union must be stated dynamically in terms of the twin assumption and sanctification of fallen human nature by Jesus

We can state the doctrine of the hypostatic union aright only if we state it in that twofold situation of the Son of God in our flesh. We cannot for a moment allow to drop out of sight here the fact that he sinlessly suffered our corruption and curse, and was made sin for us, the just for the unjust, suffering our conflict and its judgement in a way and at a depth that we can never fathom, and must never take for granted. We must therefore think of the whole life of Christ, lived out in our human nature, as a life of holy obedience to God in the midst of our disobedience, of peace with God in the midst of our enmity, of fellowship with God in the midst of our estrangement, of faithfulness to the divine covenant where we are unfaithful. Thus from first to last, the hypostatic union means such a union of the Son with our own human nature under the servitude of sin and judgement, that it is *one long act of atoning and sanctifying reconciliation,* in which he both judges our sin and enmity, and restores our human nature to its true relation with the Father and therefore to its perfection as human nature. In that light, the Chalcedonian formulation can still be used, but with profounder significance, and in a way much more faithful to the biblical revelation. In that light we can go on to make some statements about the hypostatic union.

(b) The significance of the Chalcedonian 'hypostatic union'

(i) The hypostatic union an act of grace

The first thing to be said, is that the hypostatic union must be looked at only from the perspective of God's amazing act of grace, in which God the Son freely descended into our human existence, and freely assumed human being into oneness with his divine being. That was an act of sheer grace. He did not need to do it. He did not owe it either to himself or to man to do it; it is an act grounded only in the pure overflowing love of God. It is in no sense a two-sided event, for even though there is within it, in the unity of divine and human natures, act of God and act of man, the whole act of incarnation, including all the divine and human acts within the hypostatic union, is grounded solely and entirely and exclusively in the act of God's grace.

(ii) The twofold movement of condescension and elevation

Within this one supreme act of grace, in which God assumes human being into oneness with his own divine being, and maintains it in that oneness, there is a twofold movement. There is first the act of divine condescension and humiliation, in which the Son mercifully took upon himself our alienated humanity, in order to assume our alien and creaturely human being into unity with himself. But this act of humiliation on the part of the Son is also an act of grace, elevating and exalting our poor human being into healing communion with the life of God, and into sanctification in the divine holiness. These are not two acts, but one act, which completes its 'downward' movement of grace in an 'upward' movement of sanctification, and the 'upward movement' takes place in the very act of condescension, for the coming of God down to man is as such the gathering of man into fellowship and reconciliation with God. Just as the lifting up of the Son of Man on the cross was already the beginning of his glorification and ascension to the right hand of God, so the assumption of our humanity, which was also a sanctifying and healing act, was also its elevation and exaltation into union and communion with God.

(iii) The uniqueness of the hypostatic union

The hypostatic union describes, then, the union mercifully and freely and savingly made by God in the *hypostasis* or the mode of existence of the person of the Son. That is why it is hypostatic or personal, but it is as unique as the *hypostasis* or person of God the Son is, and is entirely without parallel or analogy. It is *sui generis*[33] and to be understood only in terms of itself. It is not a personal union in our common sense of the word 'personal', which involves a mutual relation between two personalities, but personal only in the sense that it is grounded in the one unique person of God the Son. It is 'personal' because it is 'in the person of the Son' – that is the meaning of hypostatic. That is why the expression '*anhypostasia*'[34] cannot mean '*impersonality*' or what is '*impersonal*', for the expressions 'impersonal' and 'impersonality' presuppose that when we speak of 'hypostatic union' we are speaking of a personal union in our sense of the term 'personal'. Hypostatic union does not mean, then, a union between two persons and in that sense a personal union, but precisely the opposite, a union within the *one* person of the Son, so that it is only in and through the one person of the Son that we can have personal relations with the Father. And here 'personal' relations is therefore not a psychological expression, but a christological, because christocentric, expression.

---

33 Lat, 'of its own kind'.

34 *An-hypostasia*, literally 'non-personhood' (*an* being the negative prefix in Gk, cf. Eng. un-), ie. the state of being without independent personhood.

(iv) The integrity of both natures – correction of Alexandrian extremes

The hypostatic union is marked out and guarded from the extremes of Alexandrian theology by the first two Chalcedonian adverbs, *inconfuse et immutabiliter* (*asugchutōs, atreptōs*), 'without confusion' and 'without change'. There can be no intermingling or commingling of the divine and human natures, and no changing of one into the other. But that has to be restated dynamically, and so we must say something like this: in his act of humiliation, in freely uniting himself to our fallen human nature, and in savingly taking its sin and corruption upon himself in order to work out our salvation, the divine nature of Christ suffered no change, but remained truly and fully divine.

It was precisely by remaining what it ever was, that the divine nature was able to save and redeem that which it assumed into oneness with itself. On the other hand, in being assumed, healed and sanctified in the incarnate Son, and so elevated to participation in the divine, human nature also suffered no change, but remained truly and fully human. It was precisely by being kept and maintained as human nature, and in being restored to its fullness as human nature in union and communion with the divine, that human nature was redeemed as human nature. Any transubstantiation of human nature would be its dissolution. That error, upon which the whole of our salvation would be shipwrecked, is carefully and decisively set aside by the Chalcedonian formulation of the hypostatic union.

(v) The union of both natures – correction of Antiochene extremes

The hypostatic union is marked out and guarded from the extremes of Antiochene theology by the second two Chalcedonian adverbs, *indivise et inseparabiliter* (*adiaretōs, achōristōs*), 'without division' and 'without separation'. There can be no dividing or separating of the divine and human natures from one another in the incarnation. But that must be stated more dynamically. The act of the Son in humbling himself to take upon himself our humanity in the likeness of the flesh of sin and in the form of a servant, without of course sinning himself, and the act of the perfect obedience of the Son to the Father in the whole course of his life in human nature, his whole participation in the life of God, are not two independent acts or events separated from one another. In all their distinctiveness, they are fully and finally and irrevocably united in being the acts of the one person of the incarnate Son of God.

It is precisely in the impossibility of their separation that our redemption lies, for it is redemption into unbreakable union and communion with the Father, and the once and for all exaltation of our human nature in Christ, into the life of eternal God. It is because the incarnate Son and the Father are one, and cannot be divided or separated from one another, that our salvation in Christ is eternally secure in the hand of the Father, for no one can snatch us out of his hand.

(vi) Communicatio idiomatum – *the communication of properties*

The Chalcedonian formulation also asserted that 'the distinction of the natures is in no way destroyed because of the union, but rather the peculiarity of each nature is preserved'. This statement has more implications than at first appear. It states very clearly that the divine and human natures remain in their distinctiveness, and that what is proper to each is preserved in the union. That is of special importance for the preservation of the humanity of Christ. It is precisely because the humanity of Christ in all its distinctiveness is joined hypostatically to the divine nature, that the humanity of Christ remains in permanent existence; it does not pass away with the death of Christ, or with his resurrection and ascension.

Therefore the hypostatic union means that Christ continues to exist as man, risen man and true man even now at the right hand of God, and that he will come again as man, and that it is through this man, as Paul said on Mars Hill, that God would judge the world.[35] That preservation of the human nature of Christ in and through death, resurrection and ascension, is of fundamental importance for the doctrine of atonement, for Christ's heavenly sympathy and intercession, for the sacraments, and for his advent and final judgement. It is of absolute importance for the saving relevance of the gospel of the risen Christ to us who remain creatures of flesh and blood.

The properties special to the divine or human nature may be predicated of the other through their sharing in the one person of Christ

But there is more than this to the Chalcedonian statement. It means that each nature does what is proper to it in communion with the other, and not in separation from the other. Therefore, it is only right and natural, to use the much earlier language of Origen,[36] that human predicates are applied to the divine nature, and that the human nature is adorned by appellations or descriptions of divine honour. In other words, because the divine and human natures, acts and qualities are predicated of the one person of Christ, the qualities and acts predicated of the one person in virtue of his divine nature as Son of God, may be

---

35 Acts 17.31.

36 Origen (c. 185-254 AD), *De Principiis*, 2.6.3, Ante-Nicene Fathers, vol. 4 (Grand Rapids: Eerdmans repr. 1976), p. 282.

predicated of Christ under his human appellation as Son of Man, or son of David. Likewise, acts and qualities predicated of the one person of Christ in virtue of his human nature, may be predicated of Christ under his divine appellation as Son of God. That is because the one person shares equally in the names, properties, acts and experience of both natures. That measure of mutual transference of qualities was called the *communicatio idiomatum*.[37] But in Patristic theology, for example, in Cyril and Leo, this expression did not refer to a mutual interpenetration of the divine and human qualities or properties, as it came to be understood in Lutheran theology. Chalcedonian christology is careful to guard against any notion of intermingling or commingling of the natures which meant the absorption of the one into the other, or the impairing of either in its full reality and propriety.

(vii) The weakness of the logos *christology*

One other feature of the Chalcedonian christology needs to be mentioned, though it concerns more the theology of Cyril and the rejection of Nestorianism than the actual terms of the Chalcedonian formulation itself. It is the distinct tendency to avoid the problem of Nestorian separation of the two natures of Christ, with its tendency toward there being two persons in Christ, by teaching that what the Word assumed in the incarnation was not 'a man', but 'man'. Now there is a clear danger in speaking of the assumption of 'a man', for that savours of adoptionism, but on the other hand, to speak of the assumption of 'man' savours of the idea that what was assumed was only human nature in general, human nature with all its human properties and qualities. That was precisely the danger of Alexandrian theology, which ever since the *logos* christology came on the field, tended to throw into the background the significance of the historical Jesus as a single individual man. And there can be no doubt that it was this tendency which all through prevented the church for 1500 years and more, from giving full and proper place to the historical Jesus Christ. It was only because the influence of men like Irenaeus, Melito, Athanasius and Cyril of Jerusalem remained on in the church, not least in the liturgy, in spite of its monophysite tendencies, that room was kept for the historical Jesus Christ in the faith and worship of the church.

(c) Factors helping to safeguard the humanity of Jesus

But besides the influence of these men, there were four distinct factors that tended to inhibit the excesses of Alexandrian christology.

---

[37] Lat, 'communication of properties'.

(i) The condemnation of Apollinarius

In AD 381 we have the condemnation of Apollinarius, and the Apollinarians at the Council of Constantinople. Apollinarius had taught that Christ did not possess a rational human soul, but had the Word instead of a rational human soul. The affirmation that Christ did possess a human soul, was perfectly (*teleōs*) man, became normative. It was our whole human nature that he assumed, mind and will and soul, for all these come under his redemption, and unless the whole of our human nature is assumed, the whole is not redeemed.

(ii) The condemnation of Eutyches

After the triumph of Cyrillian christology over the Nestorians, an extreme Alexandrian conception of Christ was put forward by Eutyches of Constantinople, which was condemned by a synod at Constantinople in AD 448, and by Chalcedon in 451. This was the view that the act of hypostatic union meant the absorption of Christ's human nature into the divine. Nevertheless, the language of both Cyril and Leo cited at the council, gave rise to doubts in some quarters about a tendency even on their part toward monophysitism, but that was probably due to a different meaning of the term nature or *physis*.

(iii) Leontius of Byzantium – the 'enhypostatic' *humanity of Jesus*

In the sixth century, the teaching of Leontius of Byzantium (AD 485-543) played an important part in the history of christology, mainly through his work against Nestorians and Eutychians. As against the doctrine of the *an*hypostatic humanity (falsely) attributed to Cyril of Alexandria, Leontius taught the doctrine of the *en*hypostatic humanity of Christ. He repudiated the idea held by extreme Antiochenes that the human nature of Christ had an independent *hypostasis*, or independent centre of subsistence, but he taught that the true humanity of Christ was given full place within the *hypostasis* of the Son as 'enhypostatic' (*enhypostatos*). The intention of this was to give a fuller place to the humanity of Jesus Christ than appeared to be allowed by the rebuttal of Nestorianism, while asserting that the human nature of Christ was 'anhypostatic' (*anhypostatos*), that is, never existed as hypostatic apart from his deity. From its very origin, Christ's human nature was in hypostatic union with his divine nature, and as such had its subsistence *in* the *hypostasis* of God the Son, that is, '*en*hypostatically'. As Leontius himself, and as John of Damascus following Leontius, expounded this, the doctrine is not really clear, because sufficient stress is not laid upon the '*anhypostatic*' assumption in pure grace of our fallen humanity, and therefore the doctrine could not go far enough in stressing the 'enhypostatic' humanity of Christ to secure fully the place of the historical Jesus as active agent and mediator, and not simply as instrument, in revelation and reconciliation.

(iv) The condemnation of the Monothelites

The final factor of importance we must note is the condemnation of the Monothelites at the second Council of Constantinople in AD 680. That was the condemnation of those who taught that in Christ there was only one will, and the affirmation that in Christ there was a human will as well as a divine will in the hypostatic union of the two natures in his one person. That was a very important step forward, for it laid the stress not only upon nature and upon duality in unity, but upon will and action in Christ as God and man. The possession of a human will means that Christ was subject to temptation as we are, but the human will belonged to the one person of God the Son.

But again, unless we take seriously at this point the fact that Christ assumed our will, the will of estranged man in estranged adamic human nature, in order to suffer all its temptations and to resist them and condemn sin in our human nature, and then to bend the will of man back into oneness with the divine will, it is difficult to give the temptations of Christ their full place. It is difficult also therefore to give the human obedience of Christ, in struggle against the onslaught of evil and sin, its full and proper place in atoning reconciliation. If Christ assumed neutral or perfect human nature, and assumed it into oneness with his own divine person who could not choose to sin any more than he could choose not to be God, then the humanity of Christ is merely instrumental in the hands of God. But if so, then salvation is only an act of God done upon us and for us, and not also a real human act done in our place and issuing out of our humanity.

Once again we see the weakness of the Patristic christology lay in failing to adequately link up christology with the saving work of Jesus Christ, and in failing to think incarnation and atonement sufficiently into each other. Nevertheless, the condemnation of the Monothelite heresy (including incidentally the anathematising of Pope Honorius I of Rome for explicit teaching rejecting 'the two wills' of Christ, and advocating the formula of 'the one will') marked a considerable advance, if only for the reason that it kept the door wide open for full consideration of the saving significance of the humanity of Christ in the whole course of his obedience to the Father.

4 The Reformation doctrine of Christ

Return from medieval to Patristic theology and the living God of the bible

When we turn to the doctrine of Christ at the Reformation, we find a very definite turning to the teaching of the early church, and to the high Patristic doctrine of Christ, away from the scholastic formulations of the medieval church. With the Reformation there took place a decided change in the whole doctrine of God, in a move away from the Latin Stoic conception of God as *deus sive natura*[38] to the living God of the biblical revelation, who actively intervenes in history, who confronts us directly in Jesus Christ through his Word and Spirit, and who acts upon us personally. With this change from a static to a dynamic conception of God, there was also a change in regard to the conception of being and substance, grace and person, all of which have direct bearing upon the doctrine of Christ. The conception of being was related anew to the act of God the creator, who creates out of nothing, and to the being of the creator himself, who creates other creaturely beings in entire dependence upon himself.

Thus the medieval notion of a hierarchy of being between the lowest *ens*[39] and the highest *Ens* in God is set aside. The conception of substance which arose from a peculiar medieval interpretation of Aristotle was set also aside in a return to the Patristic conceptions of *ousia* and *hypostasis*,[40] and therefore the terms *subsistentia*, and *substantia*,[41] as used by the Reformers, are decidedly patristic, and not scholastic in slant and meaning. Again, the concept *persona*[42] is changed. Here there could not be a complete return to the Patristic teaching, because of the development that had arisen as a result of the Patristic teaching, but there was a definite move away from the individualism of the medieval conception of *persona*, back to the Patristic conception, but now informed with greater stress than ever upon the one supreme person of Jesus Christ, who alone is determinative of the meaning of *persona*. In the Augustinian Boethian-Thomist development, *persona* had come

---

[38] Lat, 'God or nature', a concept of God which treated God as interchangeable with nature.

[39] Lat, 'being'.

[40] Gk, *ousia* 'being'; *hypostasis* 'personal subsistence' or mode of existence.

[41] Lat, 'subsistence' and 'substance'.

[42] Lat, 'person', originally the 'mask' put on by players on the stage, hence a character or person who acts a certain part, and thus the origin of the English word 'person'.

more and more to refer to an individualised substance of rational nature, that is, to the concept of 'person' as an individual with the power of reason. That line of development was crowned with the Cartesian revival of the Augustinian *cogito ergo sum*,[43] and the attachment of ego-consciousness[44] to this individual personal substance. But all this was also bound up with the Augustinian conception of grace, which more and more, especially with the high Aristotelianism of the schoolmen, came to be construed in causal and ontological categories, so that divine grace always carried the notion of divinisation, and fullness of divinity.

The reaction from the scholasticism of the medieval church, and the renewal of theology in the biblical revelation, had the effect of making the Reformers see the dangers inherent in the Patristic formulations of the doctrine of Christ whenever the Greek philosophical terms, inevitably used in the doctrine of Christ, came to acquire a static independence over against the direct witness of the New Testament. While adhering loyally to the catholic christology of the ecumenical churches, the Reformers sought to give it fuller and more definite formulation in accordance with the saving life and work of Jesus Christ. In their reformation of the eucharist, the Reformers rejected the Roman idea of a timeless mystery and timeless repetition of the sacrifice in the mass. They sought to recover the historical perspective of the last supper, and to reincorporate in the eucharist the double stress upon the once and for all character of the incarnate work and self oblation of Christ, and upon continuous participation in his saving humanity. That doctrine of the Lord's supper, however, rested upon a corresponding doctrine of Christ which sought to recover the place of the historical Jesus Christ, and the essential integration of incarnation and atonement.

(a) The different emphases in Lutheran and Reformed theology

The Lutheran stress on the union of divine and human, and the Reformed stress on the Son as God and man

In carrying out this reformulation of the doctrine of Christ[45] there were distinct differences between the Lutheran and the Reformed[46]

---

43 Lat, 'I think, therefore I am'.

44 Self-awareness, consciousness of the *ego*, Lat for 'I'.

45 See Heinrich Schmid, *Die Dogmatik*, and Heinrich Heppe, *Reformed Dogmatics.*

46 The name used for the branch of the Reformation which, in distinction to the Lutheran, was generally Calvinist in doctrine and organisation.

theologians, differences which in some measure reflected the old Patristic distinctions between Alexandrian and Antiochene christologies. The Lutherans inclined toward the Alexandrian emphasis in New Testament exegesis, and in doctrine, and the Reformed inclined toward the Antiochene emphasis in New Testament exegesis and doctrine – and yet these distinctions are not so clear cut, for they actually criss-cross one another at significant points. Roughly speaking, however, it may be said that the Lutherans tended to stress in the doctrine of Christ the union of divine and human natures, with a tendency that appeared to the Reformed to be suspect of Eutychianism; whereas the Reformed tended to lay the stress upon the person of the Son of God as God and man, with a tendency that appeared to the Lutherans to be suspect of Nestorianism. But let it be said right away that this remarkable reflection of the twofold emphasis in the Patristic theology indicates that there is an inevitable duality in our human formulations of the doctrine of Christ, in which we must learn to see the important truths in both emphases and seek to combine them in an understanding of the whole truth of Christ. As the emphases appear between Lutherans and Reformed, they are not antitheses, but complementary and overlapping aspects of the truth.

The hypostatic union interpreted more dynamically in terms of the whole life of Jesus

Both Lutheran and Reformed theologians rightly accepted the centrality of the doctrine of the *hypostatic union*, but they sought to give that doctrine a more dynamic interpretation by drawing out the implications of the *unio* or union in terms of *communio* and *communicatio*.[47] That is to say, they sought to understand the hypostatic union not simply in terms of a state of union, but in terms of a divine movement of grace, which was translated into the *history* of the man Jesus Christ. Hence all that the Son of God as man accomplished in his historical life and work belongs to the doctrine of hypostatic union. Thus whereas Patristic theology has tended to look upon the human nature of Christ as a state assumed or appropriated in the incarnation but one looked at from the perspective of the end result, the Reformers sought to look upon the human nature of Christ also from the perspective of his healing and sanctifying assumption of our adamic humanity.

---

[47] Lat, 'communion' and 'communication'.

They asserted, of course, that Christ was without sin, but they looked upon his life and his humanity also in the light of the fact that he came to bear our sin and bear it away, that he actually entered into our sinful existence, not to become guilty of the sin which we commit, but to bear our guilt as an alien guilt, without any guilt of his own. He appropriated our corrupt and fallen existence in Adam, and within it he condemned sin in our existence, overcoming our sin by his obedience at every point to the Father. But he overcame it through humbling himself to the uttermost, entering into our estranged and sinful condition under the bondage of the law, under the judgement of God, and under the thraldom of corruption and death, and through offering within it an expiatory sacrifice for sin and guilt. In all that he was well pleasing to the Father, and the Father did not suffer him to see corruption, but raised him from the dead triumphant over all the powers of evil and darkness and death.

This is one of the points where the Alexandrian-Antiochene emphases between Luther and Calvin, for example, criss-crossed, for Luther went much further in the Alexandrian direction than ever Athanasius went, using indeed extravagant language at times, whereas Calvin was definitely more restrained in the direction of the Alexandrian theologians. But in spite of that difference, they both sought to reinterpret the hypostatic union, with Calvin laying greater stress than Luther upon the obedience of Christ, and Luther greater stress than Calvin upon the mighty act of God in redemption.

We cannot go into the Lutheran and Reformed teaching in its details, but we may single out some of the main conceptions and terms employed, seeing something of the difference, but also the basic unity of the Reformation doctrine of the hypostatic union.

(b) The problem of the 'extra-Calvinisticum'[48]

The so-called *'extra-Calvinisticum'* is a Lutheran name for Calvin's doctrine that the Son in his complete transcendence became man, and remains transcendently the Son of God, while also man in the form of a servant. The classical passage from Calvin is the following:

---

[48] On the 'extra-Calvinisticum' and the strengths and weaknesses of Lutheran thought at this point, see T.F. Torrance, *Space, Time and Incarnation* (London: OUP 1969), pp. 30-37.

> Although the boundless essence of the Word was united with human nature into one person, nevertheless we do not imagine there to be any enclosing of the Word in it. The Son of God descended miraculously from heaven, yet without abandoning heaven; was pleased to be conceived miraculously in the virgin's womb, to live on earth, to hang on the cross, in such a way that he always filled the world as from the beginning.[49]

Greek 'container' conceptions of space[50]

In order to understand the point of Calvin's statement we have to remember the teaching developed by the Greek fathers when they found they had to reject the pre-Christian Greek conceptions of space as a 'container', or 'receptacle'. Here space is thought of as something different from the things which are 'in' it: it is regarded as a container which contains things inside it.

The strictest definition of place or space along these lines was given by Aristotle[51] as the innermost limit or boundary of a container at which it is in contact with the contained body (*to peras tou periechontos sōmatos kath' ho sunaptei tō periechomenō*[52]), a conception of place as that which immediately encompasses each body. Aristotle's final definition of place (*to tou periechontos peras akinēton prōton, tout' estin ho topos*[53]) was translated by the mediaevals (St Thomas Aquinas, for example), as *terminus continentis immobilis primus* – that is, 'the immediately contiguous unmoved boundary of the containing body' or 'the first unmoved limit of the container'. That is to say, place is defined as the immobile limit within which a body is contained. This was a rather technical definition of space in terms of a container in which *what contains* and *what is contained* are *inseparable or interdependent*. It is a receptacle notion of space in which there is a relation of interdependence between the container and its contents. Since the containing body is always in immediate limiting contact with what is contained, there can, on such a receptacle view, be no void or empty space.

---

49 Calvin, *Institutes of the Christian Religion*, 2.13.4 (translation based on the Beveridge text).

50 The whole concept of space is rather difficult and takes some time to think through, but is very useful and important. For an extended discussion of Greek and modern concepts of space and time, see *Space, Time and Incarnation.*

51 See *Space, Time and Incarnation*, p. 7ff.; cf. W.D. Ross, *Aristotle* (London: Methuen 1923), p. 86.

52 Aristotle, *Physics*, 212 a 5, ed. W.D. Ross (Oxford, London & New York: Clarendon Press 1950).

53 *Ibid.* 212 a 20.

The Christian fathers found that the biblical teaching of the presence of God with us in space and time (compare Solomon's prayer at the dedication of the temple, 'the heaven of heavens cannot contain thee'[54]), and the incarnate presence of God *bodily* (*sōmatikōs*) in Jesus Christ, could not be construed in terms of any container notion of space. And so they insisted that God is present with us 'without leaving the throne of the universe', and that 'the Son of God became man, was born of the virgin Mary', and so forth, without leaving his rule over the universe.

The Patristic conception of space as 'relational'[55]

In making these statements, however, they were breaking with a notion of space as a container, as that which *contained* or *enclosed, circumscribed* or *comprehended* the presence or being of God within it. They forged instead a thoroughly relational notion of space, in which they thought of God in creation as 'containing all things by the Word of his power' and as contained by nothing, and of God coming to be with us in the realm of space and time which he created in and with the creation of the universe, yet in such a way that he did not cease to be the creator transcendent over all space and time. God 'makes room' for himself among us but in such a way that the relation of God to the 'room' is controlled by his creative and transcendent relation, and not in such a way that God becomes apparently 'boxed in' within the limits of our finite conditions.

On the one hand the fathers wanted to assert their conviction that God takes space and time so seriously in the incarnation as really to accommodate himself to our space and time existence and 'littleness'. But on the other hand, they also wanted to maintain that God accommodates himself in such a way that he remains transcendent God while becoming man, remains the creator Word while becoming flesh, remains in control of the universe while with us in our weakness.

---

[54] 1 Kings 8.27; 2 Chron 2.6.

[55] In a 'relational' view of space (and time), space is related to, or relational to, the operating active agents, and there is no concept of space as an entity in itself apart from things and agents. Thus we cannot say that space is related to the agents 'in it' since that presupposes a difference between the container (space) and the things which are 'in' it. There is no 'it' for things to be 'in'! Space and time come into being with creation as orderly functions of creaturely events, and are to be conceived as a continuum of relations given in and with created existence. A relational

It was to this Patristic way of thinking that Calvin turned, when he said that in the coming down and birth of the Son of God, he did not abandon heaven, and in being conceived in the womb of the virgin, in living on earth, or hanging on the cross, he did not cease to be the God whose presence is everywhere. Calvin is content, however, not to develop a thoroughly relational concept of space and time as the Greek fathers did; he merely rejects, with the fathers, any idea that the incarnation involves an enclosing of the deity of Christ within the limits of a containing vessel.

The difficulties of the Lutheran concept of space

The Lutherans, by contrast, operated with a receptacle notion of space. They took over in its Ockhamist[56] form the Aristotelian concept of space in which the container and what it contains are inseparable. This is what gave the mediaevals such a headache especially when they came to construe the real presence in the host ('in every bit of the host and in a thousand hosts at the same time'), but it also created difficulties with their conception of the incarnation. Operating, then, with a container notion of space of this sort, the Lutherans were aghast at Calvin's insistence that the Son of God became man in such a way as still to fill the whole world with his presence as from the beginning. And from *their* point of view they were bound to ask, 'Well, what did the Son of God leave outside (*extra*) the flesh when he became man, if he was not wholly contained in the baby and wrapped in the swaddling clothes at Bethlehem?' And so the Lutherans gave the nickname of 'the Calvinist *extra*' to Calvin's concept of the incarnation in which Calvin was followed by the Reformed tradition. It is a pity the Lutherans paid no attention to the great hymn of St Germanus, 'A great and mighty wonder . . . the Word becomes incarnate, and yet remains on high'.

The truth behind both the Lutheran and Reformed positions

In following Calvin, the Reformed theologians for their part were protesting against a Lutheran insistence that when the Word was made flesh the Word was not only for ever united to the human nature in Jesus but that the Word now exists *solely enclosed within that human*

view is a much more dynamic view since the nature of space depends on the relations between things and the speed of movement of the active agents such as light (hence space and time become related to one another), while in a container view space is viewed as a static entity, and space and time are separated from one another – Ed.

56 The mediaeval philosopher and theologian William of Ockham.

nature. (It is instructive to remember that the Anglican tradition, like the Calvinist or Reformed tradition, also broke with the Roman-Aristotelian notion of space, and therefore also with the Lutheran notion of the incarnation and the real presence interpreted in terms of a receptacle notion of space.)[57]

The Calvinists, then, felt that the Lutherans were going too far in speaking of the Son or Word of God as being for ever enclosed within the human body of Jesus. They protested that we cannot think of the incarnation of the Son in such a way as to deny his eternal transcendence to the creature, by making him a prisoner of time or the time series. The Word cannot be subordinated to the flesh it assumes nor can it be limited by the creaturely reality with which it is united, and so be altered in its transcendent and divine nature.

The Lutherans rejected this on the grounds of its alleged Nestorianism, or separation of the divine and human natures of Christ – but they on their part were only able to hold their doctrine that the Word is wholly included in the body of Jesus, by attributing to that body, divine attributes in virtue of which it could be said to fill the whole world. But the Calvinists felt that was a form of monophysite error in which the human nature of Christ was being absorbed in his divine nature, and they protested that when they spoke of the transcendence of the Word or Son, even when incarnate, the so-called 'extra' was only held *distinctive* not *separative*[58] – distinctively not separatively (*sic*).

Now there can be no doubt that in this, the Reformed theologians had the agreement of the whole of the early church behind them, and indeed Calvin's language cited above derived in part from that of John of Damascus. But the Lutherans had their important point: that with the incarnation of the Word, we must never think of the Word apart from the man Jesus, with whom the Word is for ever united, and from whom the Word is never apart. Now that the incarnation has taken place, we must say that the Son is none other than Jesus, and is identical with him. And yet the Lutherans did have their doctrine of the *deus absconditus*[59] alongside the doctrine of the *deus revelatus*, which from another perspective is in some way what Calvin and his followers were maintaining. Here then, we are not to think of alternatives or a

---

57 See Richard Hooker, *Of the Laws of Ecclesiastical Polity*, 1597, Book V, chaps. LII-LVI.

58 Lat, 'in terms of distinction' not 'in terms of separation'.

59 Lat, *deus absconditus*, 'hidden God'; *deus revelatus*, 'revealed God'.

contradiction, but rather of two complementary aspects of the truth which belong to the mystery of Christ, and which we are unable to put into precise language in such a way as to express the whole truth in a unitary way.[60]

(c) The communion of natures – communio naturarum

In using this term, the theologians of the Reformation sought to give a more dynamic account of the hypostatic *union*, and in doing so, went back to the emphasis we have in Irenaeus, who spoke of *union and communion* (*enōsis kai koinōnia*), and of the whole movement of assumption in terms of *anakephalaiōsis*,[61] which for him did not only mean the recapitulation of our fallen humanity from its origin in Adam and its restoration through obedience to union and communion with God, but the gathering up into union with God of the whole life of Christ from his birth to his mature life in a *comm-union* of two natures in one person.

This reaffirmed the Chalcedonian doctrine of a union of two natures without change, and without confusion, without division or separation, but it was meant to show clearly three things:

(i) that there is a distinction of natures which is in no way destroyed by their union in one person, for the union involves real communion;

(ii) that both natures have communion in being the natures of one person in whom the two natures are united;

(iii) that in the one person there is a mutual communion of the two natures, so that in that *mutual communion* each nature does what belongs to it.

Divergence between Lutheran and Reformed teaching on the nature of the communio[62]

Now at this point, there is a divergence again between the Lutheran and Reformed teaching. Among the Lutherans, the stress was laid upon union of two natures in a communion in which the human nature is assumed into the divine nature. The Reformed theologians refused to

---

60 Cf. Karl Barth, *Church Dogmatics*, 1/2, pp. 168ff.; 4/1, pp. 180ff. (both Eng. trans., Edinburgh: T & T Clark 1956).

61 Gk, 'recapitulation' or 'gathering up under one head'. See Eph 1.10 NIV (Gk *anakephalaiōsasthai*).

62 See the Schmid and Heppe manuals of Lutheran and of Reformed theology, Heinrich Schmid, *Die Dogmatik*, and Heinrich Heppe, *Reformed Dogmatics*.

think of an assumption of human nature into the divine, but of an assumption of human nature into the divine person of the Son, in whom there was a indirect union between the two natures. There was a *unio immediata*[63] between the human nature and the person of the Son, but a *unio mediata* between the divine and human natures through the Spirit.[64] In that way, the Reformed theologians sought to speak of an active communion between the natures without teaching a doctrine of mutual interpenetration between the natures, which is precisely what the Lutheran conception of mutual communion or participation led to. The Lutheran theologians therefore spoke of a *communio* or *communicatio naturarum*[65] in which there was in the person of Christ a mutual participation of the divine and human natures, through which the divine nature, by participating in the human nature, permeates, perfects and inhabits it, and so appropriates it to itself, while the human nature by being made participant in the divine, is permeated by it, perfected and inhabited by it. This relation was called mutual penetration in which the divine nature actively penetrates into the human nature and the human nature passively penetrates into the divine.[66] Note here that the accent is laid decisively on the divine action, but within that upon a mutual participation.

What are we to say about this mutual participation between the divine and human natures of Christ? We must emphasise with the Lutherans that there is a real difference: participation of the divine in the human is not the same as participation of the human in the divine. It is the divine act that gives, and gives to the human nature; it is the human act only to receive, and receive from the divine nature. But for that very reason, there is no reciprocity here of such a kind that the relationship can be reversed. Thus in the assumption whereby the divine Son assumed human nature into union with his divine being, there is no counterpart to that in a human appropriation of the divine into the human. God became man in Christ, but man did not, or did not also, become God. In the assumption of man into unity with the

---

63 Lat, *unio immediatia*, 'immediate union'; *unio mediata*, 'mediated union'.

64 [Cf. Heppe, *Reformed Dogmatics*, Eng. trans. G.T. Thomson (London: Allen & Unwin 1950), p. 431; square bracket references to Schmid and Heppe added to facilitate further comparison – Ed.]

65 'Communion' or 'communication of natures'.

66 Cf. H. Schmid, *Die Dogmatik*, 7th edition, p. 230f. [cf. Eng. trans. *The Doctrinal Theology of the Evangelical Lutheran Church*, 2nd Eng. edition, revised according to the 6th German edition (Philadelphia: Lutheran Publication Society 1889), p. 316f.]

divine being, human nature was not divinised, but only raised into union and communion with God. If the divine Son assumed human nature into unity with himself only then to divinise it, then that would mean that he had no sooner condescended to be our brother, than he broke off that brotherhood – the idea of a divinisation of the human nature thus makes nonsense of the incarnation and reconciliation.

(d) The communication of properties – communicatio idiomatum

This expression was used by both Lutheran and Reformed theologians to give the concept of the hypostatic union more adequate and dynamic formulation, not simply in terms of substance, but in terms of active communication of the divine and human properties of Christ in his life and work. Whereas the ancient church tended to think too much in terms of substance and its predicates, or of static natures and their attributes, the Reformers wanted to think this out in terms of the *egeneto sarx*[67] as well as the *assumptio carnis*[68] – that is, not only in terms of the once and for all event at Bethlehem, but in terms of the growth of Jesus before God and before man, and in terms of his whole historical life and work of reconciliation. In order to do this, they took over and made further use of the doctrine of the *communicatio idiomatum* of the early church. Now the Greek term *idiōma* means strictly a property of nature which cannot be communicated to another nature. The Greek fathers therefore held a very mild form of *communicatio idiomatum* as a kind of mutual metonymy, but one which did not involve mutual penetration of the two natures into one another. At this point the Reformed and the Lutheran teaching diverged again. The Reformed theologians taught that in Christ, the properties of each of the two natures coincide in one and the same person, and only in that way are they attributed to and true of both natures. But the Lutherans were not content with this, as is clear from their doctrine of the *communio naturarum*.

(i) The Lutheran doctrine of communicatio idiomatum[69]

Lutherans speak of this communication of properties as of three kinds:[70]

(1) The genus idiomaticum which speaks of the fact that the properties of either nature belong to the whole person of Christ, and therefore

---

67 Gk, 'became flesh'.

68 Lat, 'assumption of the flesh'.

69 [Cf. Schmid, *The Doctrinal Theology of the Evangelical Lutheran Church,* p. 319ff.]

70 [Cf. *loc. cit.* p. 319ff.]

we can say that 'God died', and 'the man Christ Jesus is almighty'. Here there is a reciprocal communication of properties.

(2) The genus maiestaticum, according to which it is said that the Son of God communicates his own divine majesty to the human flesh he assumed. Here, the Lutherans affirmed there is no reciprocation, no *genus tapeinoticum,* whereby the divine nature is humbled through the communication to it of properties from the human nature of Christ.

(3) The genus apotelesmaticum which refers to the co-operation of the two natures in the common purpose, and specific result, of redemption.

Now the last of these corresponds to the Reformed doctrine of the *communicatio operationum*[71] to which I shall return, but it is the second, even apart from the first, which horrified the Reformed theologians. In a real sense, of course, and not just metaphorically, we must say that God died, and that the man Jesus is almighty, but there are important senses in which we cannot say these things. We must say that God was directly present and active in the death of Christ, and that the Son of God suffered and bore the judgement on our sins in the death of Christ on the cross. We must also say the human nature is assumed into unity with the divine being of the Son, and that there is now a man on the throne of God as being of beings and Lord of Lords, but can we say that the human nature as such is so interpenetrated by divine majesty and power and all the divine attributes, that, in point of fact, its human properties are swallowed up or nullified in the divine – as for example, in the doctrine of the ubiquity or immensity of the body of Christ?

The danger of deifying the humanity of Christ

What kind of humanity is this, to which all the divine attributes can be ascribed? Have we not here compromised the true and complete humanity of Christ? And does this not really mean that God not only became man, but that man has somehow become God in Christ? Moreover, if we remember that the humanity which God assumed in Christ is our humanity, in which we are given to share, then who can stop short at applying all the divine attributes to the humanity of Jesus, and not apply them to humanity in general? Indeed, that is exactly just what German idealistic theology and philosophy did do, so that it is very difficult indeed to dissociate that deification of man which we find in nineteenth-century German

---

[71] Lat: 'communication of acts' or works.

philosophy, from the Lutheran doctrine of the incarnation in the sixteenth and seventeenth centuries with its attribution of divine properties to human nature.

Now how did the Reformed theologians deal with the problems raised by the *unio et communio naturarum*? They spoke of a *triplex* (threefold) *communio* or *communicatio* in the hypostatic union.

(ii) The Reformed doctrine of communicatio naturarum[72]

(1) Communicatio gratiarum.[73] By this, the Reformed theologians distinguished between the various gifts of grace to the human life of Jesus, who grew therefore from his earliest infancy in wisdom and grace as well as stature, and this growth was not only before man, but before God.[74] By this it is not meant that as Jesus grew into manhood there was, especially after his baptism, an increase in union between his divine and human natures, as though that were not already completed once and for all in his birth. What is meant is that from the first moment of his life, his properties as God and man, and the communication of the properties of his divine and human natures, effectively entered into operation step by step with his developing human life – and here we think especially of the graces of knowledge, will and power in which Jesus increased and grew, growing in knowledge, and learning obedience. It is at the baptism of Jesus, when he was anointed for his ministry and consecrated for his sacrificial life and death as the suffering servant, that we are surely to think of this growth and increase as reaching its culmination.

(2) Communicatio idiomatum.[75] This was stated in such a way as to preserve the fact that what is peculiar or proper to one nature, cannot be called common to another, for on being communicated to another nature, the *idiomata* of one nature would cease to be *idiomata*.[76] Thus *communicatio idiomatum* can mean only that what is proper to one nature in Christ, is attributed not to the other nature as such but to the person

---

72 [Cf. Heppe, *Reformed Dogmatics*, pp. 434-47 (*communicatio gratiarum*, p. 434f.; *communicatio idiomatum*, p. 439f.; *communicatio operationum*, p. 445f.)]

73 Lat, 'communication of graces' or of gifts of grace.

74 Luke 2.40, 52.

75 Lat,'communication of properties'.

76 *Idiōma* in Greek means a characteristic property, a 'property peculiar to' a nature, and one therefore which cannot logically be communicated to another nature.

named from the other nature, whether divine or human. Thus the properties of each of the two natures coincide in one and the same person, and are thereby also predicated of that person. But what is the property of one nature is by no means common to the other one, because of the essential and eternal difference between the natures, though it is common to the person, and to one of the natures in the person. But the real point of the *communicatio idiomatum* is seen in their co-operation in the office of the person in whom they coincide, that is, in the office of Christ as *mediator*. The mediatorial office, while requiring two natures, also requires a conjoint but distinct operation of each of the two natures. In executing the office of mediator, each nature in communion with the other effects what is proper to each. Thus the *communicatio idiomatum* cannot be expounded properly, apart from the third aspect of the *communio naturarum*, the *communicatio operationum*, the communication of acts.

(3) Communicatio operationum. Here we must think, then, of a communication of the divine and human acts in the one person of Christ. In him there takes place such a union and communion between his divine and human natures, that the divine acts are acts in his human nature, and the human acts are acts in his divine person. Each nature in communion with the other performs acts appropriate to it, but performs them as acts of the one person who embraces both natures, and is the one subject of all the divine and human acts. But *communicatio operationum* is concerned with more than that. It asserts a dynamic communion between the divine and human natures of Christ, in terms of his atoning and reconciling work. It stresses the union of two natures for mediatorial operations in such a way that these works proceed from the one person of the God-man by the distinct effectiveness of both natures. In other words, the whole dynamic movement of the hypostatic union has to be understood in terms of the fact that God was in Christ reconciling the world unto himself, and so the hypostatic union is the ontological side of the dynamic action of reconciliation. Thus we understand the meaning of the hypostatic union not merely in terms of the incarnation, but in terms of the reconciliation between God and man. And we understand the reconciliation not simply in terms of Christ's work on the cross, but in terms of his incarnation, so that the reconciling union of God and man is understood as wrought out in the incarnate person of Christ, and in the whole course of his historical life and death and resurrection from the dead.

The problem of the 'immutability' and 'impassibility' of God[77]

Now, when we look back over all these serious and difficult problems raised by the Chalcedonian christology in the theology both of the fathers and the Reformers, we find a fundamental difficulty which they all encountered in the Greek conception of the *immutability* of God. In that conception, God was regarded as too exalted to act so as to himself descend in utter humiliation in order to save us in such a way that what he did really affected him, or meant anything at all for himself. God was, so to speak, a prisoner of his own immutability, and his own impassibility. Thus, even in a doctrine of the *communicatio operationum*, Reformed theologians like Polanus insisted in speaking of participation by the divine nature in the work of atonement on the cross, as *kat'oikonomian*, by way of economy, which was meant to guard the changelessness of the divine being and nature.

The biblical view of God freely humbling himself to become a creature

But if we really take the biblical view of God, then we must think of God the Father as sending the Son into our lost existence, into unutterable humiliation in order to be really one with us. We must think of God as determining himself freely to be our God, directing himself freely to share in the profoundest way in our frail life, in all its limitations and weaknesses, and even in its lostness, all in order to be our God, and to gather us into fellowship with himself. But in this act of unspeakable humiliation, God was not simply using the humanity of Christ as his organ or instrument, while he remained transcendent to it all. *He himself* actually came, the immutable God, humbling himself to become a creature and to suffer as a creature our judgement and death, and throughout all that to maintain his sovereign freedom and initiative, even when he gave himself up to the death of the cross, in an offering as unreserved in his self-giving as it was majestically omnipotent and free in its act of grace.

That is the kind of immutability of God which we see in Jesus Christ, who is not mutable in his faithfulness, for he is the same yesterday, and today, and for ever, and who has immutably joined himself to our humanity, and immutably joined our humanity to himself, and who in becoming what we are, became what he was not, in order that we might become what we are not. That is the amazing grace of the Lord Jesus Christ, who though he was rich, for our sakes became poor, that we through his poverty might become rich.

---

[77] Cf. T.F. Torrance, *The School of Faith* (London: James Clarke 1959), p. lxxvff. and *The Trinitarian Faith*, pp. 184ff.

But it is here that in the amazing grace of God, the movement of his assumption of our humanity in the hypostatic union and in atoning reconciliation, involves a twofold participation, not only of God in the life of man but of man in the life of God, for the frail human nature which he assumed, the lowly human being which he condescended to become, is by that very act of divine self-impartation, of divine condescension, raised and exalted, not to become divine, but to share in the divine fellowship and life. What happens to this human nature, happens to it entirely in the grace of God, in the gracious will of God to exist in identity with this man, but in the grace of God it is raised far above anything we can conceive or imagine, and yet not in such a way as to cease to be what God made it, creaturely human nature. As the creator condescended to be a creature, he did not make the creature creator, but in its unity of existence with his Son, he assumed it into fellowship with his own being as God, the creator and Lord. But let us be clear about this fact, that it was the act of divine self humiliation as such which did that, and which is the exaltation of the man Jesus, and, in him, of our human nature into union and communion with the life and being of God. The whole act of the incarnation and atonement, and the whole doctrine of the hypostatic union, has to be understood only in that free and omnipotent condescension of the living and eternal God to be one with us for ever, and so to make us one with him for ever.

(e) The doctrine of anhypostasis *and* enhypostasis

The Reformed theologians insisted that the assumption of the humanity into the person of the Son of God is not an assumption of it into the divine nature, but into the *person* of the *Logos*. They made use of the concepts of *anhypostasis* and *enhypostasis*[78] to express that accurately, bringing them fully and clearly together, and thus marking real advance over the Patristic usage of these concepts. Two statements from Heidegger may be adduced here.[79] Heidegger speaks of the 'assumption of the human nature into the person of the Son of God, whereby the *Logos*, the Son of God, in the very moment of formation and sanctification assumed the human nature void of an hypostasis of its own into the unity of its own person, in

---

[78] Gk, *an-hypostasis,* literally 'not-person', ie. with no independent centre of personal being; *en-hypostasis,* literally 'in-person' or 'person-in (the person of the Son)', ie. having real personal being in the person of the Son.

[79] As quoted and cited by Heppe, *Reformed Dogmatics,* p. 427f.

order that there might be one and the same hypostasis of the *Logos* assuming and of the human nature assumed, outside of which it neither ever subsists, nor can subsist'.[80] But because the human nature assumed in the incarnation is more than human nature in general, because in the incarnation it is also as individual man that Jesus possesses human nature in the eternal Son, more must be said. 'The human [nature] is *per se anhypostatos*[81] and becomes *enhypostatos*[82] in the *Logos*, who being pre-existent, in fact existent from all eternity, has received in time the form of a servant (Phil 2.7), and assumed the seed of Abraham (Heb 2.16) as its shrine and instrument.'[83]

(i) The humanity of Jesus has no independent reality

The first thing we have to note here, is that, taken together with *anhypostasia*,[84] for the two are not to be separated, the *enhypostasia* asserts that the incarnation is an act of pure grace alone, and repudiates any form of adoptionism, that is the adoption of a pre-existing man to become Son of God. It asserts then that true man is a predicate of God's gracious action. When the Word was made flesh, God and man were so related that Jesus came to exist as man only so far as he now exists as God. In other words, there is only one Christ, one mediator, one Lord, only one person in Jesus Christ the incarnate Son of God. This one person means that his human nature had *no independent subsistence* or *hypostasis*, no independent centre of personal being. If there had been a human person to whom a divine person was added, there would have been an independent centre of personal being in Jesus over against the person of the Son of God; but the human nature of Jesus never existed apart from the incarnation of God the Son. At the first moment of the existence of his human nature, it was in hypostatic union with his Godhead. That is, the human nature from the first moment of its existence had its *hypostasis* or personal subsistence *in* the personal subsistence of God the Son. That is the meaning of *en-hypostasis*.

---

80 Heppe, op. cit. p. 427 (Heidegger XVII, 36).

81 *Per se* 'by itself' (Lat); *anhypostatos*, 'without personal being' (Gk).

82 Gk, 'possessed of, or having personal being in'.

83 Heppe, op. cit. p. 428 (Heidegger *loc. cit.*).

84 *Hypostasia* is the abstract generic form of *hypostasis*, representing something like 'personhood' as opposed to the more concrete *hypostasis*, 'person'.

(ii) The humanity of Jesus has full reality in the person of the Son

But when we have said that, we have to add that although there was no independent personal being called Jesus apart from the incarnation, that does not mean that in the incarnation there was no particular individual called Jesus existing as a particular human being, with a rational human mind and will and soul; and therefore it does not mean that he did not completely possess human nature. Jesus had a fully human mind and human soul and human will; he lived a fully human life in hypostatic union with his divine life, and in that union with his divine life, his human life had manifested the most singular and unique personality as man. That is the emphasis of *enhypostasia*. It preserves the acknowledgment of the full humanity of Jesus, and indeed of his historical person as a man among others, and as one of mankind, a true man. The *anhypostasia* stresses the *general* humanity of Jesus, the human nature assumed by the Son with its *hypostasis* in the Son, but *enhypostasia* stresses the *particular* humanity of the one man Jesus, whose person is not other than the person of the divine Son.

Therefore from the *enhypostasis* we have to go back again to the *anhypostasis* and say this: while the Son of God assumed our human nature, and became fully and really like us, nevertheless his full and complete human nature was united to God in a unique way (hypostatically in one person) as our human nature is not, and never will be. Therefore he is unlike us, not unlike us as to the humanity of his human nature, but in the unique union of his human nature to the divine nature in the one person of God the Son. (This is the baffling element in the virgin birth, which tells us that while it is our very human nature he assumed, he did not assume it in the way we share in it, because he took it in a unique relation with his deity). But it is upon the unique, hypostatic relation of his human nature to his divine nature, that the truth of our human nature depends, for it is as we share in his human nature, which is hypostatically united to God, that we are in union and communion with God.

(iii) Anhypostasis *and* enhypostasis *taken together*

The *anhypostasia* and *enhypostasia* taken together tell us that the incarnation was the union of the Word of God with mankind in solidarity with all men and women; yet it was union with one man, or rather such a union with all humanity that it was achieved and wrought out in and through this one man, Jesus of Bethlehem and Nazareth for all men and women.

It is in this connection that we are helped to see the solidarity of Jesus Christ with all humanity in his reconciling work.

(1) Jesus was at once man, and a man

The incarnation was the union of God with our human flesh in Jesus. It was the incarnation of the creator Word, by whom the whole of mankind is made and in whom all cohere. Here we have the union of the universal Word and one human creature created by that Word which makes Jesus *at once man, and a man*. Is that not the deepest significance of the expression 'Son of Man'?

(2) The anhypostatic union and solidarity of Christ with all humanity, and the enhypostatic encounter with people in personal relation

In the doctrine of *anhypostasia*, we state that the Son did not join himself to an independent personality existing on its own as an individual. That is, he so took possession of human nature, as to set aside that which divides us human beings from one another, our independent centres of personality, and to assume that which unites us with one another, the possession of the same or common human nature. But apart from the doctrine of *enhypostasia* in addition to it, *anhypostasia* could only mean a solidarity between Christ and all mankind which was, so to speak, only ontological and therefore physical and mechanical – a causal and necessitarian solidarity.

The doctrine of *enhypostasia* insists here that within that *anhypostatic* solidarity of Christ with our common human nature, he came also as an individual human being in our humanity, seeking in addition a solidarity in terms of the interaction of persons within our human and social life, in personal relations of love, commitment, responsibility, decision, etc. Thus his birth within a human family, his growing up among others, his increasing relations with people, and his public entry into a ministry of vicarious suffering and service as Son of Man, the one man for all mankind, the one man in whom all men and women are encountered in love and met by the person of God – all that ministers *enhypostatically* to his solidarity with our human life by acutely personal modes of existence, and encounter, and communion.[85]

(3) The anhypostatic assumption of fallen humanity, and the enhypostatic purity of Jesus and personal responsibility for sinners

The doctrine of *anhypostasia and enhypostasia* (put together as one concept) helps us also to understand or express how God the Son was made in the likeness of our flesh of sin, and yet was not himself a sinner; how he became one with us in the continuity of our adamic

---

85 Cf. further Torrance, *The School of Faith*, p. cxxiif.

and fallen existence in such a way as to make contact with us in the very roots of our sinning being, and yet did not himself repeat our 'original sin' but vanquished it, and broke its continuity within our human nature. He assumed our corrupt and estranged humanity, but in such a way as at the same time to heal and sanctify in himself what he assumed.

The *anhypostatic* assumption speaks of God's unconditional and amazingly humble act of grace in assuming our humanity in the concrete likeness of the flesh of sin. But within that, *enhypostasia* speaks of the fact that the person of Christ was the person of the obedient Son of the Father, who in his humanity remained in perfect holy communion with the Father from the very beginning, and so was sinless, and absolutely pure and spotless and holy. Thus he, the *enhypostatic* Son of Man, lived out a life of perfect and sinless obedience to the Father in the midst of the fallen human nature which he had *anhypostatically* assumed, and in virtue of which he had entered into solidarity with all mankind.

But as *enhypostatic* Son of Man, Jesus Christ entered deeply and acutely into personal relations with sinners, so that in personal and responsible ways of the profoundest nature, he might enter within our personal human structure of existence, and assume personally and answerably the whole burden of our sin and guilt upon himself, so that he, the just, was loaded with our unrighteousness, and he, the holy one, was loaded with our guilt, that he in our place and on our behalf might expiate our sin and guilt and make propitiation for us before God the Father, thus restoring us to the Father in purity and truth and love.

****

A note on the use of theological terms such as 'anhypostasia' *and* 'enhypostasia'

All technical theological terms such as these are to be used like 'disclosure models', as cognitive instruments, helping us to allow the reality of Christ to show through to us more clearly. As in natural science we must often cast our thought about certain connections into mathematical or algebraic form in order to see how those connections work out in the most consistent and rigorous way, so here we may well think of '*anhypostasia* and *enhypostasia*' as a sort of 'theological algebra' to help us work out the 'inner logic' in christology more consistently and purely. But once we see the connections more clearly in this way, they have to be translated back into 'the flesh and blood' of reality, translated back into terms of the person and work of Christ himself. Just as in a natural science, we may have to resort to algebra to work out the connections using algebra like a computer as it were, to compute for us what our brains are incapable of doing by themselves, but must then translate the algebra back into 'physical statements' in order to discern the real relations in empirical reality, so we must do much the same here. *Anhypostasia* and *enhypostasia* together do not themselves contain the 'stuff' of christology, but they may be, rightly used, theological instruments or lenses through which we may discern more deeply and clearly the ontological structures of the incarnation.

The **Quicunque vult** *or 'Athanasian Creed' on the Trinity*

The Catholic faith is this:

That we worship one God in trinity, and trinity in unity; neither confounding the persons nor dividing the substance (essence). For there is one person of the Father, another of the Son, and another of the Holy Spirit. But the Godhead of the Father, of the Son , and of the Holy Spirit, is all one, the glory equal, the majesty co-eternal. Such as the Father is, such is the Son, and such is the Holy Spirit. The Father uncreated, the Son uncreated, and the Holy Spirit uncreated. The Father infinite (unlimited), the Son infinite, and the Holy Spirit infinite. The Father eternal, the Son eternal, and the Holy Spirit eternal. And yet they are not three eternals, but one eternal. As also there are not three uncreated, nor three infinities, but one uncreated, and one infinite. So likewise the Father is almighty, the Son almighty, and the Holy Spirit almighty. And yet they are not three almighties but one almighty. So the Father is God, the Son is God and the Holy Spirit is God. And yet they are not three Gods, but one God. So likewise the Father is Lord, the Son is Lord, and the Holy Spirit is Lord. And yet there are not three Lords, but one Lord.

For just as we are compelled by Christian truth to acknowledge every person of the Trinity by himself to be God and Lord, so we are forbidden by the Catholic religion to say, there are three Gods, or three Lords. The Father is made of none, neither created, nor begotten. The Son is of the Father alone, not made, nor created, but begotten. The Holy Spirit is of the Father and of the Son, neither made, nor created, nor begotten, but proceeding. So there is one Father, not three Fathers, one Son, not three Sons, one Holy Spirit, not three Holy Spirits.

And in the Trinity none is before or after another: none is greater or less than another. But the whole three persons are co-eternal and co-equal. So that in all things, as has already been said, the unity in trinity, and the trinity in unity, is to be worshipped.[86]

---

[86] At the end of the text of this chapter, and after the Athanasian Creed, there is appended the following note:

On the Concept of Person

St Augustine: 'The image of the trinity is one person, but the supreme trinity himself is three persons' (*De Trinitate* XV.23; Eng. trans. *On the Trinity*, Nicene and Post-Nicene Fathers, vol. 3 (Grand Rapids, Eerdmans repr. 1956), p. 222).

Boethius: '*Persona est naturae rationalis individua substantia*' — 'Person is the individual substance of rational nature' (*De personis et duabus naturis*, Patrologiae Latinae, vol. LXIV, ed. Migne, 1891, p. 1343).

Richard of St Victor: '*Persona divina sit divinae naturae incommunicabilis exsistentia*' – 'Divine person is the incommunicable existence of divine nature' (*De Trinitate*, IV.22, Sources Chrétiennes, vol. 63, La Trinité, Latin text and translation, Paris 1959, p. 280); cf. the Duns Scotus summary of this definition, '*Persona est intellectualis naturae incommunicabilis exsistentia*' – 'Person is the incommunicable ex(s)istence of intellectual nature' ('*definitionem personae quam ponit Richardus* IV *De Trinitate* cap. 22, quod est "intellectualis naturae incommunicabilis exsistentia",' Duns Scotus, *Opera Omnia*, vol. V, Ordinatio, 1.23.1, Rome: Civitas Vaticana 1959, p. 355-6.)

Chapter Seven

THE KINGDOM OF CHRIST AND EVIL[1]

1 The breaking in of the kingdom

In this section we come to look again at the life and ministry of Jesus as the advent or *parousia* of the king who has come to claim his own and to reclaim them for the kingdom of God. Here we have in mind the parables of Jesus about the heir coming to claim the fruit of the vineyard and call his servants to account,[2] the parable of the mighty man who breaks into the house of bondage binding the strong tyrant and spoiling him of his usurped possessions;[3] and the parables of the king who sends for the poor and the outcasts, the lame and the blind, and brings them into the festive joy of the kingdom.[4] But we also have in mind the miracles of Jesus, the *dynameis*, the mighty miraculous acts of grace and power in which his words took concrete form as active intervention in the lives of men and women. It is through them that the kingdom of God's love and grace and freedom break into the midst of enslaved humanity with power and salvation. But what we are especially concerned with in this section is the light that the coming

---

1 The theme of chapter seven, complementing that of chapter four, is the human situation as revealed by Christ. Chapter four describes how in faithfulness and truth Jesus lived out the union of God and man in his person, provoking hostile attack by the powers of evil and exposing the sin of man. The focus of chapter four is on the life of Jesus, a life as Son, shepherd and king which he lived faithfully to the end knowing that the conflict it created would lead straight to the cross. The focus of chapter seven is on the conflict of Jesus with evil and the nature of the sin, guilt and evil revealed by his coming. Chapter seven examines the enmity of man and the meaning of sin in the light of the cross in order to understand them as far as is possible, in preparation for understanding more clearly and fully the atoning death and justifying resurrection of Christ.

2 Matt 21.33-46; Mark 12.1-12; Luke 20.9-19.

3 Mark 3.27; cf. Isaiah 49.24-25.

4 Matt 22.1-10; Luke 14.16-24.

of the king throws upon his work of redemption and upon the condition of those whom he has come to save and reclaim for the kingdom of heaven.

(a) The coming of the king and holy one

The coming of the king is described as the coming of the mighty one (*el gibbor* in the language of the Old Testament scriptures) and as the coming of the holy one of Israel (*qedosh yishrael*, as the Old Testament describes him). That is what we see from the very start of Jesus' ministry, from his baptism. He is the one mightier than John the Baptist who takes up John's message that the kingdom has drawn near in judgement and grace; but he fulfils it in his own life and work, for by the finger or Spirit of God he brings the power of God to bear upon the whole realm of evil and asserts the sovereignty of God's grace over and in it all. He does that, as we noted earlier, as the lowly one who breaks into the hearts of men and women through submitting to the violence of the violent and thereby storming his way by meekness and passion into the ultimate citadel of evil in order that by atonement he might bring about redemption and emancipation.

On the other hand, Jesus comes also as the holy one of Israel, that is to say, not simply as the direct radiance and glory of the divine majesty in all his holiness, but in humble obedience to the heavenly Father. It was in that perfect holy obedience of his life as true man in the midst of sinful men and women that Jesus collided with all the dark forces of evil which had entrenched themselves in the flesh (*sarx*) of humanity. The sovereign presence (*parousia*) of this king is everywhere characterised by divine authority or *exousia*, for in the coming and presence (i.e. *parousia*) of Jesus, the mighty Son of God and the holy one of Israel, the heavenly power of God himself impinges upon the fallen world in direct challenge and conflict, in struggle with the powers of darkness and in victory over all the forces of evil. It is atoning and emancipating redemption already at work reclaiming the lost and reasserting the sovereign rule of God over his creation.

(b) Conflict with the entrenched forces of evil

When we examine the witness of the Gospels we find that this atoning and redeeming *exousia*, in both the words and acts of Jesus, comes to grips with the demonic forces entrenched in the fallen world and overcomes them. Whenever Jesus proclaimed his word, that word was an assault upon the enemies of God and whenever he acted in forgiveness and healing that act was in deliverance of men and women from enslavement to the power of Satan, the prince of evil. Immediately after his baptism by John in the Jordan, Jesus was thrust into the wilderness on his mission as the servant Son, the mighty one to take the lowly road of meekness and passion, the holy one to take the humble road of obedience unto the death of the cross. There he was assailed by Satan. The battle was joined, the battleground was 'the flesh of sin', and the enemy was the devil. Jesus invaded the terrain occupied by the enemy and by his authoritative divine presence, his *exousia* in grace and holiness, he laid claim upon it for God the Father, and all through his ministry, reaching out at last to the cross and resurrection, he set out to make good that claim, in order to restore alienated humanity to the ownership of God, and to restore to humanity its truth and right as God's creation.

Hence wherever Jesus went, his presence brought conflict with the authorities or powers (*exousiai*) of this world wherever they were found, in the synagogue, in the hearts of the rulers, and in the poor bodies of the sick and possessed, the demoniacs and maniacs. Everywhere behind the outward facade of evil he came to grips with the vast forces of evil that held the world, held the mind in tyranny and darkness. He knew that the sin of man had its roots not only in the depth of the human heart and will but also in a vast evil will beyond humanity from which it could not escape. Human hostility to God was part of a whole kingdom of evil over which people had no control. It was into that kingdom of evil that Jesus penetrated in order to do battle with it and to break its power over men and women, to hew a way out of its tyranny and lead them back into the freedom of God's children. All this is an essential and an indispensable part of the whole life and ministry of Jesus; it cannot be stripped away or be demythologised without fundamental loss to the gospel. This element is so intertwined in the gospel witness to the person and work of Christ that if it is demythologised or stripped away, the essential substance of the gospel goes with it.

The indispensable place in the New Testament of Jesus' conflict with spiritual powers

This is an aspect of the New Testament witness to Christ that has been seriously neglected. It was of course set aside altogether along with the eschatology that is bound up with it during the heyday of the liberal approach to Jesus, but has to a certain extent been restored through the rediscovery of the eschatology of the New Testament. It has not yet been given its proper place, though New Testament scholars are now more and more concerned with it. Of far reaching importance was William Manson's presidential lecture to the Society for New

Testament Studies in 1952.[5] In that lecture, Manson challenged New Testament scholarship to reconsider the place of the deeper dimension in the spiritual world of the Gospels, and showed, through an examination of some of the outstanding passages and logia in the synoptic Gospels, the indispensable place of the conflict between Jesus and the powers of darkness leading up to the very end, to the hour and power of darkness that confronted him at the cross. Then he added the following:

> So the *exousia* of Jesus the Messiah comes to last mortal grips with the *exousia* of the demonic world. And the apostolic gospel from its illuminated standpoint will tell us the rest of the story. The 'archons' who dominate this present world-age, writes St Paul, did not recognise the hidden wisdom of God, for 'had they known it, they would not have crucified the Lord of glory.'[6] Christ, he writes again, 'having disarmed the principalities and powers, made a public spectacle of them, when he triumphed over them on the cross.'[7] God, we read further, by the power exerted in the raising of Christ from the dead, 'has made him sit at his right hand in the heavenly world, far above all rule and authority and power and dominion, and above every name that is named, not only in this world but in the world to come.'[8] From the Pauline, and indeed from the whole New Testament standpoint, when Christ bowed his head on the cross, all the powers of darkness, all the demonism of the cosmos, affronted him and closed with him in mortal combat. Behind all 'the fearful enmity of the carnal heart of man towards God' which arrayed itself visibly against Jesus at his trial before the Sanhedrin and at Calvary, stood the embattled hosts of the invisible world, hazarding all on a last trial of strength. And Jesus, when he faced and accepted that challenge, was taking upon himself all that hatred, all that guilt, and all that judgement of God which lay upon it, in order to complete his 'baptism', his work of delivering men from the power of the enemy and so restoring them to forgiveness and to God.[9]

That is an aspect of Christ's mercy and redemption that is particularly manifested in his works of healing which have to be placed beside his teaching, his servant ministry and his obedient

---

5 Principalities and Powers: The Spiritual Background of the Work of Jesus in the Synoptic Gospels, Bulletin of Studiorum Novi Testamenti Societas (Society for New Testament Studies), 1952, reprinted in William Manson, *Jesus and the Christian* (London: James Clarke 1967), pp. 77-88.

6 1 Cor 2.8.

7 Col 2.15.

8 Eph 1.19-21.

9 *Jesus and the Christian*, pp. 85-86.

sonship if they are to be understood aright. And only if they are fully considered is his obedience, his teaching, and his ministry in bringing the grace of God to lost men and women, properly appreciated. We are not concerned at the moment with the full doctrine of redemption as the mighty act of deliverance from the tyrant works of evil – we shall consider that in the volume on *Atonement* - but we are concerned to see that redemption is already at work in the ministry of the historical Jesus, and to see what light that sheds upon the human situation in which Jesus intervenes as the king come to reclaim his kingdom.

(c) Light and darkness

Our concern here is the light shed by the kingdom upon humanity as we try to understand something of the fearful darkness of evil that is revealed in the human situation, for it is that very darkness that Jesus has come to invade and destroy. That is a favourite theme of the Johannine writer, beginning right away with the prologue, and found in the first Epistle and Apocalypse also. Or to put it the other way round, throughout the ministry of Jesus, especially in his rescue and reclaiming of the lost and damned, we see the shadow of the cross cast ahead of it upon humanity. The cross has a light side and a shadow side. The light side is that which is revealed by the resurrection: it is the redemption of lost man into the new creation, the restoration of God's estranged children to the place of joyful and obedient sons and daughters. The shadow side is that which is revealed by the crucifixion: it is the abysmal depth of iniquity and wickedness of sin in the human heart, its entanglement in a vast evil will that brings upon the sinner the bitterness of bondage under the divine judgement upon all sin and evil.

That is the darkness that God has put behind his back, which he negates and from which he delivers us in Christ. The depth and power of that hostility to God is fully revealed at the cross but it is apparent all through the ministry of Jesus, not least in his miracles, the *dynameis*, the mighty acts of grace whereby he snatched the lost out of the jaws of hell and repelled the forces of the evil one. That is why Jesus taught the disciples to pray, 'Lead us not into temptation (that is, the assaults of evil) but deliver us from the evil one, for thine is the kingdom and the power and the glory.'[10] The very fact that Jesus inserted that into the heart of the Lord's prayer indicates how essential and central he regarded this to be. That prayer, 'Our Father', is his own prayer, which he shares with us and into which he draws us.

10 Matt 6.13.

The words and acts of Jesus the king cast an astonishing light on mankind and the way that the heavenly Father regards humanity in its plight. The miracles are not only acts of emancipating grace (*dynameis*) but signs of the kingdom (*sēmeia*). They reveal in individual acts of mercy the essential meaning of salvation in forgiveness, amnesty, emancipation from the slavery of Satan and all the forces of evil and darkness that seek to hold both the soul and the body of man under their sway; but beyond all that they reveal the fact that redemption means recreation, the restoration of the creature to uninhibited communion with the heavenly Father in a creation under the control of his holy love and grace.

Our task now is to examine what is thus revealed in two ways: *first* to set forth in general terms what is revealed about the human situation as it is seen by the eyes of the Father; and *second* in the light of that, and especially in the shadow of the cross itself, to understand as far as we may the enmity of man and the meaning of sin. This we do in the next two sections, and then we can go forward to understand more fully and clearly the atoning death and the justifying resurrection of Christ.

2 The human situation as revealed by the breaking in of the kingdom of God in Christ

The vexation and compassion of God in Christ over the distress of humanity

If we are to be true to the witness of the Gospels, the point from which we must begin here is the vexation of the heavenly Father over the condition of his children. God in Christ is burdened with the griefs and pains of men and women. He does not will their hurt or distress or destruction, but on the contrary wills that they shall be made whole, and therefore God allies himself with them against the evil that afflicts them and intervenes as the enemy of all that destroys humanity. That is the primary revelation of man in the light of the kingdom, a revelation that comes from the fact that God the Father looks upon men and women in compassion and vexation as he sees their fears and anxieties, their torments and sorrows and hunger and oppression. That is why the Acts of the Apostles can sum up what it has to say about the ministry of Jesus by the words that he went about doing good and healing all that were oppressed with the devil,[11] while the evangelists all show how much Jesus carried upon his spirit the burden of people's ills and hurts and gave himself to them in healing.[12]

---

[11] Acts 10.38.

[12] Matt 4.23-24; 8.16-17; 9.35-36; 15.30-31, etc.

But what vexes and distresses God in Christ is not simply the sickness and pain of humanity but the fact that it is engulfed in an abyss of fearful darkness, too deep for men and women themselves to understand and certainly too deep for them ever to get out of it – a pit of bottomless evil power. Mankind is entangled in sin not wholly of its own making, enmeshed in the toils of a vast evil will quite beyond it; it is chained in terror and is dragged down and down into the poisonous source or pit of evil. It is evil at its ultimate source, evil at its deepest root, in its stronghold, that God has come to attack and destroy.[13]

This revelation of the condition of humanity from the vexation of God is supported and redoubled by the fact that God in Christ acts towards mankind in its helplessness and distress in sheer grace, grace that is utterly free. Nowhere does Jesus accuse the sick of their sins before he stoops to shoulder their weakness (*astheneia*). The astounding thing is that God does not put the responsibility upon them but takes the responsibility on himself. That is the most miraculous thing about the miracles and healings, the fact that God comes among sinners and makes himself responsible for their condition and even takes their sin and culpability upon himself vicariously. But that in turn reveals the ultimate helplessness and hopelessness of man, apart from such a stupendous act of divine grace.

(a) The struggle with evil will

At this point we are faced with two profound facts of which the New Testament is deeply conscious. First, the fact that when God in Christ comes to heal or save sinners in all their helpless distress, there takes place *a struggle with evil will*, a struggle which is waged between God and evil not only in the sinner's heart, not only in their thoughts and desires, but in their bodily and spiritual existence, for the whole creaturely realm is the sphere of this struggle. Hence the Gospels see the closest relation between the spiritual and the physical. The wages of sin is death, as St Paul put it. Sin and physical disintegration and corruption are inseparable. The being and existence of man is under the sway of evil, and therefore even when Jesus heals people of physical distress he does so only through a struggle with evil will, with living and masterful evil power. Nowhere does Jesus heal as a human doctor, but always he heals as one who wrestles personally with evil and overcomes it through the conflict of his own holy will with the unholy powers of evil spirit.

---

[13] Cf. Mark 3.27; Lk 11.21-22.

We have already had occasion to see how much that cost Christ in his compassion and agony, but here we see that in the heart of it all there is a direct struggle between God and evil power. That is why Jesus had constantly to renew his strength through prayer and why prayer itself was a battle with the rebellious will of an alienated creation. The tragic situation of man revealed here is that men and women are alienated from themselves, alienated from who they were made to be, creatures and children of God. Mankind is not only estranged from God but estranged from true humanity, determined and controlled in their self-will by evil power that destroys their very being: they are subjected to evil existence and live in the shadow of death and destruction.

(b) The entry of God himself into the human situation

That is what lies at the root of human anxiety, for the deepest being of man and woman is threatened with chaos and negation, and slips away from them into corruption. It is here that we see the second profound fact of which the New Testament is conscious. Into this situation where the very being and existence of man is threatened with destruction *God himself enters*, and takes this human being and existence upon himself. That is to say, in Christ Jesus his incarnate Son, God himself enters into the destructive power of evil and so hazards, as it were, his very existence and being as God for the sake of mankind. Moreover, God enters into this estranged and threatened existence of man to live as man under all the assaults of evil, and insists in living under them all within the entire limitation of the creature under the attack of evil and under the judgement of God. It is only when we see that in the incarnation, in the entry of the Son into our alienated existence under the determinism of evil, and even into our death where evil pays its fullest wages and delivers its ultimate onslaught upon God's creatures, it is only when we see that the presence of God in all that means that God (and here we clap our hands on our mouth) has staked and risked his very being as God for our sakes, that we can begin to grasp the fearful gravity of our human condition.

That is what God does, he comes himself in order to deliver us from subjection to evil existence, from subjection to destruction and death. It is this that lies not only behind the cross and the descent of the saviour into our bottomless pit of guilt and death, but behind every act of healing and mercy in which Jesus sought to release distressed humanity from its subjection to evil and vanity, to release it from being a prisoner of chaos and disorder and disintegration, and to restore it to the truth of God's creation in which he affirms as good what he has made, and assumes it into communion with himself to share in his own divine life and glory. The miracles are concerned therefore with creation, with new creation, for God the creator assumes such responsibility for his creatures that he restores them again to creation in the teeth of everything that threatens their being and existence, restores them to natural life in a natural world in the freedom of God's creation. Thus the miracles reveal that the essential nature of redemption results in the joyful affirmation of man as God's child and creature, but that affirmation involves a total negation of all that is opposed to God and therefore opposed to God's creative will for his creatures. At no point therefore is this positive and joyful act of reclamation and recreation dissociated from the divine judgement upon evil, from the total opposition of God to all that is against God.

(c) God stakes his own being in the judgement and negation of evil

Now in that light we must look again at the two facts we have just discussed, namely, the fact that in reclaiming his creatures God enters into a struggle with evil will, and the fact that God himself enters into the human existence that is threatened with destruction and so hazards and stakes his own existence and being in the salvation of men and women. The will that God opposes and struggles with is so interwoven with the will of man in alienation from God that it is with man that God struggles, but here man under the judgement of God is given by that very judgement an obdurate and brazen character in sin – it is here that, to use language that we shall discuss later, sin gains its strength from the very law of God. That is why the 'hazard', so to speak, to which God submits as he stakes his own being in our salvation, comes not from the attack of evil itself by itself but from the divine judgement and negation of evil – it is that fact that makes the cross and the *Eli, Eli, lama sabachthani,*[14] of the Lord Jesus so indescribably terrible, makes it the sheer anguish of God bowed under his own judgement on sin, a judgement not mitigated but utterly fulfilled. Thus the menaced and threatened existence of humanity into which God the Son enters and within which he lives as the Son of Man is an existence that is under the threat of destruction not only from the inherent negation of evil but from the negation of it through the divine judgement, so that the divine negation of evil strengthens and makes obdurate and fearful that threat to destroy man's existence. It is into that very existence under the divine judgement and into its corruption and destruction under the divine negation that God enters himself in order to save humanity.

---

14 Matt 27.46, 'My God, my God, why have you forsaken me?'

The mystery of evil, in its opposition to God and in God's negation of it

Now we must admit frankly that here we are concerned with a mystery of iniquity that is far beyond our comprehension, both because evil, by its very nature as that which contradicts the good being that God has made, is contradictory and irrational, and because evil, under the judgement and negation of God is not allowed to have an independent position and in that sense a positive character, but has only a negative existence. Evil is not simply negative in the sense that it is privation or subtraction, but negative in the sense that it is direct contradiction to the holy will of God, and in that contradictory way it is positive opposition to God. Yet just because it is met by the total opposition of God, negated, disallowed, repudiated by God who does not will it but rejects it, it can be understood only as a surd[15] (to borrow for the moment a mathematical expression) or as an ultimate irrationality. It is precisely because evil has that negative irrational reality under the judgement of God that we cannot think it out into full clarity, but can think of it only under the divine negation and repudiation of it. That is the evil in which mankind is engulfed, and it is to evil existence under that divine negation that humanity is subjected in sin. It is into that evil existence that God penetrated in the incarnation of his dear Son, and in his death on the cross: he descended into hell, God the Son descended into the bottomless pit of God-forsakenness – 'My God why have you forsaken me?' – for it is in that pit of evil that man is ensnared, and willingly ensnared, and that is part of its abysmal depth.

That is what is revealed about the condition of mankind in its sin and need under the judgement of God, revealed by the shadow that the cross casts over humanity, revealed by unveiling the rooting of fallen human nature in a bottomless pit of hatred of God's grace, and hostility to his love. That brings us to the next section where what we have to do now is to examine as fully as we can the enmity of man and the meaning of sin in the light of man's crucifixion of the Son of God, the king of the kingdom of heaven.

3 Sin and alienation in the light of Christ and his crucifixion[16]

To begin with let us note the proportion of attention and of importance that the evangelists give to the crucifixion of Christ. St Mark gives ten chapters to the three years ministry of our Lord, and then devotes six chapters to the last week of his life, to his passion. Similar proportions

---

15 An 'irrational' number.

16 For what follows, cf. T.F. Torrance, *The Doctrine of Jesus Christ* (Eugene: Wipf and Stock 2002), chap. 12, 'The Background of the Cross', pp. 156-64.

are found in the other Gospels. We are pointed by all of them to the passion week as the crucial and supremely important period in the ministry of Christ, for it is there that we are given to understand as nowhere else who the saviour is, what he does for us, and what is the fearful condition of humanity from which he has come to save it. He is the mediator who has come to unite us to God, the saviour who has come to die for our sins, God himself in Jesus Christ come to enter into our condition under judgement and to stake his own self in our redemption from the pit of evil, God entering himself into our estrangement and alienation in order to reclaim us and reconcile us to himself as his dear children.

This is the point, therefore, where we must look above all to see what the estrangement of humanity is, and then to see again what God did in Christ in order to restore us from that condition to communion with himself. Quite clearly the movement of theological understanding at this point is necessarily circular, truly circular. We can proceed to deeper understanding only by allowing each aspect of Christ's work to speak of every other aspect, and each doctrine to illuminate every other. We do not understand the situation of sin in which we are involved until we see it unmasked at the cross in all its stark and dark reality where atonement for us in our sin is made. But to understand the crucifixion more fully we must understand what sin and guilt are, what the estrangement of the world is into which the saviour has come.

(a) The judgement of the cross

The Bible nowhere teaches a doctrine of sin independent of the grace and love of God

It is a very significant fact that neither in the Old Testament nor in the New Testament do we have a deliberate attempt to formulate a doctrine of sin first in an independent or abstract way and then to show over against that background the grace and love of God in redemption. We must be careful therefore to let the gospel of forgiveness and redemption guide us throughout here. As we plant the cross in the midst of our understanding of human sin and estrangement, we remember that the cross has a light side and a dark side. The light side is the glory of the resurrection and its affirmation of man in Christ, and the dark side is the shadow the cross casts on man's inhumanity. It is in that duality of revelation at the cross that we really see into the depths of sin and guilt.

No doubt humanity dislikes the shadow of the cross, the significance of Golgotha – that is why there is so much anti-semitism in the world.

That is why people try to romanticise the cross, for they will not face up to its grim factuality; they hate what it has to say about humanity and try to transmute it or soften it by aestheticism, as is so evident in many paintings of the crucifixion. But the plain fact breaks through all our camouflage and tells us that the cross is the supreme judgement on mankind, pronounced by mankind themselves in this dastardly act of crucifixion, as well as pronounced by God who submits to man's outrage and bears it all in his love.

The devastating judgement of grace and the cross

We have already noted that the very coming of God into the world in the incarnation means that the world was alienated from God, while the offer of absolute grace and forgiveness in Jesus Christ implies a devastating disqualification of our world and all its cherished riches and 'values'. That disqualification, or judgement, reaches its height in the cross, where we have unmasked the meaning of sin and the depth of man's involvement in it. Humanity is so utterly selfish and so far astray that nothing would suffice for its salvation but that the Son of God should be plucked from the bosom of the Father and be crucified in sacrifice. The indescribable horror of Golgotha is the most terrible and searching judgement on man that could possibly be made: mankind is so bad that it rose up, spat in the very face of God and slew him on a tree. None of us can dissociate ourselves from that, from those Jews and Gentiles, the representatives of church and state, and the crowd of the common people, who crucified Jesus – to do that would involve us, if possible, in even greater sin by sheer hypocrisy. If Christ came today we would still crucify him, only no doubt with a greater refinement of cruelty than even the Romans were able to think of. We cannot evade the fact that the cross is the most devastating judgement on men and women, on all of us, that could possibly be imagined. The gulf between God and man is so abysmal that Christ had to cry 'My God, my God, why have you forsaken me?' That is the midnight hour, as Kierkegaard said, when we are all unmasked.

What then does the cross have to say about the meaning of sin? Sin is revealed in its own act to be attack upon God, and to be something from which God turns away his face in judgement. Those two clauses, human rebellion and God's judgement, describe the significance of *sin* and *guilt*. Together sin and guilt separate man from God – they constitute the veil, woven within and without, which hides God from us, the very veil which in the death of Christ is torn from top to bottom. It is the rending of that veil that reveals to us what sin and guilt really are and actually involve, the utter chasm between self-willed humanity and God.

(b) Sin as alienation and contradiction

Sin presupposes the nearness of God and a two-sided relation of life with the creator

Sin is utter separation from God, alienation from God – but the distance between God and man is not constituted by any metaphysical magnitude such as the infinite distance between the creator and the creature. The distance between God and man is due precisely to the nearness of God to man, to the antagonism between God's holy will of love and our sin. The nearer God comes, the more intense the conflict and we are forced to cry, 'Depart from me, for I am a sinful man, O Lord'[17] and 'I am not worthy to have you come under my roof.'[18] Those were words spoken to God incarnate as he came near in Jesus Christ, spoken in the very presence of God, and they bring out into sharp relief the difference, the conflict between humanity and God which is minimised when God is thought of as at a distance. Sin presupposes the nearness of God.

We must go further and say: sin as severance from God presupposes a life-unity with the creator given by the Holy Spirit. The Spirit of God is God in his freedom to be present to the creature and to realise the relation of the creature to himself. The creature requires relation to the creator in order to be a creature. That relation is given and maintained by the Spirit of God who creates the existence of the creature, but of the creature as a reality distinct from God himself, yet as wholly dependent on God for what it is. There is between God and the human creature a double relation, a two-sided relation, in which the creator gives existence and life to the creature, and in which the creature depends on the creator for existence and life. That twofold relation is a continuous relation from moment to moment. The human creature, however, is made not only to have existence but to have fellowship with God, to have a relation filled with sharing in God's light, life and love.

The contradiction and severing of the life-relation – judgement and death

Sin is to be understood as the contradiction introduced into this life-relation or life-unity of man with the creator, for in sin the human creature who depends on the creator for existence and life rebels against the creator. Sin is therefore destructive of the creature – a form of suicide. By rebelling against the creator and by asserting his or her

17 Luke 5.8.

18 Luke 7.6.

independence, the creature is rebelling against the innermost relation which constitutes their very being as a creature, as human being. Sin is therefore an 'impossible possibility', as the medieval schoolmen sometimes called it.

Sin, then, involves at its very heart that twofold relation with God into which it has introduced contradiction. The central point in every human being is their relation to God, and sin means that central point has been violated. Sin means that men and women have fallen out of the central thing in their life and existence, that they have thus become ec-centric,[19] as Emil Brunner put it.

Just because the existence of the creature involves a double relation with God, because it is only one who lives in essential relation to God who can sin, the attitude between the creature constituted by its rebellion and God is qualified by a corresponding attitude of the creator toward the creature. The creator, who gives the creature life and existence, now opposes or contradicts or judges the creature, and does so precisely as God. That contradiction results in a change from the relation of life to the relation of death. To be sure the creature continues to have existence before God, but does not have the full relation of life. Into the positive life-relation with God there has come a negative factor which bears fruit in the disruption of that life-relation with God. And so while sin means that man is cut off from God precisely as and even while he or she is dependent on God, it means that man will suffer from God and suffer death.

(c) The double 'change' in attitude, of man against God, and God against man

It is false to think that in the event of sin the 'change' has come about only in the relation of man to God, and not also in the relation of God to man – in fact it is less than half the truth, for it is the relation of God to humanity that is the important thing in life and in humanity's rebellion against him in sin. Therefore we must think of sin as objectively real from the point of view of God as well as subjectively real from the point of view of man. Sin is not simply the perversion of man's mind and attitude toward God. It also means a real 'change' in God's mind and attitude toward man, his judgement on human sin, and it is that which constitutes the innermost gravity of sin. Of course, this 'change' in God's mind and attitude rests upon the fact that God

---

[19] Literally, standing 'outside the centre', from the Gk *ek* (out of), *kentron* (centre).

does not change at all. He remains the same God, ever faithful and true and loving, but it is because he is the truth and keeps truth with all humanity faithfully, because he remains love unswervingly that now in the steadfastness of his love he judges man's sin and inhumanity, opposing all that is opposed to his own being and nature as holy love.

Let us examine this more closely. God remains God whatever happens. He remains the same yesterday today and forever, he who is truth, light, life, love, holiness. He remains the 'I am who I am', and the 'I will be who I will be.'[20] God as God, precisely as God asserts himself to be God, to be true, holy, loving, and asserts that as God his truth, holiness, and love are binding on us all universally and absolutely. That self-affirmation of God is his Godness or Godhead, his majesty in which he is God, his honour, his deity.

Sin, however, means the contradiction of the Godness of God – it is sin against his majesty and is counter to his self-giving in love. If sin is an attack upon the very Godness of God, upon God precisely as God, then by his very Godness, his eternal will as God to be who he is must and does resist sin – just in being God. To be God is to be opposed to the private self-assertion of man. There can be only one God who asserts himself to be supreme: as we read in the decalogue, 'I am the Lord your God . . . You shall have no other gods before me . . . I the Lord your God am a jealous God.'[21] When men and women assert themselves against the Godness of God they are actually asserting themselves to be God, and so placing themselves in direct contradiction to the Godness of God. God resists sin in the full Godness of God – that is the meaning of the *wrath* of God. That is the negative aspect of his holiness and love, the exclusive aspect of his majesty. God would abdicate from being God, would un-God himself, if he condoned sin.

(i) The wrath of God – a sign of hope and of his reaffirmation of humanity

But let us be quite clear about what the wrath of God means. It is the *wrath of the lamb*, the wrath of redeeming love. As such the very wrath of God is a sign of hope, not of utter destruction – for if God chastises us then we are sons and daughters, and not bastards, as the scripture puts it. Judgement and wrath mean that far from casting us off, God comes within the existence and relation between the creator and the creature, and negates the contradiction we have introduced into it by and in our sin. God's wrath means that God

---

[20] Exod 3.14.

[21] Exod 20.2f.

declares in no uncertain terms that what he has made *he still affirms as his own good handiwork and will not cast it off into nothingness.* Wrath means that God asserts himself against us as holy and loving creator in the midst of our sin and perversity and alienation. God's wrath is God's judgement of sin, but it is a judgement in which God asserts that he is the God of the sinner and that the sinner is God's creature: it is a wrath that asserts God's ownership of the creature and that asserts the binding of the creature to the holy and loving God. And yet precisely as such, God's wrath is really a part of atonement, part of new creation, for it is his reaffirmation of his creature in spite of its sin and corruption. It is certainly a reaffirmation of it in judgement, for it must take the form of judgement over against sin, but a reaffirmation that the creature belongs to God and that he refuses to cease to be its God and therefore refuses to let it go. God's very wrath tells us that we are children of God. It is the rejection of evil, of our evil by the very love that God himself eternally is.

The law as the primary sign of God's grace and mercy – judgement within relation to God

That was the reason why the Jews regarded the law itself, with all its judgement, as the primary sign of God's grace and mercy – they were the commandments and ordinances that presupposed the covenant of grace. But although wrath speaks also of God's reclaiming of the perverted creature for himself, it speaks nonetheless of utter judgement, of damnation. God's wrath says that man belongs to God body and soul; that is why even if the sinner in his or her ultimate reaction should deny God's claim upon them, God's judgement cannot be equated with annihilation, but only with utter and final judgement within existential relation to God.

That must be clearly understood as we look at sin in the light of the cross and look at the cross in the light of what it reveals of the terrible guilt and sin that is judged there in Jesus' atoning sacrifice. The cross makes good God's claim upon humanity and reveals the depth of sin within its relation to its creator. Sin in itself is not simply an act done by man – it is sin *against God.* That is why the psalmist, in voicing confession, has to say, 'Against thee, thee only have I sinned.'[22] The fact that sin is against God means that sin takes its form and nature from being against God. It is not sin simply because it is against love or goodness or even against man, but because it is ultimately against God himself. As such sin is 'cursed' by God – it comes under his total ban.

[22] Psalm 51.4.

(ii) The curse of God – banishment into outer darkness

But let us be clear about what the *curse of God* means. When the Bible speaks of curse, it means that the cursed is no longer within but without, outside the covenant of God. Without the covenant relation with God man is condemned to exist as one who does not belong to it, but is an outsider. Curse means the reprobation of the elect, the casting away of those whom God has made and loves; it means separation from the face of God, banishment from creation into outer darkness. That is what Paul calls the act of God in giving mankind up to their own uncleanness and to their own reprobate mind,[23] to their own self-destruction. Cursing does not mean annihilation, the sending of the cursed into nothingness, into the *nihil* out of which man and woman were created, but *a banishment to their own denial of their being in God,* that is, into the very darkness upon which God has for ever turned his back in creation and on the cross.

That is the import of the Old Testament *sheol*, existence in darkness behind God's back, the darkness from which he has turned away in creation when he divided the light from the darkness. *Sheol* is existence in man's self-chosen perversity and blindness. That curse lies upon all sinners as their destiny in their sin and it already casts its shadow over them. In the Old Testament *sheol* is, however, a sort of suspended darkness, a suspended existence behind the back of God, waiting for his final acts of judgement and or deliverance, although the final act will mean justification for those who cast themselves on his judgement, and utter banishment for those who choose to remain in their alienation. But the Old Testament saints were all aware that the curse is the ultimate and final judgement, and that preferable to that is to fall into the hands of the living God in his wrath and judgement.

The duality of wrath and curse – God's personal 'naming' of sin as sin and guilt

Now it is only in that duality of *wrath* and *curse* that we can understand sin as sin under the divine judgement, sin as guilt against God, sin as under God's wrath and curse. Thus sin as sin is a twofold affair. It has two sides to it. On the one hand, it is the act of human rebellion against God. But if, *per impossibile,*[24] God did not resist that rebellion God would not be God, and there would be no such thing as a distinction between God's will and the sinner's will, or between good and evil. And so, on

---

23 Rom 1.24, 26, 28.

24 Lat, 'if the impossible happened'.

the other hand, sin is judged and qualified as sin by God. It is 'named' sin, judged sin and judged as sin – precisely by the act of God's resistance to it. It is this act of God – 'the handwriting' of God against us as St Paul expressed it[25] – that gives sin its depth and gravity as guilt. It does not, of course, make sin more sinful, for what makes sin so sinful is that it is sin against God, but the fact that God resists it, opposes it, makes sin something infinitely terrible, ineradicable by man, and quite irreversible by the sinner. Thus we read in the book of Exodus that Pharaoh hardened his own heart in resisting the will of God, but then we also read on the other hand, that God hardened Pharaoh's heart. The act of evil is judged sin, so to speak, as God judges it, denominates it sin, and so sin becomes guilt, 'the handwriting against us', to use the language of Paul again, the handwriting to which God appends his signature, as it were.

The innermost constitution of sin – the dual nature of the conflict

Thus in the innermost constitution of sin as sin we have the negative assertion of man against God on top of man's positive self-assertion in independence of God; and we have the negative assertion of God against the sinner on top of the positive self-assertion of God's own nature as holy love. The innermost constitution of sin is double – characterised by the act of human rebellion and by the act of divine judgement. In both cases it is personal act. God personally resists sin – that is why God's opposition to sin and his judgement upon it is called 'wrath'; for sin is a personal act against the very person of God. It is met in personal relation and is judged in personal action. There is nothing in God lower than the personal and he always acts personally, even in judging and condemning sin.

(d) The radical nature of sin

Perversion of the whole nature of human being

But sin is not an isolated act – it is not something incidental or accidental. It is constitutive and now has to do with the very existence of human being as such. We noted that sin is the contradiction introduced into the very nature of man as essentially dependent on God. Sin is only possible in the presence of God, in the relation of the creature to the creator. In sin there is brought

---

[25] Col 2.14 KJV, 'the handwriting (*cheirographon*) of ordinances that was against us'.

about a perversion of the attitude of man to God with a corresponding negative activity in the attitude of God to man. In sin the very central point in human being is altered. The whole existence of man is involved in that change – man as a sinner is altered in his and her whole relation with God. He or she *is* a sinner.

We can think here only in terms of totality. The theological terms 'radical evil', 'original sin', 'total depravity' simply express that fact. Each of these terms involves something different, and therefore there are these three terms, but the main point in each expression concerns the constitutive change in which the whole man is involved, and in which man is wholly involved. There is not such a thing as a half sin, and nor such a thing as a half sinner. Sin is a fundamental state introduced into human existence. It is the contradiction to God at the basis of human existence. Sin does not primarily refer to isolated acts of sin, for they are but the outward manifestation of this perversion at the very roots of human being. It refers primarily to a radical enmity in man and woman which amounts to a corruption of their whole existence and a disintegration of their self-relation to God. Man *is* now a sinner, and *is* bad. The law of God does not simply say that this or that is wrong, but that the person who does this or that *is* wrong, *is* a sinner.

From faith to faith, and from sin to sin

Whatever is not of faith is sin, said St Paul.[26] Sin is the negative correlative of faith. Faith is a relation of trust and surrender to God which works by love and lives by communion with Christ and in reliance upon him. Sin is contradiction of all that. It belongs to the very nature of faith, as Calvin says, to go from faith to faith, because faith receives grace for grace, but the movement of sin is in the opposite direction, from alienation to alienation. Sin as sin can go only in the direction opposite to that of faith and grace.

Now further, because sin now characterises the nature of man as fallen, and now determines their whole existence in relation to God, sin is something which men and women themselves cannot change, for all that they do for themselves is done with their autonomy which is the independence and self-will of sin. Their self-will is their free will, and they cannot escape out of their self-will. The more they strive in their self-will to save themselves, the more they sin – in fact that is the very movement of sin at its subtlest and in its very worst form, self-justification.

---

[26] Rom 14.23 KJV.

The twofold nature of guilt

Thus sin, this sin, belongs now irrevocably to the nature of man as fallen creature, and men and women cannot change their nature. This element in sin which cannot be changed, because it is determined also by God's judgement against it, is known as 'guilt'. Guilt is that element which belongs unalterably to the past and which determines the existence of every human being in the present. Guilt involves our whole past as a constituting or determining element in the present.

Man's guilty nature, that existence in sin and guilt, lies between man and God as an impassable obstacle between them. God can no longer admit men and women to his presence apart from judgement than cease to be God. Their nature as guilty is thus a nature determined not only by their inclination away from God due to sin, but by the divine reaction against them in the way of judgement. Just as sin is a two-sided affair, so now human nature as sin conditioned and sin determined is a two-sided affair. There is man's movement against God, and there is the divine reaction against that. That is the tension in which the human person exists, and it is ultimately from that root that all anxieties and disorders arise. The tragedy and the astounding fact is that men and women are so audacious and impudent as to assert that this divine reaction against sin in them is actually their own better self, or their own higher nature in evidence, so that they claim in this way to be very different from what they actually might do and are. It is thus that they try to cover up their sin but only mask themselves with a personality that is sin-born and sin determined. This self-justification, this basic hypocrisy which belongs to the personality of fallen man, is exposed at the cross where men and women see themselves for the first time in the true light and stark actuality of what they are and do.

The fact I wish to emphasise, however, is this: that guilt as belonging to man and woman and their fallen nature is that side of sin which shows their human nature is doubly determined, by their own autonomy or sin, and by the divine wrath against sin. Their nature is just as twofold as every act of sin. It represents broken fellowship. It represents the perversion of life-unity with the creator and Father of mankind. Sin is repudiated fellowship with God within mankind's existential relation to God. It is the act which seizes upon that very relation which they have in fellowship with God, the relation which constitutes the very being of humanity, and perverts it into its opposite, into separation from God, rebellion against him, in the will to be independent and autonomous. The amazing fact revealed about God over against the sinner is that God does not will that relation of existence between himself and man to cease. It is his amazing love that maintains his relation to the creature even when the creature sins and when God resists sin. He will not let the sinner go.

(e) Christ's descent into hell

That is the fact that has to be grasped profoundly if we are really to understand in all its depth the meaning of the entry of the Son of God into the world in order to assume our human nature and existence into oneness with himself and then as mediator to die for us and save us from our sin and sinful nature. Those for whom Christ died on the cross are creatures whose existence is maintained by God in relation to God, and yet their natures as sinful are natures that are determined both by their rebellion against God and God's judgement of their rebellion. It is into this humanity that God the Son entered to endure the contradiction of sinners against himself, and to shatter the bond of sin and death. That is why the cross is so terrible, because the guilt it deals with is so infinite and terrible. And guilt is terrible because at the back of it there is the full force of the divine resistance to sin, God's godly wrath. The chasm that separates man from God in the very existence of sinful man is the black abyss of hell. And Christ descended into that hell in order to redeem. He the mediator descended into the black pit of human alienation from God in order to save. In his own incarnate person he united man and God and bore the guilt of man before the presence of God. It is because the godly majesty of God, the righteous law of God, the holy love of God, stands inexorably in the path between mankind and God that the gravity of the situation is infinite. It is such that God and only God himself can deal with it, and only God in infinite anguish.

(f) The cross's exposure of infinite guilt and infinite love

It is the cross itself that shows us all this – but without looking down into the abyss which the cross reveals and spans we cannot understand the person or the work of the mediator, and we cannot understand the 'cross'. It is Christ the mediator, true God and true man, who bridges the chasm of hell in his own incarnate person, and not only in his bodily suffering, but as Calvin insisted, in the fearful pain and judgement which he bore on his soul. He bridges the chasm in his own person and all that pain he takes upon and into his person for our sakes. That is the point we have to try to grasp. While sin is the double fact of man's opposition to God and God's opposition to man, Christ came in the concrete likeness of our flesh of sin, as St Paul expressed it, condemning sin in the flesh, numbering himself with the transgressors and submitting himself to the judgement of God upon our sin. 'For us he was made sin who knew no sin'.[27] He even became a curse for us.

The depths of that are quite incomprehensible, especially when we realise that sin contains at its very heart and constitution as sin the divine wrath. By taking upon himself human guilt, Christ placed himself at the very point where God's Godness, God's holy majesty, resists sin. Jesus entered into that very situation where man's being is menaced and threatened by annihilation through separation from God, and yet held in existence by the very fact of the divine judgement against it. And so by entering into the very situation where all the divine majesty is directed against the sinner in his and her sin, the Son of God, it might well be said, 'hazarded' and 'staked' his very existence and being in order to take all that fearful tension and judgement upon himself in order to save us.

Christ's salvation is of such a kind that it expresses the ultimate reality of guilt and exposes it in all its stark actuality. It exposes it in terms of the wrath of God, but at the same time manifests in the midst of it all the infinite and overwhelming love of God, and enacts the union of God and man in a union and communion that nothing can undo. In forgiveness Jesus Christ offers himself on behalf of and in the place of the sinner, and the gulf of human sin and guilt is spanned, but in throwing a bridge over the abyss, the depth and breadth of it are made still more evident. That is why Golgotha casts such a dark shadow over the world. That is why the cross unmasks the inhumanity of man, at once exposing sin and guilt and dealing with them at their worst – in mankind's ultimate attack upon God in Jesus Christ – in God's attack of love upon the inhumanity of mankind – and out of the heart of that there come two words that reveal the infinite guilt of humanity and the infinite love of God. 'My God, my God, why have you forsaken me?'[28] 'Father forgive them, for they know not what they do.'[29]

---

27 See 2 Cor 5.21.

28 Matt 27.46.

29 Luke 23.34.

End Notes to Chapter One

E1 When Reformed theologians at the end of the sixteenth century first developed positive theology as a dogmatic science (it was they who coined the term 'dogmatics') they rejected two primary principles in Roman theology.

(i) They rejected the idea that the criterion of truth is lodged in the subject of the knower or interpreter. In all interpretation of the scriptures, for example, we are thrown back upon the truth of the word of God, which we must allow to declare itself to us as it calls in question all our preconceptions or vaunted authorities. The Reformed theologians had to fight for this on a double front: against the humanist thinkers who held the autonomous reason of the individual to be the measure of all things, and against the Roman theologians who claimed that the Roman church (the collective subject) was the supreme judge of all truth. What Reformed theology did was to transfer the centre of authority from the subject of the interpreter (the individual or Rome) to the truth itself.

(ii) They rejected the idea that the definition of the truth belongs to the truth and is a necessary extension of it. This idea had long been developed by the canon lawyers and then by the nominalist theologians (who formed the great majority at the Council of Trent), and remains inherent in the claim that whenever the Roman Church officially defines a truth, the definition becomes an extension of the truth, and as such is so binding that acceptance of it is necessary for salvation. The Reformed theologians, however, insisted that definitions or formulations of the faith are only fallible human statements that are intended to point to the truth and must never be confused with the truth itself; they can only be regarded as symbols which are always subject to correction in the light of the truth itself.

In steering a course between arbitrary individualism on the one hand, and authoritarian dogmatism on the other hand, Reformed dogmatics was battling for the principle of objectivity that now governs all branches of disciplined, scientific knowledge. At the reformation the principle of objectivity was given vivid expression in two doctrines, a) election or predestination, and b) justification by grace.

a) Pre-destination means that in all our relations with God, in thinking or acting, we have to reckon with the absolute priority of God. By his very nature as God, God always comes first. Thus our loving of God depends upon his loving of us, or our choosing of God upon his choosing of us, and even our knowing of God depends upon his knowing of us, for it is only by God that we can know God. That is the God who has revealed himself to us in Jesus Christ. There are not two 'Gods', one who comes to us in Christ, and some dark predestinarian 'God' who acts behind the back of Christ and his cross. In Christ, God's eternal Word or decree became flesh, his eternal love has become man, and so divine election goes into action in Jesus – there is no other election than what we see operating in Christ in his relations with sinners. Pre-destination then means that what God is toward us in Jesus Christ on earth and in time, he is antecedently and eternally in himself, and that everything that God is in himself he is toward us in Jesus Christ. The doctrine of predestination is corrupted when we project back into God the kind of logical or causal connections, or even the kind of temporal connections which we have on earth, for then we make it into some kind of pre-determinism or fatalism, which is very wrong, and quite unchristian.

b) Justification by grace means that in all our relations with God as moral or religious beings, we can never claim to have right or truth in ourselves, but may find our right and truth only in Christ. Justification by grace calls in question all our self-justification for it tells us that whether we are good or bad we can be saved only by the free grace of God, whether we are old or young we can enter the kingdom of God only like little children, who do not trust at all in themselves but only in their heavenly Father. But justification by faith in Christ is badly corrupted when we make our own 'faith' the justifying cause, for then our own 'faith' or our own piety usurps the place of Christ, and we are justifying ourselves. It is one of the great tragedies of Protestantism that so often justification by grace has been corrupted into a form of self-justification which easily serves to cover up gross unrighteousness. A striking example of that is the famous work of James Hogg, *The Confessions of a Justified Sinner*, in which we see justification turned into its very opposite. This was exactly what the Reformers protested against in their day.

When we apply justification by grace alone to the task of theology or dogmatics, it means that we can never claim the truth for our own statements, but must rather think of our statements as pointing away to Christ who alone is the truth. Theological statements do not carry their truth in themselves, but are true only in so far as they direct us away from ourselves to the one truth of God. Justification by grace, therefore, will never allow anyone to boast of their orthodoxy or to be dogmatic about their own formulations, for it means that all that we do is questionable and fallible. That is why justification is the most powerful statement of objectivity in theology for it throws us at every point upon God himself, and will never let us repose upon our own efforts. There is thus an immense difference between dogmatics and dogmatism. The former expounds the realities of God's self-revelation in accordance with their own objective forms, the latter works with subjective prejudice and biased or 'interested' opinions.

Now we have to ask how the Roman church reacted to the dogmatic science of the Reformed theologians. In due course the Romans themselves began to engage in dogmatics, but they meant something very different by it. 'Dogmatics', in their view, was the systematic account of the historic statements of the councils and creeds (what Reformed theology calls 'symbolics'), and of the canonical definitions and authoritative pronouncements of the Roman church on matters of faith. It was 'dogmatics' of this kind that gave rise to the notion of dogmatism, a way of thinking based on principles not tested by scientific questioning but backed only by the authority of the church. In our day, however, Roman theologians have been trying to write dogmatics in the Reformed style, building up positive knowledge of God upon a biblical basis, and testing everything in it by reference to the Word and truth of God, disclosed to us through the biblical revelation. In view of this, it is not difficult to see the far reaching importance of the statement by the late Pope John at the opening of the Vatican Council when he drew a clear distinction between the substance of the faith and its many formulations. This means that the formulations of the faith find their justification only in so far as they serve the substance of the faith itself and are open to modification and correction in the light of it. If Roman theologians are prepared to take this up seriously, then it would mean that Reformed dogmatics and a new Roman dogmatics could engage in real dialogue at last through common subjection of all our own ideas to the one truth and Word of God.

In such a dialogue, justification by grace alone would assume paramount importance – as we can see in the dialogue between Karl Barth and Hans Kung. For Romans, justification will serve to call in question their authoritarianism, and for Protestants it will serve to call in question their free thinking and individualism; and for both it will mean a readiness to submit to the masterful objectivity of the truth of God as it is in Christ Jesus. If dogmatics is the positive science in which we bring to view the basic forms of theological thinking in accordance with which we are compelled to think if we are to be faithful to the concrete act of God in Jesus Christ, then dogmatics properly pursued cannot but lead to agreement. Theological disagreements derive to a very large extent from an uncritical and unscientific approach to the basic forms of theological thinking. But if theologians in all churches all over the world would determine to let their thinking be governed by the concrete act of God in Jesus Christ above everything else then there would surely take place such an immense and powerful clarification of the basic forms of our theological thinking that we would be compelled into fundamental agreement that was both strictly theological and strictly scientific.

E2 The last two of the four original main sections of this chapter are to be found in the endnotes (the heading, **3 Procedure in christology** has been added to the main text for the sake of consistency in the headings. This means that the sections originally numbered 3 and 4 which followed it are now 4 and 5). Thus while the sections entitled, **1 The relation of Christ to history**, **2 Jesus Christ and the New Testament *kērygma***, and **3 Procedure in christology** are in the main text, the following two, entitled, **4 The relation of the *kērygma* to history: the problem of eschatology** and, **5 The relation of the *kērygma* to history: the problem of mythology and christology** are in the endnotes. As explained in the editor's introduction, this is because these sections, as with the other endnotes, contain material which though important is of a much more technical and historical nature, also more philosophical in tone, and therefore of less immediate relevance to the ordinary reader.

E3 Once the historical and the theological are divorced from one another, then we collapse them into impossible contradictions and ceaseless dialectics. That is what has happened again and again. Let us try to see how that has happened in modern times, especially since the early part of the nineteenth century when these contradictory and false problems were posed for us. Here is the question which has been asked both by theologians and historians in modern times. How can revelation and redemption that have to do with eternal verities of God, have to do also with the world of historical relativity and contingency? One persistent answer to that question which arose in the very early history of the church and again in modern times, reaching its great expression in the modern idealist view of history, is the emphasis on *gnōsis*, or the knowledge of ideas, which Jesus mediates by divine revelation within the course of his historical life, but mediates in such a way that these truths, once they are revealed, are seen to have no essential relation to the time-series, to historical existence.

Idealism: the emphasis on truths of reason at the expense of the historical

That means of course that for idealism the *incarnate person* of Christ, the person of the historical Jesus, has no ultimate place. His place lies in giving birth to certain eternal truths, and those truths are the object of faith, not the teacher himself. Strange as it may seem, the whole modern approach to the Jesus of history, which is an apparent attempt to take seriously the historical element in christology, belongs to the same idealist movement.

In Hegel or Lessing, history was ultimately reduced to mere appearance: it was the picture book of the eternal ideas which are of absolute importance. Within that quickened interest in history, and growing out of the German pietist attitude to the humanity of Jesus (cf. the Roman Catholic cult of the heart of Jesus), there arose the stress on the historical Jesus. Here it would appear that history is given its proper place, for the whole approach is historical – the Old Testament is interpreted historically, and the New Testament Epistles are interpreted historically as historical developments of the teaching found in the synoptic Gospels. And so a great attempt is made to excavate beneath the accretions and accumulations of the centuries which, it is said, have overlaid the picture of Jesus, in order to get back to the original Jesus of history.

That has certainly involved the most searching study of documents ever undertaken, and has yielded invaluable results, and yet in the end, this approach has meant the negation of the historical Christ, for the so called historical Jesus becomes only the historical dress with which truth is draped for its passage into the minds of men and women. Here, Jesus became a teacher about God, a mediator of new truth, not the truth himself. We need to get back to the original Jesus, to see clearly how the pure truth came into history, and then we see what that pure truth was and is. But once we see it, in the original Jesus, we see it to be the eternal truth of the fatherhood of God, and the brotherhood of man, truths which once seen, are self evident, and are truths of reason, apart from all historical mediation. They have no essential relation to history, and therefore no essential relation to the historical Jesus Christ. When we follow out this whole movement, the quest for the historical Jesus, we find ourselves landed up in sheer contradictions.

It is clear now that if we give up the classical christology or even approach Jesus from a purely historical angle, the historical events which belong to the life and death of Jesus fall away as of no final significance. The great dilemma is this: *either* in Jesus Christ we are confronted by God, and by one whose person is himself of the utmost importance, *or* Jesus is in the end only a teacher, a religious genius, the greatest man that ever lived but who, before the absolute importance of timeless and eternal truths, sinks into only an honourable mention.

In both liberalism and existentialism the historical Jesus is expendable

That is the denouement that comes over the idealist and liberal conception of Jesus, in which the eternal ideas mediated by Jesus finally set the historical Jesus himself aside. That is called Liberalism, but today there is a whole school of New Testament scholars who are opposed to that liberal approach to Jesus, and they lay the stress not on the ideas that he taught, but on the eschatological event which broke into the world in the historical Jesus. What is this eschatological event? The school of New Testament scholars here would call the eschatological event the act of the divine mediated in and through the historical Jesus, but they deny that the divine event is itself also an historical event. In other words, they have substituted the concept of event for that of idea, and in the same way as the idea passes through the historical Jesus and discards him, so this eschatological event passes through the historical Jesus and discards him. Just as the eternal ideas or truths mediated by Jesus had only a temporal and non-essential relation to history, so this eschatological event has only a temporal and non-essential relation to history. Again, just as the eternal truth mediated by Jesus, once it was disclosed to our knowledge, appears self evident to us as a truth of our own reason, so the eschatological event, once it is disclosed through our decision, ministers to, or is servant to, our self understanding. What is the difference between this view and the liberal one? The liberal view worked with an idealist philosophy [emphasis on ideas], and this works with an existentialist philosophy [emphasis on courageous *existence* and decision, personal action and involvement in events]; the liberal view was more concerned with static ideas, and this one more with dynamic events and decisions, but in both the result is the same: the truth of reason or self understanding is the net result, while the historical Jesus is relegated as of no ultimate importance.

All that has happened here is that the philosophical idiom has changed, the language has changed to suit the times, but we have the same radical divorce of the eternal from the temporal, the act of God from history – with the result that the historical person of Christ as God and man is no longer central or important. This is simply a new and more subtle form of liberalism. Once again the great dilemma is: *either* in Jesus Christ we are confronted by the eternal God in history, so that the person of the historical Christ as man and God is of utmost importance; *or* Jesus is only the historical medium of a confrontation between me and the act of God which summons me to decision, but in which I reach a self understanding which enables me to live my life bravely. Here christology passes away into some kind of existentialist anthropology.

Against both idealism and liberalism [here]....

(Note: words in italics at the end of a particular endnote are left in at the end of the endnote since they were part of the main text, and enable the reader to follow precisely how the endnote was part of the original text and connects to what follows in it. Words in square brackets are words which are also to be found in the main text.)

[E4] One of the most sincere and noble attempts to make this movement in modern times was that of Wilhelm Herrmann of Marburg. It was an attempt to gather from the historical analysis of the material to hand in the Gospels, as well as by the reconstructive aid of the imagination, a true historical picture of Jesus, and then in the light of that and the vivid impression it made upon the mind of the observer, to pass a judgement on the same historical level, a judgement on the ground of the value coefficient attached to the personality of the original Jesus and on his person and work. That was of course impossible – the very movement which abstracted the historical Jesus out of the context of the New Testament mystery, so stripped Jesus of his divine majesty, that any move towards his deity from his humanity was *eo ipso* (by that very fact) prevented. If you start off on a purely historical level, then the only honest inference is a purely historical one, made on a purely historical level. If you ask only historical questions, you will only get historical answers. Faith is then held to be some kind of moral appreciation of historical facts.

Now this was thought to be scientific procedure and an honest way of dealing with the historical Jesus – but leaving that aside for the moment, let us see what it involves. If the object of faith is a mere fact of history as such, then faith is simply historical inspection. But even if you go a little further, and say that this fact of history has to be appreciated morally, in terms of moral values, these moral values are only your appreciation of the historical fact which is historically perceived. But that leaves faith, even with this moral overtone attached to it, open to all the assaults of rationalist criticism, and the validity of faith will then depend on the amount of validity human reason can adduce for the historical facts in question. If there is little or no possibility of historical demonstration, then there is little or no possibility for faith. Over against the criticism of historical science, especially when historical science was becoming more and more assimilated to the natural sciences, it would be impossible for faith to exist at all. Therefore in reaction, why not separate the ground of faith entirely from historical grounds, and so secure faith from the possibility of scientific historical criticism? That is to say, separate theology from history, so that theological knowledge is not grounded at all in history, then no amount of historical criticism will destroy the foundations of theology. That was the reaction of Herrmann's great successor in Marburg – Rudolf Bultmann – but we will come to him later.

Let us meantime return to Herrmann himself, and his attempt to reach the original Jesus of history in order to let the impress of his historical personality affect the observer – no amount of exegetical alchemy can get away from the fact that if we start with only a historical picture of Jesus we will get nothing out of him except ordinary historical material, so that Jesus can mean nothing more to us than a mere figure of history alongside of others. That was thought, however, to be a scientific procedure and an honest one, but how could it be either scientific or honest when it started off by refusing to behave in terms of the nature of the object, the nature of the historical Christ as he is presented to us in the Gospels, a historical Christ set in the context of mystery, set in a context at once historical and supernatural?

E5 Now that is supremely important. We noted earlier the statement of H.R. Mackintosh that 'Jesus was not a Christian', and drew from it his conclusion that we must approach Christ from the point of view of sinners who have experienced Christ as saviour and mediator. We have, in other words, to take a *Christian and evangelical* approach to Christ. But long before H.R. Mackintosh said that 'Jesus was not a Christian', the same thing was said by Wellhausen. The Gospels were written, he said, by Christians and Jesus was not a Christian. Jesus is certainly clothed with a gospel on the pages of the New Testament but for Wellhausen it is not a gospel which he knew; it is a gospel which was put into his lips by the church. Or let us take another notorious scholar, David Friedrich Strauss, who in his *Life of Jesus,* insists that even in the earliest New Testament tradition the figure of the historical Jesus has been idealised by the faith and love of those who first proclaimed him. Now if Jesus Christ is presented to us in the pages of the New Testament from the point of view of sinners saved by him, can we possibly get away from the Christ of experience, back to a Christ who is not disguised by how people experienced him? And how can we answer the criticism that this is inevitably a distorted presentation, distorted from the very start in the minds of those who witness to him in the New Testament?

Here Wellhausen and Strauss have put their finger upon a very crucial issue which we must not run away from. Let us look at it like this, from the point of view of European pietism, whether in Germany or in Britain, pietism presents an evangelical picture of Christ, of a living Christ who confronts us in living power and whom we cannot know except in and through a personal experience of him as Lord and saviour. This is startlingly clear in Lutheran pietism which is so closely related to the fundamental question, 'How can I get a gracious God?' In other words, how can I get a God who will satisfy my need and hunger for comfort and peace? In answer to that question, pietism presents Christ as the one who satisfies all our spiritual needs. Can we deny that this presentation of Christ set in a context of 19th century piety, and interpreted according to its religious needs and satisfactions, is inevitably coloured and determined by those needs and satisfactions? Surely we cannot deny it.

The impossibility of the quest for the purely historical Jesus

But here comes the liberal scientific historian, seeking to penetrate behind these layers of interpretation which the piety of the ages has laid over the original Jesus, and trying to give us a true account of the original Jesus. Is the historian any more successful? Is not Schweitzer dead right when he examines all the lives of Jesus from Reimarus to Wrede in his *Quest of the Historical Jesus* (Tübingen: Mohr 1906, Eng. trans. London: A & C Black 1910), and tells us that what we get in all of them is simply a Jesus dressed up in the clothes and thoughts of the 19th century and not the original Jesus, and that it is in fact impossible to get back to the original Jesus at all in this way. And is Bultmann not right in his inference that if liberals and pietists cannot find the real Jesus, but inevitably distort and misinterpret him, it is also true that we cannot get behind the Gospels to the original Jesus because already from the very word 'go' the original Jesus was distorted and misinterpreted by the spiritual experience and piety of the first witnesses – so that what we get in the New Testament is only a picture of Jesus adapted to the spiritual needs and satisfactions of the first Christians?

What are we to say to this? We cannot but grant that when we approach Christ from the side of our experience of him, and make that an interpretative norm, we inevitably distort the presentation of Christ. We cannot but agree with Schweitzer's brilliant analysis of many lives of the historical Jesus – although both Schweitzer and Bultmann fall into precisely the same mistake they point out in others, but we shall come to that later. However we cannot agree that we must be as sceptical about the historical Jesus as Schweitzer and Bultmann are. That is impossible. Denney was surely right when he insisted that 'the great life of Christ that stands out before us in the Gospels is more real than anything in the world; and Jesus is so far from being hidden from us that it is no exaggeration to say that we know him better than anyone who has ever lived on earth' (article on 'Preaching Christ', Hastings, *Dictionary of Christ and the Gospels,* Vol. II, Edinburgh: T & T Clark 1908, p. 395).

On the other hand, we cannot but acknowledge, as we have already done, that in the Gospels Christ is presented from the point of view of forgiven sinners, from the point of view of the gospel of salvation, but we deny that it was the piety or religious experience of the first Christians that was determinative in this presentation of Christ. If we take the view shared by Strauss and Bultmann that the gospel as we know it is not the creation of Jesus Christ but the creation of the first Christians, which they then projected back to the historical Jesus in order to invest him with it and put its message into his mouth, then we make the incredible assumption that the original church was the true originator of the gospel, and was therefore far greater, far richer and surpassingly more creative than the original Jesus, that the gospel which has triumphed throughout the whole history of the church was the product of the amazing genius of the primitive church. Such a conclusion is fantastic in the extreme, but it does set before us in very stark fashion the ultimate alternative – *either* the gospel was the product of the creative spirituality of the first Christians, *or* it derives from Jesus Christ himself, the Son of God.

Now when we examine the actual material in the New Testament, even in the synoptic Gospels, we have to admit that there are sayings and actions attributed to Jesus which are recorded in contexts where there is, clearly discernibly at work, a pious motive which is ostensibly at any rate different from the original situation in which the incidents took place. It remains to be proved of course in each case whether or not this motive is a legitimate extension of the original motive for the saying or the action of Jesus, but it is surely entirely unscientific to set aside at once everything that looks in the least like the opinion of the reporter, or the judgement of the apostolic church which transmitted and used these sayings and reports of the action of Jesus in its liturgical worship or doctrinal instruction. It is unscientific to suppose that any historical event can be faithfully reported without a judgement, that any factual event can be apprehended, attested, and handed on in a responsible witness, without rational ideas about it. How can any rational being testify to a historical person, and hand on a responsible and authoritative tradition about him for others to apprehend and appropriate, without rational interpretation? The witness of the Gospels is certainly witness that is meaningful, but it is also deliberate witness to objective historical events and to a historical Jesus. Hence this witness is given through clear and deliberate proclamation, through the *kçrygma* [the gospel proclamation of Christ – literally, 'what is preached']. It is responsibly given in and with the proclamation of the gospel and from the point of view of the salvation that the gospel involves. But this is not to say that all this is the creation of the apostolic community.

Christ is always the kerygmatic Christ

We must agree with Bultmann that what is presented to us in the Gospels is a kerygmatic Christ, but we must disagree with him in the way he handles this *kērygma*. For one thing, Bultmann works with a thoroughly pietistic notion of preaching as preaching which is wholly concentrated upon an existential decision, and therefore preaching which is to be understood from the decisive result, or the resulting decision, and not from its actual content. This importation of an alien notion of preaching vitiates Bultmann's whole understanding of the New Testament *kērygma* and the kerygmatic Christ. That we must examine carefully when we come to discuss the relation of *kērygma* to history, but at this point, we must look again at the actual way in which Christ is presented to us in the New Testament. Certainly he is presented from the point of view of forgiven sinners who have known the power of his resurrection; certainly he is presented through the *kērygma* as a Christ clothed with the Christian gospel, but Christ is *never* presented in the New Testament simply in the context of the piety and spirituality of the primitive church, and *never* as interpreted by that piety and spirituality or by psychological or existential experience. Certainly the Christ presented in and through the *kērygma* is a Christ who challenges men and women and requires of them decision, but never in such a way that the centre of gravity passes over from Christ to that decision, and so that it is the decisive answer to Christ that in fact controls the whole complex of presentation and response. *On the contrary [here] . . .*

E6 The importance of that stands out when we think of Bultmann's conception of the *kērygma* as bound up with the decision it requires and calls forth, in which the centre of gravity passes over from the content of the *kērygma* to the result. It is probably true that for Bultmann the *kērygma* is not understood merely as a function of our own self understanding achieved in decision, because it does have its *origin in and motive power in the historical fact of the crucified Jesus*. But according to Bultmann, the historical fact of Jesus *cannot itself be the object* of the *kērygma*, for it is the *kērygma* that declares its meaning and confers upon it its value as saving event – and therefore as a historical fact Jesus is himself ultimately irrelevant for faith. In other words, for Bultmann, the historical fact of Jesus is admittedly the *occasion* for the *kērygma* and gives rise to it, but it has nothing to do with the *real meaning* of the *kērygma* which it acquires solely from the fact that it becomes a call to decision when it is preached and by its preaching awakens a new understanding. (Cf. *Kerygma and Myth, A Theological Debate*, ed. by H.W. Bartsch, trans. R.H. Fuller, London 1953, chap. 1, 'New Testament and Mythology'). But why then was Jesus needed at all, for this *kērygma* could just as easily have been occasioned by John the Baptist, and if, as Bultmann might argue, it needed the crucifixion of Jesus to give it motive power, then why was not the execution of John the Baptist able to give it motive power?

E7 That fact has been belittled by those who like Bultmann and Dodd begin with a sharp separation between the historical and the theological, for they are then forced to make this same [sharp distinction between *didachē* and *kērygma*]. *But . . .*

E8 When this [essential factor in the earliest New Testament witness] is set aside, [namely the relation of the *kērygma* to the authorised apostles and transmitters of it selected and trained by Jesus], and an alien notion of *kērygma* derived from modern pietistic preaching is imported, then we make havoc of the New Testament witness. The logic of Bultmann's position is that the *kērygma* is restricted to a call for decision. On the ground of that definition he is unable to accept much of the New Testament witness as genuine *kērygmata* (things proclaimed), and so presumes to cut them out as aberrations. Or to put it the other way round, by means of his peculiar notion of *kērygma* Bultmann claims to be able to disentangle the real kerygmatic elements from the rest, with the result that by his arbitrary method he is left with nothing that contradicts his thesis – but the whole procedure shatters itself upon this fact alone, that no such conception of *kērygma* is anywhere to be found in the pages of the New Testament. *But [and]* . . .

E9 Bultmann rightly saw the importance of this, and it has strongly influenced him, but he gave the whole thing a radically subjectivist twist which is precisely what Kierkegaard did not do.

E10 But that is precisely what Bultmann does; the historical Jesus provides for him the occasion for a decisive encounter in and through which he makes a decision, not about Christ, but about the reality and significance of his own existence, and so in this way, for the first time, he attains a full participation in existence himself. That is of course where an existentialist philosophy is substituted for the gospel.

E11 Bultmann thus makes the fundamental mistake of abstracting decision (*Entscheidung*) from its objective basis in the historical Jesus Christ, but behind that mistake lies his abstraction of the historical Christ from the objective act of God in Christ.

E12 It is this doctrine of the Holy Spirit that is ousted and supplanted by Bultmann's notion of existential decision. By existential decision I am supposed to be able to encounter the eschatological event in Christ and appropriate it to myself, yet in such a way that the historical fact of Christ is left behind *but [the]* . . .

E13 Bultmann [existentialist theology]

[E14] [Added in a separate paragraph in Torrance's text here we have the following note] NB: We should note that in all history there is some mystery, but only in this particular history, the history of Israel, the history of Jesus, does the *mystery* announce itself, utter itself. It is this fact that makes the history of Israel difficult for all other history. (Cf. Karl Barth, *Church Dogmatics*, 4.3 [first half], Eng. trans. Edinburgh: T & T Clark 1961, p. 53f).

[E15] The following sections were originally in the lectures, and the headings below summarise the content (the material itself follows).

SECTIONS 4 and 5

4 The relation of the *kērygma* to history: the problem of eschatology

Developments since 1900

(a) The work of Overbeck, Johannes Weiss, and A. Schweitzer

(b) The early Barth: dialectic of time and eternity

(c) The later Barth: union of time and eternity

5 The relation of the *kērygma* to history: the problem of mythology and christology

(a) The modern debate: the views of Rudolf Bultmann

(i) The background to Bultmann
(ii) The teaching of Bultmann
The mythology of the New Testament
Demythologisation and reinterpretation
The meaning of mythology
The meaning of authentic existence
The detaching of faith from any foundation in the historical Jesus
(iii) Chief criticisms of Bultmann's teaching

(b) Mythology and demythology in the early church
The Hebrew and Greek mind
The gnostic solution
Christian '*gnosis*'
False dichotomy between ideas and events
The healing of the dichotomies in the incarnation

4 The relation of the *kērygma* to history: the problem of eschatology

This is the problem of eschatology and of so called mythology in relation to the New Testament gospel which is such an acute question in some quarters today, particularly in Germany. Perhaps the best way to get to the heart of the matter will be to examine the investigation of the New Testament account of Christ, from this point of view, which scholars have undertaken since 1900.

Developments since 1900

We may begin with the work of Adolf von Harnack as the great scion and heir of liberal Christianity at its peak when it attempted to detach the historical Jesus from the actual presentation of the mystery of Christ in the biblical documents and in the tradition of the church. In the last 50 years, however, the situation has been radically altered. The historico-critical study of the biblical documents, with its increasingly thorough form, has brought scholars back to grapple with the enormous place occupied in them by *eschatology*, that is, the setting of the historical Jesus in the context of the divine intervention in history. Three radical changes have taken place.

(a) The work of Overbeck, Johannes Weiss, and A. Schweitzer

Of these, Albert Schweitzer has been the most influential in the English-speaking world, in his discovery that the New Testament teaching about and of Christ is lodged within an eschatological context or scheme which shapes everything in accordance with it. The New Testament documents belong to a thought world in which the central point of reference was late Jewish apocalyptic. No honest understanding of the New Testament, he claimed, can neglect that.

Under scholars like Harnack, the teaching of Jesus had been interpreted in an entirely uneschatological sense, largely because of the Kantian and Ritschlian presuppositions that the kingdom of God is the realm of moral ends or values. Then scholars like Schweitzer found themselves forced to interpret the New Testament in a thorough-going eschatological fashion, even though they themselves did not like eschatology. Moreover, late Jewish apocalyptic was essentially futurist and catastrophic, and so, he held, we must regard the kingdom of God in the teaching of the New Testament as purely futurist and abruptly supernatural. Jesus, it is said, expected only an eschatological realisation of the kingdom, and therefore everything must be projected into the coming age.

Schweitzer's views have had enormous influence, mostly in destroying reconstructions of the gospel which ignored the eschatological sayings of Jesus in their attempt to set him forth as the central figure of the kingdom of God on earth, regarded primarily as a social and ethical movement in history reaching out through human progress and evolution to utopia. Ever since Schweitzer's *The Quest of the Historical Jesus* exposed the falsity of that approach, so far as New Testament scholarship is concerned, a mere 'Jesus of history' christology has been impossible.

But what are we to say to Schweitzer's thesis today? It cannot pass uncriticised.

(i) Schweitzer grossly overstated his case, and gave a very one-sided account of the New Testament. The other side is the emphasis on fulfilled eschatology, as it was called and taught by Edwyn Hoskyns and William Manson (see his *Jesus the Messiah*), and popularised by C.H. Dodd, though unfortunately in an equally one-sided way. There can be no doubt, however, that the New Testament is pervaded with the joyful sense of God's actual presence in Jesus Christ, and with the realisation that the coming age has already broken into the present and overlaps it. That is precisely the good news of the gospel, that here and now in Christ Jesus God is present in all his royal power, not only to speak a word of pardon but actually to enact it and fulfil it in the liberation of the children of God. The account of the eschatology of Jesus as an apocalyptic eschatology of despair is simply not true – it was above all an eschatology of *good news*.

(ii) What is ultimately at stake in Schweitzer's view is the doctrine of Christ. A Jesus so utterly deluded as the figure of Schweitzer's own reconstruction, who dies with a despairing cry on the cross when events took an unforeseen course, bears no relation to the Christ actually presented in the New Testament documents, and certainly no relation to the church's faith. Schweitzer's refusal to cut out of the New Testament witness the ingredient of eschatology undoubtedly enabled him to rehabilitate the synoptic account, for example that of Mark, but his own interpretation of it abstracted it from its setting in the mystery of Christ, and left him only with an exorcist and a brave though deluded idealist. In that way Schweitzer fell into precisely the mistake he had attacked in others, except that he gave a very different picture of the so called 'historical Jesus'.

(iii) Schweitzer thought of eschatology only in a narrowly apocalyptic sense. Indeed it would appear that over and over again for Schweitzer, eschatology is little more than primitive cosmology. When he sets the gospel in a thoroughly eschatological light that really means that he sees it in the midst of an apocalyptic scenery which, as far as he can see, is inextricably bound up with unscientific views of the world. It is not surprising, therefore, that Schweitzer rejects eschatology altogether as primitive mythology, nor it is surprising that, if his critical scholarship forced him to declare that the New Testament is eschatological from end to end, he should think of the history of the Christian church as the story of the progressive elimination of eschatology. In point of fact, says Schweitzer, the kingdom of God did not come in the first generation of Christians, as was expected, and the supreme problem that has faced the church in the centuries since has been how to adjust itself accordingly and to reconstruct the gospel in an interpretation that pivots upon that actual fact. Schweitzer himself carries this elimination of eschatology to such an extreme position that all he is left with for a faith is reverence for life. Thereby he has unwittingly done another immense service to New Testament scholarship and to theology, by demonstrating that if you cut out eschatology and all that goes with it, you are left with sheer triviality. Fortunately Schweitzer himself as missionary and musician was a much greater man than he was as theologian!

(iv) Schweitzer's interpretation of the New Testament was elaborated against the eschatological views of Harnack, but it is now apparent that Schweitzer failed at the very outset because he operated with similar idealist and rationalist assumptions (Hegelian in his case – we see a parallel in Bergson) which prevented him from thinking through radically the eschatological message of the New Testament. In other words, Schweitzer's presuppositions, entirely of a Hellenic type drawn from 19th century philosophy in the west, prevented him from apprehending the *inner* eschatological form of faith – apart from which apocalypse can only appear to be rather crude, and even Jesus must then be interpreted in that crude light as well.

(b) The early Barth: dialectic of time and eternity

The great turning point after Schweitzer came undoubtedly with the publication of Barth's *Commentary on Romans* in 1918 and its rewriting in 1921. Here the problem of Schweitzer was solved by a timeless eschatology which explained the New Testament attitude to the future but imminent advent of Christ in symbolical fashion. The end of history is not thought of as an end within time, for no end within time can be real or complete. The notion of a near advent is not a mythological element in Schweitzer's sense but is an essential part of the content of the gospel. Here then, eschatology is thought of in terms of timeless crisis.

Whereas for Schweitzer eschatology was only the time conditioned mould or envelope in which the thought of the New Testament was expressed, for Barth eschatology had to do with the very roots of faith, and belongs to the inner core of the gospel. It is in its essence the relation of time to eternity, and the crisis or dialectic that inevitably involves. In this respect, Barth completed the revolution begun by Schweitzer, and it is because he took that revolution radically that his thought did not run out into triviality. Barth has been vigorously opposed at this point, and yet widely followed. The dialectic between eternity and time was expressed in terms of the infinite qualitative difference between eternity and time, and few were disposed to agree with the radical way in which Barth put it at that time, but the anti-revolutionary and non-teleological view of the coming of the kingdom in ever recurring crisis through the Spirit has been widely adopted in various forms.

(c) The later Barth: union of time and eternity

Then came Barth's second revolution, which was equally radical. He soon discovered that the position he had formulated in his *Commentary on Romans* and other early writings, necessary as it was at that stage as a corrective to the widespread and latent pantheism in theology, was untenable, for it did not square with the basic New Testament message, and the New Testament emphasis on the incarnation and the resurrection of the body, and therefore on *the reality of time* even for God. In any case, the dialectical relation between time and eternity always ends up in the elimination of time and history, and that destroys the inner eschatological tension of faith.

The upshot was that Barth repudiated a timeless eschatology, and set himself to take seriously the New Testament teaching of an imminent advent of the kingdom *in time,* and yet to see that as belonging to the inner core of faith. This meant that he did not any longer interpret the real eschatological tension in terms of an eternity/time dialectic, but in terms of the *incarnation,* of a real union between eternity and time in Jesus Christ. If the Word is made flesh, then it is also made time, and not to take that seriously is docetic heresy [the view that Christ's humanity was only apparent and not fully human]. We must take time seriously in respect of both the first advent of Christ and of his second advent. Jesus Christ risen from the dead is *man,* true *man,* and true time and true humanity belong together in him. All eschatology and all history pivot upon the resurrection of Jesus Christ in body.

More astonishing than Barth's second revolution is the fact that though Barth sloughed off the notion of a timeless eschatology (much as a snake sloughs off its skin), other theologians like Bultmann, Dodd, Niebuhr and Tillich have made it central and now teach a dialectic of eternity and time, or realised eschatology, or timeless crisis, in all of which time-relations are held to be ultimately irrelevant for faith! They end up where Barth left off nearly 30 years before. Dodd, Niebuhr, Bultmann and Tillich differ from one another in many ways, but they agree in this, that they are unable to follow Barth in his consistently realist attitude to time and history in the doctrine of Jesus Christ as true God and true man incarnate in space and time. When it comes to the resurrection of Jesus Christ in body, or the time element in the kingdom of God or in the *parousia*, they want to demythologise the *kērygma* of its necessary involvement in space-time and to transmute it into symbol, or to do docetic violence in some way to the humanity of Christ risen from the dead. They acknowledge that the time element belongs to the original *kērygma* (though Dodd has questioned it) but that is for them a mythological element which belongs to a primitive and unscientific cosmology and must therefore be demythologised, cut out, or explained away in symbolical or figurative terms. (Cf. Niebuhr on '*myth*' in *Beyond Tragedy* where he advocates a view substantially the same as that of Bultmann).

5 The relation of the *kērygma* to history: the problem of mythology and christology

What is at stake here is *the relation of* kērygma *to history*, and behind that a christological problem. The problem is not apparently the old battle between a 'Jesus of history' view and a dogmatic view of Christ. In some respects that battle had been settled with the discovery of the meaning of *kērygma*, but even there, loose interpretation (as in Bultmann) let the old false problem in by the back door again. Generally it is agreed, however, that it is a kerygmatic view of Christ that we have presented to us in the testimony of the New Testament, and that a kerygmatic approach must therefore be made to christology. But are there not elements in the *kērygma* itself which need demythologising?

That is a question that has been agitating New Testament scholarship ever since the early decades of the 19th century, that is from Lessing to Troeltsch, but which in our own day has been raised in the sharpest possible way by Rudolf Bultmann, whose views we must now consider.

(a) The modern debate: the views of Rudolf Bultmann

(i) The background to Bultmann

It may be helpful to set Bultmann in his own historical perspective. That begins with the dictum of Lessing that incidental truths of history can never establish necessary or eternal truths of reason. If therefore faith in the divine act of redemption is to survive, it must be made independent of the contingent facts of history. History certainly has a place, it was held, but only as the necessary means or occasion of launching the apprehension of the eternal truths. Thus the historical elements of Christianity can be given over to historical criticism, but the idea which is the inner truth of

Christianity remains, and indeed by means of that criticism the inner truth can even be released from its outward shell in the historical envelope into the fullness of its own power. In this line of development, there arose a sort of mediating view which gave some real importance nevertheless to the personality of Jesus from which the truth of redemption could not be altogether detached, but this personality was the spirit of Jesus, rather than the stubborn fact of his history itself. It is from that teaching that Bultmann derives his ancestry.

But there are some important differences between that approach and Bultmann's. Whereas it thought it was possible to get back to the genuinely historical Jesus by stripping away the mythical elements from the authentic elements, Bultmann realised that could not be done, and that it was impossible to get behind the tradition to the historical Jesus. If so, then the use of psychological reinterpretation of Jesus to disentangle the spirit of Jesus from its historical embodiment had to be given up, and some other principle had to be found for reinterpretation, but this would have to be a principle by which one could reinterpret the account of Jesus as given in the apostolic preaching as a whole. That principle Bultmann found in the concept of *authentic existence* which we reach through existential decision. This was also in line with his revolt from the method of Harnack, who sought to reinterpret the historical Jesus in terms of ideas, and the kingdom in terms of idealism. For the idea, Bultmann substituted the eschatological event, and so claimed to overthrow not only liberal reconstructions of Jesus, but liberal theology. Here of course, the work of Johannes Weiss and Schweitzer played an enormous part in influencing his mind, although in place of Schweitzer's method of 'tuning in' to the *Weltanschauung* (world-view) of Jesus and so leaping across the whole mythological framework in which his teaching was set, Bultmann employed the so called concept of 'existentialist decision' to reinterpret the mythological framework in which Christ is presented in the New Testament *kērygma* – cf. *Jesus Christ and Mythology* (London: SCM Press 1960), chap. 1V, 'Modern Biblical Interpretation and Existentialist Philosophy'.

In the course of this development, Bultmann was strongly influenced by two other main factors: (a) by Karl Barth's view that eschatology goes to the roots of faith itself, and cannot be eradicated from the New Testament message; but for Bultmann this is the timeless eschatology which Barth later repudiated, involving the conception of a-historical and a-temporal (non-historical and non-temporal) event; (b) by Karl Ludwig Schmidt's conception of the *kērygma* as the message of Christ crucified and risen, which gives to all the writings of the New Testament their essential unity, but for Bultmann this *kērygma* is given a twist in line with the pietist conception of preaching for subjective decision.

(ii) The teaching of Bultmann

Bultmann grants that the *kērygma* forms the very centre of the New Testament teaching and that in all the writings which are a development of it, the writers claim to reproduce the original *kērygma.* This makes a unified interpretation of the New Testament writings possible, and means the rehabilitation of biblical theology, and Bultmann himself engages in that task (see his work *Jesus and the Word* [for a highly appreciative but also critical comment on *Jesus and the Word* see T.F. Torrance, *God and Rationality* (London: OUP 1971), chap. 3, 'Cheap and Costly Grace, p. 61]) – but are we then to proclaim the Christian message to the modern world by reproducing that *kērygma,* and are we to rebuild a dogmatic theology on that basis? No, says Bultmann, we cannot do that, because the *kērygma* itself contains elements that are entirely foreign and indeed unacceptable to modern man (*Kerygma and Myth,* p. 3). It is this *kērygma* that needs to be reinterpreted in such a way that it will have the same forceful impact in our modern world as it had in the world of the New Testament. This reinterpretation must be purified from all unacceptable elements such as space and time.

Now we cannot but entirely agree with Bultmann's intention to proclaim the gospel to the modern world in such a way that it can be understood. Each generation must find the right way to communicate the gospel to men and women, but it must be the authentic gospel, or else the whole effect is self contradictory and illusory. That is the crucial point at which Bultmann must be tested.

The mythology of the New Testament

Let us then see how he looks at it and what he seeks to do. According to Bultmann, the New Testament message and particularly its eschatology are bound up with a mythical cosmology, in which the world is viewed as a three-storied structure, and a mythical anthropology in which man is regarded as a battlefield of alien powers against God (*Jesus Christ and Mythology,* p. 14-15). It is in this setting, he holds, that the New Testament presents the event of redemption which is the subject of its preaching. 'It proclaims in the language of mythology that the last time has now come. In the "fullness of time", God sent forth his Son, a pre-existent divine being, who appears on earth as a man. He dies the death of a sinner on the cross and makes atonement for the sins of men. His resurrection marks the beginning of the cosmic catastrophe. Death, the consequence of Adam's sin, is abolished, and the demonic forces are deprived of their power. The risen Christ is exalted to the right hand of God in heaven and made "Lord" and "king". He will come again on the clouds of heaven to complete the work of redemption, and the resurrection and judgement of men will follow. Sin, suffering and death will then be finally abolished. All this is to happen very soon; indeed, St Paul thinks that he himself will live to see it' (*Kerygma and Myth*, p. 2).

Demythologisation and reinterpretation

'All this', says Bultmann, 'is the language of mythology . . . To this extent the *kērygma* is incredible to modern man, for he is convinced that the mythical view of the world is obsolete. We are therefore bound to ask whether, when we preach the gospel today, we expect our converts to accept not only the gospel message, but also the mythical view of the world in which it is set. If not, does the New Testament embody a truth which is quite independent of its mythical setting? If it does, theology must undertake the task of stripping the *kērygma* from its mythical framework, of "demythologising" it' (*ibid*. p. 3). Unless we do this, Bultmann holds, the modern world will think that there is nothing more in Christianity than mythology. But this has to be done not only to such conceptions as the pre-existence of Christ, his virgin birth, his ascension and *parousia* (final presence, last advent), but also his crucifixion and resurrection, and indeed, even to the notion of the fatherhood of God. But can we actually do this? Can we recover the truth of the *kērygma* for people who do not think in mythological terms without forfeiting its character as *kērygma*?

Bultmann attacks the use of the allegorical method here which spiritualises mythological events as processes in the soul while the 'literal meaning is allowed to stand and is only dispensed with for the individual believer, who can escape into the realm of the soul' (*ibid*. p. 13). Bultmann is likewise opposed to the older liberal theologians who thought they could safely eliminate the mythological imagery as something relative and temporary, and retain only the basic principles of religion and ethics. But all that procedure succeeds in doing is to reduce the *kērygma* to a few basic principles and the *kērygma* ceases to be *kērygma*.

What then are we to do, Bultmann asks? According to him we have to accept two facts about the modern world, its scientific attitude to everything, i.e. its scientism, and also its understanding of human beings. These are both axiomatic, and it is necessarily in terms of these that the *kērygma* must be understood, and therefore in terms of them that it must be reinterpreted and presented. But in order to do this we have to show modern man that the mythological language used in the New Testament is only a medium for conveying the meaning of a past event, and that its meaning can easily be detached from the obsolete mythological framework and be communicated to the non-mythological mind of modern man.

Thus Bultmann declares that the real object of mythology is not to give an interpretation of the world as it is for its own sake, but rather to express our understanding of ourselves and our position in the world, including our awareness that we are not the lords of our own destiny. Mythology, in other words, must be interpreted not cosmologically but anthropologically, that is, in the light of the understanding of authentic human existence that the myth enshrines. In other words, it must be interpreted existentially (*ibid.* p. 10). What Bultmann seeks to do therefore is to penetrate into what he regards as the profound intention of the whole mythical framework of the New Testament *kērygma*, dislodge that intention from its antiquated forms, and transpose it into a new form acceptable to scientific man and woman through which they will be able to reach the same understanding of authentic existence as that enshrined in the New Testament *kērygma*, and therefore a new understanding of themselves.

Two expressions here require further elucidation: 'myth', and 'authentic existence'. What does Bultmann really mean by these?

The meaning of mythology

'Mythology', declares Bultmann, 'is the use of imagery to express the other-worldly in terms of this world, and the divine in terms of human life, the other side in terms of this side . . . Myth is an expression of man's conviction that the origin and purpose of the world in which he lives are to be sought not within it, but beyond it – that is, beyond the realm of known and tangible reality – and that this realm is perpetually dominated and menaced by those mysterious powers which are its source and limit. Myth is also an expression of man's awareness that he is not the lord of his own being. It expresses his sense of dependence not only within the visible world, but more especially on those forces which hold sway beyond the confines of the known. Finally, myth expresses human belief that in this state of dependence we can be delivered from the forces within the visible world. Thus myth contains elements which demand its own criticism, namely, its imagery with its apparent claim to objective validity. The real purpose of myth is to speak of a transcendent power which controls the world and human life, but that purpose is impeded and obscured by the terms in which it is expressed. Hence the importance of the New Testament mythology lies not in its imagery but in the understanding of existence which it enshrines. The real question is whether this understanding of existence is true. Faith claims that it is, and faith ought not to be tied down to the imagery of the New Testament mythology.' (*Kerygma and Myth* vol. 1, p. 10f. [quotation begins in the footnote]; cf. *Jesus Christ and Mythology* p. 19, 'It may be said that myths give to the transcendent reality an immanent, this-worldly objectivity. Myths give worldly objectivity to that which is unworldly.')

Now what does Bultmann mean by this mythical imagery in the New Testament? Is it simply the fact that the New Testament talks in spatial and temporal terms, even of the saving act of God? Yes, but it is more than that. By mythological imagery Bultmann quite definitely means the objective fact that the Son of God entered human history, was crucified, rose again, and ascended, etc. Bultmann does not deny that Jesus Christ is presented in that way in the New Testament, but that is to present Christ in mythical terms. 'Jesus Christ', he admits, 'is certainly presented as the Son of God, a pre-existent divine being, and therefore to that extent a mythical figure. But he is also a concrete figure of history – Jesus of Nazareth. His life is more than a mythical event; it is a human life which ended in the tragedy of crucifixion. We have here a unique combination of history and myth' (*Kerygma and Myth* p. 34). In other words, because Bultmann simply does not believe that God actually intervenes in terrestrial affairs – his modern positivist scientism will not allow him to, he says – he interprets all that the New Testament has to say of the coming of the Son of God, of God's action in Christ, on the cross, in the resurrection, ascension and so on, purely as 'legends', as man's mythological construction designed to explain and interpret the human tragedy of Jesus against an invisible background. And so Bultmann says, 'We are compelled to ask whether all this mythological language is not simply an attempt to express the meaning of the historical figure of Jesus and the events of his life; in other words, the significance of these as a figure and event of salvation. If that be so, we can dispense with the objective form in which they are cast' (*op. cit.* p. 35).

It is clear then that what Bultmann finds intolerable and absolutely unacceptable is the whole biblical idea that *God acts* in history, that God was at work in Israel, and that *God himself* came in Jesus Christ and intervenes in our life in order to save us, that the being of God is found within our human existence and time. Bultmann rejects in its entirety the whole concept of *Heilsgeschichte* or 'salvation history' if by that is meant that God is actually active in history. He accepts the concept of *Heilsgeschichte* only as mythology, the sole purpose of which was to convey the meaning of a past event. 'In the last resort, mythological language is only a medium for conveying the meaning of the past event' (*op. cit.* p. 37). What then does Bultmann mean by 'event'? This is the strangest thing of all – event for Bultmann has nothing whatsoever to do with space and time, it belongs entirely to the realm of word and faith, of challenge and decision. Thus the saving event of Christ has for Bultmann no ontological reality, divine or human. The logic of his position is that event is simply and solely what happens when I am challenged by the word. This word addressing me *is* the redeeming event, and my faith or decision *is* redeemed existence. Jesus was a fact of history, although we know nothing about him except that he died in tragedy, but that is not the saving event. The saving event is the challenge that I encounter in connection with the tragedy of Jesus, but it is not objectively grounded in the death of Jesus at all, and certainly not in an ontological act of God in the death of Jesus. The act of God is simply and solely this word of the cross that comes to me, and awakens me to self-understanding. In other words, the saving event is not an independent objective act of God out there, in the historical Jesus made on my behalf, but simply encounter, a subjective experience in my own heart – the saving event is my acceptance of the challenge of the word, and my decision (cf. *Kerygma and Myth* p. 41f.).

The meaning of authentic existence

In order to grasp that clearly we have to ask what Bultmann means by '*self understanding*' and '*authentic existence*'. Here Bultmann begins with Paul's concept of sin in relation to the flesh, and gives it his own very clever reinterpretation. According to Bultmann, sin describes the life of men and women without faith who seek their security in a visible and tangible world. But that is only a false security and as soon as they become aware of it, they are engulfed in *anxiety*. The false security of sin is to be seen not only in purely physical and visible existence, but in the attempt to fulfil the law for the sake of a tangible reward, or to glory in human achievement. But 'since the visible and tangible sphere is essentially transitory, the man who bases his life on it becomes the prisoner and slave of corruption' (*op. cit.* p. 19). 'Thus man becomes the slave of anxiety. Everybody tries to hold fast to his own life and property, because he has a secret feeling that it is all slipping away from him' (*ibid.*). It is out of this anxiety that a great deal of mythology arises in an attempt to give visible and tangible security to faith, so that it might even be argued that the mythologising of the faith is the very acme of sin. That is why the mythological framework of the New Testament *kērygma*, for Bultmann, actually prevents it from realising its deepest intention. What then is the intention of the *kērygma*? It is simply to release us from false security in the visible and the tangible, for only by losing our life and repudiating all security can we find it, and so find ourselves. What we need most of all is the faith in which we renounce ourselves and all self-made security and mythology, for only then will we be freed from anxiety and attain what Bultmann calls 'authentic existence', deliverance from false self-made security, deliverance, that is, from sin, into the freedom of existence without anxiety, which is what Bultmann calls the real meaning of the Christ-event. To enter into this new relation to existence is to exist eschatologically; it is to be a 'new creature'.

The detaching of faith from any foundation in the historical Jesus

From this point we can understand why Bultmann makes such a complete onslaught upon 'mythology' and upon 'the historical Jesus'. If the New Testament mythology is the projection by anxious human beings of their own visible and tangible life into the invisible and divine in order to clutch at a security above and beyond this passing life, then that is the way of false security and sin, and that way must be destroyed if we are to be saved. It is here too that we understand another puzzling feature about Bultmann, that while he denies that we can get behind the mythologised apostolic *kērygma* to the historical Jesus, he sets out with all the axioms of scientism to get beyond the *kērygma* to the historical Jesus, just in order to show its impossibility and so to destroy with uncanny ruthlessness all possibility of pinning faith on the historical fact of Jesus Christ, or on the act of God in the historical Jesus Christ. He deliberately destroys the foundations of faith in the historical Jesus. And so Bultmann is ready to accept all that positivist natural science, and a positivist historical science can do, to destroy faith in an objective divine act in Christ independent of us, in order to make room for what he conceives to be authentic faith and authentic existence in faith! The astounding fact is then that for Bultmann faith can be faith only if it is prepared in the last resort to reject the objective fact of Christ! 'This is a serious problem', he says, 'and if Christian faith is to recover its self-assurance it must be grappled with. For it can recover its certainty only if it is prepared to think through to the bitter end the possibility of its own impossibility or superfluity' (*Kerygma and Myth* p. 23).

He goes on in the same passage to describe this as the possibility of having 'a Christian understanding of Being without Christ'. That is precisely what Bultmann does do – with a desperate courage that is as incredible as it is mad. But if we can have Christian being and authentic existence without Christ, does that not make Christianity superfluous? Bultmann faces that question by actually saying that the philosophers are saying the same thing as the New Testament and saying it quite independently (*op. cit.* p. 25)! – but he also points out the difference between the way of philosophy and the Christian way of reaching authentic existence. The philosophical way is through the intellect alone, and that is not really open to the common man, but the Christian way lies through confrontation with the crucifixion of Jesus. In the tragedy and death of Jesus, the one historical fact about him, we are confronted with an image which so challenges us that in a responsive decision we deny ourselves and strip off all our false security (in clinging to the visible and tangible world we can control) and dare to live without any such false security at all. That is the function of the death of Christ, its sole value, and nothing else. In this way Bultmann demythologises it from all objective and independent reality as act of God in Christ on our behalf, and transposes its saving virtue to the spiritual event of encounter and decision. Salvation does not derive from Jesus Christ or from his unique death as a source independent of us, but is identical with an 'event' repeated in each of us as we reach a new understanding of ourselves before the appeal of the cross to conceive our existence in a new way. Nothing happened ontologically in the death of Christ for the salvation of humanity. Bultmann does say, 'the historical event of the cross acquires cosmic dimensions' (*op. cit.* p. 36), but given that he only says the cross *acquires* cosmic dimensions, and given what he says elsewhere, it is difficult to believe that for him anything really happened ontologically in the death of Christ for the salvation of humanity – such ontological happening is pure myth, what Bultmann calls 'a hotch-potch of sacrificial and juridical analogies, which have ceased to be tenable for us today' (*op. cit.* p. 35).

Now Bultmann admits of course that this is not the way the New Testament writers regarded the death of Christ – they really did believe that it was a unique event in which God intervened in history, and wrought out redemption on our behalf independent of ourselves and outside of us. But Bultmann claims that the New Testament writers were quite wrong – apart from our existential decision in front of the cross, the cross means nothing at all – the death of Jesus was actually only a human martyrdom, but God uses its image in history to be the occasion for preaching a gospel of dying in order to live, of losing our life in order to find it (cf. *op. cit.* p. 40ff.). The New Testament writers, according to Bultmann, could not help but think in their mythological way because of their unscientific cosmology, but he claims that his demythologised exposition of the cross is in accordance with the essence of the faith of the apostles and the primitive church – that at bottom this is what they really believed.

Now of course that is quite wrong – Bultmann is simply deceiving himself here. The New Testament writers certainly did believe that the actual death of Christ was the objective source of salvation, and not simply a mythical representation of some existential meaning, or the occasion of understanding ourselves. Nor was their belief in the resurrection, as Bultmann maintains, simply their way of expressing their faith in the cross as a saving event. For them the historical fact of the life, death and resurrection of Christ was the inalienable substance of the faith. For them, the saving reality and power of the cross cannot simply be resolved without remainder, as Bultmann claims, into the continued preaching of it. When therefore Bultmann says that all he is doing is to translate the New

Testament gospel into modern language so that people in the age of electricity and television can understand it, we deny that it is the same gospel; we insist that Bultmann has in point of fact entirely changed the nature of the historic Christian faith, for he has deprived it of its essential substance. The object of the New Testament faith and the object of Bultmann's faith are simply not the same. The object of Bultmann's faith is what he calls the 'Christ-event' which is identical with preaching the cross (in Bultmann's sense) or with the existential decision of faith entirely detached from history – but that is the exact opposite of the gospel and its entire destruction. It was not 'existential decision' that was crucified for us and that rose again, but Jesus Christ. The historical character of salvation in Christ, the divine intervention in the historical life and death of Christ, is of the very essence of the Christian faith – to strip Christian faith of that as if it were merely mythical husk is simply to cease to be Christian in any responsible sense at all.

(iii) Chief criticisms of Bultmann's teaching

We must now gather together our chief criticisms of Bultmann's views and seek to grapple with the deep underlying issues involved.

(1) Unlike the old liberals, whom he claims to oppose, Bultmann is not concerned with eliminating myths but with eliminating the one comprehensive myth in which the whole of the New Testament teaching is set. Therefore, he insists, 'we cannot save the *kērygma* by selecting some of its features and subtracting others, and thus reducing the amount of mythology in it . . . if we once start subtracting from the *kērygma,* where are we to draw the line?' (*Kerygma and Myth* p. 9). What Bultmann does is to reject it in its entirety ('The mythical view of the world must be accepted or rejected in its entirety', *ibid.*), not by slicing it away, but by taking it as an utterly outmoded way of saying what he wants to say in different language. In some respects this is like the method of Schweitzer who left the apocalyptic picture of Jesus intact but sought to tune in to the real spirit of Jesus behind it and then to put that into living practice, without taking over any of the New Testament theology or so called 'mythology'. But in point of fact, Bultmann does not really do what he claims, for his very narrow and pietistic definition of *kērygma,* together with his sharp form-critical methods, makes him cut out of the *kērygma* essential elements that do not accord with his initial prejudice. Thus he does actually adopt the method of subtraction as well as of reinterpretation, but in both of these ways he easily falls prey to his own philosophical presuppositions. It is here that we have a major difference between Bultmann and Schweitzer, for while the latter's presuppositions are mainly of a neo-

Hegelian variety, Bultmann's are drawn from the existential philosophy of Martin Heidegger, but on Bultmann's part that is deliberate, because, as he claims, the existence of the exegete cannot but exert a determining influence upon the work of interpretation. However, even though we were to grant that all true exegesis must in some sense be existential, it is quite unworthy of a scientific historian to presuppose from the start, as Bultmann does, that the presentation of the *kērygma* of Jesus must be distorted.

Thus the first major criticism of Bultmann must be that in spite of all his claims, his method is terribly biased, and far from being really scientific. The plain fact is that Bultmann does not offer a method of interpretation which either does justice to the distinctive character of the New Testament material, or one that is capable of laying bare its deepest meaning. In other words, Bultmann's hermeneutic or method of interpretation is not one that allows the New Testament material to disclose its own profound significance, but one that forces it into certain rigid preconceptions entirely alien to it. Nowhere is that more apparent than in Bultmann's reading of the synoptic account of the death of Jesus, which is governed by his passionate love of the Greek tragedians. There can be no doubt that Bultmann's enormous learning in the Hellenistic field, coupled with his remarkably brilliant powers in etymological and phenomenological analysis, have enabled him to perform services in New Testament scholarship, but there can also be no doubt that his philosophical preconceptions have done gross violence to the teaching of the New Testament, for in the last resort its essential theology is for him a purely mythological concept, while the eschatological tension inherent in that theology is regarded purely and simply as a necessity of finite experience when confronted with the infinite.

(2) This brings us to another important but difficult point: Bultmann's peculiar understanding of history. That is even more clear in the teaching of Gogarten, especially in his little work *Demythologisation and History*. This is the view that we are ourselves the real creators of history, and that the existence we know is historicised existence. Here two streams of thought run together, and we may best understand that by looking at those two streams of thought: one from Kant through Dilthey, and the other from Roman Catholicism through Heidegger. In Kant's famous Copernican revolution, idealist philosophers came to think of the human mind as creating its data out of a formless raw material through certain categories of the understanding, so that in the very act of knowing we give shape and form to the chaotic flux of experience. Now this notion was carried over by Dilthey to an understanding of history, and so he set himself to write a critique of the historical reason, parallel to Kant's critique

of the pure reason – for Dilthey, this was necessary if the humanistic sciences (*Geisteswissenschaften*) were not simply to take their criteria and hermeneutical method from the exact natural sciences.

But there is another line of thought that flows into this from the Roman Catholic notion of tradition, that is, of the real meaning of history in an organically developing tradition. This notion was transferred to the understanding of existence by Heidegger, for whom the real existence of a thing is found in its traditions. A thing is what its tradition is, and beyond that tradition there is no thing in itself. In this way, Heidegger transposed the medieval view of existence and essence by telescoping them into each other. For him, essence is found in existence, and on that ground, existence in essence. In Bultmann and Gogarten both these lines of interpreting history run together, and for them history is that which we make it to be, so that beyond our historicisation of existence, there is no reality.

Historical *existence* and the *history* of existence are identical. Applied to the gospel tradition, that means that what is actually historical is what the apostles made of the raw material in front of them, and behind that there is no reality. The historical reality is what they made it to be – apart from their creation there is nothing, there exists nothing. The only real historical Jesus is what *we* make of him. That helps to explain why for Bultmann the apostles (from our point of view) had to distort the picture of Jesus in their presentation – there is in fact no other Jesus than that, their creation of him. This view of history destroys what Bultmann and Gogarten call the metaphysical interpretation of the faith or the historical Jesus, and eliminates from the Christ-event anything of an objective, independent, ontological nature. Or to put it in other words, according to Bultmann and Gogarten, modern men and women cannot understand history apart from our own responsibility for it; and apart from our responsible handling of it, there is in point of fact no history, for there is no history apart from the changes human beings have introduced into it. By our decisions we give the world its particular form, so that reality is now this changing history which we create, and beyond and apart from that there is nothing real for us.

Now quite frankly this is the *biggest myth* yet created by man – that we ourselves are the creators of all history, and that apart from the history created by human beings, nothing else is real! Man is the God of history! In view of this, it is clear that it is not the New Testament but Bultmann and Gogarten themselves that need to be radically demythologised! So long as they work with such inverted conceptions of history, scientific interpretation of the New Testament is quite impossible.

(Cf. also the influence of Kierkegaard – misinterpreted here. According to Kierkegaard, if we are to grasp a historical reality directly, we must first transpose it back to the reality of its *becoming* in order to assimilate it to the reality of our own life. But for Bultmann that meant that the historical is always only the raw material which we appropriate to ourselves if we can reduce it to its *posse* [what it is able to be – its *poss*ibilities] in order then to assimilate it in its *esse* [what it is – its *esse*nce]. Thus if in historical matters we are concerned with a conceived reality which relates itself to our own personal reality in that it summons us to realise its possibilities, the question of actuality (*Tatsächlichkeit*) of an event is of minor importance – for it does not contribute anything to the understanding of the historical. It was easy therefore for the existentialists to cut away that objective actuality and interpret the historical solely in terms of its *posse* in abstraction from its *esse*. But for Kierkegaard that would have been ludicrously impossible.)

[There are several short sections here in the text which are in brackets and which begin with 'cf.', 'compare'. They would appear to be notes in the text to indicate other connections of ideas, either notes for Torrance himself, and not necessarily part of the lectures, or reminders of the possibility of saying something to students at this point.]

(Cf. also the influence of the Hegelian idea that God comes to self-consciousness in our human ratiocination. Applied to history, that would mean that God comes to consciousness in our historical self-consciousness. Something of this is apparent in the application of the Hegelian teaching to history in Croce, the Italian neo-Hegelian philosopher – but whether this had any direct influence upon Bultmann is doubtful. Certainly the early writings of Hegel have considerable bearing upon existentialism).

(3) When Bultmann wishes to reinterpret the objective facts of *kērygma*, e.g. as given in the Apostles' Creed, in terms of an existential decision which we have to make in order to understand, not God or Christ or the world, but ourselves, we are converting the gospel of the New Testament into something quite different, converting christology into anthropology. It is shockingly subjective. It is not Christ that really counts, but my decision in which I find myself. At this point one sees Bultmann's involvement in the theological tradition of Schleiermacher and Ritschl that grew out of German pietism and subjectivism, and also in the tradition of the Marburg school of philosophy which tried in vain to break out of phenomenology by existential decision. Moreover, the existential decision with which Bultmann works is not that of Kierkegaard in which the fact and person of Christ is all determining, but that of the Roman Catholic but atheistic Heidegger, who took Kierkegaard's idea, and altered it by abstracting it

entirely from its objective ground in Christ and attaching it to a secularised notion of tradition which he retained from his Roman Catholic upbringing.

(Cf. here Bultmann's interpretation of the resurrection of Christ as simply and solely what takes place in our hearts in endless repetition. An objective resurrection of Christ, outside of us and for us, is for him purely mythical. But that is the exact antithesis of the gospel which lays the greatest stress upon the objective fact of the resurrection, while the 'Christ in us' is a subjective actualisation of that real event through the communion of the Spirit. Cf. here also the concept of 'indwelling grace' in German pietism, and the correspondence between Harnack and Peterson – and then cf. Schleiermacher! The eternal repetition of the Christ-event in the heart is remarkably parallel to the eternal repetition of the crucifixion of Christ in the mass.)

(4) But can we agree at all with what Bultmann has to say about myth itself, and about the criteria he uses for determining what is myth and what is not, namely, the positivistic scientific axiom that all the realities of this world are explained by the determinism of natural laws, and the modern scientific understanding of man which can be gained quite apart from Christ altogether? There is a profound issue here that we must go into later, but at this point let us note that in his conception of myth Bultmann fails to distinguish adequately between the mythological and the analogical and therefore tends to confuse them. In all analogical language about God there is an essential element of unlikeness and difference, but it is not for that reason mythological. Or as Calvin used to put it, in all our language about God and his acts in history there is an essential element of 'impropriety', especially when it is the language of sinners, but it is not for that reason untrue. All revelation is given by way of a divine accommodation to man. Even the incarnation is such an act, in which God has adapted his Word to man, in the likeness of man, but it is not therefore false. Thus all the language of revelation and of faith is eschatological, for it points beyond itself to God, and is essentially of a sacramental character. (Cf. the old scholastic distinction between *veritas increata* [uncreated truth] and *veritas creata* [created truth].) The difficulty of Bultmann's position becomes clear when we find that even the fatherhood of God becomes problematic. In *Jesus Christ and Mythology* (p. 69), Bultmann says, 'in the conception of God as Father the mythological sense vanished long ago', but he says that we can speak of God as Father in an analogical sense. However, he also says that 'we cannot speak of God as he is in himself, but only of what he is doing to us and with us' (*op. cit.* p. 73). We cannot make general statements about God, only existential statements about our relation to him. 'The affirmation that God is creator

cannot be a theoretical statement about God as *creator mundi* (creator of the world) in a general sense. The affirmation can only be a personal confession that I understand myself to be a creature which owes its existence to God' (*op. cit.* p. 69). Statements about God are not to be understood as objective (that is mythology) – they have to be understood as existential statements (*op. cit.* p. 61ff). But if we can say nothing about God in himself or about what he does objectively, can we still give any content to his actions in relation to ourselves, and can we really say anything at all of God, even in analogical language? Can Bultmann discard what he thinks of as mythological and still retain the analogical? If we are really to demythologise the fatherhood of God, what are we landed with, and where are we to stop? Are we to transpose all theological language into abstract symbol after the fashion of mathematical logic, and if so, then is demythologisation not only the de-deification of theology, but its complete dehumanisation?

(Cf. here Bultmann's relation to logical positivism and its programme of the demythologisation of philosophy or of the disenchantment of the world of values, and also to similar movements in art and music.)

On the other hand, Bultmann forgets that he cannot avoid what he calls 'myth' by translating or adapting the language of the New Testament to the so-called modern scientific mind, for modern science has its own 'myths' as we see, for example, in evolution or atomic physics. Even Martin Heidegger, Bultmann's great hero, regards science as 'a human project (*Entwurf*), a sketch of meaning introduced into one particular view of the world from the human perspective', so that at best it can give us only what he calls 'a co-ordinate perspective' of the world. 'Science deals with objects from a definitely limited point of view determined in advance, limits its interest to certain phenomena and on that basis settles its methods and its criteria . . . Science is not privileged but specialised, not *the* interpretation of the world, but a selected aspect, not an experience in the use of a concrete object handled in the perspective of man's projects, but a breakdown into abstractions taken out of the system of concrete relations and assimilated to another system of meanings determined by special questions raised within the perspective of the project of nature.' (James Brown, *Subject & Object in Modern Theology*, chap. IV, 'The subject makes itself: Heidegger and existentialism' (London: SCM Press 1955, p. 87.)

(5) In his demythologised reinterpretation of the *kērygma* of God (*logos*) and human speech (*lalia*) in which the human language is purified, made perfect through being purged of all improprieties. Only *kērygma* in which the word of God is joined to *pure* speech can be *kērygma* intelligible to scientific man. And so it is the business of scientific New Testament

criticism to clarify that issue, to strip the *kērygma* of its primitive imperfections, of its outmoded and obsolete forms, and of unscientific cosmologies to give us the pure truth. Apart altogether from the fact that this is to turn christology into anthropology, a question of primary importance is raised even on the christological level. When the Word was made flesh, was that flesh some immortal perfect flesh, or was it flesh of our flesh? Did the Son of God become incarnate in our fallen humanity, yet without sin, or did he assume some kind of pure humanity which we know nothing about? Now of course Bultmann would say that the Son of God never assumed our flesh at all, and that it is precisely this which is the mythology. That is ultimately the question on which we must take sides here, for everything else depends on it. But suppose it was the *Son of God* who took flesh, as all the New Testament writers certainly believe – (cf. 1 John 4.2-3, where every spirit who does not believe that Christ is come in the flesh is anti-Christ!) – then *our* answer to the question whether Christ assumed flesh of our flesh, or some other kind of flesh, will determine *our* answer to Bultmann's demand that in the *kērygma* we must find a reinterpretation of it in which the *Logos* is expressed not in the speech of our fallen flesh, but in some scientifically purified and rarified speech of flesh. There can be no doubt that ultimately it is on christological grounds like these that we have to repudiate Bultmann's position as involving a docetic christology, as well as Socinianism (denial of the divinity of Christ).

(6) In point of fact, then, Bultmann's demythologisation of the *kērygma* means stripping it of its physical elements – its setting in physical history and the physical world of space and time in which we live. The whole process which takes the *kērygma* out of that setting and plants it in some setting of existential decision, cuts out of the gospel its historical particularity, and cuts out of the incarnation its *ephapax*, its '*once and for all*' finality. It cuts the *kērygma* adrift from history altogether. Now Bultmann declares that he does not do that, for the existential decision is in historical encounter with the crucified Jesus, but once that decision is made, history as we know it is set aside, and in point of fact he does therefore cut the *kērygma* adrift from history, for history has no essential relation to the substance and content of faith. The historical event of Christ, apart from the appeal it addresses to us, signifies nothing for our salvation, for it is not a source of salvation independent of ourselves. The historical fact of Christ cannot be the object of the *kērygma*, since it is the *kērygma*, says Bultmann, that is, the *kērygma* as he understands it, that declares its meaning and confers on it its value as saving event. It is only because the *kērygma* is a function of man's self understanding that it invests the historical fact of

the crucified Christ with a meaning and an existential reality which it does not have in itself.

Here we must say to Bultmann that in spite of all his protests to the contrary, he is simply a child of subjective idealism, and that all he has done is to change the idiom of 19th century idealism to that of existentialism. The position that Bultmann adopts towards the relation of the *kērygma* to the physical realities of flesh and blood, becomes very apparent when you compare him to Karl Marx. The latter revolted from the idealism which had cut Christianity adrift altogether from physical history and our flesh and blood existence, and sought desperately to ground the concept of salvation or the community of the saved in physical existence; that is, he materialised the whole message of Christianity and secularised its eschatology. Whatever we say about scientific man, modern man is Marxist man, that is to say, man who labours with the body, lives in it, and seeks salvation in it – and Bultmann's flight from history, from the *Word made flesh*, is as far removed as anything could be from the understanding of the common man of today. The only way to make the gospel relevant is to follow the incarnation, for in it the Word was already made flesh, already made relevant to our physical existence in the fact of Christ.

(7) The plain fact is that Bultmann shies away from the weakness of God on the cross, as Paul called it, and so is offended at the cross. The fact that the eternal God is there in all that weakness is a scandal to his 'Greek' mind, and the fact that his eternal salvation must repose upon a contingent fact of history in Jesus frightens him – and therefore it is Bultmann himself above all who seeks false security by cutting the *kērygma* adrift from history and all its weakness, so that it will not be open to the criticisms of rationalism. Or, paradoxically, he deliberately uses all the weapons of positivist science in order to destroy the historical foundations of faith, so that faith may rest on something that is not subject to weakness and change and relativity and contingency. He thus has not the courage to rest his faith upon the weakness of God in the historical Jesus, and so seeks falsely to secure himself and his self-understanding within the limits of scientism.

(b) Mythology and demythology in the early church

Now we must try to understand the basic issue underlying the whole of this controversy over the so-called mythology of the New Testament. It is important to see that the problem of mythology and demythology is not a new one, but one that faced the New Testament gospel immediately it was proclaimed in the Graeco-Roman world. That is nowhere more apparent than in Alexandria, where we find a thoroughgoing attempt to interpret the biblical gospel to the philosophical culture of Greece. The concept used there was *gnôsis*, particularly in the teaching of Clement of Alexandria. Clement rejected the mythological apparatus of gnosticism in all its fantasies, but nevertheless by means of *gnōsis*, a higher knowledge that transcends faith, the biblical message with its realist history and eschatology was subjected to scientific and philosophical treatment (i.e. *epistēmē*, understanding) in order to make it intelligible. It was the sincere intention of the Alexandrian scholars to bring Christian faith to the mature and lofty place it deserved in Hellenic culture, and so to make it accessible to everyone with reason and science. But that was not achieved by Clement, but rather through the theological science of John Philoponos in the great Academy in Alexandria, in the sixth century.

The Hebrew and Greek mind

In order to understand the situation which the biblical gospel faced in circumstances like that, we must recall the profound difference between the biblical outlook – even in language – and that of the Greek world. The Hebrew outlook is well reflected in the very structure of the Hebrew language which is built upon the basis of verbs and verbal relation involving an essential polarity. This is very apparent in the philosophical work of Martin Buber, especially in his little work *I and Thou*, with its concept of *meeting* as the essential relationship. Buber's whole position in that remarkable book can be fairly said to arise out of the very structure of Hebrew language and thought. The Greek language on the other hand, at least in its classical form, is largely built up with substantives and attributes, with abstract nouns and adjectives, which corresponds remarkably with the basic Hellenic separation between the realm of ideas and the realm of events. To the Hebraic mind, that was a false dichotomy. The biblical revelation knows no such radical dichotomy, for the spiritual and the material are bound up together in God's creation, and indeed it is precisely in the material realm that we encounter God at work. To the classical Greek mind on the other hand, the whole physical realm of matter and events was ultimately unimportant. It was the study of the world of ideas, the world of spirit, it was held, that leads to the knowledge of God, to *gnôsis*. That outlook, with its radical dichotomy between the realm of ideas and the realm of events, was second nature to the Greek mind, and the habit of thinking it involved was quite unquestioned and its presuppositions axiomatic. It was quite unthinkable that any other approach to truth, to God or salvation was either possible or rational.

To this pre-Christian Greek mind any idea of an actual incarnation was philosophically irrational, in fact impossible, if it was realistically conceived. But the Greeks had their notions of theophany, of mythologically conceived divine appearances among mankind and it was quite naturally in that light that they looked upon the incarnation. It was the death of Jesus, the atonement, however, which completely baffled them – the idea, as Melito of Sardis put it, that God almighty should be bound and judged by humanity and murdered in order to bring about the forgiveness of sins, was simply irrational and impossible. And so through the second century at least, and for much later, the atonement failed, on the whole, to meet with any deep understanding in the Greek world (except for people like the writer of the *Epistle to Diognetus*, Melito of Sardis and Irenaeus, and later of course, Athanasius). But the death of Jesus the Son of God on earth brought into sharp focus the whole historical and eschatological message of the bible: that our salvation, and our knowledge of God, are grounded upon *divine action in time*. Now the whole notion of God coming into time and doing battle with the powers of darkness, overcoming law, sin and death by his own suffering and death and resurrection, inevitably appeared fictitious and quite unreal, and therefore not to be taken literally. To the Hellenic mind, therefore, *the historical realism of the* kērygma *could only be conceived mythologically.*

A signal instance of this problem is to be seen in Justin Martyr, who has left us writings of two quite different kinds. In his *Dialogue with Trypho, a Jew*, Justin is a biblical theologian accepting quite realistically all the biblical realism of the Old Testament and New Testament, and in this account the abstract concept of the *logos* does not really figure at all. But we also have Justin's apologies, in which he sought as a philosopher to commend the Christian gospel to the Greeks in terms of the prevailing rational conception of the *logos*. The remarkable thing is that both these accounts of the Christian faith were held side by side in the thought of Justin Martyr. He could not put them together, and they could not be held together in that uneasy juxtaposition for very long. How was the problem to be solved?

The gnostic solution

The gnostics offered their solution in their attempt to conceive the historical realism of the gospel mythologically, but instead of seeking to strip away the mythology or to eliminate it, the gnostics pushed the mythology into a transcendental realm, and gave everything a 'high-falutin' or grandiose philosophical name. It was a spiritualised and philosophised mythology that they taught, and in that way they tried to combine a rationalisation of Christianity with a notion of redemption. It is worth noting that it was this gnostic mythologising of Christianity that found considerable place for ritual, for religious ceremonies were multiplied as visible counterparts to heavenly mythological patterns – and it was through the gnostic combination of myth and ritual that the later church became inundated with so many fanciful ceremonies and elaborate rituals.

Christian 'gnōsis'

That was the gnostic way of solving the problem, but in Alexandria some early theologians of the church moved in an opposite direction – and it is here that we have the beginning of demythologising. Through *gnōsis* the historical gospel is subjected here to a demythologising process by which its real essence is said to be brought out. By scientific *epistēmē* (knowledge, understanding), crude faith is made to yield a higher *gnōsis*, that is, pure knowledge of divine truth scientifically intelligible. Later on, the allegorical method used by Origen allowed a freer use of biblical material, but the historical realism of theology, and especially the eschatology of the gospel, were transmuted into mystical, symbolic truth.

Now that process of transmutation began as soon as the biblical gospel began to be preached on Greek soil – and we get clear glimpses of what happened in 2 Timothy 4.4, and 2 Peter 1.16. It is worth while studying these passages – both are strongly eschatological and they both present biblical truth (*alētheia*) in a way that is to be distinguished from myths (*muthoi*), and in a way that cannot be turned into myths. Thus we read in 2 Peter 1.16, 'we did not follow cleverly devised myths (*sesophismenois muthois*) when we made known to you the power and coming of our Lord Jesus Christ, but we were eyewitnesses of his majesty.' For the New Testament, it is decisive that the message of the mighty action of God in history for our salvation is *truth* or *reality*, and *not myth*. That applies both to the oriental type of gnosticism with its cunningly devised philosophical myths, and to the more sober Greek gnosticism which regarded the eschatological drama of the biblical gospel as a mythological way of expressing rational insights. To the typically Hellenic mind, even to so-called Christian 'gnostics', all talk about two aeons or ages, the birth of the Son of God on earth, the death of God's Son on the cross, the resurrection of the body, the ascension of Jesus, the *parousia*, a new heaven and a new earth, and all talk about apocalyptic conflict, is unreal, or at the very best the expression, in terms of an out of date cosmology and obsolete framework, of a meagrely apprehended truth. The biblical gospel, therefore, with all its historical realism and apocalyptic imagery about God's intervention in history, was held as needing to be demythologised.

False dichotomy between ideas and events

Now there can be no doubt that this so-called demythologising of the historical gospel really involves robbing the gospel of its historical realism – and indeed robbing it of the historical Jesus, as happened in the second and third centuries through the *logos*-christologies – but the whole approach involves a false alternative. The alternative is not between a mythological gospel and a demythologised gospel, for *that alternative itself rests on a false dichotomy between ideas and events*. In fact the whole notion of myth arises only when this false dichotomy between the realm of ideas and the realm of events is posited, for there myth means, as in Plato, a crude counterpart in temporal terms of a timeless idea.

In point of fact, the whole idea of *myth* and the reading of mythology into the Old Testament and New Testament means that we are approaching the biblical gospel with alien presuppositions and so are misunderstanding the gospel. That is what happened in the second century, in the great conflict between the biblical faith and gnostic heresies of various kinds, and what went on happening all through the christological controversies of the next few centuries. People standing within the philosophical and cultural perspective, mainly of Greece, had deeply ingrained habits of thinking so customary that they appeared self-evident and were unconscious canons of thought. Hence when they tried to understand the gospel, they understood it *not out of the gospel itself*, but in terms of conceptions alien to it, and so misunderstood it. That fact is very clearly and fully brought out by Irenaeus the first great biblical theologian of the church, who attacked the whole attempt to understand the gospel out of alien preconceptions.

What happened then was this: imagining the historical gospel to be mythological because it did not fit in with their preconceptions or way of looking at truth, the gnostics attempted to strip it of its attributed mythical character, but in reality what they did was to transpose the reality of the gospel into a myth of their own. And so we discover gnostics transposing the gospel into astral myths of Iranian and Mandaean character, and the 'Christian gnostics' like Clement of Alexandria transposing the gospel into a more intellectual myth, a myth of highly attenuated symbols, but a myth nevertheless.

An obvious instance of that is the demythologisation of the resurrection of the body, expounded by Origen in terms of Plato's *Timaeus* (spherical bodies!). But what in point of fact needs demythologising is not the gospel with its wholly realistic understanding of salvation through the incarnation of the Son of God in our real world of space and time, but the demythologising of those elements in our human presuppositions which make the gospel message falsely to appear mythological. In other words, it was not the teaching of Jesus and the apostles that needed demythologising, but the unconscious presuppositions of Clement of Alexandria and his school of philosophical thought!

As we have seen, this whole false alternative of mythology/ demythology has been raised in our generation by Albert Schweitzer, and now by Bultmann. Bultmann's fault is precisely that of the Alexandrian theologians and scholars in the 2nd and 3rd centuries. He looks at the historical gospel and its eschatological realism from the perspective of the 'Enlightenment', from the perspective of the Hellenic mind to which he is so thoroughly assimilated. From that alien standpoint, with its false dichotomy between ideas and events, he imagines the New Testament not simply to be infected with certain mythologising elements, but to be fundamentally cast in one supreme mythological framework, but all Bultmann succeeds in doing – apart from helping us to see the falsity of the problem! – is to transpose the truth and reality of the New Testament *kērygma* into a great modern myth of the 20th century which goes under the 'high-falutin' name of existentialism! But it is no less a myth because it makes use of philosophical terms and symbols instead of images derived from ancient cosmology. It is only a myth that is even more cunningly devised than any the gnostics invented! There is nothing we need more, therefore, it might be said, than the demythologising of nineteenth- and twentieth-century biblical scholars.

What we are up against in the demand for demythologisation is a revolt against actual human history in its physical and concrete particularity. The gospel can no more be stripped of its physical event character, than the *Logos* can be stripped of the flesh he assumed in the incarnation. But the whole problem is a false one, resting on a false alternative, the dichotomy between a realm of ideas and a realm of events. The only way to solve the problem is to get behind it and to cut away the false starting point, to get back to the biblical way of thought in which idea and event are thought of in a unity, and only as distinctions within a unity. That is what actually took place in Alexandria under the profound theology of Athanasius and Cyril.

But we can go even further and ask, why is it that this dichotomy between idea and event constantly arises? Why is it, for example, that in modern education the power to think in terms of ideas is divorced from the power to think in terms of images? Why is it that a child for whom the world of ideas is so wonderfully real, soon grows out of that unity between the spiritual and the physical? (Cf. T.F. Torrance, *The School of Faith* (London: James Clarke 1959), pp. xxviii-xxix.)

The healing of the dichotomies in the incarnation

From the perspective of the incarnation the answer is clear: it is the distortion of the fall and of human sin that lies behind this disruption or dichotomy between knowing and being, word and event, theology and history, and it is that very rupture in our human existence that God has come to heal in the incarnation. When the Word was made flesh, the rupture between our true being in communion with God and our physical existence in space and time was healed. It is precisely about this that the sacraments have so much to say in the unity of word and physical elements in the ordinances of baptism and eucharist. The sacraments are designed in the midst of our brokenness and dividedness to hold together in one, spirit and flesh, word and event, spiritual and material, until the new creation. Sacraments are thus the *amen* to the incarnation, the experienced counterpart to the Word made flesh. Here, then, in the Word made flesh we have truth in the form of personal being, truth in the form of concrete physical existence, truth indissolubly one with space and time, with historical and physical being. To demythologise the truth of its physical and temporal elements is to try to disrupt the incarnation, to attempt to tear apart the Word from the flesh assumed in Jesus Christ. Thus demythologisation belongs to the essential distortion of sin – the sin that brought about the dichotomy in us, that refuses to accept the limitations of our creatureliness in speech and language and in the thought forms of space and time, that wants to conceive the truth in some imaginary form of pure being instead of the form of human flesh which it has assumed once and for all in the incarnation. The relation of the *kērygma* to history belongs to the very essence of the Christian faith, for it is grounded in the unity of reconciliation and revelation in Jesus Christ, in his unity of word and act, person and work, in the union of true God and true man.

E16 [Let us not forget, however,] that there are elements here which we must not avoid, although they have been so falsely construed in the notion of demythologisation and twisted to an alien end. [*It is the fact*]

Addendum:

ESCHATOLOGY[1]

Editor's note

This appears to be one of Torrance's very early works (from around the early 1950s or at least containing material which derives from then), and while containing material of considerable interest, never to have been revised for publication. The language and the thought in parts are more condensed and sometimes rougher, and there are a few places where the meaning is expressed so cryptically as to be difficult to follow. Torrance did a great deal of work in the late 1940s and throughout the 1950s on church and order, the sacraments and eschatology, and while much of that was published in the two volumes of *Conflict and Agreement*, most of the material here has never been fully revised and expanded for publication (although some of it was used in *Conflict and Agreement*, volume 2 – see the relevant footnotes below). There are clearly points where the thoughts are compacted together and Torrance has not had occasion to amplify them and expand them into his usual clarity of expression. Where the thought is difficult, accordingly, explanatory words or phrases have either been inserted in italics, or the text has been revised and the original put in a footnote.

Rather than being placed at the end of the Soteriology volume *Atonement*, the Eschatology 'Addendum', with its more technical discussions, has been positioned here in full at the end of the Christology volume *Incarnation* where it can be studied alongside the overlapping and similarly more technical 'endnotes' from the 'Introduction to Christology'.

---

[1] See further T.F. Torrance, *Conflict and Agreement in the Church*, vol. 2, Lutterworth, London 1960, esp. 'Eschatology and the Eucharist' pp. 154-202. Cf. also the epilogue to *Atonement*, the soteriology volume of Torrance's lectures, 'Christ the First and the Last', a lecture originally given in 1953 and reprinted from *Conflict and Agreement in the Church*, vol. 1 (London: Lutterworth 1959), pp. 304-15.

1 Eschatology in history – the Reformation, and Calvin and his legacy

Three periods appear to stand out in the history of the church as rich in eschatology, the first century, the age of the Reformation, and the present day. No period has ever been without its eschatology, but as a general rule theologians have been content to give only the last chapters of their works to eschatology, as if it were a mere addendum to faith and not the 'fibre of the living strand'.[2] The great question that must force itself upon us immediately is this: Why was it that the church failed so early to grasp and absorb into her whole life and thought the eschatological teaching of the New Testament? And why was it that after the Reformation the Lutheran, Reformed, and Anglican churches largely lost the eschatological note in spite of the fact that their hymns and liturgies are resonant with it?

Whatever be the final answer or answers we must give to these questions, it seems clear that the deepest significance of the best biblical scholarship of our day (as represented, for example, in Kittel's *Theologisches Wörterbuch zum Neuen Testament* (Theological Dictionary of the New Testament) is that it is wrestling with precisely this problem, with the result that the new biblical scholarship is producing an understanding of the bible unparalleled in the history of the church since the first century. No one can read the volumes of Kittel without being profoundly impressed with the fact that scholars from all sides and of many varieties have this in common, that their lexicographical and lexicological studies have forced them back into an exposition of the faith that bears something of the eschatological cast that characterises all the scriptures. Undoubtedly the renewed understanding of the Old Testament and its relation to the thought of the New Testament has a great deal to do with this, which would seem to justify the historian in the judgement that whenever the church has been tempted to tear Christianity from its God-given roots in Hebraic soil it has destroyed something so essential that its effects bear strange fruit for centuries afterwards.

The Reformation and the centrality of eschatology for Calvin

Undoubtedly the Reformation represented a tremendous recoil from a Latin conception of God, worked out into an almost impeccable

---

[2] Cf. H.R. Mackintosh, *Immortality and the Future* (London: Hodder & Stoughton 1915), p. 107f. (quote p. 108).

structure with the aid of Aristotelian logic, and a return to the living God and the dynamic faith of the bible. But what was it even in the age of the Reformation, something lacking or something misconceived, that led the church down the road from Luther to Ritschl, or from Calvin to Schleiermacher, for whom eschatology came to count for little or nothing at all? It was not that the eschatological element did not pervade the thought of the Reformation, though it was not held so consciously as it often is today. It is sometimes said, with grave injustice, that there is no real place given to the doctrine of the last things in Calvin – perhaps because in modern style he had no last chapters on the subject. The significant thing is that Calvin inserted his definite teaching on this subject into the third book of the *Institute* in connection with the doctrines of the Spirit, faith, and justification. The same procedure is true of his *Commentaries* and *Sermons*, and appears to be one which Calvin learned from St Paul himself who never set himself deliberately to give teaching on the last things (e.g. in *Romans* – but cf. the *Thessalonian Epistles*) but gives it only incidentally as the need arises, although the whole of his teaching is cast in strong eschatological terms. That is just the way in which it is given in his writings by John Calvin, for with him every doctrine entails what we now call the *eschatological tension*.

The influence of christology

It was a decided return to christology which first brought this about (cf. Bernard of Clairvaux whom Calvin cites more than anyone else apart from Augustine), for when salvation is lodged fully in Christ then he in his own person fills the whole vista of faith, while the reality of his presence through the Spirit means the reality of the presence of the kingdom here and now. But as he has ascended and withdrawn himself from worldly visibility, without detracting from his personal nearness, faith inevitably looks for the hour when the veil will be torn aside, and Christ will appear in glory and completely substantiate the faith of the church. Until then the faith of the church is nourished by justification and the sacraments which are thought of in terms of the God-manhood of Christ as seen particularly in the light of the cross and resurrection. That means that the eschatological tension that reached its acutest point in the person and work of the mediator is enshrined in the tension between *justus et peccator* (justified and yet a sinner) and between real presence and bread and wine. To the word of justification, the sacraments add the pressure of imminence, so that the two together on their christological basis contain the heart of Reformation eschatology.

Christology and the eschatological relation

Another way in which Calvin expressed that eschatological relation is thus: if Christ himself is our salvation, supremely in his own person, then the gift of grace is identical with the giver. Christ gives himself to us personally through the unity and yet duality of word and Spirit. Therefore faith rests upon a dual ground, *knowledge of the ascended Christ in his word, through the Spirit,* and carries the eschatological relation at its very heart. It is faith that has apprehended Christ through the Spirit, but in order to apprehend him faith must reach out still to comprehend him ever more fully, and so faith exists in the tension of having and not having, but a tension that is secure in the hand of God because it rests upon the fact that believers are once and for all apprehended by God, and no one can pluck them out of God's hand. That is the absolute certainty behind the humble uncertainty 'I believe; help my unbelief'.[3] This transmutation of medieval doubt or pusillanimity into the humble certainty of faith is particularly clear in Luther.

The eschatological relation is, however, bound up essentially with the historical revelation and action of Christ, as Calvin made clear through the stress upon the word, and indeed upon the historical continuity of the word as the preached word. *The word mediates the event, and* the word is thus the historically mediated event, but because it is bound up inextricably with the Spirit, through the word preached and through the Spirit as dual but indivisible act, the living Jesus Christ becomes present to faith – and not simply the mystical Son of God, but Jesus Christ himself the incarnate and historical Son of God. The more seriously the person of this Jesus is taken, and the more the emphasis upon the word throws faith back upon the historical events of Jesus Christ, the more faith is poised upon historical fulfilment, that is upon the expectation that this same Jesus will reveal himself personally in the actuality of history. And so faith is made to rest essentially upon a future event as well as upon a past event, and faith must inevitably be expressed in terms of hope also.

The controversy with Rome and the Reformers' reaction to Anabaptist apocalyptic

We must not forget, however, that the Reformers' conception of faith was marked and to a certain extent shaped by the battles in which they were engaged. Because faith has to do essentially with a transcendent act, a word about the new man or the new creation,

---

[3] Matt 9.24.

the coming age, it is thrown into tension, with, and often into contradiction to, this world and its processes. Thus Calvin sets faith in opposition on the one hand, to the worldly view of the kingdom which identified it with the *Imperium Romanum*,[4] but in opposition on the other hand, to the present kingdom of the mystic conceived as a static and timeless reality. The doctrines of justification and the sacraments reflect this double tension supremely and are inevitably misunderstood by those who have no real eschatological understanding, or who have not thought eschatology into the foundation of faith itself. This was the point that came out most strongly in the controversy over *imputation*,[5] the doctrine which was so grievously misunderstood by the Roman church and which became the pivot upon which the Counter-Reformation reacted in denunciation of the Reformed faith.

But the Reformers had still another battle to fight – this time against the Anabaptists who conceived of the kingdom too literally in terms of history and apocalyptic, and of salvation too much in terms of the future. Unfortunately, the recoil of the leading Reformers from the excesses of these *Schwärmer* or 'enthusiasts' carried with it a recoil from apocalyptic, or at least from thinking out fully the implications of apocalyptic. They tended to restrict eschatology to the eschatological tension, and definite teaching about the last things to the subjects of death, judgement, and resurrection. In other words, the separation of eschatological tension from apocalyptic really meant a movement to cut eschatology adrift from history. Looking back we may say that this was a decided weakness in the theology of the Reformation – not so much, however, in its prayers and hymns, particularly the eucharistic prayers and hymns!

---

4 Roman rule, empire, authority [as though the realisation of the kingdom could be identified, for example, with the conversion of the empire and the identification of church and state after Constantine, or the perpetuation of temporal and spiritual power in the Roman church. Cf. the last paragraph in this section, '. . . unless one is to follow Rome in her false elision or conflation of the temporal and the eternal, or the mystics in their ultimate denial of history', and also the paragraph below headed, 'The two ends held partially apart until the parousia . . .', where Torrance refers to 'the Roman Catholic totalitarian eschatology with the virtual deification of the historical church' – Ed].

5 The doctrine, based on Romans 4, that we are reckoned as righteous, or that righteousness is imputed to us.

The weakness of Calvin's doctrine of election and its influence on eschatology

But when eschatology tends to be cut adrift from history it is governed not so much by the logic of action (divine intervention), as by the logic of ideas (determinism). That is particularly evident in Calvin's more systematic works where the kingdom of God is conceived too generally in terms of an overarching sovereignty of God, and Calvin's doctrine of election is conceived in terms of an act of predestination which is pushed back to some still point before and behind time, rather than as the living action of the eternal in time. That on its part tended to deaden the relation between the kingdom of God and history, and to throw the urgency of judgement almost entirely into the future. At any rate, the result was that a view of providence and election with the major emphasis laid upon the past, upon a pre-temporal eternity, prevented the inner eschatological tension which characterised every doctrine from reaching its full development in clear teaching about the second advent of Christ, or at least in preventing the teaching about the second advent from conditioning the attitude to history. Thus it came to lack the urgency so characteristic of the New Testament view of the kingdom as imminent in time. The nearest approach to an integration of eschatology and history is to be found in the post-Reformation federal (covenant) theology, but that was too predestinarian and had borrowed too much from Aristotle and the Schoolmen to leave room for a living eschatology.

The New Testament looks toward a historical future, and a redemption of the whole world, but from the angle of the fallen world and its history that only can be expressed apocalyptically – unless one is to follow Rome in her false elision *or conflation* of the temporal and the eternal, or the mystics in their ultimate denial of history. The Reformation failed to bring out this New Testament emphasis with sufficient strength, and so paved the way for the denial of eschatology in neo-Protestantism. To weaken the relation between eschatology and history means that the inner eschatological form of faith becomes lost.

2 The gradual elimination of eschatology from its central place in the church

We cannot undertake here any account of the history of the doctrine through the centuries till the present day, except to say that it is the story of the gradual elimination of the eschatological element from its central place in the church and of its increasing secularisation, which in Marxian socialism becomes a movement of great power. The rise of this secularised eschatology cannot but be regarded as a severe judgement on the Christian church, for it means that the church has so failed to bear witness to the cross and resurrection of Christ as the power of God (for the weakness of God is stronger than man), that the nations have separated the eschatological and social message of the church from Christ Jesus, and have harnessed it to the ruthless forces of Newtonian science. The gradual de-eschatologising or *Enteschatologisierung* (as the Germans call it) has had effects within the churches themselves which must be noted.

The effects on the churches

(a) The loss of mainstream eschatology and the divorce of apocalyptic from prophetic

The main teaching about the last things in the West (apart from isolated thinkers like Bengel) has largely been left to sects whose roots go back into the Anabaptist tradition. Although the extremes of those early *Schwärmer* have not been repeated to the same extent in modern times, it still remains true that their modern successors have developed an eschatological emphasis that is one sided in its divorce of the apocalyptic view of the kingdom as other-worldly, coming at the end of time, from the prophetic view of the kingdom as breaking into the midst of time and involving history, and therefore that is constantly on the brink of becoming fantastic. Against this apocalyptic eschatology divorced from actual history, the church will always be in revolt, for apocalypse can only have Christian meaning in the closest association with present history.

(b) The relegation of eschatology from the centre to the end of dogmatics

When the church came to formulate her teaching about such doctrines as death and judgement, the life everlasting and the return of Christ, she tended to append it to the end of dogmatics rather uncertainly, failing to grasp these doctrines aright in themselves, and failing to take up the New Testament stress upon eschatology as integral to the very heart of the gospel and to every doctrine of the faith. With a tradition such as this in the church, the words of H.R. Mackintosh have great relevance and point: 'It is a just and illumining thought that every system of theology should be read backwards at least once, commencing with the last things, since it is in the conclusion that we find the truest index of the whole.'[6]

(c) *Idealism in place of eschatology*

When the church came to relate the kingdom of God to history, idealism took the place of eschatology. The church cannot live or work without an ideal, a goal, an end or *telos*, and without having some idea of the *eschaton*, the final end. But there is a vast difference between an ideal end in the Greek sense and the New Testament *eschaton*, the end that has in Christ broken into time, for all the formal similarity that they may bear. The difference between the two conceptions is precisely the core of the Christian gospel.[7] The Greek end is always an ideal end. As human beings, we are not what we ought to be, but no matter how much we try individually or in history to be what we ought to be, the end is still ideal and beyond our grasp. In the Christian gospel, this end has broken into the present and is even now operative in the world through the message of the gospel. Because it has actually entered history, the whole of Christian thought and action can no longer be conceived in terms of idealism. The Christian's end remains the final end, but because that end has broken into time and yet transcends time we are conscious of it here and now.

3 The modern recovery of eschatology

In the last two generations, however, the whole picture has been decisively altered, and that has been due to two main factors:

(i) The influence of evangelisation: the rising tide of evangelical witness which led to the great missionary movement of modern times has forced the church in the home countries to think anew of the relation between the evangel and history, and evangel and the whole world. The actual task of the gospel succeeded in throwing an urgency back into the church's faith which the theologians and scholars had belittled and almost destroyed.

(ii) Modern historico-critical study: the historico-critical study of the biblical documents with its increasing thoroughness brought scholars

---

6 Mackintosh, *op. cit.* p. 109.

7 Cf. *Conflict and Agreement*, vol. 1, p. 306f. (or see the epilogue to *Atonement* under the heading 'The difference between the Hebrew eternal "end" which enters time and history, and the Greek timeless and ideal "end".'

back to grapple with the enormous place occupied in them by eschatology. It is particularly with this movement that we are concerned here.

The rediscovery of the central place of eschatology in the New Testament

Right in the forefront of this return to the understanding of the eschatological character of the New Testament stand the names of Overbeck, Johannes Weiss, and Schweitzer, though the influence of the last named has been most dramatic in this country. The 'discovery' associated with these scholars was that all New Testament teaching is lodged within an eschatological scheme which gives to each doctrine its peculiar form. Or to put this the other way round, the New Testament thought-world has a central point which gives its otherwise varied character an essential unity, so that the individual ideas and doctrines that come up fall within its orbit and have their deepest meaning in relation to its central point. This central point is declared to be a specially modified form of late Jewish apocalyptic eschatology. This means that as against the uneschatological views of scholars like Harnack, the New Testament must be interpreted in a thorough going eschatological fashion, and further, that as late-Jewish apocalyptic eschatology was essentially futurist and catastrophic, we must regard the kingdom of God in the gospel as purely future and abruptly supernatural. Jesus, it is said, expected only an eschatological realisation of the kingdom, and therefore everything must be projected into the coming age.

The influence of Schweitzer

Schweitzer's views have had enormous influence, particularly in destroying those reconstructions of the gospel which chose to ignore the eschatological sayings of Jesus in an attempt to set him forth as the central figure of the kingdom of God on earth, a kingdom regarded primarily as a social and ethical movement in history reaching out through human progress toward utopia. But there can be no doubt that Schweitzer has overstated the case, and given a very one-sided account of the New Testament. He ignores almost entirely the element of teleology[8] in the teaching of Jesus with its roots in the prophetic view of the kingdom. At the same time it is simply not true that the teaching of Jesus has only a future reference, as C.H. Dodd has made magnificently clear, for there is constant insistence upon the fact that

---

[8] From the Gk *telos*, end, goal: the interpretation of nature or history in terms of its ends or goals, which means here, a looking forward to the fulfilment of the divine purpose in history.

the kingdom has come already, while throughout it all there is a joyful sense of God's actual presence in Jesus Christ. He is the king of the kingdom, and is here now to redeem and to save with the very finger of God. What is at stake ultimately in Schweitzer's view therefore is the doctrine of Christ, for a Jesus who is so utterly deluded as the figure of Schweitzer's reconstruction, who dies with a despairing cry when events take an unforeseen course, cannot be the Son of God as the church believes him to be.

But behind all this it must be said that Schweitzer misunderstands the nature of eschatology itself when he thinks of it only in a narrow apocalyptist sense. Indeed again and again it would appear that in eschatology Schweitzer sees little more than a primitive cosmology. When therefore he sets the Gospels in a thoroughly eschatological setting, that really means that they are set in the midst of an apocalyptic scenery which, as far as he can see, is bound up with unscientific views of the world. It is not surprising therefore that he rejects eschatology almost *in toto* or in full as primitive mythology, nor surprising that if his scholarship forces him to declare the New Testament to be eschatological from end to end then he should think of the story of the church as the story of a progressive elimination of eschatology. Schweitzer himself carries that position to its ultimate conclusion which significantly ends in the trivial declaration of faith as simply reverence for life.

Schweitzer's interpretation of the New Testament was elaborated in opposition to the uneschatological views of Harnack, but it is now apparent that Schweitzer really failed because he operated with similar idealist and rationalist assumptions which prevented him from radically thinking through the eschatological message of the New Testament. In other words, his essentially Hellenic presuppositions prevented him from apprehending the inner eschatological form of faith, apart from which apocalypse can appear only rather crude. For him therefore, the supreme problem which faces the church, and has faced the church throughout her long history, is a reinterpretation of the gospel message that must be pivoted upon the *actual fact* that the kingdom of God did not come in the first generation as the early Christians expected it would – the so called problem of the 'delayed advent' (*das Problem der ausgebliebenen Parusie*). Schweitzer has done a tremendous service to biblical studies in calling attention to the eschatological nature of early Christian faith, but by propounding the problem in this way he has unfortunately set the whole discussion off on a false scent.[9]

---

9 Cf. especially W. Michaelis, *Der Herr verzieht nicht seine,* Verheissung, 1942 (The Lord does not withdraw [or delay] his promise).

Developments after Schweitzer

Most of the literature on eschatology of recent years has started from this problem, and has either gone on after taking the 'actual fact' for granted, or tried to explain it away. Schweitzer has had direct descendants to his views in Werner and Buri in Switzerland who begin with the fact that the whole of the New Testament eschatology is bound up with a very definite historical situation which cannot be repeated, and who go on to restate the whole Christian position in such a way that it is no longer vitiated by the delusion of the near advent of Christ, but theirs is a theology that runs out into the same trivialities in which very little that is vital of the original gospel is left. On the other hand, there had arisen a *timeless eschatology* which explained away in symbolical fashion the New Testament attitude to a future but imminent advent of the kingdom, and to this belong people so varied as the early Barth, Bultmann, Hoskyns, and Dodd, and many others. Apart from such people as these whose eschatological thought is closely bound up with New Testament scholarship, there are others who might conveniently be grouped into three categories.

(a) Behind all the discussion there has been a tradition that has maintained a close relation to the teaching of the Reformation, and has thought out the problems of biblical theology that have been thrown up but without losing the inner eschatological tension of faith that one finds in Calvin and Luther – the most notable and influential of these on the continent was undoubtedly Martin Kähler, who in many ways is coming back into appreciation today, and in this country, P.T. Forsyth and H.R. Mackintosh.

(b) At the same time there has been a movement among those who still operate within the idealist tradition to get to grips with eschatology and to set it forth with a new understanding of what were called 'values'. Into this group one might put Althaus, von Hügel, and John Baillie, and to a lesser extent Emil Brunner.

(c) Still a third group comprises those who have what is often called a more 'naive' attitude to time and to the kingdom, a serious reinterpretation of the New Testament which received great impetus from the eschatological fervour of the elder Blumhardt (with his stress upon the resurrection) and the evangelical sects.

It is impossible to go into these various conceptions of eschatology here, though it is time that most New Testament scholars paid more attention to the work of the theologians which has been going on parallel to that of biblical studies.

4 The eschatological tension of time and eternity in modern theology

The early Barth

The great turning point after Albert Schweitzer came undoubtedly with the publication of Barth's *Romans*.[10] Here the problem of Schweitzer was at first solved by a timeless eschatology,[11] and it was pointed out that in Schweitzer's sense the New Testament is not eschatological in any thorough going way, for the stress is as much upon the past and present as it is upon the future. Here the end of history is not to be interpreted as an end within time, for no end within time can be a real or complete end. The end is also the beginning, *for the end is to be found in the eternal which lies behind time,* and so the nearness of the end is interpreted as the transcendental relation of the present to its origin in the eternal. Hence the notion of a near *parousia,* the second coming of Christ, far from being part of the mythological element that must be left behind, is an essential part of the content of faith itself. It depends on the infinite qualitative distinction between time and eternity. Such a view of eschatology as timeless crisis appears to empty history of its worth, and there was definite reaction against it even by those who like Althaus learned from it. Over against Schweitzer, the significance of Barth's early view was this, that whereas for Schweitzer eschatology was only the time-conditioned mould in which the thought of the New Testament was expressed, for Barth eschatology has to do with the very roots of faith and belongs to the inner core of the gospel. We cannot therefore either in Harnackian or Schweitzerian fashion slough it off in favour of some essence which remains uncontaminated by it. In this respect, Barth completed the revolution made by Schweitzer in biblical studies, and indeed it is just because he took it full circle that his thought does not run out into triviality.

The later Barth

The extraordinary thing is that Barth soon discovered that the position as he had formulated it in the *Epistle to the Romans* and other early

---

10 Karl Barth, *Der Römerbrief* (Commentary on Romans) 1919.

11 A doctrine of the extreme proximity to us in time of the eternal which presses in on us and continually throws us into crisis but without itself entering time and becoming history, ie. as though eternity and time were adjacent but not overlapping circles (an illustration regularly used by Torrance), so that eternity touches time but does not enter into it.

writings, necessary as it was at that stage, was untenable, both because it did not square with the New Testament emphasis upon time, and because it involved, contradictorily enough, a dialectic between time and eternity that cut across the essentially eschatological tension of faith. The result was that Barth gave up a timeless eschatology, and set himself to take seriously the New Testament teaching of an imminent advent of the kingdom *in time* and yet to see that as belonging to the inner core of faith. This meant that the real eschatological tension was not interpreted in terms of an eternity/time dialectic, which always means in the end a refusal to take time seriously, but rather in terms of the new and the old, of a new time in reconciliation and union with the eternal, and an old time which is the time of this fallen world, which through sin exists in mysterious contradiction to God. Here the whole content of eschatology is thought through christologically in terms of the incarnation, the God-manhood of Christ, and the events of the crucifixion, resurrection and ascension. In this way eschatology is nothing but a thorough going expression of the doctrine of grace as it concerns history, while the important word is not *eschaton* (the last event) but *Eschatos* (the last one).

The impact of Barth and the reaction to his views

This is not the point to expound Barth's views, but to note the result of his early impact upon the history of thought on the subject. Perhaps more extraordinary than Barth's own development is the fact that so many writers have entered into the very elements which Barth has sloughed off and have made them central to their eschatology. In other words, starting at the stage of Barth's *Römerbrief* (Commentary on Romans) and often in reaction against important parts of it, writers like Bultmann, Hoskyns, Dodd and Niebuhr have continued to develop an eschatology which is concerned mainly with the dialectic between time and eternity, not always with the sharpness of Barth's early 'infinite qualitative distinction between time and eternity', but nevertheless a doctrine of timeless crisis, which is anti-evolutionary and non-teleological.[12] In all this it is Niebuhr who takes time most seriously, and Bultmann and Dodd least seriously.

But more significant than this distinction *between Barth and the others* is another which cuts across the views of all four, and concerns their relation to Barth's fundamental point maintained throughout, that the eschatological relation has to do with the very meaning of revelation and lies at the foundation of the biblical teaching about faith and

12 Interpreting history in terms of an end or goal of history which fulfils it.

knowledge. Bultmann, and Dodd, and ultimately even Niebuhr deny this, and still operate with what might be called (for lack of a better expression) Hellenic epistemology.[13] Hoskyns on the other hand, had learned too deeply from the Old Testament and from Barth to read so naïvely into the New Testament Platonic categories and rationalist presuppositions, but it is a pity that he did not work out his views into a full and consistent account.

Bultmann

In many ways the views of Bultmann are really parallel to those of Schweitzer except that Bultmann realises that a profound eschatological element must remain in faith even after the mythological elements have been discarded (*Entmythologisierung* or demythologisation). Here it is form-criticism which has been used as the means by which scholars try to get into the essence of the New Testament faith and yet discard those elements which appear to be accretions to, or in contradiction to, the original message. But it is becoming increasingly apparent in those who use the form-critical knife, even in C.H. Dodd himself, that too much is apt to be cut away and that form-criticism is too easily made the tool of philosophical presuppositions. The major difference between Bultmann and Schweitzer in this respect is that whereas Schweitzer's presuppositions were largely Hegelian, Bultmann's are taken from the existential philosophy associated with the work of Martin Heidegger. There can be no doubt that Bultmann (in his earlier thought) gets much more deeply into the issues and has done tremendous service in New Testament scholarship, but his philosophical assumptions actually do gross violence to his scholarship, for in the last resort they make him think of the eschatological tension as but a necessity of finite experience confronted with the eternal in time. In a deeper sense than for the merely form-critical, eschatology *for Bultmann* has its roots in an essential time-conditioning of faith. It arises in our encounter with the eternal in history, but because the historical element is involved we must always learn to distinguish between the form and the content of eschatology. *For Bultmann* this means that all eschatological expressions have a certain impropriety: they are ultimately symbolical and give time-conditioned expression for a reality that cannot be conveyed conceptually.

---

[13] Cf. especially Bultmann's *Glaube und Verstehen* vol. 1 (Faith and Understanding) 1933 and *Offenbarung und Heilsgeschehen* (Revelation and Redemption-Event) 1941, and Dodd's *The Parables of the Kingdom*, 3rd edition (London: Nisbet 1936), particularly chapter 1.

Brunner and Kähler

There is undoubtedly a great truth here particularly when we come to think of apocalyptic, but much of it goes back to idealist roots and even to the thought of Schleiermacher. Its great fault lies in its failure to do justice to the event-character of revelation which is essential to its fundamental historicity. It is here that Brunner has come to grapple with the problem. He shares the view, much more than Barth for example, that eschatological terms are ultimately symbolical, but refuses to work that out in any way that will lead to a docetic view of history. There are times when his utterances have tended in that direction, but he is very aware of the difficulty, and it is never his intention to do anything but the fullest justice to history. Without it eschatology has no meaning whatsoever. Brunner links up here with the work of Martin Kähler (as also does Barth) and the scholars (sometimes called 'biblicist' by the descendants of Schweitzer) who lay great emphasis upon the *Heilsgeschichte* (salvation history) – that is to say, not *Heilsgeschichte* in the supra-temporal sense of the early dialectical theology but as the sacred story of the divine intervention in actual history which reaches its great climax in the incarnation and final fulfilment in the *parousia.*

Althaus – 'The last things'

Side by side with this, is the great work of Paul Althaus who in four editions of his *Die Letzten Dinge*[14] (The Last Things) has struggled with a view of eschatology which tries to take seriously the eschatological tension as having to do here and now with an eternal experience within time, and yet with a real end which is both the judgement and goal of history. Although Althaus still operates within the philosophical presuppositions inherited from Ritschlianism, his is really a magnificent attempt to grapple with all the major problems, and in particular to bring eschatology and teleology together so as to give a positive account to ongoing history, and yet to relate all history to a transcendent end in which history is fulfilled from beyond itself. Throughout all he makes great efforts to keep eschatology thoroughly christological, for it is only when the actuality of the end is placed fully in Christ Jesus that belief in the *parousia,* and in the *parousia* as a near-advent, becomes an essential notion of faith. His view of the eschatological tension might be described as a both/and paradox in

---

[14] 1st 1922, 2nd 1924, 3rd revised 1926, 4th revised 1933 (5th Bertelsmann, *Gütersloh* 1949).

distinction from the early dialectical either/or paradox. The significance and value of his work lie in that debate, and in the fact that he tries to get at eschatology from its centre in the Christian faith. But in the last analysis his is a supra-temporal eschatology that does not escape from an idealist view of time.

The work of Karl Heim

Even more significant than the work of Althaus, however, has been the work of Karl Heim. On the one hand, his significance lies in the fact that he stands in a closer relation to the biblical message, working out an eschatology in terms of justification and forgiveness, and bringing into history the acute tension manifest in the death of Christ in the contradiction between the powers of evil and the holy love of God. On the other hand, Heim's significance lies in his efforts to break with the idealist conception of time that has for so long done violence to our understanding of the biblical message. For help in his interpretation, Heim turns partly to Bergson and partly to the changes in modern notions of time due to the new physics, and certainly he manages to introduce into his views something of a Heraclitean tension.

Critics argue that this is only to understand primitive mythology in terms of modern mythology, but although it is not always easy to understand or agree with Heim's notions of time, particularly when they are influenced by transient scientific theories, he has done us great service both in thinking eschatology and soteriology into each other, and in overthrowing what he calls a static (*stabil*) view of time in favour of a dynamic (*labil*) view as the time-form of the Ego.[15] The latter means that he works out a view of eschatology in close association with the life of the church, for our Christian view of time must inevitably be bound up with God's action in history through the church as the place where eternity is so to speak within time. Eternity does not stand forth only at the end of time but is the frontier of time all along the line. It is the other side of time and beyond time, the final reality that bears upon time. That reality is supremely manifest in the incarnation, and through the death of Christ and through the church in her proclamation of the gospel, it gets to grip with time in the matter of guilt. Thus history, particularly history in relation to the church, is read in terms of the contradiction of sinners against the man of Cavalry, and the whole panorama of time has its meaning unfolded there in terms of a dynamic tension so acute that every time is seen to be the last time. Heim does not think in terms of alternatives such as realised

[15] *Ego,* the Latin for 'I', used for the human self.

eschatology or a future coming of the kingdom at the end of time, but in terms of both.

It is characteristic of Heim that he speaks of these difficult matters again and again through illustrations. Thus he likens the church of the New Testament to a vast iron bridge which spans the torrent of time with a single arch supported by only two pillars, the cross of Christ which stands on this side of time and the coming of Christ in power which stands on the other side of time.[16] The church of Christ in history is maintained from age to age by these two supports and its very being is bound up with the essential unity of these two events, the perfected event of the death and resurrection of Christ and the future event of the parousia. It is because the very being of the church is proleptically conditioned by a new creation to be revealed at the parousia, the return of Christ, that she lives in dynamic tension here and now at the very frontiers of eternity.

This tension is throughout the tension that lies at the heart of justification, the relation that exists in the conflict between guilt and the power of evil (in which Heim sees behind the outward façade of world history the embattled array of Satanic forces) and the redeeming purpose of God.[17] It is because that struggle was supremely concentrated in the cross, and because Jesus Christ emerged there as absolute victor over all evil that God confronts time through Jesus Christ by whom at last the world will be judged and all history brought to its great consummation. But because it is through Jesus Christ that God confronts the world in its history, history will inevitably repeat on the full scale of humanity the conflict of the cross, but it will be a conflict or cataclysm in which Jesus Christ will emerge triumphant with his new creation of heaven and earth. Because we are concerned throughout all this with a dynamic or fluid (*labil*) view of time we cannot think of the consummation by a lengthening of time but in terms only of God's moment fulfilling and ending our time. Hence we cannot say in what day or hour the *parousia* will take place.[18] All we

---

16 Karl Heim, *Jesus the World's Perfecter*, Eng. trans. (Edinburgh: Oliver & Boyd 1959), chap. 16, p. 153.

17 The original here reads: 'This tension is throughout the tension that lies in the heart of justification, the relation between guilt and power in which Heim sees behind the outward façade of world history the embattled array of Satanic forces against the redeeming purpose of God.'

18 The original text reads, 'we cannot think of the consummation by a lengthening, but in terms only of God's moment, so that we cannot say in what day or hour . . .'

know is that we are confronted now through the gospel with God's will and with eternity as though this were the last time.

5 The nature of New Testament eschatology

These theological discussions, as well as the discussions of biblical scholars, have demanded a fresh and thorough investigation of the teaching of both Old and New Testaments on the kingdom of God, and the nature of the eschatological cast of all the doctrines of the faith. A vast amount has been done in commentaries and journals, as well as in Kittel's *Theological Dictionary*, that has yet to be gathered together and focused on eschatology proper. It is significant, however, that more and more recent writers have determined to ask questions such as: What is the biblical view of time? How do the scriptures think of the relation between the kingdom of God and history? How are we to think of the kingdom as present in the church? What do we really mean by 'eschatological', if it does not simply refer to final judgement and death and resurrection? It is only now after several generations of intense discussion that the issues are beginning to emerge clearly into the open.

The roots of New Testament eschatology in the prophetic view of the kingdom of God

The Christian view of the kingdom of God and the last things undoubtedly goes back to roots in the Old Testament, and particularly to the double consciousness in the Hebrew mind of the kingdom as bound up with creation, and yet as the pure act of God. In the world of history and trouble, the reality of that kingdom can be imaged forth only dimly, but the Old Testament prophets are mastered with the consciousness that it will be fully realised in the same sphere of reality in which people daily live and suffer, for God is the Lord of all the earth who will not forego his purpose in creation. At the same time they are equally conscious that though the kingdom is imaged in the pattern that has been given to Israelite society and history, it is not something that will arise out of history but will supervene upon it until it breaks out into apocalyptic vision. But the Old Testament apocalyptic eschatology is still rooted and grounded in history, and speaks proleptically in anticipation of the kingdom as a state in time. No doubt it is bound up with a transcendent community, but it is one that will be realised only in cosmic circumstances perfected by the word of God when creation and kingdom come together. That duality which holds together in unshakeable unity the redeemed community and a redeemed earth, carrying with it the seeds of the Christian doctrine of the resurrection of the body, lies at the heart of the New Testament eschatology, and it is there that its most decisive expression is found.

The Old Testament emphasis on the future has now been shifted to the present

In the Old Testament, the kingdom of God was revealed at certain decisive points in the history of Israel, but because its domain stretched necessarily over the whole creation it reached beyond Israel, and because the world was a world in estrangement from God, it could be manifest only as a mystery behind it and yet impinging upon history. In the New Testament, the kingdom is regarded as having broken into time and is overtaking men and women in Jesus Christ, but because it comes into the particularity of history, its universal domain is as yet hidden from the eyes of humanity. It confronts them not first extensively in its universality, but intensively in decisive encounter. This means that though the kingdom of God is present among mankind it is nevertheless known only in a continuation of the double consciousness of the Old Testament where the kingdom is seen as bound up with creation, and yet as the pure act of God. But the whole emphasis has been shifted. In the Old Testament the main accent lay upon the future; in the New Testament the main accent lies upon the present, but here the accent on the present has no meaning apart from the future when the kingdom of God now realised intensively in temporal and historical encounter, *in Christ and his encounter with people,* will be realised extensively in a new heaven and a new earth.

The New Testament kingdom is both present and future

It is precisely the tension between those two stresses which is at the root of what we call today the eschatological element in the New Testament. The kingdom is both future and present. The Christian's relation to salvation is both a having and hoping. 'The hour is coming,' said Jesus, 'and now is'.[19] It is that double significance which makes *parousia* such a difficult thought, for the New Testament teaching about the *parousia* alternates between a future advent and a realised presence here and now. Thus in the fourteenth chapter of the fourth Gospel, particularly as seen in the light of the first epistle of John, the advent presence of Christ undoubtedly refers both to his presence through

---

19 John 5.25.

the Spirit and to his presence on the last day, and that doubleness is very apparent in the Johannine teaching about judgement.

On the lips of Jesus himself, as we see in the Synoptics, the emphasis is upon the presence of the kingdom in his own person, and as he himself was then present in the flesh the accent fell largely upon the present, though there are undoubted references, as several recent scholars have demonstrated (notably, Stauffer, Kümmel, Michaelis and Cullmann)[20] to a future coming not to be wholly identified with resurrection, ascension and Pentecost. After the ascension, however, from the angle of the redeemed sinner to whom Jesus is no longer present according to the flesh, the emphasis necessarily falls as much upon the advent hope as upon communion in the real presence here and now, while the intense personal nearness of the risen Christ impresses itself inevitably upon faith as always imminent. That means that redeemed sinners can only think of their reconciliation with Christ eschatologically, but also that they cannot think of the advent in purely futurist terms. That is why the New Testament constantly thinks of the *parousia* in terms of epiphany, for the relation between the *today* and the *eschaton* is much more a tension between the hidden and the manifest, the veiled and the unveiled, than between dates in calendar time. What is still in the future is the full unveiling of a reality, but the reality itself is fully present here and now.

The continuity between synoptic and apostolic eschatology

The attempt by some scholars to read the eschatology of the apostles as contradicting the eschatology of the Synoptics shows a failure to understand the interior logic of this eschatological relation, besides

---

[20] The indications are that this was written in the early 1950s or even earlier. Parts of the material here overlap closely in content and language with *Conflict and Agreement* vol. 2, some of which, e.g. pp. 154-202, 'Eschatology and the Eucharist', dates from 1952 (cf. for example the similarities referred to in footnotes below between passages here and *Conflict and Agreement* pp. 164f., 171f., and 172-75). In *Christus und die Zeit*, first published in 1946 (Eng. trans. *Christ and Time* 1951), Cullman refers to E. Stauffer, *Die Theologie des Neuen Testaments* 1941, W.G. Kümmel *Verheissung und Erfüllung* 1945, and Michaelis *Der Herr verzieht nicht seine* Verheissung 1942. In his writing here, Torrance mentions only the German text of *Christ and Time*, [in section 9 below, for example, he refers to '*Christus und die Zeit* (also available in a French translation)'], and appears therefore not to know of an English translation which would indicate a date prior to 1951, the date of Cullmann's first appearance in English.

forgetting, as the late H.R. Mackintosh used to say, that Jesus was not a Christian, that is to say, that his *ipsissima verba* or own words were not given from the perspective of the sinner redeemed by Christ. If the *eschaton* in Jesus Christ has really come into the present then it must invade and shape the thought of the redeemed, so that the Synoptic revelation of the kingdom attains its full fruition only through the apostolic witness to it. And that is precisely the significance of the eschatological teaching in the closing chapters of the fourth Gospel, and the constant teaching of the Acts of the Apostles. What 'Jesus began to do and teach' in the flesh is continued and completed by himself through the Spirit in the witness and work of the apostolate.[21] It is upon this rock that the church is built, and to this apostolic witness that the keys of the kingdom are given. Any *Gleichschaltung* or harmonisation of the New Testament in terms of a purely futurist eschatology or in terms of a realised eschatology based one-sidedly upon one emphasis in the Synoptics is both to do violence to the Synoptics and to mutilate the completeness of the New Testament witness.

The New Testament holds the prophetic and the apocalyptic together

Another way of expressing the eschatological relation is in terms of 'end' described in the New Testament both as *telos* and *eschaton*,[22] the roots of the teleological end going back to the prophetic view of the kingdom, and the roots of the eschatological end to the apocalyptic view of the kingdom. In using both terms, the New Testament clearly refuses to teach an eschatology of judgement and new creation that is divorced from a teleological conception of creation and history, or is not controlled by God's creative purpose in time. Therefore while the kingdom of God means that the fashion of this world will pass away before the eschatological rule coming from above and beyond, yet that rule actually enters into the course of history and its saving action cannot be divorced from God's original and eternal purpose in creation. This double view of the end is magnificently combined, as H.H. Farmer has pointed out[23] in the eighth chapter of the epistle to the Romans.

---

[21] Acts 1.2ff.

[22] *Telos*, end, goal; *eschaton*, final consummation – for *telos* see particularly Luke 22.37; John 13.1; Rom 10.4; 1 Cor 10.11; 2 Cor 3.13. Cf. E. Stauffer, *Die Theologie des Neuen Testaments*, 4th (and 5th) revised edition, Bertelsmann, *Gütersloh* 1948, chap. 51 'Die Wege der Vorsehung (The Ways of Providence)', p. 187 [Eng. trans. from the 5th edition, J. Marsh, *New Testament Theology*, London: SCM Press 1955, p. 208f.].

[23] H.H. Farmer, *The World and God*, (London: Nisbet 1935), p. 223.

6 'Realised eschatology' – the views of C.H. Dodd

The view which demands special consideration in this country, and which must be fully discussed before we can see our way ahead either in biblical studies or in theology, is the so called 'fulfilled eschatology' championed by the late Sir Edwyn Hoskyns, or as it is more popularly known, the 'realised eschatology' championed by C.H. Dodd. This is an eschatology which has arisen directly out of the debacle of liberal thought occasioned by Schweitzer and is to be understood largely in that setting. It is a thorough going eschatology which wholly repudiates the principle of evolutionism, but as we have already noted still operates with an epistemology that does not appear to be too biblical.

The transmutation of horizontal relations into the vertical

In its earliest forms (as in von Dobschütz, *The Eschatology of the Gospels*) the kingdom of God tends to be interpreted in terms of the divine idea, but in Hoskyns and Dodd the emphasis is upon the breaking in of the kingdom of God as *event*, so that the *eschaton* is now a matter of actual experience. The kingdom of God has already come. It is 'fulfilled' or 'realised' eschatology. The crisis of personal decision and the final judgement of the world are telescoped into each other – they are one and the same thing. All horizontal relations are transmuted into a vertical relation in which the kingdom is perfectly fulfilled, so that every moment in time is heavy with present significance and meaning not because of a future reference but because it points to eternity and is fulfilled in it. But if this were true, one would be at a loss to see what the real distinction is between the Old Testament view of the kingdom and that of the Gospels. In this sense the kingdom was just as present then as it is now, and so the real significance of 'realised' as something distinctive is lost. It does not take much to see that such a view in the hands of a consistent form-critic really dissolves the historical element into mist and empties it of reality.

There is no doubt however, that 'realised eschatology' has thrown a flood of light upon the New Testament, particularly upon some of the parables, while the emphasis upon the *eschaton* here and now has done New Testament scholarship invaluable service in helping it to free itself from evolutionism. It is a view, however, that can be maintained only by rigorous application of form-critical methods to the Gospels, particularly to those passages which do not fit the theory, not to speak of the Epistles and the Apocalypse. The overall impression given by the works of C.H. Dodd is that 'realised eschatology' is as much a ready-made formula for the solving of New Testament problems as an interpretation arising out of the New Testament itself. It is indeed sometimes so much a *tour de force* that the whole New Testament teaching about the second advent of Christ is set aside as a mistake; that parables and *logia* which appear to speak of a lapse of time between two eschatological moments are declared to have been adapted by the tradition to strengthen the illusory hope of the early church, or if genuine are only an accommodation of language, while apocalyptic elements are set aside as misunderstandings. Such a drastic excision of '*maranatha*'[24] out of the New Testament witness and the earliest Christian confession of faith betrays a handling of the New Testament that leaves much to be desired, for it denies that the keys of the kingdom (the knowledge of the mystery) lie with the apostolic witness to Christ.

A comparison of Dodd and Schweitzer

It might be helpful at this point to throw Dodd's views into comparison with Schweitzer's, for that is the setting they seem to have, though Schweitzer is rarely ever mentioned by Dodd. Dodd takes for granted that the problem is the so-called *Parusieverzögerung* or 'delayed advent', but he wants to solve it by setting out an eschatology that does not give up the high christology of the church. Schweitzer's christology was frankly Ebionite[25] – Jesus was terribly mistaken. Dodd shrinks from that conclusion and prefers to lay the misapprehension at the door of the early church which is then made answerable for the false construction of the sayings of Jesus in terms of a futurist eschatology. But by eliminating the time-element inherent in the gospel message as we have it, Dodd tends toward docetism in spite of himself. Again both Dodd and Schweitzer take up a similar attitude to the second advent in the sense of a futurist eschatology, but in Schweitzer and more so in his descendants that tends to be transmuted into an idealist utopia after all in which a *parousia* is an impossibility. For Dodd, who occasionally allows himself references to a future advent or judgement, only to deny them in almost the next breath, the *parousia* would appear to be quite unnecessary, for strictly speaking it has already come, and is fully realised. In other words, the *parousia* is made out to be an event

---

24 The Aramaic 'come, Lord', 1 Cor 16.22.

25 In Ebionite teaching, Jesus was a purely human figure, anointed by God at baptism and adopted to be son of God because of his obedience to Mosaic law.

of the transcendental or supernal[26] world, so that the notion of a second advent is purely symbolical. In Schweitzer's view there is no final judgement at all; in Dodd's view history itself is the judgement of mankind. Undoubtedly there is much in the 'realised eschatology' of Dodd that is a decided advance over the so called 'consistent eschatology' of Schweitzer, for it completely refutes the notion that Jesus is simply an exponent of late-Jewish apocalyptic ideas, but 'consistent eschatology' has the great advantage of offering an interpretation of the New Testament with a minimum of mutilation and reconstruction, whereas 'realised eschatology' can only be established by radical reconstruction, and at times dubious interpretations of certain passages.[27]

The difficulties of 'realised eschatology'

Theologically, there are insuperable difficulties to such a view. The teaching that the kingdom of God refers to a transcendent order beyond history, to a supernal world which enters history purely as the *eschaton*, carries with it the idea that 'the time-scale is irrelevant to the ultimate significance of history.'[28] That is such a reaction from the teleological view of the kingdom as to become an equally one-sided eschatological view. Indeed such a one-sided[29] eschatology really means the denial of eschatology altogether, for there is no eschatological expectation left. Everything has happened already. When the time-element is eliminated like that the eschatological tension is transmuted into a dialectic between the supernal world, and this world, and the kingdom of God becomes ultimately docetic, almost a Platonic magnitude[30] *or form*, and the word *eschaton* loses its original meaning. This inflation of

---

26 Relating to things above or in a higher place, celestial. The use of the word supernal, rather than the much more common supernatural, would appear to be a deliberate avoidance of the rather different connotations associated with the latter. See the note on magnitude below.

27 E.g. Matt 12.28; Mark 1.15, etc.

28 C.H. Dodd, *op. cit*. p. 71.

29 The text here has 'consistent', but it is not in the inverted commas of the previous paragraph (ie. a reference to 'consistent eschatology', as Schweitzer's views were commonly called – see e.g. Cullman, *op. cit.* 3rd edition, p. vii, xviii, 30), and in the context here can perhaps be better understood as '*one-sided*' to avoid confusion – Ed.

30 Torrance's use of the unusual words 'supernal' and 'magnitude' may reflect a reading of Karl Heim's essay 'Time and Eternity' in *The New Divine Order* (London: SCM Press 1930), pp. 51-94 – for 'supernal' see p. 57, and for

the eschatological element of the New Testament (particularly in the hands of Bultmann) is so serious that (to borrow an expression from Harnack) the term eschatological is rapidly becoming a *Zauberbegriff*, or magical concept to solve all problems.

The merit and demerit of 'realised eschatology'

The great merit of 'realised eschatology' is its insistence that the decisively new factor must be located wholly in the life, death and resurrection of Jesus, but its great demerit is that it entails a divorce of redemption from creation, of eschatological end from teleological end – except perhaps in retrospect, for the parables of growth are made to refer only to what led up to the coming of the kingdom, not to the action of the kingdom in time. The Old Testament prophets pointed to the coming of the kingdom as a state in time, for they taught that the kingdom could only be realised among humanity in a perfect environment, that is to say, in harmony with God's purpose of creation. It is a kingdom therefore with cosmic and historical significance, and to be realised in the same sphere of reality as that to which we belong. With the kingdom as C.H. Dodd envisages it, on the other hand, it is difficult to understand how it is actually realised at all, if it only discounts history and does not gather it up into fulfilment.

The prophetic view of a kingdom hidden until the time of its fulfilment

The prophets also taught, as we have had occasion to see, that the presence of the kingdom in a fallen world must mean that it comes as a hidden kingdom, at least until the apocalyptic moment when it is fully revealed in a new heaven and a new earth. That is surely the thought of the New Testament which it holds all the more decidedly just because the *eschaton* has entered time. No doubt it cannot be discerned by observation in the passing fashion of this fallen world, but it necessarily entails within the world the creation of a new community through which the kingdom is actual in conditions of time. That is indeed the mystery of the kingdom, but unlike the messianic remnant of the Old Testament which had not yet received the promise, this community is actual in the fullness of time, rooted and grounded

'magnitude' p. 52, 53, 65). Cf. the similar use of 'magnitude' in *Conflict and Agreement*, vol. 1, p. 203, where Torrance speaks of the view which often thinks 'of the Church as if there were over against the visible Church an invisible Platonic magnitude' (i.e. a transcendent ideal church), a reference to the concept in Plato's thought of eternal realities called 'forms', such as the form of the Good, of which earthly realities were only imperfect copies.

in the incarnation, a community that has foundations. But while its builder and maker is God,[31] and just because it is actual in time, it partakes also of the contradictions and conflicts of history, with another law in its members warring against the law of God.[32] In spite of being in the likeness of sinful flesh the new community is indeed the body of Christ, the mystery through which the unveiling of the righteousness of God takes place in the world in the preaching of the Gospel, but therefore also the unveiling of the wrath of God as the redeeming purpose of divine love in effective conflict with the forces of evil.

The coming of the kingdom in Jesus but the holding apart of final judgement

In the earthly ministry of Jesus, when the word was broadcast to all and sundry, the *eschaton* confronted people in the person of Christ standing in their very midst as the mystery of the kingdom, the *eschatos*, invading the realm of their choices and decisions, throwing them into ferment and crisis, and (as C.H. Dodd has described so well) acting selectively upon them so that their reaction to it is itself the divine judgement. That inevitably happens when the kingdom of God comes into the midst, for the king takes charge of the situation and his word acts upon people whether they will or no giving their own choices and decisions an essential form *vis à vis* the kingdom. Nevertheless this breaking in of the last judgement is veiled in the form of the parable and presented as it were obliquely in order both to bring men and women face to face with the last things in crucial decision and yet to leave them room for decision, which could not happen if the *eschaton* were wholly realised, as C.H. Dodd would have it, and the time-element were eliminated. And so the fourth Gospel puts very clearly the whole Synoptic teaching of the parables when Jesus says: 'I judge you not, but the word that I have spoken to you, that shall judge you at the last day.'[33] That final judgement confronts people here and now, but its full action is delayed until the last day. Had the *eschaton* encountered men and women in its unveiled openness they would have been damned on the spot without room or freedom for the decision of faith – that is why Jesus held apart the prophetic and the apocalyptic views of the kingdom.[34]

---

31 Cf. Heb 11.10.

32 Cf. Rom 7.23.

33 See John 12.47-48.

34 Cf. Reinhold Niebuhr, *The Nature and Destiny of Man* (London: Nisbet 1943), Gifford Lectures vol. II, p. 49.

The mystery of evil

However, just because room and time are given for reaction, the terrible possibility is allowed for the reaction of evil in its final and intense contradiction to the kingdom of God. That is what the New Testament calls 'the mystery of iniquity',[35] which is also unveiled through the preaching of the gospel, and will be unveiled fully at the last day and be destroyed. But just as in the earthly ministry of Jesus, that mystery of iniquity was provoked out of its mystery and pressed by the finger of God to the point of ultimate decision in the terrible conflict that issued in the cross, so the church as the body of Christ, proclaiming the same word of the kingdom in order that all may repent and believe the gospel, also provokes such a reaction of evil in the conflicts of history that there is also an eschatological fulfilment of evil culminating in the last judgement. The tares and the wheat grow side by side,[36] and so as Niebuhr has said, history is 'the story of an ever-increasing cosmos, creating ever-increasing possibilities of chaos.'[37]

The final inadequacy of 'realised eschatology'

'Realised eschatology' does not do justice to the New Testament teaching of this mystery of iniquity *vis-à-vis* the mystery of the kingdom and can therefore have no teleological word to say to the desperate conflicts of history, *no assurance of a coming fulfilment of the kingdom.* It is precisely because the New Testament thinks of the kingdom as a present but as yet veiled reality, because it refuses to identify the kingdom with the church or teach the unveiling and complete realisation of the kingdom in the conditions of this present evil world, that it carries with it a doctrine of final justification and consummation that gives meaning and sacred purpose to all things as working together for good. To dissolve the distinction, in the actual continuation of the fallen world, between the kingdom as present veiled reality and unveiled reality yet to come, is to dissolve the New Testament eschatology and indeed the New Testament gospel.

---

35 Cf. 2 Thess 2.7.

36 Matt 13.24-30.

37 Reinhold Niebuhr, *An Interpretation of Christian Ethics* (London: SCM Press 1936), p. 108.

7 The views of W. Manson – the coming of the kingdom in Jesus

A much more satisfactory view of the New Testament eschatology has been sketched by W. Manson of Edinburgh in a profound study of the Gospels, *Jesus the Messiah*. (This registers a considerable advance upon his earlier views in *Christ's View of the Kingdom of God*). Manson has taken pains to point out that in his thought of the kingdom Jesus starts and 'reasons from present events and experiences to the coming of the kingdom, not vice-versa.'[38] He takes his stand on the prophetic view of history, but what was new in that was the importance that Jesus attached to his own acts among people. 'If I by the finger of God cast out demons, then has the kingdom of God unexpectedly reached even you.'[39] And so 'Jesus becomes the presentation-point, so to speak, of the divine working in history, the focus through which all lines of the divine plan concerning the past and the future are drawn'.[40] 'The kingdom of God hitherto only a dream, a transcendent object of hope or aspiration, had come into immediate and verifiable relation to history. The advent and claim of the end had been registered'.[41] The decisive factor in all this is not only that he proclaimed the kingdom of God as a glorious event in the future, but the complete identification of Jesus with the coming of that kingdom, and indeed of its actual arrival in himself.

In Judaism 'all righteousness or "justification" is denied to, and withdrawn from, the present order and existence of things in the world, and is transferred to a world to come, a new age in which the righteous will of God will be the only source and perfect norm of life',[42] but in Jesus that absolute will of God is realised, and realised not only as demand but as grace, and it is in the fulfilment of the kingdom as such that Jesus goes toward the cross as the Son of Man who represents the fullness of the sacrifice by which men and women are made sharers in the kingdom. It is thus that the kingdom enters time and becomes actual in the human midst.

---

38 W. Manson, *Jesus the Messiah* (London: Hodder & Stoughton 1943), p. 50.

39 See Luke 11.20; cf. Matt 12.28.

40 Manson, *op. cit.* p. 13.

41 Manson, *op. cit.* p. 12-13.

42 Manson, *op. cit.* p. 16.

The retention of apocalypse – the consummation of redemption in the world to come

The crucial fact for eschatology, however, is the bearing of this absolute on us as we are placed in the world. There is no doubt that the kingdom of God is already at work in power, forcing its way (*biazetai*),[43] demanding that people break with the existing order of this world, but its full power is concealed and has yet to be revealed. Here and now the kingdom of God intersects the orbit of our mundane existence, but that intersecting is necessarily partial. It at once comes into time with Jesus Christ as its focus, but it remains infinite in its recession. To use Manson's spatial figure (which of course is only metaphor), the revelation is not a circle or an ellipse which can *wholly* pass into and be absorbed into our orbit. It is rather like a parabola or hyperbola which, while entering into time, runs wholly and at all points into infinity. The boundary of its entrance into history is the boundary line of time and eternity. History does not coincide with it but is asymptotic.[44] An eschatology such as 'realised eschatology', which does not deal faithfully with this infinite recession, lacks vision and does not take the measure of the mystery involved. It is because that mystery remains that apocalypse remains an essential element at the heart of faith. Christianity cannot abandon the 'apocalyptic opposition of the then and the now. It looks for the consummation of redemption to take place only in the world to come.'[45]

The transcending of the apocalyptic dualism

However, continues Manson, 'a change has, nevertheless, come over its attitude to the present sphere of existence in that this shadowed world of sin is now seen under the immediate sign and power of the world to come. *The future and higher sphere of glory already in a real sense penetrates and intersects this sphere of humiliation through the power of the Spirit.* Something has crossed the dividing-line, and this not merely a *vox*, a summons from the world beyond to repent and believe, but a higher manifestation. While much of the traditional apparatus of apocalyptic ideas is retained in the Synoptic records and in the New Testament, the thing which is new and distinctive in the Christian revelation of God is the experience which expresses itself already in the words of Jesus about his mighty works: "The kingdom of God has

---

43 Matt 11.12.

44 'Not falling together', from the Gk *asumptōtos*.

45 Manson, *op. cit.* p. 152.

come upon you." "The kingdom of God is in your midst." "The kingdom of God is as if a man should cast seed into the ground." This is not all an enthusiastic prolepsis of things to come. It means that the world is not left wholly to itself but stands, despite all demonism, under the power, and, by grace, within the range of the salvation of God'.[46] It is thus that the apocalyptic dualism is transcended.

8 'Realised teleology' – the views of G.F. MacLeod

There is still another interpretation of the Christian hope that must be discussed for it has a great deal to teach us. It is more a tendency than a clearly articulated view. Here the kingdom of God is thought of as so present in space and time that the eschatological tension tends to disappear in spite of the intention of the sponsors themselves. This idea, which might well be called 'realised teleology', is traceable (with very differing emphases) in the younger Blumhardt, H. Kutter, Ragaz and in this country in people like G.F. MacLeod and other 'incarnationists' for whom 'community' occupies a supreme place in their thought. It is the tendency to think of the church not as eschatologically identical with the kingdom of God but as the extension of the incarnation, and to think also of the unbroken wholeness of Christ as a possession possible in the conditions of space and time. It is not content with the eschatological relation between having and hoping, but insists on the possession of total salvation secure in the continuity of this-worldly reality. Nor is it content with the sacramental confirmation of faith but insists upon transmuting it at every point and every moment into objectivity. To a certain extent this runs parallel to the totalitarian eschatology of Rome, but whereas in Roman doctrine the earthly realities are transubstantiated into realities of grace, here the realities of grace are transubstantiated into the earthly realities of daily life. 'God is earthed', as Dr MacLeod says.

The realising of the kingdom on earth – the mission of the church

Like realised eschatology, realised teleology repudiates evolutionary utopianism, for it thinks of salvation as wholeness realisable here and now, and refuses to throw the kingdom of God forward into the future, either in the way of a futurist eschatology or an ultimate ideal. The decisive event has already taken place in the incarnation which means not only the union of God and man but the integration of the material

---

[46] *Ibid.*

and the spiritual. In some sense the whole creation has been renewed already, though it waits for its manifestation through the action of the church as the sphere within which and through which that integration is made good.

If realised eschatology tends to take its stand one-sidedly on the end as *eschaton*, this eschatology tends on the contrary to take its stand one-sidedly on the end as *telos*, which correspondingly is conceived as capable of fulfilment here and now in the conditions of time and space. In other words, this is *realised teleology*. Thus, for example, faith in the integration of the material and the spiritual carries with it the doctrine of the healing of the body as an essential part of whole salvation. That refers not simply to healing from disease but the healing of the body social and politic as the extension of the incarnation. That has already been accomplished in the body of Christ and is therefore to be realised in the obedience of the church as earthed in the material world.

Dissatisfaction with the 'now' but 'still to come' of salvation and redemption

In all this there is a manifest dissatisfaction with the eschatological tension between salvation as once and for all accomplished in the death and resurrection of Christ, and yet as one still to be realised in its fullness, a tension which is enshrined in the two sacraments of baptism and holy communion. Realised teleology refuses to hold this doubleness in eschatological tension, and so tends to slip in a third sacrament or other sacraments in which the two elements are fully integrated. Thus while the New Testament thinks of the fullness of Christ as the final goal of the church and indeed of all things in heaven and earth, Dr MacLeod thinks of it as the cosmic fullness which must be realised here and now in the total healing of soul and body. The teaching of St Paul that while we are redeemed already we must also wait for the redemption of the purchased possession seems to receive little place in this thought.

Healing the hurt of God's creation too lightly

Unquestionably we have laid hold of here one of the most important elements in the Christian faith, the resurrection of the body, the resurrection as historical fact, and a great attempt is being made to work out its deep implications for daily Christian life and thought already on earth. There is no separation between creation and redemption here, and yet it must be said that this is to heal the hurt of God's creation too lightly. It does not see the incarnation sufficiently in the light of the death of Christ, and therefore that the incarnation terminates this world as well as fulfils it, so that, in the words of H.H. Farmer, 'an essential element in the whole experience of forgiveness, which lies at the heart of the Christian's reconciliation with God, is eschatological, is a pointing forward to a divine consummation which involves the cessation of the present sinful order in which man now is. As Althaus says: "Without eschatology the doctrine of forgiveness in view of our present abiding state of sinfulness, cannot be saved from falling either into frivolity or into rank scepticism".'[47]

The judgement of the cross and its critical tension with the world

Dr MacLeod has indeed pointed the church to a fullness of its duty in the world which is a pressing challenge, but it is a mission that is far profounder and more difficult than he apparently realises. It is without doubt the function of the church to live out the atonement, or at-one-ment, as he would say, in the world, that is, to be in the flesh the bodily instrument of God's crucial intervention, and so become the sphere in which the great reconciliation already wrought out in the body of Christ is realised among humanity, so that the life and action of the church, now the suffering servant in the world, becomes as it were sacramentally correlative to the life and passion of Jesus Christ. But in realising at-one-ment in the world, the church must learn to enter into the judgement of God in the death of Christ upon humanity, and to enter thereby into the travail of Christ for the new universal humanity. The church cannot be at one with the world, for its at-one-ment with God brings it into critical tension with the world reflecting the judgement of the cross, but that is precisely the point at which there is introduced into the world the gospel of a new humanity at one with God, and indeed of a new heaven and a new earth.

There is no doubt that the Christian ethic is an absolute ethic and not an interim-ethic, and that it requires an absolute obedience organic to existence in this world and to its orders of life which have been given divine sanction. For that very reason, however, as W. Manson has pointed out, love towards God cannot require people either to abandon the ordinary obligations of citizenship or to 'press upon the state ideals of action such as non-resistance to armed aggression, which under given circumstances would overthrow the foundations of law and order and defeat the good which the state exists to serve.'[48] 'It would seem, therefore, at this point', continues Dr Manson, 'that it is not Christian to press the Christian absolute, understood in its true

---

[47] Althaus, *The World and God*, p. 218.

[48] Manson, *op. cit.* p. 93.

character as love, upon orders of life which stand outside of the powers of the kingdom of God. As the ethic of a spiritual life revealed by Jesus Christ, the Christian ideal binds all who have been brought by him to see God, and as such it will determine the spirit of their citizenship in the state and their whole life in the world. In this manner Christianity will ultimately affect the state's conception of its functions. But so long as the kingdom of God only intersects our mundane existence, and does not fill the whole sphere of it, there will be limits to what can be demanded of the state in its name, and to what can be set up as definition of social duty. What the Christian ethic does here is not to provide a law for society, but to create a tension in its midst which cannot but have transforming results. The kingdom of heaven is as leaven.'[49]

The failure of 'realised teleology' to understand the essential eschatological tension

'Realised teleology' does not really enter into this critical situation and is therefore unable to understand the tension of world-denial and world-affirmation that belongs to the heart of Christian experience.[50] Consequently, it is the tendency of theologians who espouse realised teleology to believe the regulative idea of communism, or of a secularised eschatology, that the perfection of the indirect relationships of the community of labour and of society will in fact be the realisation of the kingdom of God. No doubt the church must encourage every effort to produce the kind of society in which community can best be realised, but the church that lives in repentance acknowledges that sin can be fully realised (or as St Paul would say, fulfilled) in the collective as well as the individual life,[51] and therefore must acknowledge before the judgement of God that even the form and fashion of the historical church must pass away as a compromised form of the will of God.

In the words of H.H. Farmer, 'Eschatological faith provides a solution for this world which does not evacuate the world of its meaning as a sphere in which God's presence may now be known and his will served, even though these will never be perfectly realised. It does this by conceiving the divine kingdom as the end of the present order in the double sense of the word end. Somehow there is at work within the

---

49 *Ibid.*

50 See O. Cullmann, *Christus und die Zeit* (Zurich, Evangelischer Verlag A.G. Zollikon [EVZ] 1946), pp. 186-9, (Eng. trans. *Christ and Time,* 3rd edition [London: SCM Press 1962], part III.4, pp. 211-13).

51 See Niebuhr, *The Nature and Destiny of Man,* vol. II, p. 149.

limitations and frustrations of this world a divine purpose which transcends it and cannot be comprehended in terms of it. The consummation of that purpose will therefore at one and the same time mark the end of this world and be the fulfilment and justification of it. And the divine will, which will be fully realised only then, can nonetheless be served now, even as the far-off ocean may swell the water of an inland creek and lift the boats of those who have never seen its infinite horizons. Eschatological faith is thus both pessimistic and optimistic in regard to this world. It says yes and no to it at the same time. It is God's world and yet it is not God's world in the fullest sense, being only preparatory to it.'[52]

The church must remain an eschatological community, proclaiming the new creation

Throughout this the accent must undoubtedly fall upon the triumphant certainty of the finished work of Christ (much more than it does in Farmer's thought), for Christ is already the new man in whom all things are become new, and in whom we have proleptically even now the consummation of the divine purpose of creation. Just because that is complete already we cannot think in terms of an extension of the incarnation, but only of an eschatological 'repetition' of the incarnation (including the death and resurrection), which is the doctrine enshrined in the sacrament of holy communion. The proclamation of this new humanity is the most explosive force in the world not only because it is proleptic to the final judgement of holy love and proleptic to the new heaven and new earth, but because in it the last things actually confront people creatively here and now in time. It is therefore only as an eschatological *community*[53] that the church can really carry out her divine mission in the world, to confront all humanity with the crucial word of the gospel, and so penetrate every aspect of human life with the power of the resurrection, intensively as well as extensively. The great missionary task of the church lies therefore both in the evangelisation of the world and in being the instrument by which the dynamic word of this gospel intervenes in every form of human

---

52 H.H. Farmer, *The World and God,* p. 214-5.

53 The text here has 'magnitude' – cf. here the 'Epilogue' to the *Soteriology* volume, under the heading 'The main features of apostolic eschatology', section (v), where Torrance speaks of 'the church in history as the eschatological community, the community that reaches out beyond this present age into the age to come' (*Conflict and Agreement,* vol. 1, p. 312).

existence and action, social, national and international. Without such thorough going fermentation in the world the church will not be in a position to proclaim the gospel in any way proportionate to her great passion, nor will she have the power to alter the face of present human society so as to make it by the very power of God an instrument in the furtherance of his redeeming purposes.

9 The biblical tension of present and future – the views of O. Cullmann

The most exciting work on the eschatology of the New Testament since that of Albert Schweitzer is *Christus und die Zeit*[54] (also available in a French translation) by Oscar Cullmann. This is a great attempt to turn eschatological thought away from the dialectic of this-worldly/other-worldly, or of time/eternity to the deeply biblical tension between the present and the future. The main emphasis is placed where 'realised eschatology' places it, in the person of Christ, but here we have a formulation of eschatology that both brings creation and redemption together and yet takes the time element with the utmost seriousness. Because the teleological and eschatological ends are brought together in this way, Cullmann can also give within his eschatology a doctrine of history or rather of salvation-history in two main phases as *first* the narrowing of the universal purpose of God's creation through Israel, then through the remnant of the people of God *a widening* until it reaches out at last to the fullness of the new heaven and the new earth in the complete purpose of God. 'Thus salvation-history progresses in two movements: the one goes from the many to the one, that is the old covenant, and the other from the one to the many, that is the new covenant. Exactly in the centre stands the atoning deed of the death and resurrection of Christ. Both these movements have this in common that they are fulfilled according to the principle of election and substitution. This is supremely regulative for the present period which runs out from the centre. According to the New Testament the earthly church, in which the body of Christ manifests itself, plays a central part for the redemption of all mankind and for the whole creation'.[55]

---

[54] *Christ and Time.*

[55] *Christus und die Zeit*, pp. 101-2 – cf. the translation in *Christ and Time*, p. 117, which is rather different although essentially the same in content.

The distinction between the kingdom of God and the reign of Christ

Two thoughts run throughout this which have importance both for realised eschatology and realised teleology: the distinction which Cullmann draws between the kingdom of God and the reign of Christ,[56] and a linear conception of time. The kingdom of God has come decisively among humanity in Christ, but it remains essentially a future reality. The reign of Christ on the other hand, has already begun and continues through the church, and is actualised in the word of the gospel reaching out to the whole world, so that all worldly powers and authorities are made to function only within the lordship of Christ. This means that we are really living in the last times, for the reign of Christ is essentially proleptic to the kingdom of God which will be established at the end of this present age. The conception of the kingdom of God carries with it the element of judgement upon this present evil world whose form and fashion must pass away. Apart from final judgement history becomes meaningless, but with the final judgement it is given the teleological end of the conflicts of history. In the conception of the kingdom of Christ, on the other hand, the essential oneness of God's purpose in creation and redemption is maintained, inasmuch as in Christ there is a new creation, carried through history into the kingdom of God, where it entails the eschatological judgement of all history.

The two 'ends' held partially apart until the parousia, but both sides of the eschatological tension given full weight

Because in the eschatological reserve of the New Testament those two ends are held partially apart until the *parousia* and the completion of both ends in one, the new creation is as yet a hidden creation, hidden with Christ in God, but always on the point of becoming manifest. Until then the church lives in the eschatological tension between the first coming of the kingdom and the final coming, and carries out her task as the crucified body in the realm where sin and the flesh are still found and where the subordinate powers still try to break free from the lordship of Christ. Nevertheless the church lives in the Spirit on the day of the Lord, that is to say, on the victory side of the kingdom, and the song in her mouth is the triumphant chant of Psalm 2, 'Why do the nations conspire, and the peoples plot in vain? . . . I have set my king on Zion, my holy hill . . . Ask of me, and I will make the nations your heritage, and the ends of the earth your possession.'[57]

---

[56] O. Cullman, *Christ and Time,* 3rd (revised) edition (London: SCM Press 1962), p. 151f., 208.

[57] Psalm 2.1,6,8.

The distinctive thing about this faith is that both sides of the eschatological tension are given full weight, and consequently the eschatological tension is not transmuted into a dialectic between other-worldly/this-worldly as it is with C.H. Dodd, or eternity/time as it is with Niebuhr, nor on the other hand, into an integration of spirit/matter as it is with George MacLeod. It is essentially a tension between time and time, redeemed time and time waiting for the full reality of its redemption. It is with this view of time that the distinction between the two eschatological moments of the first *parousia* and the second *parousia*, or the kingdom of Christ and the kingdom of God is given. There can be no doubt that some such distinction must be made else we have on the one hand, the Roman Catholic totalitarian eschatology with the virtual deification of the historical church, or on the other hand, the Protestant[58] totalitarian eschatology with the virtual denial of history in the distortion by 'realised eschatology' of the kingdom of God into a timeless supernal world beyond history. Both these views cut the nerve of the biblical teaching on the kingdom.

The adequacy of a purely linear view of time?

At the same time it is doubtful if the bible does operate with the strictly linear conception of time attributed to it by Cullmann. Is he not confusing time (*chronos*) with duration (*aiōn)*, for example when he says that 'time and eternity have temporality in common'?[59] Does not the fact that guilt has entered into time destroying humanity's freedom toward God, binding them hand and foot, a slave of *Chronos*, the god of this *aiōn*, mean that time has itself fallen from grace and been changed for man? Is it not part of our faith that Christ Jesus was both born of a virgin and rose again from the dead, and that therefore there is already a new creation which is neither the product of the old world nor constrained by the sin and the necessities of guilt-impregnated time, and therefore that the powers of this world, including *Chronos* (cf. Rev 10.6, 'that there should be time, *chronos*, no longer' KJV), have been dethroned? Do not the resurrection as a historical fact (in Martin Kähler's sense) and the forty days between the resurrection and the ascension mean that the reality of the new creation is temporal fact now though its reality is veiled since the ascended Lord is yet to be unveiled in the

[58] The text has 'Roman Catholic' again, which is surely an error in transcription.

[59] Cullman, *op. cit.* p. 55 – cf. English translation (ET), *op. cit.* p. 63, 'Thus time and eternity share this time quality.'

parousia? Must we not think of the kingdom of God and with it the new creation as interpenetrating our old world within the reign of Christ here and now, if only in some contrapuntal fashion?

The New Testament emphasis is not on the future reality of the kingdom, but on the future of its full manifestation – the constant expectation of its nearness

At any rate we must say that the New Testament emphasis upon the future of the kingdom's full manifestation is not on the future of the reality but the future of its full manifestation, so that the eschatological tension in linear time must be modified into eschatological tension between the time of a present but hidden reality and the time of the same reality manifest in the future. It is that very modification which lies at the back of the constant expectation in the New Testament of the proximate nearness in time of the Lord – '*maranatha*'. That was felt just as poignantly at the close of St Paul's ministry as at the beginning. The very nearness of the Lord[60] cuts short the time.[61] And that is surely the thought that St Paul puts into the otherwise puzzling citation from Isaiah: 'He will consummate and cut short the work of his word upon the earth'.[62]

It is a mistake therefore to speak of the expectation of an early return of the Lord as illusory or false – the mistake lies rather in reading either a realised eschatology or a purely linear view of time into New Testament eschatology.

10 The concept of time in New Testament eschatology – the nature of the eschatological tension

There seems little doubt that the New Testament gives us teaching on eschatology without committing itself to any specific conception of time. It is usually content to express the truth in terms of limited or limitless duration. On the analogy of the doctrine of the Trinity, however, where a formed doctrine is not given either, it may be that the eschatological teaching of the New Testament requires definite clarification in our theology. If so must we not go on to form a time-

---

60 Phil 4.5.

61 1 Cor 7.29.

62 See Rom 9.28 KJV, *logon gar suntelōn kai suntemnōn poiēsei Kyrios epi tēs gēs* – cf. Isaiah 28.22 LXX.

concept on the analogy of the incarnation? Must we not say with Karl Barth that because the Word has become flesh it has also become time?[63]

The tension between old time as we know it and the new time of the new creation

And must we not say further, that we have to do with that new time here and now even in the midst of old time? That would mean that the eschatological tension is to be thought of as between new time in the new creation, and old time as we still know it in the continuation of this fallen world. That would also mean that new time is as yet concealed under the form and fashion of old time, or (shall we say?) under the likeness of sinful time.

To work out this relation carefully we must undoubtedly go back to its ground in the incarnation, for in the person of Jesus Christ, in his God-manhood, we have consummated already the union of the eternal and the temporal.[64] And may we not think of that helpfully in terms of the great Chalcedonian doctrine of the hypostatic union? Just as in Christ God and man are united in such a way that there is neither fusion on the one hand, nor yet separation on the other, a union without any diminishing of the completeness or perfection of deity or of humanity, so here too we may think of there having taken place in the incarnation, as it were, a sort of hypostatic union between the eternal and the temporal in the form of new time. And just as Christ for ever lives our mediator and our atonement, in whom all things cohere, and in whom all things in heaven and earth will be brought back to the fullness of God, so we must think here of a union between the eternal kingdom of God and the new creation, indeed a union between the eternal and time made new in Christ Jesus, and of that as an abiding union even in the heart of our world's estrangement.

But here we must go a step beyond Chalcedon, and remembering that the captain of our salvation was made perfect through suffering, carry the hypostatic union in our thought through the cross to its

---

63 *Kirchliche Dogmatik* (KD) 1/2 (Zurich: Verlag der Evangelischen Buchhandlung Zollikon [EBZ] 1938), p. 55 – ET, *Church Dogmatics* (CD) 1/2 (Edinburgh: T & T Clark 1956), p. 50; see KD 2/1 (Zurich: EBZ 1940), p. 66-7 – ET, CD 2/1 (Edinburgh: T & T Clark 1957), p. 61-2); and KD 3/2 (Zurich: Evangelischer Verlag A.G. Zollikon [EVZ] 1948), p. 524ff. – ET, CD 3/2 (Edinburgh: T & T Clark 1960), p. 437ff. [English refs. added – Ed].

64 Cf. T.F. Torrance, *Conflict and Agreement*, vol. 2 (London: Lutterworth 1960), p. 171f.

perfection in the resurrection. We must think therefore of the union between the kingdom of God and new time as having in Christ entered into the heart of our alienation from God, into the heart of the conflicts of history, and, in the teeth of all the contradictions of sin and all the abstractions (in T.E. Hulme's sense of the word) of fallen time, as having perfected itself through the cross and resurrection into the abiding triumph of a perfection in God which both consummates the original purposes of creation and crowns it with glory.

The twofold nature of the eschatological tension, between eternity and time, and between new time and old time

Now we are able to see that the eschatological tension is really twofold. It is the union achieved in the tension between the eternal and the temporal, and also in the tension between the holy and sinful. The central fact in this for eschatology is this: that the union of the eternal and the temporal, or as we have spoken of it earlier, the bringing together of the apocalyptic and prophetic views of the kingdom, in the conditions of our humanity and our history inevitably creates a new tension, that between the new creation and the fallen world. Eschatologies make shipwreck of themselves when they concentrate on one or the other of those two tensions.

'Realised teleology' and 'realised eschatology' each concentrate on one side of the tension

'Realised teleology' concentrates upon the relation between the new creation and the old as if it were the perfected union of the eternal and the temporal, where the tendency is to jump straight into the kingdom of heaven from the incarnational fact of Bethlehem, without due acknowledgement of a perfection achieved only through the cross. 'Realised eschatology' concentrates upon the relation between the eternal and the temporal in terms of the tension between the new and the old, where the tendency is to think of the kingdom of God as jumping into the midst through the crucial fact of the cross and the resurrection without due acknowledgement of the incarnational tension here and now – the former because it thinks of the teleological end as realised here and now, the latter because it thinks of the eschatological end as realised here and now. However, against both these views christology teaches us that the entry at Bethlehem of an abiding union between God and man and its perfection in the cross and resurrection, because it is the first-fruits of the new creation, inevitably entails conflict in the conditions of time and history. That is why, although we must say that the kingdom of God has come already and come in power, we must also say that the conflict continues in time just because the new creation is here and now breaking up the old, until the hour when the veil of sense and time in the fallen world will be torn aside, and the kingdom of God will come at last with observation in the new heaven and the new earth.

The teleological 'end' must be interpreted eschatologically, and the eschatological 'end' teleologically

It is because the teleological end must be interpreted eschatologically, placing the decisive event in the birth, death and resurrection of Jesus Christ, that we must reject all liberal doctrines of a kingdom of progress. It is because the eschatological end must be interpreted teleologically that we must reject equally the view that the *parousia* is past and gone and the kingdom fully present because it has been completely realised in the resurrection and ascension of Christ. Behind both views there lies a faulty christology. But just because the decisive event in the birth, death and resurrection of Christ entails in our fallen world a new creation we must go on to teach a doctrine of eschatological fulfilment or development through history. That is why the New Testament ends with the Apocalypse.

Apocalypse is the unveiling of the hidden reality of the new creation in Jesus Christ

Apocalypse in its deepest sense is the unveiling of Jesus Christ, who has come into our world and history as the suffering servant or the lamb of God, the transcendent Son of God. At his death and resurrection the veil of the temple was torn aside and men and women beheld the glory of the only begotten of the Father full of grace and truth.[65] In Jesus Christ we think of the kingdom of God as having entered our world, as veiled behind history, behind the forms and fashions of this age, so that we are unable to see it directly, just as people were unable to discern the Christ behind the likeness of the sinful flesh of our fallen humanity except by revelation or apocalypse. The pattern of that kingdom cannot be discerned by the inspection of the course of history. But in the Spirit of the day of the Lord it is possible for faith to see proleptically, if only under the shadow of God's hand, something of the glory of God that passes through history.[66] Apocalypse therefore is the unveiling to faith of history already invaded and conquered by the

---

65 John 1.14 KJV.

66 Cf. Exod 33.18-23.

lamb of God. Apocalypse is the unveiling to faith of the new creation as yet hidden from our eyes behind the ugly shapes of sinful history, but a new creation already consummated and waiting for eschatological unfolding or fulfilment in the advent presence of Christ. No doubt we are unable to trace the lineaments of the kingdom of God in history, but it is nevertheless a fact that even now God governs and orders the course of the world so as to make all things to work together for good,[67] and even the wrath of man to praise him.

The key to history is the lamb of God who must reign until his enemies are under his feet

The key of the ages, the clue to history, is Christ crucified, the lamb of God. It is the person who in faith has seen the veiling and unveiling of Jesus Christ who can penetrate apocalyptically behind the guilt and wrath of history and see the veiling and unveiling of God's kingdom in it all. And yet even the children of faith will be surprised at the last day, as our Lord taught in a parable.[68] The achievements of the church in time are not what they appear, for even when she has done what she ought to do she must confess that she is an unprofitable servant.[69] The kingdom of God is concealed even behind the temporal forms and fashions of the church all of which must pass away at the final judgement. Only God can fulfil the purpose of history. The new Jerusalem comes down from above.[70] God has already put everything under the feet of Christ, but Christ must reign nevertheless until all his enemies are put under his feet.[71] We do not see that as yet, but we do see Jesus already crowned with glory and honour and wait for the fulfilment of his reign.[72] That is the faith and hope of the church.

Between the times, faith and hope are confirmed and nourished by the two sacraments of the Word made flesh, baptism and holy communion, which are essentially signs belonging to the fullness of time, that is to say, filled with the complete incarnate presence of the Son of God, who gives himself to us in forgiveness and reconciliation through the cross and the resurrection. In baptism that is communicated in a once and for all sense, and here the wholeness of Christ and the

---

[67] Rom 8.28 KJV.

[68] Matt 25.31f.

[69] See Luke 17.10.

[70] Rev 21.2.

[71] 1 Cor 15.27.

[72] The text has simply '. . . but we do see Jesus (Heb 2.8-9).'

completeness of our salvation are particularly enshrined. In baptism we have to do with the new creation, the perfect body of Christ into which we become incorporated. In holy communion, on the other hand, we have to do with the continuance of that in conditions of time, with the church as the bodying forth in this fallen world of communion with Christ.

The correspondence of the sacraments to the twofold tension of Christian eschatology

These two sacraments correspond to the twofold tension of Christian eschatology.[73] The doubleness of the eschatological tension of the *parousia* as both a presence and a coming, as something once for all and yet as the showing forth of that until the Lord come, is enshrined in both of them, but the emphasis upon the once and for all union of God and man, of the eternal and the temporal falls most heavily upon the sacrament of baptism, while in the eucharist or sacrament of holy communion we have the emphasis most upon the continuation of that in the contradictions and abstractions of fallen time. If in the sacrament of baptism there is enshrined the faith that once for all we have been put in the right with God through Jesus Christ, in the sacrament of holy communion we have the unshakeable conviction that in the presence of Christ we are in the wrong and we need constantly to receive communion in his body and blood for 'he who has washed does not need to wash, except for his feet'.[74] If at baptism we think of our union with Christ as *opus dei*, work of God which takes place in and for its own sake, at communion we think of the same union inserted into our flesh and blood, into time and history as by faith we partake of Christ's flesh and blood. If at baptism we think of our having died and risen with Christ, new creatures, so that old things are passed away and all things are become new,[75] at holy communion we think of that creation not only as a *datum*, a given, but as a *dandum*, that is a given which must ever be given from moment to moment in the conditions of our passing and sinful world, so that every time we communicate is eschatological time (*kairos*) until we drink it new in the kingdom.

Unquestionably, therefore, the two sacraments are given to us to enshrine the double consciousness of the New Testament

---

[73] Cf. *Conflict and Agreement*, vol. 2, pp. 164ff.

[74] John 13.10 KJV/RSV.

[75] Rom 6.3f.; 2 Cor 5.17.

eschatological faith and hope, to enable us to hold in the grasp of our faith and hope the *parousia* as both a real presence here and now and yet as an advent presence still to come. At the same time both sacraments make it quite clear that the kingdom of God is amongst us not in word only with suspended action, not in Spirit only, but in deed and in power, as real act in time, as word-deed enacted in our flesh and blood and inserted into history. But precisely because it is both, it is both an abiding reality and also an eschatologically repeated event until Christ comes.

In view of this teaching from the sacraments there are several things that must be said about the eschatological relation when the union with God in Christ is inserted into history.[76]

The sacraments and the eschatological relation

(a) The eschatological relation is not an easy one – the sacraments' twin emphasis

The eschatological relation is not easy. Just as it became fact and reality for us once and for all only through the desperate passion of the cross, so we can follow Christ only by bearing the cross daily. 'I have been crucified with Christ; it is no longer I who live, but Christ who lives in me; and the life which I now live in the flesh I live by the faith of the Son of God, who loved me and gave himself for me'.[77] While on the one hand, we are given the real presence of the whole Christ, yet on the other hand, that is to be realised in sacramental obedience enacted in our daily life. It is a reconciliation, as we have seen, thrust into a world that continues in its estrangement from and contradiction to God, and that is why in addition to the sacrament of baptism we have the eucharist. We are taught by this that while in new time we are complete in Christ Jesus, yet in the conflicts and abstractions of fallen time we are unable to realise that wholeness, but must nevertheless reckon that we are dead to the old life and created again in the new. That means that while in faith we are a new creation yet we are unable as yet to join body and soul, the invisible and the visible, the material and the spiritual, etc,[78] in any closer union than is given to us in the

---

[76] For what follows cf. *Conflict and Agreement*, vol. 2, pp. 172-75.

[77] Gal 2.20 RSV/KJV.

tensions of the cross through holy communion. The two sides are joined together only in the death and resurrection of Christ.

To add therefore a sacrament of wholeness, of body-soul union, or to transmute the gift of healing from the strenuous domain of petitionary prayer to the sacramental domain *as though we could have a sacrament of healing, or any programme of healing here and now*[79] is to deny the sacrament of the eucharist that we must take up our cross daily, die daily, and constantly communicate in the body and blood of Christ. It is to heal the hurt of God's people too lightly, and to evade the fact that the cross must be inserted into the conditions of time, into the heart of our struggles and conflicts, redeeming the time. It is to deny that although we are redeemed, we wait for the redemption of the purchased possession. It is to deny the eschatology of the eucharist: 'For as often as you eat this bread and drink the cup, *you proclaim the Lord's death until he comes.*'[80] However, although the tension between the invisible and the visible, the new and the old, cannot be resolved in time as we know it, it remains the function of the church in the world to carry the union already perfected in Christ into all the conditions of time, and how the church is constrained until it is accomplished![81] The church has therefore the sacrament set at the heart of her worship in order that she may indeed be the suffering servant in the world, although no doubt she will pray desperately, 'Father if it be possible let this cup pass from me'. But let it be quite clear that unless the church that communicates in the body and blood of our Lord is prepared to throw herself into the heart of the world's trouble, however costly that may be, and act out there the communion which

---

[78] This would be appear to be an earlier way of expressing things. Torrance's later thought appears to be expressed in more integrative terms, although clearly with the same tension between the new and the old. Cf. T.F. Torrance, *The Mediation of Christ*, new edition (Edinburgh: T & T Clark, 1992), p. 15-17 – Ed.

[79] Cf. *Atonement*, the soteriology volume of these lectures, chap. 9, sec. 5.(b).(2): 'This does not mean that it may not please God throughout history to answer the prayer of his people for direct miraculous healing, but it does mean that with the withdrawal of the resurrected body of Christ from visible and physical contact with us in the world, there is no appointed programme of anything like "faith healing" or miraculous activity of a kindred sort.'

[80] 1 Cor 11.26 (Torrance's italics).

[81] Cf. Luke 12.50.

is her very life, she does not take up the cross and follow her Lord. It is thus that 'the kingdom of God presses in and men of determined purpose lay impatient hands on it'.[82] The church can do that because she knows her Lord in the power of his resurrection.

(b) The eucharist points to an eschatological fullness still to be unveiled

The perfect union of God and man that has broken into time in the virgin birth, inserted itself into history at the cross, and yet is not the prisoner of fallen time because of the resurrection, entails a new creation that travels through old time inasmuch as Christ Jesus lives on. Although we must communicate again and again in the ever given presence of Christ in the sacrament of holy communion, there is a sense in which faith is continuously feeding upon the flesh and blood of Christ, and the church has eternal life abiding in her (John 6 & 15). That is the reality which churches can strive to grasp in a doctrine of apostolic succession construed as temporal and historical continuity. But the danger is that when so construed it can fail to realise the important eschatological element in the eucharist in which the church, every time she communicates, receives the judgement of the cross upon the forms and fashions of this passing world, even upon the orders of the church so far as they partake of the forms and fashions of this world. And that judgement in the death of Christ must be shown forth until he comes.[83]

The church must continually transcend herself and her forms in the new creation

Nevertheless, behind it all there is the ever-living continuity of Christ himself, the new creation. And it is precisely because there is that continuity travelling through and under the visible and historical continuities that the latter are disrupted, and inevitably break up, for the axe is already laid to the root of the tree.[84] Whenever the church denies that eschatological element in the eucharist it becomes a human church for then it denies that the church transcends herself in the new creation, and tries to perpetuate in faith an un-crucified Christ who has not really made

---

[82] Matt 11.12, W. Manson's translation, *Jesus the Messiah*, p. 65; cf. Luke 16.16.

[83] On the eschatological element in the eucharist, and the implication that there can be no final validity in any church structure or historical continuity, see *Conflict and Agreement*, vol. 1, pp. 196ff.

[84] Matt 3.10; Luke 3.9.

all things new in the power of the resurrection. It is precisely because the church lives on in the power of the resurrection that she must refuse to be imprisoned in the wrappings of human systems and decisions. Because she is already a resurrected body the church cannot claim, without arresting repentance[85] and quenching the Holy Spirit, that in this fallen world historical succession is of the *esse*, the very nature of the church. Nevertheless, we have in the sacraments, in the union between the visible and the invisible, the material and the spiritual, eschatological pointers to the fact that the complete union which we possess in faith here and now will be unveiled finally in a new heaven and new earth, when not only in faith but in the fullness of sight there will be perfect union between the visible and the invisible, material and spiritual, sense and faith.[86] Apart from that consummation the sacrament of communion has no final meaning, for that consummation is the fulfilled joy of triumph. 'Be of good cheer. I have overcome the world.'[87]

(c) *The wholeness of Christ is a matter of eschatological expectation and not of temporal repetition*

It is apparent, therefore, that the wholeness of Christ given to us in the sacraments can be thought of only in terms of eschatological expectation and eschatological repetition.[88] That is the way in which the continuity of the new creation and of new time is manifest in the midst of old time. It could not be otherwise. Temporal repetition, on the other hand, as the way the doctrine of the mass or the doctrine of episcopal succession has been interpreted, strikes at the heart of the sacrament as *opus dei* or work of God and at its once-for-all character. Temporal repetition in whatever form is the attempt to perpetuate the particularity of the incarnation as extension in fallen time, as something that can continually be taken up and handled, as temporal object, secure in the conditions of a fallen world, as though Jesus Christ had not risen again. It is a desire to possess God, and to domesticate the Spirit in the continuity of space and

---

85 Cf. Visser t 'Hooft, *The Kingship of Christ* (London: SCM Press 1948), p. 69f.

86 See the note above suggesting that in Torrance's later thought this would be expressed in more integrative terms.

87 John 16.33.

88 Cf. the footnote, *Conflict and Agreement*, vol. 2. p. 72.

time, and confounds the wholeness of the risen Christ with a historical catholicity here and now.

We walk by faith and not by sight, until Christ returns and we see him as he is

The New Testament Gospels, in their accounts of the transfiguration and the resurrection appearances, teach us that the transfigured and risen Christ cannot be perpetuated in the institutions and conditions of this passing world. He inevitably vanishes out of our sight. We cannot anticipate the second advent: of that hour not even the Son of Man knew.[89] Without any doubt whatsoever his real presence is with us, and yet he is still to come. Christ does not communicate himself to us here and now as he will at the second advent, nevertheless his presence is as fully real as it will be then. In the repeated communicating in the body and blood of Christ in the sacrament, the continual feeding of faith upon Christ (John 6) is crowned with vision, but because Christ is wholly identical with himself, and the new creation is a new creation and cannot be identified with this present evil world, it is a Christ who vanishes out of our sight again and again, for as yet we walk by faith not by sight. It is, however, because faith is nourished and crowned with vision in the sacrament again and again, the vision of the transcendent Christ – the *alpha* and the *ōmega*, the beginning and the end who cannot be expressed in terms of this fallen world[90] – that apocalyptic images are an inner necessity for faith. It is faith reaching forward in eager expectation of sight because it is faith that has already seen invisibly the risen saviour. And faith knows that day will come when Jesus Christ, the incarnate Son of God, will return and the veil will be torn aside and we shall see him as he is and become like him.[91]

---

89 See Mark 13.32.

90 See Rev 1.13ff.

91 1 John 3.2.

GLOSSARY OF THEOLOGICAL TERMS

As most theological and philosophical terms are defined in the text, the glossary contains only the most important or those most useful for reference here. Where possible, the definitions have been taken or adapted from the text.

Accommodation – associated with Calvin, the term refers to God's 'coming down' to meet us at our level and make himself known in human language and in ways the human mind can understand.

Active and passive obedience – active obedience refers to Jesus' active fulfilment of the will and law of God and his life of positive human righteousness, while passive obedience refers to his suffering the consequences and judgment of sin.

Adoptionism – the theory that Jesus was born human but adopted to be the Son of God.

Anabaptist (literally 're-baptising') – a term generally referring to movements of the 16th century which rejected infant baptism and advocated the baptism (or rebaptism) of believers able to decide for themselves.

Anhypostasis and enhypostasis – *anhypostasis* refers to the fact that the humanity of Jesus had no independent reality of its own apart from the incarnation of the Son, while *enhypostasis* refers to the fact that the humanity of Jesus did have real personal being *in* the person of the Son as a result of the incarnation (Gk, *an-hypostasis*, literally 'not-person', ie. with no personal being except in the Son; *en-hypostasis*, literally 'in-person' or 'person-in [the person of the Son]', ie. having real personal existence *in* the person of the Son).

Apollinarianism (Apollinarius c.310-c.390) – the doctrine that in the incarnation the eternal Word took the place of the human spirit or mind (*nous*). This was condemned at Constantinople in 381 on the ground that it impaired the perfect humanity of Christ because it meant Jesus did not have a normal human mind.

A posteriori – from experience, by empirical investigation (Lat, 'from after', hence following events or experience).

A priori – from first principles, by reason alone, independent of experience (Lat, 'from the first').

Arianism (Arius c.250-c.336) – the doctrine, condemned at Nicaea in 325, that Jesus was not of the same being as God and therefore not God but the highest of creatures, created by God for a mediatory and creative role.

Arminianism (Arminius 1560-1609) – a system of doctrine which attempts to hold together divine sovereignty and human free-will, teaching that Christ died for all and that God's predestination is based on foreknowledge of human decision to accept or reject Christ.

Atonement – the divine work of covering and putting away sin, thus creating 'at-one-ment' between God and man. The term is especially used of Christ's work of salvation which culminated on the cross.

Christian Dogmatics – the church's orderly understanding of scripture and articulation of doctrine in the light of Christ and their coherence in him.

Christology – the doctrine of Christ, particularly of the person of Christ.

Contingency – the fact that the universe is not necessary and does not have to be the way it is, but is 'contingent' on the freedom of God to create it and might have been otherwise.

Councils – the great ecumenical councils were formal gatherings of bishops of the whole church assembled together to take key decisions on doctrine and creed. The most important councils, listed together with their central affirmations, were:

(i) *The Council of Nicaea* in AD 325 affirmed that Jesus Christ is truly God, of one being (*homoousios*) with the Father, in an affirmation of faith against the Arians.
(ii) *The Council of Constantinople* in AD 381 affirmed that Jesus Christ was perfectly man, against the Apollinarians whose teaching impaired the perfect humanity of Christ.

(iii) *The Council of Ephesus* in AD 431 affirmed that Jesus Christ is one person, against the Nestorians who divided Christ into two persons.

(iv) *The Council of Chalcedon* in AD 451 affirmed that in Jesus Christ there are two distinct natures in one person, and that in the one person of Christ they were hypostatically united 'unconfusedly, unchangeably, indivisibly, inseparably' ('without confusion, change, division or separation'). The first two adverbs specifically targeted the Eutychians and Monophysites, while the last two targeted the Nestorians.

(v) *The Council of Constantinople* in AD 680 asserted that Jesus Christ possessed a human will as well as a divine will, against the Monothelites who asserted that in Jesus Christ there was only one single will.

Creatio ex nihilo – 'creation out of nothing'.

Decalogue – the 'ten commandments' (from *deka logoi*, 'ten words', the Greek translation of the Hebrew equivalent).

Deism – the view of God as the creator who, having brought the universe into being, leaves it to run according to natural law.

Docetism – the theory that while Jesus was God, he only *appeared* to be human (from the Gk, *dokeō*, to seem or appear). Generally, any theory which denies the full reality of Jesus' humanity.

Dogma – the church's authoritative formulation of doctrine in accordance with apostolic teaching.

Dogmatics – see Christian Dogmatics.

Doxological – giving praise or glory to God (from the Gk, *doxos*, glory).

Dyophysitism – the view that after the incarnation Christ had two natures, divine and human (from the Gk, '*duo*' two, and '*physis*' nature).

Ebionism – the view that Jesus was not God but an ordinary man, adopted to become Son of God.

Enhypostasis – see Anhypostasis and enhypostasis

Exegesis – the interpretation of biblical texts.

Epistemology – the philosophy of knowledge, its nature, methods, sources and limits.

Eschatology – generally, the doctrine of 'the last days' or end of history (from the Gk, *eschatos*, last). New Testament eschatology thinks in terms of 'the last days' as having begun in the coming of Christ and of his second coming as imminent, not simply in terms of time, but in terms of Christ's nearness through his resurrection as the beginning of the new creation and through his continual breaking into history in the Spirit.

Eschaton – the end, the last word and final act of God in Christ. The eschaton is the end of history, but not an event beyond it but within it, which means its transformation into the new creation.

Eutychianism (Eutyches c.378-454) – a doctrine of 'two natures before the incarnation and one after'. This was condemned at Chalcedon in 451 on the ground that it implied Christ's human nature was no longer the same as ours but had been swallowed up by his divinity.

Existentialism – the philosophy which emphasises personal *existence*, courageous decision and living in the present moment.

Gnosticism – the belief in a secret, higher spiritual realm of knowledge (*gnôsis*) to which an enlightened person could gradually attain in order to reach God and be liberated from the material realm.

Hermeneutics – the art or science of interpretation, especially of scripture.

Homoousion – the term used of Jesus' identity of being with the Father and adopted at the council of Nicaea in 325 (from the Gk, *homo–ousios*, 'same-being' or 'of one being' with . . .).

Hypostatic union – the doctrine, first formally adopted at Chalcedon in 451, that in Jesus there are two distinct natures, divine and human, in one person.

Hypostasis – a term with two distinct meanings, originally objective or substantial reality (from the Gk *hypo-stasis*, standing under; the Lat *sub-stantia*, substance) but then used to denote the unique reality or 'personal subsistence' of the three persons in the one being of God. From the time of the Council of Constantinople in 381, the formula 'three *hypostaseis* in one *ousia*', 'three persons in one being', became the orthodox doctrine of the Trinity.

Idealism – a philosophy of knowledge which generally emphasises ideas and the contribution of the human mind to knowledge. In a stronger form, idealism emphasises the 'necessary truths of reason' at the expense of the 'accidental truths of history'.

Incarnation – God's becoming man (from the Lat, *in carne*, in flesh).

Kerygma – the New Testament proclamation of Christ (from the Gk, *kērygma* proclamation, preaching), in which the apostolic proclamation, that Jesus is the Christ, was inseparable both from what Jesus was and did in history and from his own self-proclamation in the apostolic kerygma by the Spirit.

Limited atonement – the doctrine that Jesus did not die for all humanity but only for the elect.

Marcionism (Marcion died c. 160) – the doctrine of the incompatibility of the Old Testament God, the creator God of law and judgement, with the New Testament God of love and grace.

Monophysitism – the view that there is only one nature (divine) in Christ not two (divine and human), [from the Gk, '*monos*' one, and '*physis*' nature]. Condemned at Chalcedon in 451.

Monothelitism – the view that Christ only has 'one will' (a divine will) and not two (a divine and a human), [from the Gk, *monos* one, and *thelein* 'to will']. Condemned at Constantinople in 680.

Moral influence theory – a theory of the atonement, associated mostly with Abelard (1079-1142), that emphasises the power of the cross, as a demonstration of the love of God, to evoke the response of repentance and love.

Nestorianism – the theory of a conjunction of two persons, divine and human, in Christ. Although Nestorius (died c.451) did affirm the oneness of Christ, his doctrine of a conjunction of divine and human in Christ and a union of will, rather than a hypostatic union of divine and human in one person, was seen as compromising the unity of Christ and was condemned at the Council of Ephesus in 431.

Ontological – referring to the nature of things in their being or inner reality.

Passive obedience – see Active and passive obedience of Jesus

Patristic theology – the theology of the early church 'fathers' (from the Gk, *patēr*, father).

Parousia – normally used of the last advent of Christ, *parousia* more accurately refers to the first and second advents as one whole coming-and-real-presence of Christ in the flesh (from the Gk, *parousia*, 'presence, coming').

Pelagianism (Pelagius c.354-415) – the belief in human capacity and freedom to co-operate with divine grace for salvation.

Perichôresis – the mutual indwelling and communion of persons, Father, Son and Holy Spirit, in the one God.

Recapitulation – the theory associated with Irenaeus (c.130-c.200) that Jesus in his human life summed up the human race and its history. He undid its sin and disobedience by his obedience and gathered it up as a new humanity under his headship as the new Adam.

Reformed – name used for the branch of the Reformation which, in distinction to the Lutheran, was generally Calvinist in doctrine and organisation.

Sabellianism – a form of *modalism*, that Father, Son and Spirit are not eternal persons in God himself but modes or ways that he successively reveals himself.

Septuagint – the Greek translation of the Old Testament, also known as the LXX, the Roman numerals for 70 since it was translated by '70 scholars' (the actual number was 72).

Socinianism (Socinus (1539-64)) – a unitarian theology which teaches that Christ is not divine, but a mortal man begotten through the Holy Spirit and then re-begotten in the resurrection to be immortal. Though not an atoning sacrifice, his death was accepted as a ground for forgiveness and was important for its revelation of the love of God.

Soteriology – the doctrine of salvation, especially of the work of Christ (Gk, *sōtēr*, saviour).

Torah – Hebrew, 'law', or 'instruction in the law'.

Total depravity – the doctrine of the constitutive change introduced by sin into the whole being of humanity, such that every part of the human person, body, mind and soul is affected.

Trinity – the central doctrine of the Christian faith that the one God exists in three eternal persons.

Unitarianism – the doctrine of the unity and unipersonality of God which denies the doctrines of the Trinity and the divinity of Christ.

Universalism – the doctrine of universal salvation, that in the end all will be saved.

Vicarious humanity of Christ – term referring to the fact that Christ in his humanity stands in our place and represents us, so that what is true of his humanity is true of us, and that what he did in his (our) humanity is ours (Lat, *vicarius*, 'acting in the place of another').

GENERAL INDEX

A

B

C

D

E

F

G

I

K

L

M

N

O

P

Q

R

S

T

INDEX OF BIBLICAL REFERENCES

ATONEMENT

The Person and Work of Christ

Thomas F. Torrance

(edited by Robert T. Walker)

In his forthcoming book *Atonement*, Thomas F. Torrance shows how Jesus Christ brings his work of salvation to its climax in his atoning death on the cross, bodily resurrection, ascension in our humanity and sending of the Spirit. The union of God and man begun at Bethlehem comes to fruition at Pentecost. United to him through the Spirit, the church waits expectantly for his coming again when the salvation already complete in his person will be actualised in the redemption of all creation.

> Nowhere else in T. F. Torrance's writings will you find the kind of synthesis of the entire sweep of his dogmatics as you will find in *Incarnation* and its companion volume *Atonement*. Everyone concerned with constructive systematic theology in general, or with Torrance's theology in particular, will want to acquire and read these books. They reveal the heart and soul of Torrance's theological vision.

Elmer M. Colyer,
Professor of Historical Theology,
Stanley Professor of Wesley Studies, University
of Dubuque Theological Seminary, USA,
and author of *How to Read T. F. Torrance: Understanding his Trinitarian & Scientific Theology*

Published by Paternoster and IVP in October 2009